MW00903001

This Book Belongs To:
Brian Edwards

Pricing and Cost Accounting

A HANDBOOK FOR GOVERNMENT CONTRACTORS

THIRD EDITION

Pricing and Cost Accounting

A HANDBOOK FOR GOVERNMENT CONTRACTORS

THIRD EDITION

Darrell J. Oyer, CPA

MANAGEMENTCONCEPTS

Management Concepts, Inc.
8230 Leesburg Pike, Suite 800
Vienna, Virginia 22182
Phone: (703) 790-9595
Fax: (703) 790-1371
Web: www.managementconcepts.com

Printed in the United States of America

Library of Congress Cataloging-in-Publication Data

Oyer, Darrell, 1941–
   Pricing and cost accounting: a handbook for government contractors/Darrell J. Oyer.—
3rd ed.
     p. cm.
   ISBN 978-1-56726-325-1
   1. Public contracts—United States.   2. Cost accounting.   I. Title.

HD3861.U6O94 2011
657′.835042—dc22

2011003516

About the Author

Darrell J. Oyer, CPA, is president of Darrell J. Oyer Co., a consulting firm that provides accounting services and training to government contractors and federal government employees. He is highly experienced in developing and reviewing contractor estimating systems, cost accounting structures, and cost control systems to ensure compliance with federal procurement requirements. Prior to forming his own firm in 1991, Mr. Oyer was a partner in the Deloitte & Touche government contracts advisory practice. Previously, he worked for the Defense Contract Audit Agency and the U.S. Air Force Auditor General's office.

Dedication

To Irving J. Sandler, my long-time mentor, in gratitude for his contributions to my knowledge of the contracting business.

Acknowledgments

The author would like to thank Margaret Worthington, CPA, and Carl Ford for their thorough and careful review during the development of this book. Their insightful and pertinent comments proved invaluable to the completeness and accuracy of the final product.

Table of Contents

Preface

Government contracting is unique. Its intricacies often cannot be understood using common sense and experience in the commercial marketplace. The terminology alone is confusing to the uninitiated. However, the rules are not mysterious—they simply need to be understood. The purpose of this book is to help demystify the process of winning and carrying out a government contract.

Obtaining government business is often very different from obtaining commercial business, largely because extensive rules are in place to ensure fairness in the award of contracts that use public funds. Contractual arrangements with the government feature documents that contain numerous contract clauses, all of which need to be read and understood—even in the haste of preparing a contract bid. The nature of determining contract price is often significantly different because of the various alternatives to the firm-fixed-price arrangement most common in the commercial marketplace.

Not only is the government your customer, but it also acts as your overseer in some contract situations. Accordingly, both estimating and accounting systems may have to be audited before you can successfully obtain and conclude a government contract. A key issue is that not all costs can be included in your price to the government. Detailed rules on reimbursement are designed to prevent the taxpayer from paying for costs that are "against public policy."

Current and potential contractors must be aware of and understand the rules. Most contractors are at least familiar with the Federal Acquisition Regulation (FAR); importantly, however, rules and regulations related to the cost accounting standards (CAS) may also be applicable to a contract.

Government contracting rules and regulations are constantly changing. Contractors need to be current on the often-changing requirements.

Since 1999 the thresholds for certification of cost and pricing data have changed twice, the threshold for CAS coverage has been substantially revised, new issues have arisen in commercial item contracting, profit guidelines have been revised by several major agencies, cost principles have been revised, and audit initiatives have been redirected. This third edition incorporates these changes and many others.

Without current information you could be attempting to comply with rules and regulations that are no longer current. Or, you could be in noncompliance with unknown new rules. The former is costly and the latter can be fatal to a business entity.

This book is intended to serve as a practical guide for contracting with the federal government. To help guide current and potential contractors in dealing with the myriad issues that can arise from contract bid through contract closeout, the book follows the life cycle of a government contract.

Chapter 1 describes the methods that the government uses to award contracts. The focus of the remainder of the book is on those situations where government involvement in contractor operations is most significant. Chapter 2 describes the various types of government contracts, generally falling under the categories of fixed-price and cost-reimbursement. The pricing and administration of the various contract types are often closely related to their unique features.

Chapter 3 addresses what a contractor must include in an accounting system that will be considered adequate for government contracting. Key requirements are written policies and procedures, labor recording practices, designation of direct vs. indirect costs, establishment of indirect cost pools, establishment of cost controls, and consistency in application. Contractors should establish an accounting system before pricing or bidding on a contract.

Not all business costs are allowable in pricing and billing costs under many government contracts. A cost must generally be reasonable in nature and amount, allocable to the contract, in accord with generally accepted accounting principles and practices, and in compliance with the contract terms. Chapter 4 addresses these aspects of pricing and billing. In addition, Chapter 5 addresses individual cost allowability rules contained in the FAR.

Some contracts and subcontracts are subject to the CAS. Chapter 6 addresses which contracts are covered by the CAS, who must submit a CAS disclosure statement, the difference between full and modified coverage, the ramifications of the CAS contract clause, the dreaded cost impact statement, and the key aspects of the 19 standards.

With an understanding of the contract types and the cost rules described in the preceding chapters, a contractor can turn to estimating costs or developing prices as described in Chapter 7. Generally, a contractor should have established estimating policies and procedures, and provide for estimating techniques by cost element. Chapter 8

contains advice on the second element of a price: markup on cost or estimated cost. The FAR and individual agencies have their own rules on how markup is to be evaluated; these guidelines are described.

Chapter 9 addresses a unique aspect of government contracts when prices are negotiated based on cost and pricing data: the Truth in Negotiations Act. The basics provisions of this act—specifically, defective pricing and postaward reviews—are described in detail. The chapter addresses penalties, reasons for the law, basic requirements, covered pricing actions, government proofs of defective pricing, and contract price adjustments.

Chapter 10 covers matters related to contract administration. These include contract modifications, subcontracting responsibilities, cost monitoring and reporting, and contract closeout. In addition, the government may terminate a contract for convenience. Cost-reimbursement rules for these terminations are described.

The final chapter, Chapter 11, addresses the various audits that may be performed during contract performance. These audits include price proposals, incurred costs, contract modification pricing, postaward reviews, termination settlements, interim payment requests, the CAS, accounting systems, estimating systems, operations audits, financial jeopardy audits, and contract closeouts.

Contracting with the federal government can be a worthwhile, profitable undertaking. The key is to understand the applicable rules and regulations—and to be prepared to carry them out in a way that enables the contracting relationship to be mutually beneficial for both the contractor and the federal government. It can be done!

Darrell J. Oyer, CPA
February 2011

Instructor materials available. Please contact pubsupport@managementconcepts.com.

CHAPTER 1   Federal Government Procurement Methods

The federal government uses three primary methods for soliciting and awarding contracts: commercial items, sealed bids, and negotiations. Commercial items are addressed in Part 12 of the Federal Acquisition Regulation (FAR), with special coverage of Federal Supply Service (FSS) contracts in Part 38. Sealed bids are covered by FAR Part 14, Sealed Bidding. Negotiations, which usually involve some interface between the government and the contractor, are classified as either competitive or sole source and are subject to FAR Part 15, Contracting by Negotiation. The difference between FAR Parts 12 and 15 is often not fully understood. Part 12 pertains to commercial purchases by the government and Part 15 pertains to commercial purchases as exemptions from submission of cost or pricing data.

Effective April 1, 1985, the Competition in Contracting Act (CICA) of 1984 made sweeping changes to the government's competitive procedures. Overall, the aim of CICA was to promote full and open competition in the acquisition process. More specifically, Congress intended to put competitive proposals on the same level with sealed bids, and to significantly limit the use of "other than competitive," or sole source proposals. The Federal Acquisition Streamlining Act of 1994 set forth the government's preference for the acquisition of commerical items by establishing acquisition policies more closely resembling those of the commercial marketplace and encouraging the acquisition of commercial items and components. Since these reforms in the mid-1990s, government procurement officials have gradually reverted to pre-1990s practices.

COMMERCIAL ITEMS

The federal government's policy is to first conduct market research to determine whether commercial items or nondevelopmental items are available that could meet the agency's requirements. Agencies are to acquire commercial items or nondevelopmental items when they are available to meet agency needs and are to require prime contractors and subcontractors at all tiers to incorporate, to the maximum extent practicable, commercial items or nondevelopmental items as components of items supplied to the agency.

A commercial item is defined in FAR Part 2.101 as:

> (1) Any item, other than real property, that is of a type customarily used by the general public or by nongovernmental entities for purposes other than governmental purposes, and —
>
> (i) Has been sold, leased, or licensed to the general public; or
>
> (ii) Has been offered for sale, lease, or license to the general public;
>
> (2) Any item that evolved from an item described in paragraph (1) of

this definition through advances in technology or performance and that is not yet available in the commercial marketplace, but will be available in the commercial marketplace in time to satisfy the delivery requirements under a Government solicitation;

(3) Any item that would satisfy a criterion expressed in paragraphs (1) or (2) of this definition, but for —

(i) Modifications of a type customarily available in the commercial marketplace; or

(ii) Minor modifications of a type not customarily available in the commercial marketplace made to meet Federal Government requirements. Minor modifications means modifications that do not significantly alter the nongovernmental function or essential physical characteristics of an item or component, or change the purpose of a process. Factors to be considered in determining whether a modification is minor include the value and size of the modification and the comparative value and size of the final product. Dollar values and percentages may be used as guideposts, but are not conclusive evidence that a modification is minor;

(4) Any combination of items meeting the requirements of paragraphs (1), (2), (3), or (5) of this definition that are of a type customarily combined and sold in combination to the general public;

(5) Installation services, maintenance services, repair services, training services, and other services if —

(i) Such services are procured for support of an item referred to in paragraph (1), (2), (3), or (4) of this definition, regardless of whether such services are provided by the same source or at the same time as the item; and

(ii) The source of such services provides similar services contemporaneously to the general public under terms and conditions similar to those offered to the Federal Government;

(6) Services of a type offered and sold competitively in substantial quantities in the commercial marketplace based on established catalog or market prices for specific tasks performed or specific outcomes to be achieved and under standard commercial terms and conditions. This does not include services that are sold based on hourly rates without an established catalog or market price for a specific service performed or a specific outcome to be achieved. For purposes of these services —

(i) "Catalog price" means a price included in a catalog, price list, schedule, or other form that is regularly maintained by the manufacturer or vendor, is either published or otherwise available for inspection by customers, and states prices at which sales are currently, or were last, made to a significant number of buyers constituting the general public; and

(ii) "Market prices" means current prices that are established in the course of ordinary trade between buyers and sellers free to bargain and that can be substantiated through competition or from sources independent of the offerors.

(7) Any item, combination of items, or service referred to in paragraphs (1) through (6) of this definition, notwithstanding the fact that the item, combination of items, or service is transferred between or among separate divisions, subsidiaries, or affiliates of a contractor; or

(8) A nondevelopmental item, if the procuring agency determines the item was developed exclusively at

private expense and sold in substantial quantities, on a competitive basis, to multiple State and local governments.

Agencies must use firm-fixed-price contracts, fixed-price contracts with economic price adjustment, or time-and-material/labor-hour contracts for the acquisition of commercial items. Use of any other contract type to acquire commercial items is prohibited. These contract types may be used in conjunction with an award fee and performance or delivery incentives when the award fee or incentive is based solely on factors other than cost.

Although the contracting officer must establish price reasonableness, customary commercial terms and conditions should be used when pricing commercial items. Commercial item prices are affected by factors that include speed of delivery, length and extent of warranty, limitations of seller's liability, quantities ordered, length of the performance period, and specific performance requirements. The contracting officer must ensure that contract terms, conditions, and prices are commensurate with the government's need. Government agency guidance often limits the use of the commercial item classification.

The Federal Supply Schedule program is directed and managed by the General Services Administration (GSA). GSA may delegate certain responsibilities to other agencies. The FSS program provides federal agencies with a simplified process for acquiring commercial supplies and services in varying quantities while obtaining volume discounts. Indefinite-delivery contracts are awarded using competitive procedures to firms. The firms provide supplies and services at stated prices for given periods of time, for delivery within a stated geographic area such as the 48 contiguous states, the District of Columbia, Alaska, Hawaii, and overseas. The schedule contracting office issues publications that contain a general overview of the FSS program and ad-

dress pertinent topics. Always remember that if an item is on a Federal Supply Schedule, it is conclusively a commercial item.

SEALED BIDS

The sealed bid method of contracting is used to select contractors solely on the basis of the lowest price, when certain FAR conditions permit. The sealed bid method can be used if: (1) time permits; (2) award is based on price (i.e., not cost) and price-related factors; (3) discussions with the bidders are unnecessary; and (4) more than one sealed bid is expected. The sealed bid method of contracting operates most effectively when two conditions exist:

1. The government is able to describe its needs in sufficient detail to permit bids to be prepared and evaluated on a common basis.

2. The number of competitors and the quantity being purchased are sufficient to ensure real competition.

The government's requirements and the terms and conditions of the proposed contract are announced publicly and circulated widely to potential bidders by way of an Invitation for Bids (IFB). Formal advertising eliminates the need for the government to negotiate with competitors about their bids and provides an objective means for distinguishing among capable competitors. Essentially, the government feels confident that the established market price has been subject to arm's-length transaction. Furthermore, the government is focusing on price and not on contractor cost and profit.

A sealed bid effectively serves as a contract offer. It may be withdrawn or modified before opening, but once opened, a bid generally cannot be revoked or modified. In developing a bid price under a sealed bid solicitation, the contractor is responsible for estimating cost and profit in any manner deemed appropriate to best accomplish its objectives. Contractors submit price information only; they do not have to disclose cost data and profit rates to the government.

The contractor's bid need not be based on cost. Instead, it may be based primarily on the contractor's assessment of its risk and its competitive position. For example, if the contractor has a unique item that no one else can sell, its price—and therefore its profit— might be higher. If the contractor is trying to break into a market, its price might be lower to meet or beat the competition. Similarly, a contractor operating at full capacity may decide to increase its estimated labor costs because overtime will be required to accomplish the work. In this case, the contractor may feel comfortable increasing its profit rate as well. Conversely, a contractor operating at less than full capacity, or one relatively new to the industry, may determine that a more aggressive price and lower profit are required to win the contract. Of course, the contractor must balance its form of pricing against the risk as well as its ability to absorb any potential loss.

When preparing a response to a sealed bid solicitation, a contractor must be sensitive to 41 U.S.C. 253(B)(e) and 10 U.S. C. 2305(b) (5). The objective of these laws is to ferret out antitrust violations—practices by contractors designed to eliminate competition or restrain trade. This order requires government agencies to report to the attorney general each sealed bid procurement over $10,000 that involves identical bids. Identical bids are defined as two or more bids that are identical in terms of unit price or total amount after giving effect to discounts and all other relevant factors. Contracts resulting from sealed bidding are to be firm-fixed-price contracts or fixed-price contracts with economic price adjustment.

CONTRACTING BY NEGOTIATION

Negotiation means contracting through the use of competitive or other-than-competitive (i.e., sole source) proposals. Simply put, a negotiated contract is any contract awarded without using sealed bidding. The single element that most distinguishes contracting by negotiation from contracting by sealed bid is the subjective judgment required in a negotiation to weigh quality and other factors against price. Overall, negotiation permits the government greater latitude in selecting contractors (see Figure 1).

The basic elements in a sealed bid procurement—the existence of an established price and a functioning marketplace—are not as well defined in negotiation. The procedures used in negotiating a contract vary depending on the competitive environment; specifically, multiple bidders vs. sole source awards. The government's focus shifts from price analysis to a combination of price and cost analysis. And the contracts are subject to various complicated federal regulations that mandate how costs should be determined, accumulated, and allocated.

For each government acquisition, the relative importance of cost or price will likely vary. In acquisitions where the requirement is clearly definable and the risk of unsuccessful contract performance is minimal, cost or price may be dominant in source selection. The less definitive the requirement, the more development work required, or the greater the contract performance risk, the more dominant technical or past performance considerations will likely be.

If the acquisition selection is to consider award to other than the lowest priced offeror or other than the highest technically rated offeror, the solicitation will state the relative importance of all evaluation factors and whether all evaluation factors other than cost or price are together significantly more important than, approximately equal to, or significantly less important than cost or price.

Figure 1
Contracting by Sealed Bid vs. Negotiation

Procurement Characteristic	Sealed Bid	Negotiation
Initiating document	Invitation for Bids (IFB)	Request for Proposals (RFP)
Response	Bid	Proposal
Specifications	Precisely stated	May not be precise
Minimum offerors	Two*	One
Selection criteria	Low price from responsible and responsive bidder	Various evaluation factors
Types of contracts	Firm fixed-price	Any type
Government access to records	Limited	Yes

*Can be one bidder under certain circumstances.

This permits tradeoffs among cost or price and non-cost factors, and allows the government to accept other than the lowest priced proposal. Any perceived benefits of a higher priced proposal must merit the additional cost.

The lowest priced, technically acceptable source selection basis is appropriate when best value is expected to result from the process. Under this process, the evaluation factors and significant subfactors that establish the requirements of acceptability will be presented in the solicitation. Solicitations must specify that award will be made on the basis of the lowest evaluated price of proposals meeting or exceeding the acceptability standards for non-cost factors. Past performance need not be an evaluation factor in lowest price, technically acceptable source selections. If the government determines that a small business concern's past performance is not acceptable, the matter is referred to the Small Business Administration for a Certificate of Competency determination. Proposals are evaluated for acceptability but not ranked using the non-cost/price factors.

Oral presentations by offerors as requested by the government may substitute for, or augment, written information at any time in the acquisition process, and are subject to the same restrictions as written information

regarding timing and content. Prerecorded videotaped presentations are generally not considered oral presentations, although they may be included in offeror submissions. The solicitation may require each offeror to submit part of its proposal through oral presentations. However, certifications, representations, and a signed offer sheet (including any exceptions to the government's terms and conditions) must be submitted in writing. Information pertaining to areas such as an offeror's capability, past performance, work plans or approaches, staffing resources, transition plans, or sample tasks (or other types of tests) may be suitable for oral presentations. When oral presentations are required, the solicitation must provide offerors with sufficient information to prepare for those presentations.

The government must maintain a record of oral presentations. A copy of the record placed in the file may be provided to the offeror. When an oral presentation includes information that the parties intend to include in the contract as material terms or conditions, the information must be put in writing. Incorporation by reference of oral statements is not permitted.

Exchanges of information among all interested parties, from the earliest identification of a requirement through receipt of proposals, must be consistent with pro-cure-ment integrity requirements. The purpose of exchanging information is to improve the understanding of government requirements and industry capabilities. This allows potential offerors to judge whether or how they can satisfy the government's requirements, enhances the government's ability to obtain quality supplies and services at reasonable prices, and increases efficiency in proposal preparation, proposal evaluation, negotiation, and contract award.

An early exchange of information among participants in the acquisition process can identify and resolve concerns regarding the acquisition strategy. This includes proposed contract type, terms and conditions, and acquisition planning schedules; the feasibility of the requirement, including performance requirements, statements of work, and data requirements; the suitability of the proposal instructions and evaluation criteria, including the approach for assessing past performance information; the availability of reference documents; and any other industry concerns or questions. Early exchanges of information can be accomplished through industry or small business conferences, public hearings, market research, one-on-one meetings with potential offerors, presolicitation notices, draft Requests For Proposals (RFPs), Requests For Information (RFIs), presolicitation or preproposal conferences, and site visits.

Special notices of procurement matters or electronic notices may be used to publicize the government's requirement or to solicit information from industry. RFIs may be used when the government does not presently intend to award a contract, but wants to obtain price, delivery, other market information, or capabilities for planning purposes. Responses to these notices are not offers and cannot be accepted by the government to form a binding contract. There is no required format for RFIs.

After release of a solicitation, the contracting officer is the focal point for any exchange with potential offerors. When specific information about a proposed ac-quisition that would be necessary for the preparation of proposals is disclosed to one or more potential offerors, that information is to be made available to the public as soon as practicable, but no later than the next general release of information, in order to avoid creating an unfair competitive advantage. Information provided to a particular offeror in response to that offeror's request must not be disclosed if doing so would reveal the potential offeror's confidential business strategy. When a presolicitation or preproposal conference is conducted, materials distributed at the conference are made available to all potential offerors upon request.

This process invites potential offerors to submit information that allows the government to advise the offerors about their potential to be viable competitors. A pre-soli-ci-tation notice identifies the information that must be submitted and the criteria that will be used in making the initial evaluation. Information sought may be limited to a statement of qualifications and other appropriate information (e.g., proposed technical concept, past performance, limited pricing information). At a minimum, the notice contains sufficient information to permit a potential offeror to make an informed decision about whether to participate in the acquisition. This process should not be used for multistep acquisitions where it would result in offerors being required to submit identical information in response to the notice and in response to the initial step of the acquisition.

The government evaluates responses and advises each respondent in writing either that it will be invited to participate in the resultant acquisition or, based on the information submitted, that it is unlikely to be a viable competitor. The agency advises respondents considered not to be viable competitors of the general basis for that opinion. The agency informs all respondents that, notwithstanding the advice provided by the government in response to their submissions, they may participate in the resultant acquisition.

RFPs are used in negotiated acquisitions to communicate government requirements to prospective contractors and to solicit proposals. RFPs for competitive acquisitions describe the government's requirement, the anticipated terms and conditions that will apply to the contract, information required to be in the offeror's proposal, and factors and significant subfactors that will be used to evaluate the proposal and their relative importance. The solicitation may authorize offerors to propose alternative terms and conditions, including the contract line item number (CLIN) structure. When alternative CLIN structures are permitted, the evaluation considers the potential impact on other terms and conditions or the contract requirement.

An RFP may be issued for Office of Management and Budget (OMB) Circular A-76 studies, which involve cost comparisons between government and contractor performance. Electronic commerce may be used to issue RFPs and to receive proposals, modifications, and revisions. If facsimile proposals are authorized, contracting officers may request offeror(s) to provide the complete, original signed proposal at a later date. Oral RFPs generally are authorized when processing a written solicitation would delay the acquisition of supplies or services to the detriment of the government. Use of an oral RFP does not relieve the government from complying with other FAR requirements.

TIMELINESS—SEALED BID AND COMPETITIVE PROPOSALS

Offerors are responsible for submitting offers, and any revisions and modifications to them, so that they reach the government office designated in the solicitation on time.

If an emergency or unanticipated event interrupts normal government processes so that proposals cannot be received at the office designated for receipt of proposals by the exact time specified in the solicitation, and urgent government requirements preclude amendment of the solicitation closing date, the time specified for receipt of proposals will be deemed to be extended to the same time of day specified in the solicitation on the first work day on which normal government processes resume. If no time is specified in the solicitation, the time for receipt is 4:30 p.m., local time, for the designated government office on the date that proposals are due.

Proposals, and modifications to them, that are received in the designated government office after the exact time specified are "late" and will be considered only if they are received before award is made and one of the following conditions is met:

1. The proposal was sent by registered or certified mail not later than the fifth calendar day before the date specified for receipt of offers.

2. The proposal was sent by mail (or telegram or facsimile, if authorized) or hand-carried (including delivery by a commercial carrier) if it is determined by the government that the late receipt was due primarily to government mishandling after receipt at the government installation.

3. The proposal was sent by U.S. Postal Service Express Mail Next Day Service-Post Office to Addressee, not later than 5:00 p.m. at the place of mailing two working days prior to the date specified for receipt of proposals. (The term "working days" excludes weekends and U.S. federal holidays.)

4. The proposal was transmitted through an electronic commerce method au-

thorized by the solicitation and was received at the initial point of entry to the government infrastructure not later than 5:00 p.m. one working day prior to the date specified for receipt of proposals.

5. There is acceptable evidence to establish that the proposal was received at the activity designated for receipt of offers and was under the government's control prior to the time set for receipt of offers, and the contracting officer determines that accepting the late offer would not unduly delay the procurement.

6. The proposal was the only one received.

The government will promptly notify any offeror if its proposal, modification, or revision was received late, and inform the offeror whether or not it will be considered, unless contract award is imminent.

When a late proposal or modification is transmitted within the United States or Canada by registered or certified mail or by U.S. Postal Service Express Mail Next Day Service-Post Office to Addressee and is received before award, the offeror will be promptly notified that the offeror must establish that the proposal was sent by either: (1) registered or certified mail showing a date of mailing not later than the fifth calendar day before the date specified for opening; or (2) U.S. Postal Service Express Mail Next Day Service-Post Office to Addressee showing a date of mailing not later than 5:00 p.m. two federal working days prior to the date specified. Late proposals and modifications that are not considered will be held unopened, unless opened for identification, until after award and then retained with other unsuccessful proposals.

Proposals may be withdrawn at any time before award. Written proposals are withdrawn upon receipt by the government of a written notice of withdrawal. Oral pro-posals in response to oral solicitations may be withdrawn orally. Upon withdrawal of an electronically transmitted proposal, the data received will not be viewed and will be purged from primary and backup data storage systems.

EVALUATION PROCESS—COMPETITIVE PROPOSALS

An award decision is based on evaluation factors and significant subfactors that are tailored to the acquisition. Evaluation factors and significant subfactors must represent the key areas of importance and emphasis to be considered in the source selection decision and support meaningful comparison and discrimination between and among competing proposals. The evaluation factors and significant subfactors that apply to an acquisition and their relative importance are subject to the following requirements:

1. Price or cost to the government will be evaluated in every source selection.

2. The quality of the product or service will be addressed in every source selection through consideration of one or more non-cost evaluation factors such as past performance, compliance with solicitation requirements, technical excellence, management capability, personnel qualifications, and prior experience.

3. Generally, past performance will be evaluated in all source selections for negotiated competitive acquisitions expected to exceed $1,000,000.

Generally, the extent of participation of small disadvantaged business concerns in performance of the contract will be evaluated in unrestricted acquisitions expected to exceed $500,000 ($1,000,000 for construction).

All factors and significant subfactors that will affect contract award and their relative importance must be stated clearly in the solicitation. Although the rating method need not be disclosed in the solicitation, the general approach for evaluating past performance information must be described. The solicitation must state whether all evaluation factors other than cost or price, when combined, are significantly more important than cost or price, approximately equal to cost or price, or significantly less important than cost or price.

Proposal evaluation is an assessment of the proposal and the offeror's ability to perform the prospective contract successfully. The government evaluates competitive proposals and then assesses their relative qualities based solely on the factors and subfactors specified in the solicitation. Evaluations may be conducted using any rating method or combination of methods, including color or adjectival ratings, numerical weights, and ordinal rankings. The relative strengths, deficiencies, significant weaknesses, and risks supporting proposal evaluation must be documented.

Normally, competition establishes price reasonableness. When contracting on a firm-fixed-price or fixed-price with economic price adjustment basis, comparison of the proposed prices will usually satisfy the requirement to perform a price analysis. In very limited situations, a cost analysis may be appropriate to establish the reasonableness of the successful offeror's price. When contracting on a cost-reimbursement basis, evaluations include a cost realism analysis to determine what the government should realistically expect to pay for the proposed effort, the offeror's understanding of the work, and the offeror's ability to perform the contract. Cost realism analyses may also be used on fixed-price incentive contracts or, in very exceptional cases, on other competitive fixed-price-type contracts.

The currency and relevance of past performance information, the source of the information, the context of the data, and general trends in the contractor's performance are considered. A solicitation describes the approach for evaluating past performance, including evaluating offerors with no relevant performance history, and provides offerors an opportunity to identify past or current contracts (including federal, state, and local government and private) for efforts similar to the government requirement. A solicitation authorizes offerors to provide information on problems encountered on the identified contracts and the offeror's corrective actions. The government considers this information, as well as information obtained from any other sources, when evaluating the offeror's past performance.

The evaluation should take into account past performance information regarding predecessor companies, key personnel who have relevant experience, or subcontractors that will perform major or critical aspects of the requirement when such information is relevant to the acquisition. In the case of an offeror without a record of relevant past performance or for whom information on past performance is not available, the offeror may not be evaluated favorably or unfavorably on past performance. The evaluation includes the past performance of offerors in complying with subcontracting plan goals for small disadvantaged business (SDB) concerns and monetary targets for SDB participation.

Cost information may be provided to members of the technical evaluation team in accordance with agency procedures. The government may reject all proposals received in response to a solicitation, if doing so is in the best interest of the government.

COMMUNICATIONS—COMPETITIVE PROPOSALS

If contract award will be made without discussions, offerors may be given the opportunity to clarify certain aspects of proposals or to resolve minor or clerical errors.

An example of the former is the relevance of an offeror's past performance information and adverse past performance information to which the offeror has not previously had an opportunity to respond.

Award may be made without discussions if the solicitation states that the government intends to evaluate proposals and make award without discussions. If the solicitation contains such a notice, the government may later determine that it is necessary to conduct discussions. Communications are exchanges between the government and offerors after receipt of proposals, leading to establishment of the competitive range.

If a competitive range is to be established, these communications:

1. Are limited to the offerors whose past performance information is the determining factor preventing them from being placed within the competitive range and those offerors whose exclusion from, or inclusion in, the competitive range is uncertain.

2. May be conducted to enhance government understanding of a proposal, allow reasonable interpretation of the proposal, or facilitate the government's evaluation process. (Such communications are not to be used to cure proposal deficiencies or material omissions, materially alter the technical or cost elements of the proposal, and/or otherwise revise the proposal. Such communications may be considered in rating proposals for the purpose of establishing the competitive range.)

3. Are for the purpose of addressing issues that must be explored to determine whether a proposal should be placed in the competitive range. (Such communications are not to provide an opportunity for the offeror to revise its proposal, but may address ambiguities in the proposal or other concerns, e.g., perceived deficiencies, weaknesses, errors, omissions, or mistakes and information relating to relevant past performance.)

4. Will address adverse past performance information on which the offeror has not previously had an opportunity to comment.

If discussions are to be conducted, the government must establish a competitive range based on the ratings of each proposal against all evaluation criteria. The government must establish a competitive range comprising all the most highly rated proposals, unless the range is further reduced for purposes of efficiency. The government may determine that the number of most highly rated proposals that might otherwise be included in the competitive range exceeds the number at which an efficient competition can be conducted. If the solicitation notifies offerors that the competitive range can be limited for purposes of efficiency, the government may limit the number of proposals in the competitive range. Offerors excluded or otherwise eliminated from the competitive range may request a debriefing.

After establishment of the competitive range, the government and offerors begin negotiations with the intent of allowing the offerors to revise their proposals. These negotiations may include persuasion, alteration of assumptions and positions, and give-and-take, and may apply to price, schedule, technical requirements, type of contract, or other terms of a proposed contract.

When negotiations are conducted in a competitive acquisition, they take place after establishment of the competitive range and are called discussions. Discussions are tailored to each offeror's proposal, and are conducted by the contracting officer with each offeror within the competitive range. The primary objective of discussions is to maximize the government's ability to obtain best value, based on the requirement and the evaluation.

The government must indicate to, or discuss with, each offeror still being considered for award, significant weaknesses, deficiencies, and other aspects of its proposal (such as cost, price, technical approach, past performance, and terms and conditions) that could be altered or explained to enhance materially the proposal's potential for award. The scope and extent of discussions are a matter of contracting officer judgment. In discussing other aspects of the proposal, the government may, in situations where the solicitation stated that evaluation credit would be given for technical solutions exceeding any mandatory minimums, negotiate with offerors for increased performance beyond any mandatory minimums, and the government may suggest to offerors that have exceeded any mandatory minimums (in ways that are not integral to the design) that their proposals would be more competitive if the excesses were removed and the offered price decreased.

If, after discussions have begun, an offeror originally in the competitive range is no longer considered to be among the most highly rated offerors being considered for award, that offeror may be eliminated from the competitive range whether or not all material aspects of the proposal have been discussed, and whether or not the offeror has been afforded an opportunity to submit a proposal revision. Government personnel involved in the acquisition may not engage in conduct that: (1) favors one offeror over another; (2) reveals an offeror's technical solution, including unique technology, innovative and unique uses of commercial items, or any information that would compromise an offeror's intellectual property to another offeror; (3) reveals an offeror's price without that offeror's permission; or (4) reveals the names of individuals providing reference information about an offeror's past performance or knowingly furnishes source selection information. However, the government may inform an offeror that its price is considered by the government to be too high or too low, and reveal the results of the analysis supporting that conclusion. It is also permissible, at the government's discretion, to indicate to all offerors the cost or price that the govern-ment's price analysis, market research, and other reviews have identified as reasonable.

If an offeror's proposal is eliminated or otherwise removed from the competitive range, no further revisions to that offeror's proposal are considered. The government may request or allow proposal revisions to clarify and document understandings reached during negotiations. At the conclusion of discussions, each offeror still in the competitive range will be given an opportunity to submit a final proposal revision. The government must establish a common cut-off date only for receipt of final proposal revisions. Requests for final proposal revisions advise offerors that the final proposal revisions must be in writing and that the government intends to make award without obtaining further revisions.

TRUTH IN NEGOTIATIONS—COMPETITIVE COST-TYPE PROPOSALS AND ALL NON-COMPETITIVE PROPOSALS

The Truth in Negotiations Act, Public Law 87-653, is of primary importance to contractors as it relates to the development and submittal of cost and pricing data for negotiated contracts. Unless certain exceptions apply, this act requires that both prime contractors and subcontractors submit cost or pricing data and certify that, to the best of their knowledge and belief, the cost or pricing data submitted are accurate, current, and complete, in certain situations:

1. Before award of a negotiated prime contract over $700,000[1]

---

[1]This threshold is based on an index and is reestablished in October of each year divisible by 5.

2. Before pricing of a contract change or modification over $700,000

3. Before award of a negotiated subcontract in excess of $700,000, at any tier, if prime and higher tier subcontractors have furnished certified cost or pricing data

4. Before pricing of a change or modification over $700,000 to such a subcontract.

The thresholds for submission and certification of cost or pricing data should not be confused with government agency practices regarding the audit of price proposals. Beginning in late 2010, the Defense Contract Audit Agency (DCAA) determined that cost-type proposals under $100 million and fixed-price type proposals under $10 million will no longer be reviewed. However, these proposals are still subject to the Truth in Negotiations Act and are subject to an after-the-fact review to determine if accurate, current , and complete cost or pricing data were disclosed.

Given the requirements of the Truth in Negotiations Act, it is important to define cost analysis and price analysis. Cost analysis involves the evaluation of the judgmental factors used by the contractor in estimating costs. Profits are also subjected to separate review using specific criteria. Cost analysis includes the following considerations: (1) verification of cost or pricing data; (2) evaluation of the effect of the offeror's current practices on future costs; (3) comparisons of costs proposed for individual cost elements; (4) compliance with government cost principles and regulations; (5) analysis of make-or-buy programs; and (6) should-cost analysis, which is a technique that evaluates contractor prices based on what an item should cost rather than based on historical costs.

Price analysis is the process of examining and evaluating a contractor's proposed price without separately evaluating individual cost and profit elements. Some methods of price analysis include: (1) comparison of prices submitted by various contractors; (2) comparison with prices of prior quotations for similar items; (3) comparison with prices set forth in published price lists, published market prices of commodities, etc.; and (4) comparison with estimates of cost developed independently by government personnel.

CHAPTER 2 — Types of Government Contracts

A flexible selection of contract types is available to the government for acquiring the variety and volume of goods and services it requires. Contract types vary according to the degree and timing of the responsibility assumed by the contractor for the costs of performance, and the amount and nature of the profit incentive offered to the contractor for achieving or exceeding specified standards or goals.

Two factors are significant in the government's selection of contract type: (1) the government's ability to state precisely a quantity of goods or services; and (2) the government's ability to define precisely the work to be performed. When uncertainties are limited, the contracting arrangement will be precise with respect to price and performance. When uncertainties are great, the contractual arrangement will have much more flexibility.

The government uses two major categories of contract type: fixed-price and cost-reimbursement. Numerous variations exist within each of these two categories. Specific contract types range from firm-fixed-price, in which the contractor has full responsibility for the performance costs and the resulting profit or loss, to cost-plus-fixed-fee, in which the contractor has minimal responsibility for the performance costs, and the negotiated fee or profit is fixed. For a fixed-price contract, the contractor is obligated to provide an end product or service at an established price. Thus, the profit or loss on the contract will be directly affected by any difference between the estimated cost and the actual cost of performance.

By comparison, in a cost-reimbursement contract, the contractor is responsible only for whatever product or service evolves as a result of the effort, up to the estimated costs established in the contract. The contractor's fee or profit is fixed by the contract and, thus, the contractor's interest in cost performance factors is not as significant as in a fixed-price contract. In between the firm-fixed-price contract and the cost-plus-fixed-fee contract are various incentive contracts, in which the contractor's responsibility for the performance costs and the profit or fee incentives offered are tailored to the uncertainties involved in contract performance.

The government's concern in monitoring contractor costs is greatest under cost-reimbursement contracts. The government imposes strict regulations on contractors regarding the accumulation, allowability, and allocation of costs. In addition, the government takes steps to ensure that the accounting systems of contractors with cost-reimbursement contracts are adequate to establish actual costs. The same regulations apply to the negotiation of fixed-price contracts; however, the emphasis on cost monitoring is not as rigid.

Negotiated contracts may be of any contract type that promotes the government's interest. Contract types not described in the FAR are not to be used without a formal deviation. The cost-plus-a-percentage-of-cost system of contracting is prohibited by legislation. Prime contracts other than firm-fixed-price contracts must prohibit cost-plus-a-percentage-of-cost subcontracts.

During the federal government's early years, the use of firm-fixed-price contracts was essentially exclusive. Purchased goods and services were rather simple—horses, guns, cannons, etc. World War I temporarily popularized the cost-reimbursement contract type. Because of the contractor risks involved in designing, developing, and producing new items, this contract type was necessary for equitable contracting arrangements. World War II expanded the use of cost-reimbursement contracts, which became institutionalized in regulations shortly thereafter.

The development of cost allowability rules parallels the expanded usage of cost-reimbursement contracts. From World War II through about the 1960s, contracts were either firm-fixed-price or a variation of cost-reimbursement. The next additions to contract types were the variations on the fixed-price contract. These variations permitted more risk to be shifted to a contractor than under a cost-reimbursement contract. However, both fixed-price incentive and cost-reimbursement contracts depended on the determination of actual costs in establishing a final contract price.

In the mid-1990s, a new trend developed to minimize administrative requirements by using other than cost-based pricing of contracts. The definition of commercial items was expanded to allow more purchases under fixed-price contracts without prices being cost-based. The government began to use "other transaction" authority instead of traditional contracting to obtain goods and services. This approach greatly limited the amount of audited cost-based pricing. Initiatives were directed at eliminating or reducing the extent of cost-based pricing throughout the government procurement process.

GOVERNMENT SELECTION OF CONTRACT TYPES

The government generally determines the contract type to be used. However, contract type is theoretically a matter for negotiation. The contract type and the contract price are closely related and are usually considered together. The government's overall objective is to establish a contract type and price that will result in reasonable contractor risk and provide a contractor with the greatest incentive for efficient and economical performance. Generally, a firm-fixed-price contract, which makes best use of the inherent profit motive, is used when the contractor risk involved is minimal or can be predicted with an acceptable degree of certainty. When a reasonable basis for firm pricing does not exist, other contract types are used.

For major acquisition programs, a series of contracts may result in a different contract type in later periods than that used at the start of the program. Contracting officers are discouraged from protracted use of a cost-reimbursement or time-and-materials contract if experience provides a basis for firmer pricing. Fixed-price contracts have been found unacceptable for research and development work. Under these contracts, a contractor may be required to research and/or develop an item at a fixed price, which may be impractical. The use of fixed-price contracts for research and development has proven to be disastrous. Contractors cannot afford the risks under these conditions, and when failure occurs the outcome is not good—default, lawsuits, etc. A contractor invariably loses money and the government may not get the work expected.

The government considers many factors in selecting the contract type. Effective price competition results in realistic pricing and thus a fixed-price contract is usually appropriate. Price analysis with or without actual price competition may also provide a basis for selecting the contract type. The government also considers the degree to which price analysis can provide a realistic pricing standard.

In the absence of effective price competition and if price analysis is not sufficient, the cost estimates of the offeror and the government may provide the basis for negotiating contract pricing arrangements. The uncertainties involved in performance and the possible impact on costs are evaluated, so that a contract type that places a reasonable degree of cost responsibility on the contractor can be negotiated.

A firm-fixed-price contract is suitable for acquiring commercial items or for acquiring other supplies or services on the basis of reasonably definite functional or detailed specifications when the contracting officer can establish fair and reasonable prices at the outset. This occurs when: (1) price competition is adequate; (2) price comparisons with prior purchases of the same or similar supplies or services made on a competitive basis or supported by valid cost or pricing data are reasonable; (3) available cost or pricing information permits realistic estimates of the probable costs of performance; or (4) performance uncertainties can be identified and reasonable estimates of their cost impact can be made.

If urgency is a primary factor, the government may choose to assume a greater proportion of risk or it may offer incentives to ensure timely contract performance. In times of economic uncertainty, contracts extending over a relatively long period may require economic price adjustment terms. Before a contract type other than firm-fixed-price is used, a contractor's accounting system must permit development of all necessary cost data required by the proposed contract type. This factor may be critical when a contractor is being considered for a cost-reimbursement contract. If performance under a proposed contract involves concurrent operations under existing contracts, the impact of those contracts should be considered in selecting a contract type.

FIXED-PRICE CONTRACTS

Fixed-price contracts specify a firm price for work to be performed. These contracts may provide for adjustable prices under certain circumstances and/or provide ceiling prices. Fixed-price contracts providing for an adjustable price may include a ceiling price, a target price (including target cost), or both. Normally, the ceiling price or target price is subject to adjustment in the event of an equitable price adjustment. Firm-fixed-price or fixed-price with economic price adjustment contracts are used for acquiring commercial items. The fixed-price contract provides maximum incentive for a contractor to control costs and perform effectively because the contractor bears full responsibility for the resulting profit or loss.

The most frequently used fixed-price contract types are firm-fixed-price and fixed-price-incentive. Several other variations of the fixed-price contract are also available.

Firm-Fixed-Price Contract

Of all the various types of contracts, the firm-fixed-price (FFP) contract has the greatest potential for contractor financial reward and risk. Because the contract price is fixed at the date of award and the contractor is obligated to provide the product or service under contract, a highly efficient and cost-effective operation will generally result in greater contractor profits.

Obviously, the opposite is also true. A firm-fixed-price contract provides for a price that is not subject to any adjustment on the basis of the contractor's cost experience in performing the contract. This contract type provides maximum incentive for the contractor to control costs and perform effectively, and imposes a minimum administrative burden on the contracting parties.

Fixed-Price-Incentive Contract

A fixed-price-incentive (FPI) contract provides for adjusting profit and establishing the final contract price by applying a formula based on the relationship of total allowable cost to target cost. The final price is subject to a price ceiling established upon award of the contract. An FPI contract is most appropriate when: (1) a firm-fixed-price contract is not suitable (i.e., the nature of the product is such that the costs to be incurred in producing the product cannot be accurately estimated); (2) the nature of the goods or services being acquired and the circumstances of the acquisition are such that the contractor's assumption of a degree of cost responsibility will provide a positive profit incentive for effective cost control and performance; or (3) the contract also includes incentives on technical performance and/or delivery.

When predetermined formula-type incentives on technical performance or delivery are included, increases in profit or fee are provided only for achievement that surpasses the targets, and decreases are provided to the extent that such targets are not met. The incentive increases or decreases are applied to performance targets rather than minimum performance requirements. With an FPI contractual arrangement, a contractor has a high incentive to be cost-efficient and performance-effective. If successful in lowering contract costs below the target costs, a contractor can realize a higher profit through application of the incentive formula. Essentially, the contractor and the government become partners when the costs incurred are less than the costs estimated.

The five elements commonly negotiated into the terms of an FPI contract are: (1) target cost; (2) target profit; (3) target price (the sum of (1) plus (2)); (4) a fee adjustment formula target cost; and (5) a price ceiling (an amount in excess of the target price). The sharing ratio is a formula specifying how the government and the contractor will share any cost underrun or overrun.

Figures 2 through 4 depict how this contract type is applied. For each of these figures, the following basic assumptions are the same: (1) the target cost is $1,000,000; (2) the target profit is $85,000; (3) the target price is $1,085,000; (4) the government share of any cost over/underrun is 70 percent; and (5) the ceiling price is $1,160,000.

Figure 2 is a fixed-price-incentive contract where the actual cost of $900,000 is under the target price. This results in a $100,000 underrun. The contract price is computed by starting with the target price on line (i). The price is then reduced on line (j) by the government's share of the cost underrun or $70,000, which is 70 percent of $100,000. This results in a contract price of $1,015,000 on line (k). The profit on this contract is $115,000, which is $1,015,000 minus $900,000.

Figure 3 is a fixed-price-incentive contract where the actual cost of $1,100,000 is over the target price. This results in a $100,000 overrun. The contract price is computed by starting with the target price on line (i). The price is then increased on line (j) by the government's share of the cost overrun or $70,000, which is 70 percent of $100,000. This results in a contract price of $1,155,000 on line (k). The profit on this contract is $55,000, which is $1,155,000 minus $1,100,000.

Figure 4 is a fixed-price-incentive contract where the actual cost of $1,200,000 is over the target price and the ceiling price. This results in a $200,000 overrun. The contract price is computed by starting with the target price on line (i). The price is then increased on line (j) by the government's share of the cost overrun or $140,000, which is 70 percent of $200,000. This results in a contract price of $1,255,000 on line (k). However, this exceeds the ceiling price of $1,160,000; thus, the ceiling price becomes the contract price. The loss on this contract is $40,000, which is $1,200,000 minus $1,160,000.

Figure 2
FIXED-PRICE-INCENTIVE CONTRACT
Under Target Price

Facts:	Amount	Ref.	Source
Target Cost	$1,000,000	(a)	Negotiated
Target Profit	85,000	(b)	Negotiated
Target Price	$1,085,000	(c)	(a) + (b)
Contractor Share	30%	(d)	Negotiated
Government Share	70%	(e)	Negotiated
Ceiling Price	$1,160,000	(f)	Negotiated
Actual Cost	$900,000	(g)	
Overrun (Underrun)	($100,000)	(h)	(g) – (a)
Price:			
Target Price	$1,085,000	(i)	(c)
Government Share	(70,000)	(j)	(e) * (h)
Total Calculated Price	$1,015,000	(k)	(i) + (j)
Total Price	$1,015,000	(l)	Lesser of (d) or (k)
Profit (Loss)	$115,000		(l) – (g)

Figure 3
FIXED-PRICE-INCENTIVE CONTRACT
Over Target Price

Facts:	Amount	Ref.	Source
Target Cost	$1,000,000	(a)	Negotiated
Target Profit	85,000	(b)	Negotiated
Target Price	$1,085,000	(c)	(a) + (b)
Contractor Share	30%	(d)	Negotiated
Government Share	70%	(e)	Negotiated
Ceiling Price	$1,160,000	(f)	Negotiated
Actual Cost	$1,100,000	(g)	
Overrun (Underrun)	$100,000	(h)	(g) – (a)
Price:			
Target Price	$1,085,000	(i)	(c)
Government Share	70,000	(j)	(e) * (h)
Total Calculated Price	$1,155,000	(k)	(i) + (j)
Total Price	$1,155,000	(l)	Lesser of (d) or (k)
Profit (Loss)	$55,000		(l) – (g)

Facts:	Amount	Ref.	Source
Target Cost	$1,000,000	(a)	Negotiated
Target Profit	85,000	(b)	Negotiated
Target Price	$1,085,000	(c)	(a) + (b)
Contractor Share	30%	(d)	Negotiated
Government Share	70%	(e)	Negotiated
Ceiling Price	$1,160,000	(f)	Negotiated
Actual Cost	$1,200,000	(g)	
Overrun (Underrun)	$200,000	(h)	(g) – (a)
Price:			
Target Price	$1,085,000	(i)	(c)
Government Share	140,000	(j)	(e) * (h)
Total Calculated Price	$1,225,000	(k)	(i) + (j)
Total Price	$1,160,000	(l)	Lesser of (d) or (k)
Profit (Loss)	($40,000)		(l) – (g)

Figure 4
FIXED-PRICE-INCENTIVE CONTRACT
Over Ceiling Price

Figure 5 contains the spreadsheet formulas for the calculations in Figures 2 through 4.

Most incentive contracts include only cost incentives, which take the form of a profit or fee adjustment formula and are intended to motivate the contractor to manage costs effectively. No incentive contract may provide for other incentives without also providing a cost incentive. The FPI contract can be a profitable and lucrative endeavor for both the contractor and the government. The contractor must adhere closely to the federal regulations in estimating and accumulating contract costs, however, since these costs will be the basis for determining the eventual price to be paid by the government.

Incentives Contract

Performance incentives include such aspects as a missile's range, an aircraft's speed, an engine's thrust, or a vehicle's maneuver-ability. Both positive and negative performance incentives may be used with service contracts. Technical performance incentives are often used in development and in production for major weapon systems and may involve a variety of specific characteristics that contribute to the overall performance of the end item.

Delivery incentives are used when improvement from a required delivery schedule is an important government objective. Incentive arrangements on delivery should specify the application of the reward-penalty structure in the event of government-caused delays or other delays beyond the control—and without the fault or -negligence—of the contractor or subcontractor.

A fixed-price-incentive (firm target) contract specifies a: (1) target cost; (2) target profit; (3) price ceiling (but not a profit ceiling or floor); and (4) profit adjustment formula. These elements are all negotiated at the outset. The price ceiling is the maximum that may be

Facts:	Amount	Ref.	Source
Target Cost	$1,000,000	(a)	Negotiated
Target Profit	$85,000	(b)	Negotiated
Target Price	=P7+P8*	(c)	(a) + (b)
Ceiling Price	$1,160,000	(d)	Negotiated
Contractor Share	0.3	(e)	Negotiated
Government Share	0.7	(f)	Negotiated
Actual Cost	$900,000	(g)	
Overrun (Underrun)	=P14–P7	(h)	(g) – (a)
Price:			
Target Price	=P9	(i)	(c)
Government Share	=P12*P15	(j)	(f) * (h)
Total Calculated Price	=P18+P19	(k)	(i) + (j)
Total Price	=IF(P20>P10,P10,P20)	(l)	Lesser of (d) or (k)
Profit (Loss)	=P20–P14	(l) – (g)	

**Figure 5
SPREADSHEET FORMULAS FOR FIXED-PRICE-INCENTIVE CONTRACT**

*Formula references in "Amount" column are Excel spreadsheet cell references

paid to the contractor, except for any price adjustment under the contract terms. When the contract is completed, the parties negotiate the final cost, and the final price is established by applying the formula. If the final cost is less than the target cost, application of the formula results in a final profit greater than the target profit. Conversely, if the final cost is more than the target cost, application of the formula results in a final profit less than the target profit, or even a net loss. If the final negotiated cost exceeds the price ceiling, the contractor absorbs the difference as a loss.

Firm-Fixed-Price with Economic Adjustment Contract

A fixed-price contract with economic price adjustment provides for upward and downward revision of the contract price upon the occurrence of specified contingencies. A fixed-price contract with economic price ad-justment is used when there is serious doubt concerning the stability of market or labor conditions that will exist during an extended period of contract performance. Price adjustments based on labor and material costs are generally limited to contingencies beyond the contractor's control. Commonly, an economic adjustment provision adjusts the contract price only if the actual escalation exceeds or falls short of a stated percentage. Economic price adjustments are determined on one of three bases: (1) established prices; (2) actual costs of labor and/or materials; and (3) cost indexes for labor and/or materials.

Adjustments based on established prices are based on increases or decreases from an agreed-upon level in published or otherwise established prices of specific items or the contract end items. For example, a contract that requires a substantial amount of a special metal might provide for an annual price adjustment if the change in a published price of the metal exceeds a certain percent.

Adjustments based on actual costs of labor or materials are based on increases or decreases in specified costs of labor or materials that the contractor actually experiences during contract performance. For example, a contract that requires significant costs for an operating crew might provide for an annual price adjustment if the change in actual labor costs exceeds a certain percent. When this method is used, the contract terms must specifically identify the labor costs by category (e.g., type of personnel) and cost elements (e.g., labor rates, fringe benefits) to avoid subsequent disputes.

Adjustments based on cost indexes of labor or material are based on increases or decreases in labor or materials cost standards or indexes that are specifically identified in the contract. For example, a contract might provide for an annual price adjustment if the consumer price index changes by more than x percent.

Fixed-Price Redeterminable Contract

A fixed-price redeterminable (FPR) contract with retroactive price redetermination provides for a fixed ceiling price and retroactive price redetermination within the ceiling after completion of the contract. This contract type is used primarily for research and development contracts of $100,000 or less.

Firm-Fixed-Price Contract with Successive Targets

A fixed-price contract with prospective price redetermination provides for a firm fixed price for an initial period of contract deliveries or performance and prospective redetermination, at a stated time or times during performance, of the price for subsequent periods of performance. A fixed-price contract with prospective price redetermination is used in acquisitions of quantity production or services for which it is possible to establish

a firm fixed price for an initial period, but not for subsequent periods of contract performance. The initial period is generally the longest period possible. Each subsequent pricing period should be at least 12 months. The contract may provide for a ceiling price and may be adjusted only by operation of contract clauses providing for equitable adjustment.

A fixed-price-incentive (successive targets) contract specifies the following elements, all of which are negotiated at the outset: (1) an initial target cost; (2) an initial target profit; (3) an initial profit adjustment formula to be used for establishing the firm target profit, including a ceiling and floor for the firm target profit; (4) a ceiling target profit; (5) a floor target profit; (6) a ceiling price that is the maximum that may be paid to the contractor, except for any equitable price adjustment; and (7) the production point at which the firm target cost and firm target profit will be negotiated.

When the production point specified in the contract is reached, the parties negotiate the firm target cost and the firm target profit. The firm target profit is established by an initially negotiated formula. At this point, the parties have two alternatives: (1) negotiate a firm fixed price, using the firm target cost plus the firm target profit as a guide; or (2) negotiate a formula for establishing the final price using the firm target cost and firm target profit (an FPIF contract).

A contractor's accounting system must be adequate for providing data for negotiating firm targets and a realistic profit adjustment formula. It must also be adequate to establish a framework for later negotiation of final costs. Cost or pricing information adequate for establishing a reasonable firm target cost must be available at an early point in contract performance.

If the total firm target cost is more than the total initial target cost, the total initial target profit will be decreased. If the total firm target cost is less than the total initial target cost, the total initial target profit will be increased. The initial target profit will be increased or decreased by the contractually stated percentage of the difference between the total initial target cost and the total firm target cost. The resulting amount will be the total firm target profit, provided that in no event is the total firm target profit more or less than a contractually stated percentage of the total initial target cost.

Figures 6 through 10 show how this contract type works. The same basic data are assumed for five outcomes. The initial target cost, initial target profit, ceiling contract price, ceiling target profit percentage, and floor target profit percentage are negotiated at contract award. Also, a formula is negotiated for price adjustment purposes. The adjustment will be to the initial target profit. The formula will state that the initial target profit will be adjusted downward by x percent of the excess of the firm target cost over the initial target cost. Likewise, the formula will state that the initial target profit will be adjusted upward by y percent of the excess of the initial target cost over the firm target cost.

At a specified point in time (which is negotiated at the time the contract is awarded), a firm target cost is negotiated based on new cost data. The formula is applied to the initial target profit. The contract price can then be completed as either a firm-fixed-price (FFP) or a fixed-price-incentive fee (FPIF) contract.

Figure 6 FIXED-PRICE-INCENTIVE SUCCESSIVE TARGET CONTRACT Well Under Initial Target Price			
Facts:	Amount	Ref.	Source
Initial Target Cost	$1,000,000	(a)	Negotiated
Initial Target Profit Percentage	12%	(b)	Negotiated
Initial Target Profit Amount	120,000	(c)	(a) * (b)
Initial Target Price	$1,120,000	(d)	(a) + (c)
Formula for Adjustment of Target Profit Percentage	25%	(e)	Negotiated
Ceiling Price	$1,300,000	(f)	Negotiated
Floor Target Profit Percentage	9%	(g)	Negotiatcd
Floor Target Profit Percentage Amount	$90,000	(h)	(a) * (g)
Ceiling Target Profit Percentage	15%	(i)	Negotiated
Ceiling Target Profit Percentage Amount	$150,000	(j)	(a) * (i)
Firm Target Cost	$800,000	(k)	Negotiated Later
Price:			
Firm Target Cost	$800,000	(l)	(k)
Initial Target Profit	$120,000	(m)	(c)
Profit Formula Adjustment	$50,000	(n)	(e) * ((a) - (l))
Total	$170,000	(o)	(m) + (n)
Firm Target Profit	$150,000	(p)	(o) but < (j) and > (h)
Total Price	$950,000	(q)	(l) + (p) but < (f)
Expected Profit (Loss)	$150,000	(r)	(q) - (k)

Figure 7 FIXED-PRICE-INCENTIVE SUCCESSIVE TARGET CONTRACT Under Initial Target Price			
Facts:	Amount	Ref.	Source
Initial Target Cost	$1,000,000	(a)	Negotiated
Initial Target Profit Percentage	12%	(b)	Negotiated
Initial Target Profit Amount	120,000	(c)	(a) * (b)
Initial Target Price	$1,120,000	(d)	(a) + (c)
Formula for Adjustment of Target Profit Percentage	25%	(e)	Negotiated
Ceiling Price	$1,300,000	(f)	Negotiated
Floor Target Profit Percentage	9%	(g)	Negotiated
Floor Target Profit Percentage Amount	$90,000	(h)	(a) * (g)
Ceiling Target Profit Percentage	15%	(i)	Negotiated
Ceiling Target Profit Percentage Amount	$150,000	(j)	(a) * (i)
Firm Target Cost	$900,000	(k)	Negotiated Later
Price:			
Firm Target Cost	$900,000	(l)	(k)
Initial Target Profit	$120,000	(m)	(c)
Profit Formula Adjustment	$25,000	(n)	(e) * ((a) - (l))
Total	$145,000	(o)	(m) + (n)
Firm Target Profit	$145,000	(p)	(l) but < (j) and > (h)
Total Price	$1,045,000	(q)	(l) + (p) but < (f)
Expected Profit (Loss)	$145,000	(r)	(q) - (k)

The examples include five scenarios for the firm target cost: (1) well under the initial target cost; (2) under the initial target cost; (3) over the initial target cost; (4) well over the initial target cost; and (5) extremely over the initial target cost. Assuming a firm fixed price rather than adding more complications for a FPIF contract, the expected profit or loss line is based on meeting the firm target cost.

Figure 6 is for the well under initial target price scenario, in which the ceiling target profit is attained. (The cost underrun is so great that the contracts maximum profit provision applies.) Figure 7 is for the under initial target price scenario. Figure 8 is for the over initial target price scenario. Figure 9 is for the well over initial target price scenario, in which the floor target profit is applied. (The cost overrun is so great that the contract's minimum profit provision applies.) Figure 10 is for the extremely over initial target price scenario and the ceiling price is applied. Figure 11 contains the formulas for these scenarios. Figure 12 displays the relationship of the various components of this contract type.

Fixed-Price, Level-of-Effort Contract

A firm-fixed-price, level-of-effort (FP-LOE) term contract provides for a specified level of effort, over a stated period of time, on work

Figure 8 FIXED-PRICE-INCENTIVE SUCCESSIVE TARGET CONTRACT Over Initial Target Price			
Facts:	Amount	Ref.	Source
Initial Target Cost	$1,000,000	(a)	Negotiated
Initial Target Profit Percentage	12%	(b)	Negotiated
Initial Target Profit Amount	120,000	(c)	(a) * (b)
Initial Target Price	$1,120,000	(d)	(a) + (c)
Formula for Adjustment of Target Profit Percentage	25%	(e)	Negotiated
Ceiling Price	$1,300,000	(f)	Negotiated
Floor Target Profit Percentage	9%	(g)	Negotiated
Floor Target Profit Percentage Amount	$90,000	(h)	(a) * (g)
Ceiling Target Profit Percentage	15%	(i)	Negotiated
Ceiling Target Profit Percentage Amount	$150,000	(j)	(a) * (i)
Firm Target Cost	$1,100,000	(k)	Negotiated Later
Price:			
Firm Target Cost	$1,100,000	(l)	(k)
Initial Target Profit	$120,000	(m)	(c)
Profit Formula Adjustment	($25,000)	(n)	(e) * ((a) - (l))
Total	$95,000	(o)	(m) + (n)
Firm Target Profit	$95,000	(p)	(l) but < (j) and > (h)
Total Price	$1,195,000	(q)	(l) + (p) but < (f)
Expected Profit (Loss)	$95,000	(r)	(q) - (k)

that can be stated only in general terms. This contract type is suitable for investigation or study in a specific research and development area where the product is usually a report showing the results achieved through application of the required level of effort. However, payment is based on the effort expended rather than on the results achieved.

Some FP-LOE contracts contain price adjustment provisions that are based on the estimated versus actual labor provided. For example, the provision might require a price adjustment if more or less than 15 percent of the estimated hours is incurred. This provision could be on the total hours for the contract or on individual labor categories.

Fixed-Price, Award-Fee Contract

Award-fee provisions are used infrequently in a fixed-price contract. Such contracts establish a fixed price (including normal profit) for the effort. This price will be paid for satisfactory contract performance. Award fee earned (if any) will be paid in addition to that fixed price based on periodic formal evaluation of the contractor's performance against an award-fee plan.

COST-REIMBURSEMENT CONTRACTS

Cost-reimbursement contracts provide for payment of actual allowable costs, as gov-

Figure 9 FIXED-PRICE-INCENTIVE SUCCESSIVE TARGET CONTRACT Well Over Initial Target Price			
Facts:	Amount	Ref.	Source
Initial Target Cost	$1,000,000	(a)	Negotiated
Initial Target Profit Percentage	12%	(b)	Negotiated
Initial Target Profit Amount	120,000	(c)	(a) * (b)
Initial Target Price	$1,120,000	(d)	(a) + (c)
Formula for Adjustment of Target Profit Percentage	25%	(e)	Negotiated
Ceiling Price	$1,300,000	(f)	Negotiated
Floor Target Profit Percentage	9%	(g)	Negotiated
Floor Target Profit Percentage Amount	$90,000	(h)	(a) * (g)
Ceiling Target Profit Percentage	9%	(i)	Negotiated
Ceiling Target Profit Percentage Amount	$90,000	(j)	(a) * (i)
Firm Target Cost	$1,200,000	(k)	Negotiated Later
Price:			
Firm Target Cost	$1,200,000	(l)	(k)
Initial Target Profit	$120,000	(m)	(c)
Profit Formula Adjustment	($50,000)	(n)	(e) * ((a) - (l))
Total	$70,000	(o)	(m) + (n)
Firm Target Profit	$90,000	(p)	(l) but < (j) and > (h)
Total Price	$1,290,000	(q)	(l) + (p) but < (f)
Expected Profit (Loss)	$90,000	(r)	(q) - (k)

erned by Part 31 of the FAR. Cost-reimbursement contracts establish estimates of total cost for the purpose of obligating funds. If a contractor exceeds the funds without contracting officer approval, such costs are incurred at the contractor's risk.

A cost-reimbursement contract is used when the uncertainties of performance do not permit costs to be estimated with enough accuracy to use a fixed-price contract. Cost-reimbursement contracts entail minimal contractor financial responsibility. Under these contracts, the contractor is reimbursed for actual allowable costs up to the contract ceiling, plus the established fee. The contractor usually is not allowed to invoice for more than 85 percent of the fee until the contract

is completed. The remaining 15 percent is held by the government as a reserve for contractual problems and/or final indirect rate adjustments.

Once awarded a cost-reimbursement contract, a contractor is subject to numerous federal regulations and contract clauses. One of the more troublesome clauses, the limitation of cost clause (LOCC), is found in FAR 52.232-20. This clause requires a contractor to notify the contracting officer in writing whenever he has reason to believe that: (1) the costs he expects to incur under the contract in the next 60 days (or an alternative number of days ranging from 30 to 90) when added to costs previously incurred, will exceed 75 percent (or an alternative percentage

Figure 10 FIXED-PRICE-INCENTIVE SUCCESSIVE TARGET CONTRACT Extremely Over Initial Target Price			
Facts:	Amount	Ref.	Source
Initial Target Cost	$1,000,000	(a)	Negotiated
Initial Target Profit Percentage	12%	(b)	Negotiated
Initial Target Profit Amount	120,000	(c)	(a) * (b)
Initial Target Price	$1,120,000	(d)	(a) + (c)
Formula for Adjustment of Target Profit Percentage	25%	(e)	Negotiated
Ceiling Price	$1,300,000	(f)	Negotiated
Floor Target Profit Percentage	9%	(g)	Negotiated
Floor Target Profit Percentage Amount	$90,000	(h)	(a) * (g)
Ceiling Target Profit Percentage	15%	(i)	Negotiated
Ceiling Target Profit Percentage Amount	$150,000	(j)	(a) * (i)
Firm Target Cost	$1,350,000	(k)	Negotiated Later
Price:			
Firm Target Cost	$1,350,000	(l)	(k)
Initial Target Profit	$120,000	(m)	(c)
Profit Formula Adjustment	($87,500)	(n)	(e) * ((a) - (l))
Total	$32,500	(o)	(m) + (n)
Firm Target Profit	$90,000	(p)	(l) but < (j) and > (h)
Total Price	$1,300,000	(q)	(l) + (p) but < (f)
Expected Profit (Loss)	($50,000)	(r)	(q) - (k)

ranging from 75 to 85) of the estimated costs specified in the contract; or (2) the total cost for the performance of the contract, exclusive of any fee, will be either greater or substantially less than estimated.

The primary purpose of the LOCC is to protect the government from unauthorized and unexpected cost overruns. Once the contractor notifies the government of a potential overrun, the government must decide whether or not to extend the work and grant additional funding, or to revise the contract scope of work.

Several decisions by the Board of Contract Appeals (BCA) construed a pre-1966 LOCC liberally, allowing contractors to recover for cost overruns in a variety of situations. Since

then a revised LOCC, adopted in October 1966, has made it extremely difficult for a contractor to be reimbursed for a cost overrun. If a contractor with an adequate accounting system can show that he could not reasonably foresee a cost overrun, he can be excepted from the requirement. In establishing this exception to the no-reimbursement for overrun rule, the Court of Claims has stated that it is an abuse of discretion for the contracting officer to refuse to fund the cost overrun because of the contractor's failure to give notice when it was impossible to do so.

The best example of when a contractor may not be aware of a potential overrun is a contractor who had submitted indirect cost billing rates for audit. The government auditor

Figure 11 SPREADSHEET FORMULAS FOR FIXED-PRICE-INCENTIVE SUCCESSIVE TARGET CONTRACT			
Facts:	Amount	Ref.	Source
Initial Target Cost	$1,000,000	(a)	Negotiated
Initial Target Profit Percentage	12%	(b)	Negotiated
Initial Target Profit Amount	=+C8*C7	(c)	(a) * (b)
Initial Target Price	=+C9+C7	(d)	(a) + (c)
Formula for Adjustment of Target Profit Percentage	25%	(e)	Negotiated
Ceiling Price	$1,300,000	(f)	Negotiated
Floor Target Profit Percentage	9%	(g)	Negotiated
Floor Target Profit Percentage Amount	=+C13*C7	(h)	(a) * (g)
Ceiling Target Profit Percentage	9%	(i)	Negotiated
Ceiling Target Profit Percentage Amount	=+C15*C7	(j)	(a) * (i)
Firm Target Cost	$1,200,000	(k)	Negotiated Later
Price:			
Firm Target Cost	=+C17	(l)	(k)
Initial Target Profit	=+C9	(m)	(c)
Profit Formula Adjustment	=+C11*(+C7-C20)	(n)	(e) * ((a) - (l))
Total	=+C22+C21	(o)	(m) + (n)
Firm Target Profit	=IF(C23<C14,C14,IF(C23>C16,C16,C23))	(p)	(o) but < (j) and > (h)
Total Price	=IF(C24+C20>C12,C12, +C20+C24)	(q)	(l) + (p) but < (f)
Expected Profit (Loss)	=+C25-C20	(r)	(q) - (k)

*Formula references in "Amount" column are Excel spreadsheet cell references

challenged certain pension costs and reduced the billing rate substantially. The contract funds were substantially expended using this lower billing rate. When the government auditor performed the final indirect cost audit several years later, the auditor changed his mind and did not disallow any pension costs.

Another practical danger is the government's unilateral removal of funds from a contract before final audited rates have been established. In some cases, funds expire after three or five years. In other cases, funds may simply not be available to cover increases be-

cause final indirect cost rates are more than the interim billing rates.

Types of cost-reimbursement contracts available include cost-sharing, cost-reimbursement-only, cost-plus-fixed-fee, cost-plus-incentive-fee, and cost-plus-award-fee.

Cost-Sharing Contract

A cost-sharing contract is one in which the contractor receives no fee and is reimbursed only for an agreed-upon percentage (e.g., 80

Figure 12

RELATIONSHIP OF PROFIT TO DIFFERENCES BETWEEN INITIAL TARGET COST AND FIRM TARGET COST

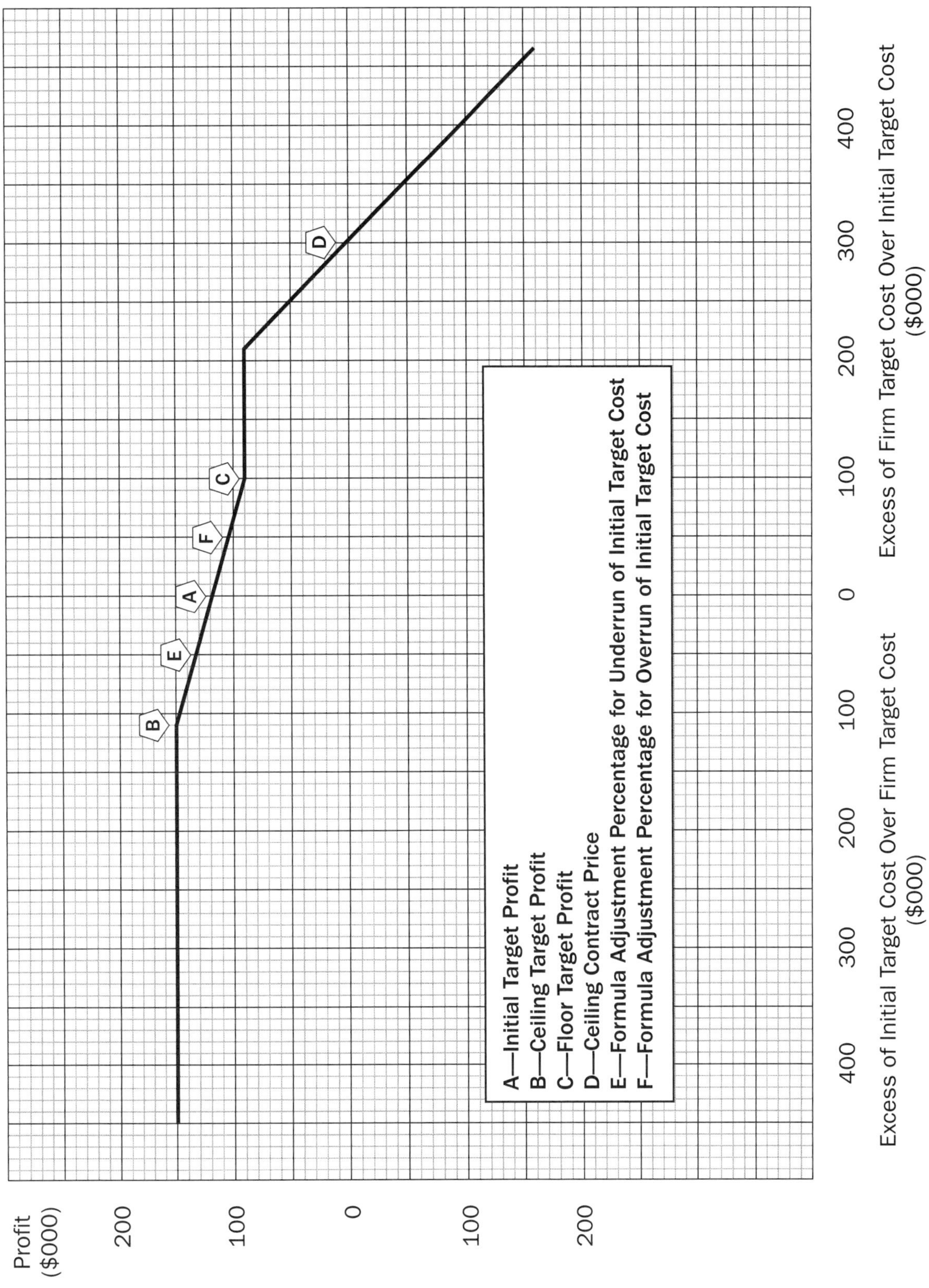

A—Initial Target Profit
B—Ceiling Target Profit
C—Floor Target Profit
D—Ceiling Contract Price
E—Formula Adjustment Percentage for Underrun of Initial Target Cost
F—Formula Adjustment Percentage for Overrun of Initial Target Cost

percent) of allowable costs. A cost-sharing contract is used when a contractor agrees to absorb a portion of the costs, in the expectation of substantial compensating benefits. For example, a contractor might agree to share in the development costs of a weapon systems in anticipation of being awarded any resulting production contract. This contract type is more widely used for educational institutions and nonprofit entities than commercial organizations.

Cost-Reimbursement-Only Contract

A cost-reimbursement-only contract is one in which the contractor receives no fee. This contract type is more appropriate for research and development work, particularly with nonprofit educational institutions or other nonprofits.

Cost-Plus-Fixed-Fee Contract

A cost-plus-fixed-fee (CPFF) contract provides for payment to the contractor of a negotiated fee that is fixed at the inception of the contract. This contract type permits contracting for efforts that might otherwise present too great a risk to contractors, but it provides the contractor only a minimum incentive to control costs.

A cost-plus-fixed-fee contract may take one of two basic forms—completion or term. The completion form describes the scope of work by stating a definite goal or target and specifying an end product. This form of contract normally requires the contractor to complete and deliver the specified end product (e.g., a final report of research accomplishing the goal or target) within the estimated cost, if possible, as a condition for payment of the entire fixed fee. However, in the event that the work cannot be completed within the estimated cost, the government may require completion of the work without increase in

fee, provided that the government increases the estimated cost. Additional fee under these circumstances depends on whether the "cost overrun" is due simply to more cost than anticipated or to increased scope of work. Simple cost overruns for the scope of work contemplated in the contract do not warrant additional fee. Cost increases due to change in the scope of work and contract risk do warrant additional fee (or less fee if the government believes a reduced scope of work has occurred).

The term form describes the scope of work in general terms and obligates the contractor to devote a specified level of effort for a stated time period. Under this form, if the government considers performance to be satisfactory, the fixed fee is payable at the expiration of the agreed-upon period—upon contractor statement that the level of effort specified in the contract has been expended in performing the contract work. Renewal for further periods of performance is a new acquisition that involves new cost and fee arrangements.

Because of the differences in obligation assumed by the contractor, the completion form is preferred over the term form whenever the work, or specific milestones for the work, can be defined well enough to permit development of estimates within which the contractor can be expected to complete the work. The term form should not be used unless the contractor is obligated by the contract to provide a specific level of effort within a definite time period.

Cost-Plus-Incentive-Fee Contract

The cost-plus-incentive-fee (CPIF) contract is a cost-reimbursement contract that provides for the initially negotiated fee to be adjusted later by a formula based on the relationship of total allowable costs to total target costs. This contract type specifies: (1) a target cost; (2) a target fee; (3) a minimum fee; (4) a maximum fee; and (5) a fee adjustment formula. The formula provides, within limits, for increases in fee above the target fee when total allowable costs are less than target costs, and decreases in fee below the target fee when total allowable costs exceed target costs. When total allowable costs are greater or less than the range of costs within which the fee-adjustment formula operates, the contractor is paid total allowable costs, plus the minimum or maximum fee.

Figures 13 through 16 describe how this contract type is applied. For each of these figures, the following basic assumptions are the same: (1) the estimated cost is $1,000,000; (2) the stated fee is $85,000; (3) the minimum fee is $60,000; (4) the maximum fee is $110,000; and (5) the contractor share of any cost over/underrun is 30 percent.

Figure 13 is a cost-plus-incentive-fee contract where the actual cost of $900,000 is well under the estimated cost. This results in a $100,000 underrun. The contract price is computed by starting with the actual cost on line (i). The fee calculation begins with the stated fee, $85,000, on line (j). The fee is then increased on line (k) by the contractor's share of the cost underrun or $30,000, which is 30 percent of $100,000. This results in a calculated fee of $115,000 on line (l). However, this fee exceeds the maximum fee, so the allowable fee amount is the maximum or $110,000. The price on the contract is then $1,010,000, which is the sum of the actual cost and the allowable fee. The profit on this contract is $110,000, which is $1,010,000 minus $900,000.

Figure 14 is a cost-plus-incentive-fee contract where the actual cost of $950,000 is slightly under the estimated cost. This results in a $50,000 underrun. The contract price is computed by starting with the actual cost on line (i). The fee calculation begins with the stated fee, $85,000, on line (j). The fee is then increased on line (k) by the contractor's share of the cost underrun or $15,000, which is 30 percent of $50,000. This results in a calculated fee of $100,000 on line (l). The price on

the contract is then $1,050,000, which is the sum of the actual cost and the allowable fee. The profit on this contract is $100,000, which is $1,050,000 minus $950,000.

Figure 15 is a cost-plus-incentive-fee contract where the actual cost of $1,050,000 is slightly over the estimated cost. This results in a $50,000 overrun. The contract price is computed by starting with the actual cost on line (i). The fee calculation begins with the stated fee, $85,000, on line (j). The fee is then decreased on line (k) by the contractor's share of the cost overrun or $15,000, which is 30 percent of $50,000. This results in a calculated fee of $70,000 on line (l). The price on the contract is then $1,120,000, which is the sum of the actual cost and the allowable fee. The profit on this contract is 70,000, which is $1,120,000 minus $1,050,000.

Figure 16 is a cost-plus-incentive-fee contract where the actual cost of $1,150,000 is well over the estimated cost. This results in a $100,000 overrun. The contract price is computed by starting with the actual cost on line (i). The fee calculation begins with the stated fee, $85,000, on line (j). The fee is then decreased on linc (k) by the contractor's share of the cost overrun or $45,000, which is 30 percent of $150,000. This results in a calculated fee of $40,000 on line (l). However, this fee is less than the minimum fee so the allowable fee amount is the minimum, or $60,000. The price on the contract is then $1,210,000, which is the sum of the actual cost and the allowable fee. The profit on this contract is 60,000, which is $1,210,000 minus $1,150,000.

Figure 17 contains the spreadsheet formulas for the calculations in Figures 13 through 16.

Cost-Plus-Award-Fee Contract

A cost-plus-award-fee (CPAF) contract is a cost-reimbursement contract that provides for a fee consisting of: (1) a base amount fixed at inception of the contract (which may be

Figure 13
COST-PLUS-INCENTIVE-FEE CONTRACT
Well Under Estimated Cost

Facts:		Amount	Ref.	Source
Estimated Cost		$1,000,000	(a)	Negotiated
Fee		$85,000	(b)	Negotiated
Minimum Fee		$60,000	(c)	Negotiated
Maximum Fee		$110,000	(d)	Negotiated
Contractor Share		30%	(e)	Negotiated
Government Share		70%	(f)	Negotiated
Actual Cost		$900,000	(g)	
Overrun (Underrun)		($100,000)	(h)	(g) – (a)
Price:				
Actual Cost		$900,000	(i)	(g)
Fee	$85,000		(j)	(b)
Contractor Share	30,000		(k)	(e) * (–h)
Total Calculated Fee	$115,000		(l)	(j) + (k)
Total Allowable Fee		$110,000	(m)	(l), but not more than (d) or less than (c)
Total Price		$1,010,000	(n)	(i) + (m)
Profit (Loss)		$110,000		(n) – (g)

zero); and (2) an award amount that the contractor may earn in whole or in part during performance. The amount of the award fee to be paid is determined by the government's judgmental evaluation of the contractor's performance in terms of the criteria stated in the contract.

OTHER CONTRACT TYPES

Other contract types include time-and-materials, labor-hour, indefinite-delivery, letter, basic agreement, and basic ordering agreement.

Time-and-Materials Contract

A time-and-materials (T&M) contract provides for acquiring supplies or services on the basis of: (1) direct labor hours at specified fixed hourly rates that include wages, overhead, general and administrative (G&A) expenses, and profit; and (2) materials at cost, including, if appropriate, material handling costs. A time-and-materials contract provides little positive profit incentive to the contractor for cost control or labor efficiency. T&M rates are sometimes referred to as "wrap-rates" because all costs are included in the price per labor hour.

Materials and other direct costs are paid on a cost-reimbursement basis without a fee. All appropriate indirect costs allocated to direct materials in accordance with the contractor's usual accounting procedures consistent with Part 31 are permitted. This includes G&A expenses and indirect material handling costs—only if the contractor has an established material handling cost pool.

Facts:		Amount	Ref.	Source
Estimated Cost		$1,000,000	(a)	Negotiated
Fee		$85,000	(b)	Negotiated
Minimum Fee		$60,000	(c)	Negotiated
Maximum Fee		$110,000	(d)	Negotiated
Contractor Share		30%	(e)	Negotiated
Government Share		70%	(f)	Negotiated
Actual Cost		$950,000	(g)	
Overrun (Underrun)		($50,000)	(h)	(g) – (a)
Price:				
Actual Cost		$950,000	(i)	(g)
Fee	$85,000		(j)	(b)
Contractor Share	15,000		(k)	(e) * (–h)
Total Calculated Fee	$100,000		(l)	(j) + (k)
Total Allowable Fee		$100,000	(m)	(l), but not more than (d) or less than (c)
Total Price		$1,050,000	(n)	(i) + (m)
Profit (Loss)		$100,000		(n) – (g)

Figure 14
COST-PLUS-INCENTIVE-FEE CONTRACT
Slightly Under Estimated Cost

T&M contracts have been popular for inspect-and-repair-as-needed (IRAN) contracts. Under these contracts, the contractor is paid a fixed hourly rate for labor and related costs, and actual costs for materials identified as needed for repairs. The purpose of the contract not allowing a profit on materials is to avoid an incentive for a contractor to identify repairs that might be of questionable need.

Whether a T&M contract is a fixed-price type contract or a cost-type contract is an ongoing disagreement between the government and some nongovernment people. The government considers these contracts to be cost-type because the ultimate price is based on the quantity of goods or services delivered, which the government views as being at the discretion of a contractor rather than determined by the government buyer. The opposing view is that a T&M contract is both fixed-price and cost-type. The time portion is a fixed unit cost per item delivered. The materials portion is cost-reimbursement.

In the late 2000s it became necessary to segregate T&M contracts into two categories, commercial and non-commercial, for purposes of establishing whether subcontracted work should be invoiced as time or materials under a prime contract. The ramifications of this distinction are clear: A prime contractor receives no profit or fee on work performed by a subcontractor if the work is treated as a subcontract. For commercial T&M contracts, the labor for the prime contractor, subcontractors, and affiliates of the prime contractor may be invoiced to the government based on the labor rate specified in the prime contract. For T&M contracts awarded based on adequate price competition for other than the Department of Defense, the labor may also be

Figure 15
COST-PLUS-INCENTIVE-FEE CONTRACT
Slightly Over Estimated Cost

Facts:		Amount	Ref.	Source
Estimated Cost		$1,000,000	(a)	Negotiated
Fee		$85,000	(b)	Negotiated
Minimum Fee		$60,000	(c)	Negotiated
Maximum Fee		$110,000	(d)	Negotiated
Contractor Share		30%	(e)	Negotiated
Government Share		70%	(f)	Negotiated
Actual Cost		$1,050,000	(g)	
Overrun (Underrun)		$50,000	(h)	(g) – (a)
Price:				
Actual Cost		$1,050,000	(i)	(g)
Fee	$85,000		(j)	(b)
Contractor Share	(15,000)		(k)	(e) * (–h)
Total Calculated Fee	$70,000		(l)	(j) + (k)
Total Allowable Fee		$70,000	(m)	(l), but not more than (d) or less than (c)
Total Price		$1,120,000	(n)	(i) + (m)
Profit (Loss)		$70,000		(n) – (g)

invoiced in this manner. For the Department of Defense, such contracts must be invoiced as non-commercial items would be invoiced. For non-commercial items the labor of subcontractors and affiliates is invoiced based on actual cost, i.e., as the materials portion of the T&M contract.

Labor-Hour Contract

A labor-hour contract is a variation of a time-and-materials contract, differing only in that no materials are to be supplied by the contractor.

Indefinite-Delivery Contract

The indefinite delivery (ID) contract type relates to multiple awards of indefinite-quan-

tity contracts. The two categories of ID contracts are: (1) a delivery-order contract, which does not procure or specify a firm quantity of supplies (other than a minimum or maximum quantity) and which provides for the issuance of orders for the delivery of supplies during the period of the contract; and (2) a task-order contract, which does not procure or specify a firm quantity of services (other than a minimum or maximum quantity) and which provides for the issuance of orders for the performance of tasks during the period of the contract.

There are three types of indefinite-delivery contracts: (1) definite-quantity contracts; (2) requirements contracts; and (3) indefinite-quantity contracts. Indefinite-quantity contracts and requirements contracts permit flexibility in both quantities and in delivery scheduling and ordering of supplies or servic-

Figure 16
COST-PLUS-INCENTIVE-FEE CONTRACT
Well Over Estimated Cost

Facts:		Amount	Ref.	Source
Estimated Cost		$1,000,000	(a)	Negotiated
Fee		$85,000	(b)	Negotiated
Minimum Fee		$60,000	(c)	Negotiated
Maximum Fee		$110,000	(d)	Negotiated
Contractor Share		30%	(e)	Negotiated
Government Share		70%	(f)	Negotiated
Actual Cost		$1,150,000	(g)	
Overrun (Underrun)		$150,000	(h)	(g) – (a)
Price:				
Actual Cost		$1,150,000	(i)	(g)
Fee	$85,000		(j)	(b)
Contractor Share	(45,000)		(k)	(e) * (–h)
Total Calculated Fee	$40,000		(l)	(j) + (k)
Total Allowable Fee		$60,000	(m)	(l), but not more than (d) or less than (c)
Total Price		$1,210,000	(n)	(i) + (m)
Profit (Loss)		$60,000		(n) – (g)

es after requirements materialize. Indefinite-quantity contracts limit the government's obligation to the minimum quantity specified in the contract. Requirements contracts may permit faster deliveries when production lead time is involved, because contractors are usually willing to maintain limited stocks when the government will obtain all of its actual purchase requirements from the contractor.

Definite-Quantity Contract

A definite-quantity contract provides for delivery of a definite quantity of specific supplies or services for a fixed period, with deliveries or performance to be scheduled at designated locations upon order. A definite-quantity contract is often used when it can be determined in advance that a definite quantity of supplies or services will be required

during the contract period, and the supplies or services are regularly available or will be available after a short lead time.

Requirements Contract

A requirements contract provides for filling all actual purchase requirements of designated government activities for supplies or services during a specified contract period, with deliveries or performance to be scheduled by placing orders with the contractor. The solicitation and resulting contract state that an estimated quantity will be required or ordered, or that conditions affecting requirements will be stable or normal. The contract may also specify maximum or minimum quantities that the government may order under each individual order and the maximum that it may order during a specified period of time.

Figure 17
SPREADSHEET FORMULAS FOR COST-PLUS-INCENTIVE-FEE CONTRACT

Facts:		Amount	Ref.	Source
Estimated Cost		$1,000,000	(a)	Negotiated
Fee		$85,000	(b)	Negotiated
Minimum Fee		$60,000	(c)	Negotiated
Maximum Fee		$110,000	(d)	Negotiated
Contractor Share		0.3	(e)	Negotiated
Government Share		0.7	(f)	Negotiated
Actual Cost		$900,000	(g)	
Overrun (Underrun)		=W14–W17*	(h)	(g) – (a)
Price:				
Actual Cost		=W14	(i)	(g)
Fee	$85,000		(j)	(b)
Contractor Share	=W15*W11		(k)	(e) * (–h)
Total Calculated Fee	=V19+V20		(l)	(j) + (k)
Total Allowable Fee		IF(V21>W10,W10,IF(V21<W9,W9,V21))	(m)	(l), but not more than (d) or less than (c)
Total Price		=W22+W18	(n)	(i) + (m)
Profit (Loss)		=W24–W18		(n) – (g)

*Formula references in "Amount" column are Excel spreadsheet cell references

Indefinite-Quantity Contract

An indefinite-delivery, indefinite-quantity (IDIQ) contract provides for an indefinite quantity, within stated limits, of supplies or services to be furnished during a fixed period, with deliveries or performance to be scheduled by placing orders with the contractor.

The contract requires the government to order and the contractor to furnish at least a stated minimum quantity of supplies or services, and requires the contractor to furnish any additional quantities ordered, not to exceed a stated maximum. To ensure that the contract is binding, the minimum quantity must be more than a nominal quantity, but it should not exceed the amount that the government is fairly certain to order. The contract may also specify maximum or mini-

mum quantities that the government may order under each task or delivery order and the maximum that it may order during a specific period of time.

There are two types of IDIQ contracts—single awardee and multiple awardee. For a single awardee contract, only one contractor is selected for award and the contract operates as described. A multiple-awardee contract results in several awardees being selected as eligible to bid on delivery orders or task orders issued subsequent to contract award. For orders issued under multiple-delivery order contracts or multiple-task order contracts, each awardee is to be provided a fair opportunity to be considered for each order in excess of $2,500. Winning a multiple-award contract is similar to "winning air." There is no guarantee of any work unless the awardee is successful in the individual order competition stage. In most instances, a contractor may not protest an agency award of an individual order.

Letter Contract

A letter contract is a written contractual instrument that authorizes the contractor to begin immediately manufacturing supplies or performing services. A letter contract may be used when the government's interests demand that the contractor be given a binding commitment so that work can start immediately and negotiating a definitive contract is not possible in sufficient time to meet the requirement. However, a letter contract should be as complete and definite as feasible under the circumstances. When a letter contract is awarded, the contracting officer will include an overall price ceiling in the letter contract.

Each letter contract must specify a definite schedule, including: (1) dates for submission of the contractor's price proposal, required cost or pricing data, and, if required, make-or-buy and subcontracting plans; (2) a date for the start of negotiations; and (3) a target date for definitization, which is to be the earliest practicable date. The schedule will provide for definitization of the contract within 180 days after the date of the letter contract or before completion of 40 percent of the work to be performed, whichever occurs first.

However, the contracting officer may, in extreme cases and according to agency procedures, authorize an additional period. In practice, many definitizations take much longer than 180 days. Generally, this delay is more advantageous to the government than the contractor because the letter contract contains a not-to-exceed (NTE) or ceiling price. Thus, if the cost estimate decreases, the price will likely be negotiated downward, but if the cost estimate increases, the price may not be negotiated in excess of the ceiling. Contractors are advised to avoid letter contracts.

Basic Agreement

A basic agreement is a written instrument of understanding, negotiated between the government and a contractor, that: (1) contains contract clauses applying to future contracts between the parties during its term; and (2) contemplates separate future contracts that will incorporate by reference or attachment the required and applicable clauses agreed upon in the basic agreement. Importantly, a basic agreement is not a contract. A basic agreement is used when a substantial number of separate contracts may be awarded to a contractor during a particular period. Basic agreements are used with negotiated fixed-price or cost-reimbursement contracts.

Basic agreements provide for discontinuing their future applicability upon 30 days' written notice by either party. A basic agreement will not obligate funds, state or imply any agreement by the government to place future contracts or orders with the contractor, or be used in any manner to restrict competition. Each contract incorporating a basic agreement includes a scope of work and price, delivery, and other appropriate terms that apply to the particular contract.

Basic Ordering Agreement

A basic ordering agreement (BOA) is a written instrument of understanding, negotiated between an agency, contracting activity, or contracting office and a contractor, that contains: (1) terms and clauses applying to future contracts (orders) between the parties during its term; (2) a description, as specific as practicable, of supplies or services to be provided; and (3) methods for pricing, issuing, and delivering future orders. Importantly, a basic ordering agreement is not a contract.

A basic ordering agreement is used to expedite contracting for uncertain requirements for supplies or services when specific items, quantities, and prices are not known at the time the agreement is executed, but a substantial number of supplies or services covered by the agreement is anticipated to be purchased from the contractor. The use of these procedures can result in economies in ordering parts for equipment support by reducing administrative lead-time, inventory investment, and inventory obsolescence resulting from design changes.

A basic ordering agreement does not state or imply any agreement by the government to place future contracts or orders with the contractor or be used in any manner to restrict competition. Each basic ordering agreement describes the method for determining prices to be paid to the contractor for the supplies or services. Common application is for ordering spare parts. The agreement may provide a formula for pricing spare parts based on agreed-upon direct labor rates and indirect cost rates plus other factors.

UNAUTHORIZED CONTRACT TYPES AND VARIATIONS

The FAR very specifically states that contract types other than those authorized by the regulations are not permitted. However, approved and unapproved variations occasionally exist. For example, a major weapon system contract was converted to a "cost-plus-fixed-loss" contract as part of an agreement to ensure delivery when the contractor had a significant financial problem. This contractual arrangement had to be approved at the highest level of the agency.

Other unauthorized variations typically attempt to provide downward-only adjustments to fixed-price contracts. For example, some contracting officers seek a downward-only adjustment clause in T&M contracts. In other words, the price will be the lower of the negotiated fixed hourly rate and the actual hourly rate determined on an after-the-fact basis. This is an inequitable contract type and

is not authorized. Any "maverick" provision that violates the sanctity of a fixed-price contract should be rejected.

OTHER TRANSACTIONS

Beginning in the early 1990s, the government expanded the use of arrangements other than contracts to obtain certain goods and services. A transaction other than a contract does not require most of the contract clauses that are mandatory for government contracting. The most notable of these are the clauses for compliance with cost accounting standards (CAS), cost allowability rules, and government audit rights. The initial usage of this vehicle was under the Small Business Innovative Research Program.

The goal of the other-transaction (OT) approach was to entice commercial organizations into providing goods and services to the government. Often strictly commercial organizations refuse to accept government contracts because of the excessive administrative and government oversight that accompanies contracts. The use of other transactions has expanded from research to prototype development and beyond. This approach is beneficial to the government because it attracts sellers that would not otherwise deal with the government, and is beneficial to the sellers because it avoids the most negative aspects of contracting with the government.

CONTRACT TYPE AND POTENTIAL FINANCIAL REWARD

The fixed-price contract offers the greatest opportunity for profit or loss and the cost-plus-fixed-fee contract offers the least potential variability in profit. The term "profit" is used here in terms of the difference between the contract price and allowable costs. Potential profit must be further reduced by any unallowable costs, including federal income taxes.

Figure 18 displays the relative profit at various levels of cost incurrence for: (1) firm-fixed-price contracts; (2) fixed-price-incentive contracts; (3) cost-plus-incentive-fee contracts; and (4) cost-plus-fixed-fee contracts. The vertical scale is profit or loss, with the breakeven point noted. The horizontal scale is the allowable cost. As allowable costs increase, the profit decreases in all instances. However, the pattern is different for each contract type. The figure incorporates the differences in profit levels associated with the various contract types as well as the relationship to allowable cost.

The firm-fixed-price contract profit has a constant relationship to allowable costs, i.e., a dollar for dollar correlation. The fixed-price-incentive contract involves a 30 percent sharing of any allowable cost variance from the estimate up to a maximum price. The cost-plus-incentive-fee contract provides for a similar sharing; however, both a minimum and maximum profit are established. The cost-plus-fixed-fee contract maintains a constant profit regardless of allowable costs.

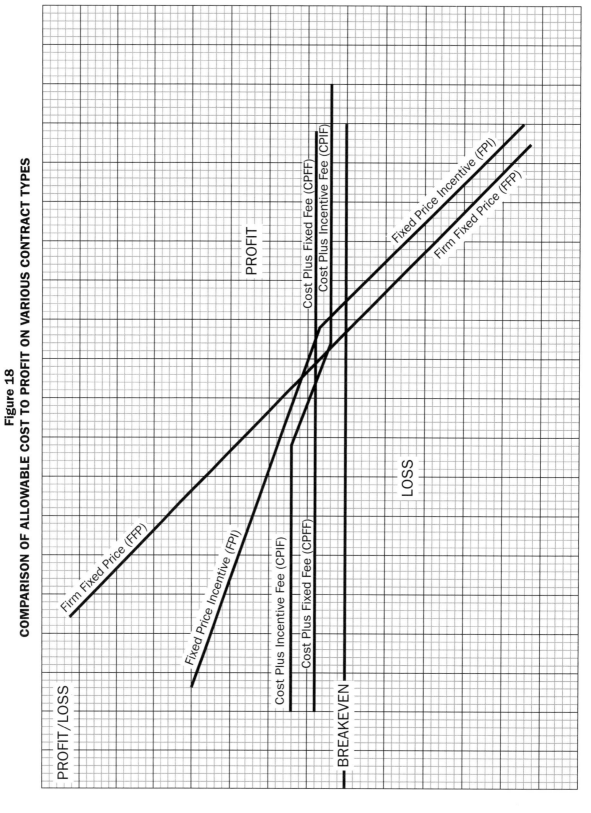

Figure 18
COMPARISON OF ALLOWABLE COST TO PROFIT ON VARIOUS CONTRACT TYPES

CHAPTER 3

Accounting System Requirements

An accounting system is a combination of records, internal controls, and written policies and procedures, all of which function together in the process of estimating, accumulating, and reporting financial data. An adequate accounting system is important for any business; however, an adequate accounting system is especially important for government contractors. A government contractor must establish an accounting system consistent with "generally accepted accounting principles" (GAAP) and any other contractual requirements.

In addition to establishing an accounting system that meets GAAP requirements for financial reporting, government contractors must establish a system that records the incurrence of contract costs in accordance with government laws and regulations, particularly the cost accounting standards (CAS) and the Federal Acquisition Regulation (FAR) cost principles. Basically, contractors must establish an accounting system that accomplishes the following:

1. Segregates costs by contract and contract line item, depending on the type of contract and the work being performed

2. Provides actual cost data at interim periods to allow for contract repricing or negotiating revised contract targets

3. Accounts for specific unallowable costs as established in FAR Subpart 31.2, and augmented by CAS 405

4. Separates preproduction and nonrecurring costs from production and recurring costs

5. Generates reliable data for purposes of pricing new and/or follow-on procurements

6. Identifies and segregates direct and indirect costs

7. Identifies varying levels of indirect costs (e.g., fringe benefits, labor-related overhead, material-related overhead, services usage, and general and administrative—G&A—cost).

The Defense Contract Audit Agency often includes additional criteria, such as a contractor being current on the annual indirect cost rate submission and timely submission of adjustment vouchers for cost-type contracts. The government cost regulations do not require the use of any specific or uniform cost accounting system or method of determining contract costs. Accordingly, contractors are free to develop and use the type of accounting system that is most appropriate for their business. For example, there are no requirements regarding use of either a job order cost system or a process cost system. In addition, no specific direction requiring the use of actual costs versus standard costs in costing and pricing contracts is provided. However, contractors are required to incorporate certain basic elements into an accounting system before it is considered to be adequate for government contracts.

The size of the firm and the extent of its government contracts can also dictate the depth and breadth of a cost accounting system. Smaller companies with fewer government contracts can probably generate the necessary cost data using a relatively simple manual system. However, a multidivisional or multinational company engaged in developing or manufacturing complex products may require much more. In this case, it would be almost mandatory that the company establish some type of computerized cost system to ensure that its own and the government's interests are adequately addressed. Certainly, in any enterprise engaged in government contracting, regardless of its size, costs must be addressed in logical, sensible, and suitable terms.

Manually maintained books and records are acceptable. Software that does not accommodate government contracting requirements may be supplemented with spreadsheet analyses. However, if a contractor follows this approach, care should be taken to ensure that the spreadsheets are reconcilable to the official books and records. Software especially designed for government contractors is commercially available as well.

If a contractor wants to advance into the increasingly complex government contracting arena but does not currently use a commercially available government contract-oriented accounting software package, the contactor should consider initiating a Request for Proposal (RFP) process. Through this process the contractor can seek to replace its current system with government-compliant software that will interface as necessary with corporate transaction and reporting requirements. The RFP should emphasize project management,

government cost accounting and reporting, timekeeping, labor distribution, billing, revenue recognition, contract management, and financial reporting functionality.

Historically, very few cost accounting systems have met the specific needs of the government contracting marketplace. In fact, this marketplace was once dominated by a single major vendor. Recently, several products with national and international market reach have entered the market, providing more choice to the government contractor customer. These packages have been tried and tested in the commercial market as well as in the government contracting arena. These new packages offer substantial functionality, ease of use, and flexibility.

Deltek has been the major supplier of enterprise resource planning (ERP) software to both large and small corporations; one of the company's key market areas has been defense contractors. Recently, Microsoft and other vendors have begun competing in this area. Through some careful acquisitions and development efforts, Microsoft has rolled out a suite of products targeted at government contractors. The company has developed software specifically for government contractors as well as other types of companies.

Project-based software packages such as Deltek GCS and Costpoint are geared to service contractors. While the original Deltek GCS is less expensive, the code and file formats present certain limitations. Costpoint is more robust and better for larger firms. Manufacturers might consider SAP or Oracle, being careful to understand that additional configurations may be necessary for government contracting compliance. For example, SAP often incorporates standard cost features that are not relevant to a company circumstance. Microsoft's Dynamics SL or Dynamics NAV provide benefits to both service contractors and manufacturers based on their ease of use and seamless integration with Microsoft Office applications and Microsoft technologies. Microsoft systems also tend to be more open; therefore, a contractor is not dependent on just the Microsoft suite of products to handle all its ERP needs. However, any software can be supplemented sufficiently for use on government contracts. Modifications are even available to permit the use of Quick-Books for government contract purposes.

When configured correctly and implemented properly, these project-based packages provide major benefits. Billing, allocations, revenue recognition, time and expense recording, project profitability analysis, access rights, and organizational restructuring can be quickly and easily completed in accordance with federal and internal corporate requirements.

BASIC RECORD KEEPING

The types of books and records used in any accounting system are based on what is most suitable for a contractor's business. The overall objective is to provide cost accounting and financial data that are adequate for government contract costing purposes. The basic record keeping system must provide sufficiently detailed contract costs so that costs can be determined at interim levels for purposes of repricing, negotiating revised targets, and determining billings. Although the use and design of certain specific accounting records may vary from contractor to contractor, the record keeping systems for all government contractors must include a general ledger, a job cost ledger, labor distribution records, time records, subsidiary journals, a chart of accounts, and financial statements.

Several key functions are essential to the adequacy of any basic record keeping system:

1. Segregate direct costs by contract or job and then by cost element (e.g., labor, materials, other direct charges)

2. Segregate indirect costs by account and title (e.g., fringe benefits, labor-related

overhead, material-related overhead, service usage, G&A cost)

3. Accumulate costs on both a current and cumulative basis (i.e., year to date and project to date)

4. Establish the accounting period and perform reconciliations of time sheets to labor costs included in job cost ledgers and of basic cost records to the general books of account

5. Enter costs to the books on a current basis

6. Separately identify unallowable costs in the regular books of account (or by way of a less formal cost accounting technique, as long as adequate cost identification is established).

The cost of labor is often the most sensitive cost element. Labor costs impact a contrac-tor's cost structure and thus the price paid by the government. Direct and indirect labor costs are generally the single most significant cost element charged to government contracts. In addition, certain areas of labor (e.g., direct labor dollars or hours) are commonly used as the base element for indirect cost rates. Labor costs or hours are also an essential element in a contractor's estimating system used in providing quantitative and qualitative historical data necessary for determining estimated costs for follow-on government contracts.

Thus, the accurate recording of labor costs by contractor employees is of utmost importance. Unlike other cost items, labor is not supported by third-party documentation such as an invoice, purchase order, or other receipt. The key document in a manual time-keeping system is the timecard prepared by individual employees. Since timecards can be easily altered or controlled by other persons, it is essential that individual employees be made aware of their responsibility and realize the importance of accurate timecard preparation. The government relies heavily on basic internal controls to ensure the propriety of labor costs presented for payment, contract costing, and estimating. It is therefore essential that the internal controls related to labor recording and distribution be firmly established and periodically reviewed by management.

Manual timecards and timesheets should include the following information: employee name, employee identification number, time period, employee signature, daily entries, project name, project number, daily totals, project totals, tax location identification, and a comments section to note changes or other significant matters. Figure 19 presents a sample time report for hourly employees and Figure 20 presents a sample time report for salaried employees.

Electronic timekeeping systems are acceptable, but must have adequate internal controls. For example, only the employee should be authorized to make entries and changes to the timesheet information. Any changes after initial entries have been made must be maintained in the system to provide an audit trail.

Figure 19
TIME REPORT—HOURLY EMPLOYEES
XYZ Company

Employee
Week Ended

Employee Signature

Direct Labor	Sun	Mon	Tue	Wed	Thr	Fri	Sat	Total
Total Direct Labor								
Indirect Labor								
Administration								
Bid/Proposal								
Time Off								
Leave								
Holiday								
Total Indirect Labor								
Grand Total								

Figure 20
TIME REPORT—SALARIED EMPLOYEES
XYZ Company

Employee _____

Month _____

Year _____

	1	2	3	4	5	6	7	8	9	10	11	12	13	14	15	16	17	18	19	20	21	22	23	24	25	26	27	28	29	30	31	Total
Direct Labor																																
Total Direct Labor																																
Indirect Labor																																
Overhead																																
G&A																																
Administration																																
Bid/Proposal																																
Absences																																
Leave																																
Holiday																																
Total Indirect Labor																																
Grand Total																																

Employee Signature _____

INTERNAL CONTROLS AND WRITTEN POLICIES AND PROCEDURES

Good internal controls and established, written policies and procedures are the backbones of a good accounting system. Although government cost regulations do not prescribe specific internal control procedures, the CAS require the establishment and use of written procedures for several areas of cost accumulation and allocation. Some of the cost areas include depreciation, capitalization of tangible assets, accounting for acquisition of material costs, and allocation of direct and indirect costs.

In addition, government auditors evaluate the strengths and weaknesses of contractor internal control systems by measuring the contractor's adherence to its written policies and procedures. Auditors review these written policies and procedures to determine the overall adequacy of a contractor's accounting system. If auditors find significant deficiencies, they qualify their audit reports by stating that the contractor's record keeping system is inadequate for government contract costing purposes. This type of audit response obviously works against an organization's efforts to establish itself as a responsible contractor.

The more significant internal control features of an acceptable accounting system for government contract costing purposes include the following:

1. Separation of authority between key accounting functions (e.g., payroll vs. timekeeping; requisition of materials and services vs. purchasing; purchasing vs. an accounts payable function; billing function vs. accounts receivable)

2. Written policies and procedures establishing the purpose and requirements of the accounting system (e.g., timekeeping, payroll, purchased services and materials, direct and indirect cost control, asset capitalization and utilization, post-retirement benefits and deferred compensation)

3. Internal reviews by management to ascertain employee compliance with the policies and procedures

4. Periodic reconciliations of cost control records from the point of original entry through cost accumulation summaries to billing records and accounts receivable

5. Management authorizations of critical accounting activities (e.g., issuance of payroll checks, signing of timesheets) and requisitioning/purchasing of materials and services

6. Budget control procedures for comparing actual cost to budget and contract financial status

7. Productivity measurement techniques to allow management to focus on problem areas and improve overall economy and efficiency (e.g., engineered or estimated standards)

8. Organizational charts to define lines of authority and responsibility and to provide for division of responsibility in operating, recording, and custodial functions

9. In-house suggestion boxes and hot-lines to encourage employees to make recommendations and ask questions about proper procedures or to inform management of possible areas of employee wrongdoing or fraud.

The extent of internal controls depends on the size of the organization. Obviously in a one-person organization, internal controls are very limited. This does not mean that the accounting system is unacceptable. It just means that an auditor will likely want to perform additional tests to obtain assurances.

Contractors are are advised to have written policies and procedures in the following areas:

- Definition of direct costs
- Description of indirect cost structure
- Job cost accumulation process
- Labor recording
- Cost transfers between segments
- Interim invoicing
- Preparation of incurred cost submission
- Final invoicing
- Asset capitalization
- Contract briefs
- Documentation of expenses
- Incentive compensation plans
- Paid time off
- Consultant costs
- Employee travel expenses
- Monitoring indirect costs
- Employee benefits
- Limitation of cost clause requirements
- Segregation of unallowable costs
- Adjustment vouchers
- Cash discounts
- Severance pay
- Closing statements
- Uncompensated overtime.

MANAGING CONTRACT COSTS

During contract performance, a contractor is generally paid by two methods—public vouchers and progress payments. Public vouchers are generally used for cost-reimbursement contracts. Progress payments apply to fixed-price type contracts. In either case, the contractor's accounting system must be adequate to support the payment of costs incurred.

Costs included in a standard public voucher must reflect contract costs incurred both in the current period and cumulatively. Direct costs should be included as actually incurred, and the applied indirect costs should reflect a billing rate that is based on an estimate of year-end allowable actual costs or contractually established provisional costs. Any cost limitations resulting from a contractually established cost ceiling or limitations also must be reflected in the voucher. As a general rule, cost-reimbursement contracts are subject to a withholding of 15 percent of fee until the contract is completed and the contractor submits a final voucher. This reserve helps protect the government's interest, including possible contractor overbillings. FAR 52.216-7, Allowable Cost and Payment, governs cost reimbursements.

FAR 52.232-16, Progress Payments, governs a contractor's submittal of progress payments based on incurred costs. This contract clause requires that costs that are claimed have actually been paid or incurred, depending on the contract terms. The standard progress payment clause requires that the costs of "supplies and services" purchased by the contractor directly for the contract may be included in the progress payment claim only after actual payment by cash, check, etc. On the other hand, the clause allows costs for such items as direct labor, materials issued from inventory, and indirect costs, to be simply incurred, not necessarily paid, at the time the progress payment is submitted. It does require, however, that the contractor maintain a current payment status on those items. Government auditors will review the contractor's historical payment records to ascertain that delinquency is not a problem. As of October 1, 1999, a proposed FAR change would remove the requirement to pay subcontractors before seeking reimbursement from the government.

With regard to the submittal of progress payment requests, the government requires that the contractor have reasonable visibility of the percentage of contract completion. This requirement illustrates the need for the contractor's accounting system to accumulate costs by contract and to allow for visibility of actual costs incurred compared to budgeted costs. The accounting data will have to be merged with production data and engineering estimates to enable management to fully assess project status. This requirement also permits the government to see whether the contractor is incurring costs at the budgeted rate, or is in an overrun position. If the latter is the case, the request for progress payment will be reduced by the equivalent overrun percentage as the government attempts to protect itself from paying overrun dollars.

Another category of expenditures that is not reflected on the company books should be controlled. Those costs are open commitments, which are basically purchase orders that have been placed but remain unrecorded or unpaid because a vendor service has not been rendered or a product has not been received. A contractor needs to establish a system to track those open commitments and measure them along with their actual expended costs to ascertain valid cost-to-budget comparisons. Normally, open commitment costs are not included for cost reimbursement or progress payment requests. But measurement to budget and well-founded estimated costs to complete calculations must include this area of potential cost.

Cost-reimbursement contracts contain a limitation of cost clause (LOCC) to protect the government from unauthorized and unexpected cost overruns. This clause requires a contractor to notify the contracting officer in writing whenever he has reason to believe that: (1) the costs he expects to incur under the contract in the next 60 days (or an alternative number of days ranging from 30 to 90), when added to costs previously incurred, will exceed 75 percent (or an alternative percentage ranging from 75 to 85) of the estimated costs specified in the contract; or (2) the total cost for the performance of the contract, exclusive of any fee, will be either greater or substantially less than estimated. This clause is discussed in detail in Chapter 2.

ALLOCATING COSTS

The government will pay only for costs that it believes relate to or benefit its work. The process of assigning costs to government and commercial contracts is known as cost allocation. When the government requires that a cost be allocable to a government contract, it means that the cost is for something that benefits the government work or is necessary for the government work.

Proper cost allocation requires an understanding of the types of costs involved on a contract. Costs must then be applied consistently within an acceptable cost structure.

Direct and Indirect Costs

Direct costs are costs incurred solely for the benefit of a single final cost objective, such as a contract. Indirect costs benefit more than one contract. FAR 31.202 defines a direct cost as any cost that "can be identified specifically with a particular final cost objective. No final cost objective shall have allocated to it as direct cost any cost, if other costs incurred for the same purpose in like circumstances have been included in any indirect cost pool to be allocated to that or any other final cost objective. Costs identified specifically with the contract are direct costs of the contract and are to be charged directly to the contract. All costs specifically identified with other final cost objectives of the contractor are direct costs of those cost objectives and are not to be charged to the contract directly or indirectly."

Direct costs are those specifically identified to various cost objectives within the company. They normally include the salaries and wages of personnel directly associated with these objectives, materials or services directly used in manufacturing the product, subcontracted costs, and other direct costs directly related to the cost objectives. A direct cost may be one for materials or services incorporated into the product or the production process.

Indirect costs are all costs that cannot be specifically identified with a single contract or with units of output because the cost either is incurred for more than one contract or unit of output or is not susceptible to measurement at the unit of output level. Such costs are necessary to produce units of output and are as much a cost of producing goods and services as costs that are specifically identified, such as direct labor and direct material.

FAR Subpart 31.203 defines an indirect cost as "any cost not directly identified with a single, final cost objective, but identified with two or more final cost objectives or an intermediate cost objective. It is not subject to treatment as a direct cost. After direct costs have been determined and charged directly to the contract or other work, indirect costs are those remaining to be allocated to the several cost objectives. An indirect cost shall not be allocated to a final cost objective if other costs incurred for the same purpose in like circumstances have been included as a direct cost of that or any other final cost objective."

Indirect costs are commonly separated into overhead and G&A costs. A business may have several overhead cost pools, but only one G&A cost pool. Small companies often combine overhead and G&A into a single cost pool, whose title might be indirect cost pool, overhead cost pool, or G&A cost pool. The number of overhead cost pools at a business depends on the circumstances.

A small company might have one indirect cost pool and rate for both overhead and G&A costs. A larger company might have a single overhead pool for indirect costs related to contract performance and a G&A cost pool for overall operations costs. Additionally, a large contractor that has several functions or locations might use overhead pools. For example, the contractor could have one overhead cost pool for plant A and another for Plant B. There could also be one overhead pool and rate for work performed at the customer site and another for work performed at the contractor site. The contractor could have a separate overhead cost pool for materials and subcontract functions. In this latter example, the production overhead would likely be allocated based on direct labor dollars and the overhead related to ordering and handling materials would likely be allocated based on material and subcontract dollars.

Overhead Costs

Overhead costs are those not directly related to cost objectives but are support-type costs necessary for the production of goods or services. These costs may be associated with general product lines, organizational groups, or groups of contracts. Overhead costs commonly include salaries and wages of support and production personnel, facilities costs, and supplies.

Overhead costs are accumulated into overhead pools. The number of pools can vary depending on the complexity of operations. Each overhead pool is allocated to cost objectives in reasonable proportion to the beneficial or causal relationship of the pool(s) to cost objectives. Overhead costs are commonly expressed in a rate as follows:

Direct manufacturing labor costs	
2,000 hours @ $15.00	$30,000
Manufacturing overhead costs	$45,000
Manufacturing overhead rate	
as percentage of labor cost	<u>150%</u>
($45,000 divided by $30,000)	
or	
Manufacturing overhead rate as a	
cost per hour of labor	<u>$22.50</u>
($45,000 divided by 2,000 hours)	

Manufacturing automation has grown immensely and has created another aspect of overhead allocation. As direct labor disappears in an automated environment, using direct labor as an allocation base no longer is logical. Activity-based costing (ABC) seeks cost drivers as cost allocation bases. For example, instead of allocating overhead based on direct labor dollars or hours, overhead is allocated based on machine time, operator-maintained work stations, etc. Instead of allocating material-related overhead based on material costs, this overhead is allocated based on the number of items purchased, the quantity of items passing through inventory, the number of times material is moved, etc.

Service Centers

A contractor service center furnishes services to others within a company. Good examples are the computer mainframe installations that provide shared services for other corporate segments. Complex algorithms are usually calculated for work done in these centers. The algorithms will include charges for mainframe time as well as ancillary equipment utilized in running programs for users.

Another example of a service center is a testing facility, which can range from a wind tunnel to an environmental test lab. A type of machine utilization rate may be calculated for the type of tests being performed. Some of the testing service center rates can be quite large due to the expensive original cost of the equipment and the specialized housing necessary for this equipment. Other service center examples include copying or reproduction centers, graphic arts, technical library, automobiles, and aircraft.

General and Administrative Costs

G&A costs are defined as "Any management, financial, and other cost which is incurred by or allocated to a business unit and which is for the general management and administration of the business unit as a whole." These costs normally include compensation of company executives and their related fringe benefits, legal and professional fees, and other administrative personnel and costs.

G&A costs are frequently accumulated in a single pool and are allocated to the entire business unit based on the total cost input by way of a rate expressed as follows:

Direct manufacturing labor cost	$ 30,000
Direct material costs	$ 25,000
Manufacturing overhead costs	$ 35,000
Other direct costs	$ 10,000
Total cost input	$100,000
G&A costs	$ 10,000
G&A rate ($8,500 divided by $85,000)	10.00%

In the total cost input G&A allocation method, all costs (labor, overhead, material, and other direct charges) are included in the G&A allocation base. An alternative G&A allocation method is called the "value added" method and would be expressed as follows:

Direct manufacturing labor cost	$ 30,000
Direct material costs	$ 25,000
Manufacturing overhead costs	$ 35,000
Other direct costs	$ 10,000
Value added (total cost input less materials and subcontracts)	$ 75,000
G&A costs	$ 10,000
G&A rate ($10,000 divided by $75,000)	13.33%

A third allocation method is called the single element method. This method uses only one cost element (e.g., labor as an element of the base) to allocate G&A costs. It is not used too often, however, because the smaller the base employed, the larger the G&A rate will be. This unfortunately does not present a readily acceptable, saleable G&A rate. In most instances, the lowest G&A rate possible presents a more acceptable selling point:

Direct manufacturing labor cost	$ 30,000
Direct material costs	$ 25,000

Manufacturing overhead costs	$ 35,000
Other direct costs	$ 10,000
G&A costs	$ 10,000
G&A rate ($10,000 divided by $30,000)	33.33%

There have been numerous debates and a few court decisions regarding which G&A allocation method is the most acceptable. The CAS allow any of these methods. However, a non-CAS-covered business unit is not restricted to the use of only these three G&A allocation bases.

The Defense Contract Audit Agency (DCAA) has generally advocated the total cost input method as the only acceptable method. Case history indicates that the courts have not agreed with that philosophy and have allowed any of the three methods to be used based on the contractor's selection and the equity of the resulting allocations.

Another aspect of G&A costs is multiple layers of G&A costs. These layers are represented by several different labels, such as a group or a sector. These units usually have cognizance over a number of divisions or segments producing goods and services. For contracts subject to full CAS coverage, corporate allocations are governed by CAS 403. Basically, corporate or group costs are identified as much as possible to specific segments, or groups of segments. The residual expenses, which cannot be identified, are then reviewed as a percentage of total revenue. If the residual expenses exceed specified percentages, these expenses must be allocated by a method called the "three factor formula." This formula includes revenues, payroll, and net book value of assets.

Consistent Application

With regard to the accumulation and allocation of direct and indirect costs, both the FAR and the CAS emphasize the need for consistent allocation of costs incurred for the same purpose in similar circumstances. This fundamental requirement of government contract costing serves as a foundation in the development of any accounting system. The CAS provide specific criteria for the accumulation and allocation of both direct and indirect costs. They describe the nature of these costs and include guidance in determining acceptable, indirect allocation bases. In circumstances where the CAS do not apply to contracts, the method of allocation is to be in accordance with consistently applied GAAP and causal-beneficial relationships.

According to the FAR, the base period for allocating costs is the cost accounting period during which such costs are incurred and accumulated for distribution to work performed in that period. For contracts subject to full CAS coverage, the cost accounting periods to be used in allocating indirect costs are governed by CAS 406. This requirement is also incorporated in the FAR. For contracts subject to modified CAS coverage and for contracts not subject to CAS coverage, the base period for allocating indirect costs will normally be the contractor's fiscal year.

Establishing a Cost Structure

When an offeror or a contractor must create a cost structure for government contracting, a spreadsheet application is helpful. The first column of such a spreadsheet contains all the nominal accounts, i.e., revenue and expense accounts. The second column presents the amount from the most recent cost accounting period or an estimate for the current cost accounting period, if this is available.

Each amount is then assigned to a column for direct labor costs, material and subcontract costs, other direct costs, fringe benefit costs (if applicable), overhead cost pool(s), and G&A. Columns for unallowable costs should also be included. The totals on these columns are used to develop cost allocation bases and cost pool amounts. A check figure can be developed to ensure that all general ledger costs are accounted for in the government cost structure. Figure 21 demonstrates this application.

Many variations are possible in Figure 21. For example, multiple overhead cost pools are common; the most common is an overhead cost pool for materials and subcontracts. Other overhead cost pools might be for contractor site and client site work, physical location, business line, profession discipline, etc.

Monitoring Indirect Costs

Indirect cost rates should be monitored to prevent over- or under-invoicing of cost-type contracts and to ensure that business decisions are based on accurate information. Rates should be monitored at least monthly, preferably quarterly. Annual revisions to interim billing rates are not required by the FAR, but agencies such as DCAA may demand that such revisions be submitted in advance of each fiscal year. Interim billing rate adjustments should be requested at any time rates are expected to vary significantly from actual rates at year-end. The test is what is expected at year end, not the year-to-date rate. At the completion of the year, DCAA encourages contractors to adjust indirect cost rates to reflect actual rates prior to audit. This is not required by the FAR, but is often a good idea to prevent under- or over-billings.

OTHER COST ACCOUNTING CONCEPTS

FAR 31.201-1, Composition of Total Costs, states "(a) The total cost of a contract is the sum of the allowable direct and indirect costs allocable to the contract, incurred or to be incurred, less any allocable credits, plus any allocable cost of money pursuant to FAR 31.205-10. In ascertaining what constitutes a cost, any generally accepted method of determining or estimating costs that is equitable

and is consistently applied may be used, including standard costs properly adjusted for applicable variances."

There are two methods of recording costs in an accounting system: a job order system and a process cost system. Similarly, there are two bases for measuring cost: actual cost and standard cost. A job order cost system accumulates costs by job or task. In other words, this system assigns costs, such as direct labor, direct material, and overhead, to specific jobs within a contract. It may assign costs to individual production units or to a lot that consists of several units. The job order cost system is common in manufacturing contracts, where the production items are dissimilar in design, processing, or cost. It is also used in research and development contracts and service contracts. Costs in job order systems are recorded at actual cost.

A process cost system accumulates costs by a specific process or by a department that may represent several processes. This system assigns the various costs to the units introduced by the department during a specific time period. It is common in manufacturing of products where identical units of production are involved, such as chemical, petroleum, and computer chips.

In a process system, costs are assigned either at actual cost or at a standard cost. A standard cost accounting system, as defined in the FAR, uses costs that have been computed using preestablished measures (e.g., estimated or engineered standards). These measures pertain to both the quantity of services (e.g., labor hours, material units) and the value per quantity of resource. Standard cost accounting systems are acceptable as long as standard costs are properly adjusted for applicable variances. The recognition that standard cost accounting systems are capable of producing actual costs (i.e., standard plus or minus variances) is important because actual costs are the basis for determining allowable contract costs and in establishing costs for contract payments.

Figure 21
INDIRECT COST STRUCTURE DEVELOPMENT

Account	Total	Direct Labor	IR&D/B&P Labor	Materials & Subcontractors	Direct Costs	Unallow. ODCs	Fringe Benefits	Overhead	G&A Gross	G&A Unallowable	G&A Allowable	
Direct Labor	$325,600	$325,600										
IR&D/B&P Labor	55,400		$55,400									
Subcontractors	365,100			$365,100								
Materials	107,100			107,100								
Auto, Taxi and Subway	2,300				$2,300							
Airfare	8,500				8,500							
Hotel/Rent	3,000				3,000							
Meals	1,000				1,000							
Conferences	1,300				1,300							
Other Direct Costs	2,000				1,900	$100						
Bank Charges	900								$900		$900	
Publications & Subscriptions	600							$600			0	
Dues & Memberships	600							600			0	
Equipment Rental	4,600							3,680	920		920	*
Expendable Equipment	600							480	120		120	*
Insurance	18,500						$18,200		300		300	
Leave—Holidays	14,000						14,000				0	
Leave—Vacations	28,700						28,700				0	
Leave—Others	2,700						2,700				0	
Office Supplies	3,500							2,800	700		700	*
Office Expenses	2,900							2,320	580		580	*
Operating Spplies	1,300							1,040	260		260	*
Payroll Taxes	48,500						48,500				0	
Postage & Delivery	2,700							2,160	540		540	*
Printing and Reproduction	100							80	20		20	*
Professional Fees—Accounting	7,900								7,900		7,900	
Professional Fees—Legal	8,200								8,200		8,200	
Professional Fees—Patent	4,800								4,800		4,800	
Professional Fees—Other	100								100		100	
Rent—Office	24,100							19,280	4,820		4,820	*
Rent—Storage	2,400							1,920	480		480	*
Salaries and Wages	168,000							161,400	6,600		6,600	
Services—Computer	200							160	40		40	*
Taxes—Property	500								500		500	
Taxes—Federal Income	1,000								1,100	$1,000	0	
Taxes—State Income	100								100		100	
Taxes—Other	400								400		400	
Telephone	8,400							6,720	1,680		1,680	*
Seminars and Conferences	100							80	20		20	*
Travel & Lodging	3,500							2,800	700	64	636	*
Interest Expense	2,000								2,000	2,000	0	
Penalties	100								100	100	0	
Entertainment and Morale	100								100	100	0	
Fringe Benefits on Indirect Labor	0								34,304		34,304	
IR&D/B&P Labor	0								55,400		55,400	
IR&D/B&P Fringe Benefits	0								11,312		11,312	
IR&D/B&P Overhead	0								29,971		29,971	
Total Expenses	$1,233,400	$325,600	$55,400	$472,200	$18,000	$100	$112,100	$206,120	$174,867	$3,264	$171,603	
Allocation Base	Direct Labor plus IR&D/B&P Labor plus Indirect Labor						$549,000					
	Direct Labor plus IR&D/B&P Labor plus Fringes on Both							$458,796				
	Total Costs less G&A								$1,058,533	$1,058,533	$1,058,533	
Rate							20.42%	44.93%	16.52%	0.31%	16.21%	

Check		Rate	Amount	Multiple-Lbr	Multiplier-Tot	
Direct Labor			$325,600			
Fringe Benefits at		20.42%	66,484	1.20		
Subtotal			$392,084			
Overhead at		44.93%	176,149	1.75		
Subtotal			$568,233			
Other Direct Costs			490,300			
Subtotal			$1,058,533			
Allowable G&A at		16.21%	171,603	2.03		
Subtotal			$1,230,136			
Unallowable G&A		0.31%	3,264	2.03	2.79	
Total			$1,233,400			
Check:			$1,233,400			
Difference			$ –			

Government auditors often have difficulty reviewing process cost systems because they are unfamiliar with such systems. As a result, memorandum records might be necessary to present costs on a job cost basis. Government auditors also often have difficulty reviewing standard cost systems for the same reason. Similarly, memorandum records might be necessary to present standard costs on an actual cost basis.

CAS 407 provides criteria under which standard costs may be used for estimating, accumulating, and reporting costs of direct material and direct labor, and provides guidance relating to the establishment of standards, accumulation of standard costs, and accumulation and disposition of variances.

When a contract is not subject to the CAS, only the FAR cost principles and GAAP will apply. For the most part, the FAR cost principles are not as specific as the CAS; however, many of the same cost accounting concepts are included in both. In fact, some of the CAS are incorporated by reference or by restatement in the FAR cost principles.

CREDITS

FAR 31.201-5, Credits, states "The applicable portion of any income, rebate, allowance, or other credit relating to any allowable cost received by or accruing to the contractor shall be credited to the Government either as a cost reduction or by cash refund."

This requirement compels contractors to analyze any and all credits received to ascertain their direct or indirect impact on government contracts. For example, a vendor may issue credit for direct material that was not used and was returned. This would be credited directly back to the applicable contract or contracts.

Sometimes contractors receive an annual or semiannual credit from the travel agency they employ for airline tickets purchased. This credit, because it covers all tickets written in the period, would usually be credited into overhead and/or G&A pools. This would be an indirect type of credit and the most equitable method of relaying it to the government is via the indirect pools. Another indirect credit is found in the income from the sale of scrap. These credits, which resulted from working on many contracts, are again most equitably handled by credits to an indirect pool. In these instances of contractors receiving credit for some reason, it is important to avoid automatically taking the credit to "Other Income."

Any credit received needs to be scrutinized to ensure that the government receives its due cost reduction. For cost-reimbursement contracts, any credits must be given to the government even after the contract has been closed.

CHAPTER 4

Cost Allowability

Knowing what costs can be claimed is essential in preparing price proposals and indirect cost rate proposals, as well as understanding how profit is affected by unallowable costs. In addition, knowing what costs are allowable will aid in avoiding penalties for claiming expressly unallowable costs as well as government allegations of defective pricing, criminal or civil false claims, or fraud.

ORIGIN OF GOVERNMENT CONTRACT COST PRINCIPLES

The first U.S. government purchases were on a firm-fixed-price basis for such items as horses, guns, and cannons. Over the years, the rules and regulations on the allowability of costs under government contracts have evolved from simple directives first developed during World War I into rather complex and substantial rules. The Revenue Act of 1916 contained the first cost principles, which consisted of a mere one page of cost allowability rules. In the late 1930s, the Treasury Department began to issue Treasury Decisions (TDs) regarding cost-type contract costs and profits. TD 5000, which was issued in 1940, contained only about six pages of guidelines on both cost allowability and cost allocability. TD 5000 continued to be used as the basic cost rules until the first Armed Services Procurement Regulation (ASPR) was published in 1949. A major revision of the ASPR was promulgated in 1959. In 1978, the title of the ASPR was changed to the Defense Acquisition Regulation (DAR).

The Federal Procurement Regulation (FPR) was developed almost concurrently with the ASPR and the DAR and, for the most part, was modeled after the defense regulations. Civilian (nondefense) agencies used the FPR, although several (e.g., National Aeronautics and Space Administration, Department of Energy) developed their own regulations based either on the ASPR and the DAR or on the FPR.

After several years of study and development, governmentwide acquisition regulations were issued as the Federal Acquisition Regulation (FAR) on April 1, 1984. To accommodate special departmental and agency needs, organizations were authorized to publish supplemental regulations to the FAR. These supplemental regulations could be more stringent than those in the FAR, but they could not contradict or establish as allowable any cost made specifically unallowable by the FAR. In addition to the FAR (and the agencies' supplemental regulations), promulgations by the Cost Accounting Standards Board (CASB), generally accepted accounting principles (GAAP), and federal and state laws all play important roles in determining contract cost allowability.

APPLICABILITY OF GOVERNMENT COST REGULATIONS

All contracts and contract modifications for supplies and services or experimental, developmental, and research work negotiated on the basis of cost with commercial organizations must adhere to the cost principles and procedures set forth in FAR Part 31.2. These cost principles must be used in pricing negotiated supplies, services, research contracts, and contract modifications with commercial organizations whenever the contract or subcontract exceeds $550,000. The cost principles and procedures must be used under the following circumstances:

1. Determining reimbursable costs under cost-reimbursement contracts, including any cost-reimbursement subcontracts, and the cost-reimbursement portion of T&M contracts

2. Negotiating overhead rates

3. Proposing, negotiating, or determining costs under firm-fixed price and cost-reimbursement contracts

4. Revising fixed-price-incentive contracts

5. Redetermining prices of prospective and retroactive price redetermination contracts

6. Pricing changes and other contract modifications.

Cost allowability provisions did not always apply to fixed-price contracts. By 1959, various versions of fixed-price contracts had become more common and the government designated the allowability provisions as "guides" to pricing fixed-price contracts. In July 1970, the regulations were revised to make cost allowability provisions applicable to both fixed-price contracts and cost-type contracts. This aspect was reinforced in a Board of Contract Appeals case involving the Lockheed-Georgia Co. (ASBCA No. 27660), where the Board accepted interest expense as an allowable cost despite the specific cost principle that states that interest expense for financing purposes is unallowable.

The cost allowability rules do not apply to U.S. government contracts awarded to the Canadian governmental agency known as the Canadian Commercial Corporation. This agency was established as a conduit for U.S. government contract awards to commercial organizations in Canada. By agreement between the two nations, such awards will be treated as exempt from cost rules because the awards are to the sovereign Canadian government, which has its own cost regulations.

FAR 31.102 states: ". . .application of cost principles to fixed-price contracts and subcontracts shall not be construed as a requirement to negotiate agreements on individual elements of cost in arriving at agreement on the total price. The final price accepted by the parties reflects agreement only on the total price. Further, notwithstanding the mandatory use of cost principles, the objective will continue to be to negotiate prices that are fair and reasonable, cost and other factors considered."

The final price eventually agreed to by the parties reflects agreement only on the total price, not on line-item cost and profit amounts. This FAR provision anticipates disagreement in certain cases between the government and a contractor on the allow-ability and allocability of particular types of costs. Furthermore, this FAR provision recognizes that differences of opinion are certain to arise in interpreting the regulations, including the structure of cost allocation bases and indirect cost pools, as well as the allocation to cost objectives. The FAR focuses on the real objective of negotiating a bottom-line price for the work and not necessarily agreeing on each line item of cost and profit, such as labor, material, or overhead.

In this connection, the contractor may reach a bottom-line price quite differently from the way the government does. For example, the contractor might have a different concept of which cost items are allowable and allocable to the contract, such as certain items of labor and material, overhead, and G&A expenses. In addition, the contractor might believe that it was successful in negotiating

15 percent profit on the work, but the government might believe that it negotiated only a 7 percent profit. Again, the only amount on which there should be no difference of opinion is the bottom-line price incorporated into the contract.

FAR CONCEPT OF TOTAL COST

FAR 31.201-1 discusses total cost: "The total cost of a contract is the sum of the allowable direct and indirect cost allocable to the contract, incurred or to be incurred, less any allocable credits, plus any allocable cost of money pursuant to 31.205-10. In ascertaining what constitutes a cost, any generally accepted method of determining or estimating costs that is equitable and is consistently applied may be used, including standard costs properly adjusted for applicable variances. See 31.201-2(b) and (c) for CAS requirements."

Thus, the FAR neither requires nor mandates a single accounting system or method of determining total cost. Contractors are free to develop and use the type of accounting system they deem appropriate to reflect the financial results of their operations properly, considering the nature of their services or products. A contractor can still choose many of the accounting techniques to use, including the differentiation of direct and indirect costs, the number and content of overhead cost pools, and the method of allocating overhead costs to cost objectives.

CREDITS

In defining total contract costs as allowable costs less any allocable credits, FAR 31.201-5 recognizes that certain receipts should be credited against the cost to which those items relate, instead of being recorded as revenue. These receipts are not truly revenues from the sale of goods or services but are, in effect, a reduction of the cost of the transactions to which they relate. To treat them as revenues would distort both revenues and cost. The applicable portion of any income, rebate, allowance, or other credit relating to any allowable cost and received by or accruing to the contractor is to be credited to the government either as a cost reduction or by cash refund.

For example, the following receipts should be treated as credits: (1) prompt payment and trade discounts on the cost of materials or services; (2) refunds on materials returned to the vendor; (3) receipts from the sale of scrap; (4) dividends and rebates received under insurance policies; (5) rebates from travel agencies on airline tickets; and (6) entries to correct accounting errors such as overpayments.

If a refund relates to more than one transaction, the credit should be allocated on a pro rata basis to the various transactions to which it belongs. In those cases, the government is entitled to only its pro rata share of the credit. Many times this type of transaction credit is accomplished through an overhead or G&A pool. State and local tax credits can be quite complex as they are usually very location-specific. An analysis of location-specific government contract activity is usually warranted to ensure that: (1) proper credit is forwarded to the government; and (2) the proper amount is credited to the other business of the contractor.

Northrop Corporation is a good example of how the credit rule is applied (ASBCA No. 8502). After the Renegotiation Board reduced the contractor's profits, the contractor applied to the state of California for a refund of the California franchise tax that it had paid on the basis of profits before renegotiation. When the contractor recovered the excess franchise tax and the interest on it, the government demanded its portion of the refunded franchise tax, with interest, for which the contractor had been reimbursed under its negotiated CPFF contracts. The ASBCA held for the government.

Over the past few years, many ASBCA cases have established case law for determining the division of credits. Companies have been very aggressive in trying to ensure that equity is served in determining credit allocation. Often, the contractor's commercial business was not receiving the recognition it deserved. Sometimes a facility housed both government and commercial business. As a result, any credits received an enormous amount of scrutiny to determine an equitable distribution.

Another aspect of contracting that affects the distribution of credits is the mix of contracts. A contractor may begin a period of business activity with a large number of fixed-price contracts. During the period, the mix of contracts may shift toward more cost-reimbursable contracts. Credits would have to be scrutinized carefully to ascertain which period they applied to and to what degree government contracts, if any, would have been affected. The problem of contract mix has been a thorny issue in allocating credits.

For instance, a fixed-price contract bid awarded early in the accounting period was not costed/priced to include a credit for taxes that, at the time, was not known would occur. Subsequently, when the credit was issued by the taxing authority, no credit was due to the fixed-price contract. The government can argue to have credit issued. However, if instead of a credit an additional tax had been levied, the fixed-price contract would not have been increased to cover that additional cost. Fixed-price contracts carry a certain sanctity for not having their price adjusted for occurrences, either plus or minus, during contract performance.

INCURRED COSTS

Ordinarily, a cost is incurred when an obligation to pay another party arises. Under accrual accounting, costs come into existence when a liability occurs. This matter is not clear-cut, however. Problems (such as payments without obligation) have resulted in various court actions stemming from the

attempt to decide when costs have been incurred for government contract purposes. Sometimes payment may clearly be necessary for contract performance to be considered an incurred cost.

In Wyman-Gordon (ASBCA No. 5100), a contractor lent money to a subcontractor who successfully completed the work but was unable to repay the loan because he went broke. The contracting officer disallowed the loan as a bad debt. The ASBCA disagreed and ruled that the cost was necessary under the circumstances. On the other hand, in Westinghouse Electric Corp., where no payment had actually been made, the ASBCA refused to recognize the prime contractor's claim for an overrun by the subcontractor.

In Norcoast Constructors Inc. and Morrison-Knudsen (ASBCA. No. 16483), the government took possession of storage tanks the contractor was entitled to keep under the contract. The ASBCA stated that the contractor was due an equitable adjustment amounting to the value of the tanks. Although the government argued that the contractor's costs were not increased, the ASBCA said that the contractor could have sold the tanks, thus lowering the contract costs.

"Contingent liabilities" have also created some problems. In General Dynamics Corp. (ASBCA No. 8867), the ASBCA did not permit accrued "potential" liabilities related to layoff benefits for employees, since future payments were not certain and no funds had been set aside.

The problem of contingent liability was also present in A.C.F. Brill Motors Co. (ASBCA No. 2470). A subcontractor closed a plant, laying off employees, which raised the state unemployment insurance rate. The subcontractor included as a contract cost the increased payments already made and those to be made in the future. In denying the contractor's claim, the ASBCA observed that the future payments were contingent on a variety of factors, all of which might not necessarily have been related to the employee layoff issue.

Another area of costs that is challenged is "to be incurred" costs. The government usually expresses skepticism that these costs will ever materialize. However, contractors can quite frequently rely on the incurrence of like costs in past activities. Some examples are: certain recurring taxes, equipment-specific depreciation costs, and in certain instances "compelled" post-retirement cost, including medical and pension expenses. In cases of plant closures, for instance, many potential areas of cost must be recognized. These could include items such as severance pay, unpaid taxes, environmental impact costs, and underfunded pension plans. Conversely, overfunded pension plans have created havoc in attempting to close a plant segment.

The "paid cost" rule is another area that was briefly applied and then rescinded. While this rule was in effect, a cost for a product or service performed by a vendor or subcontractor had to be paid before it could be claimed by a prime contractor. Small businesses did not have this requirement. In 2000, this rule was deleted from the regulations. This permits payment when a contractor is not delinquent in paying costs of contract performance in the ordinary course of business. This would allow a cost to be recognized (and thus subsequently billed to the government) when it was entered on the books of a company as an "unaudited liability." In other words, if a shipment or an invoice had been received, and not yet paid, there would be recognition of a liability that would have to be met in a future period.

ALLOWABILITY OF COSTS

FAR Subsection 31.201-2 states that the factors to be considered in determining whether a cost is allowable include the following:

1. Reasonableness

2. Allocability

3. Standards promulgated by the CAS Board, if applicable; otherwise, generally accepted accounting principles and practices appropriate to the particular circumstances

4. Terms of the contract

5. Any limitations set forth in FAR 31.2.

Although a particular cost meets these criteria, another aspect sometimes determines cost allowability: perception. Perception has nothing to do with true allowability. A case in point involves costs for kenneling a dog. During the congressional hearings in the 1980s, the *Washington Post* ran an article about how taxpayers were paying the cost of kenneling a dog owned by an aerospace executive. Although the costs were allowable, there was an appearance of impropriety. Needless to say, from that time on, government contractors have had to view virtually every cost not only from the aspect of cost allowability but also from the aspect of "front page perception."

To the extent that a contractor's costs are subject to the CAS and a method of cost allocation is inconsistent with the standard(s), that method is unacceptable and must be altered to conform to the standard. However, if the CASB has not issued a standard on a particular matter and the cost is not deemed "unallowable" per the FAR, a contractor may apply GAAP to its cost accounting system to account for the cost. Note that not all CASB promulgations are included in the FAR allowablity criteria: Only the CAS standards are included; CAS rules and regulations (such as those related to cost impact statements and accounting changes) are not included.

Although GAAP is noted as an alternative, it is rarely used for determining allowability. Usually, as soon as GAAP is used to determine allowability, the government rule makers amend the FAR to make such costs specifically unallowable. An outstanding example is a case involving Gould Co. (ASBCA No.

24881) accounting for goodwill costs. The Board ruled that goodwill was allowable in writing up assets. The government changed the FAR to make goodwill unallowable as quickly as it could. In another instance, stock purchase agreements governed by IRS rules were determined by case law to be allowable. Once again, the FAR was amended to make these costs unallowable.

It is important to recognize that *all* allowability criteria must be met for a cost to be allowable. For example, if a cost complies with the CAS or GAAP but not with the FAR, the cost is unallowable. Furthermore, even if a cost is in compliance with the CAS, with GAAP, and with the FAR, the government could still negotiate a contract clause that would restrict reimbursement of that cost.

For questions of allocability, the Armed Services Board of Contract Appeals has ruled that a conflict between a CAS and a specific FAR principle should be decided in favor of the terms of the CAS, because the purpose of the CAS was to establish cost allocability (Boeing Corp., ASBCA No. 28342). However, in another case (Emerson Electric, ASBCA No. 30090), the Board ruled that where the CAS permit several accounting choices, the FAR can effectively limit those choices to a single alternative. In these cases, no conflict exists, because the FAR-dictated choice complies with both the CAS and the FAR.

A court decision involving General Electric Co. (US Cls Ct No. 25492) adds confusion to any attempt to separate the concepts of allowability and allocability. In this case, the focus was on the terminology of the 1979-1985 Defense Acquisition Regulation and the FAR provision on foreign selling expenses. During this period, the regulation terms these expenses unallocable. In 1985, the regulation was revised to recognize that the correct term should have been "unallowable." In deciding this case, the court ignored this revision and took the position that the term "allowability"

was understood to be the applicable term despite the actual wording in the regulation.

In reversing the Martin decision (ASBCA No. 35895) on the allowability of G&A expenses that are applied to an unallowable G&A base, the U.S. Court of Appeals stated essentially that any FAR provision by its nature relates to cost allowability rather than allocability. Thus, no matter how the allowability criteria are expressed in the FAR (i.e., even if allowability is in terms of allocability), no conflict exists because the FAR has jurisdiction over allowability issues.

One of the specific functions of the reestablished CAS Board (1989) is to resolve inconsistencies between the CAS and the FAR. The administrator of the Office of Federal Procurement Policy (OFPP) is directed to resolve these inconsistencies. If an inconsistency is not resolved, the regulation that is inconsistent with the CAS may be ignored.

Government agencies are permitted to publish supplemental regulations to meet their special needs. These rules may add allow-ability criteria to the FAR criteria but cannot render allowable any cost made specifically unallowable by the FAR. Federal departments and agencies that have published regulations include Agriculture, the Agency for International Development, Commerce, Defense, Energy, the Environmental Protection Agency, the Federal Emergency Management Agency, the General Services Administration, Health and Human Services, Housing and Urban Development, Interior, Justice, the National Aeronautics and Space Administration, the Small Business Administration, Transportation, Treasury, and the Veteran Administration. The Air Force, Air Force Systems Command, Army, and Navy have published regulations along with the Department of Defense. Agency regulations have significantly modified the FAR on the allowability of independent research and development (IR&D), bid and proposal (B&P), and precontract costs.

Reasonableness

What is reasonable? Why is the government interested in controlling costs on this basis? How is reasonableness applied to contractors in a complex business world? These valid questions have no easy answers. Obviously, the government is concerned about protecting its interests and ensuring that work is done in an efficient and economical manner. The factor of reasonableness is often the government's entrée to cost recovery as well as to an evaluation of areas that are essentially limited to management prerogative. Needless to say, this area often involves controversy.

Any determination of reasonableness must be evaluated on a case-by-case basis. This precept is illustrated in Bruce Construction Corporation (324 F.2d 516). The court stated that reasonableness should be determined by evaluating the circumstances at the time the cost was incurred, rather than by applying any universal principle. The court also noted that where a cost has already been incurred, a presumption of reasonableness may apply. Congressional direction shifted this burden of proof regarding reasonableness from the government to the contractor.

An expense may be disallowed as unreasonable in "amount." This area involves complicated issues and interpretations. Several different factors may come into play, including relative amount, public policy, custom, and usage. In Stanley Aviation Corporation (ASBCA No. 12292), the government alleged that the contractor's indirect rates were far in excess of estimated amounts and challenged the costs on the basis of reasonableness. The ASBCA disagreed and said that the government should have examined the underlying circumstances in more detail, including an evaluation of the indirect cost pools on an item-by-item basis. Furthermore, the court recognized that the contractor was acting under the strongest possible economic motivation to reduce its costs.

In the determination of reasonableness, everything is relative. Cost comparisons involving the same items under similar circumstances are important in justifying a reasonable amount. A key case that illustrates this concept is Lulejian and Association, Inc. (ASBCA No. 20094). In this case, the government attempted to make cost comparisons of items involving the contractor's compensation, but the ASBCA rejected the comparisons as insufficient because: (1) they involved years different from the one at issue; (2) they were incurred by organizations of a different type from the contractor's; and (3) they involved services of lesser duty and responsibility than those at issue. In ruling for the contractor, the ASBCA stated that "... the overall cost was reasonable compared to the cost of such benefits in the industry in general, and the cost of its relatively liberal pension plan and group life insurance plan was offset by the absence of other benefits commonly available to employees in the industry."

The reasonableness of specific costs must be examined closely in firms or divisions not subject to effective competitive restraints. What is reasonable depends on a variety of considerations and circumstances involving both the nature and the amount of the cost in question. In determining the reasonableness of a specific cost, the contracting officer is to consider:

- Whether it is the type of cost generally recognized as ordinary and necessary for the conduct of the contractor's business or the contract performance
- Generally accepted sound business practices, arm's-length bargaining, and federal and state laws and regulations
- The contractor's responsibilities to the government, other customers, the owners of the business, employees, and the public at large
- Any significant deviations from the contractor's established practices.

Ordinary and Necessary

In a commercial setting, a cost that is ordinary for the conduct of a business or necessary to advance performance on a contract may be presumed to be reasonable. Other considerations come into play when contracting with the government. The terms "ordinary" and "necessary" are not defined precisely in the FAR. Therefore, they are somewhat open to interpretation. Contracting officers often attempt to define what is ordinary and necessary by establishing contract ceilings on particular direct or indirect costs. For example, they often establish limits on travel costs, fringe benefits, and escalation rates. Government auditors also play a key role in determining what is ordinary and necessary. They may question the cost associated with using a private plane or conducting periodic management meetings at distant, exotic locations as unnecessary and out of the ordinary. Any determination of this kind should consider a number of factors, including the contractor's size versus relative cost of the questioned item, type of business, industry custom, and reasonable alternatives.

In Vare Industries, Inc. (ASBCA 12126, et al.), for example, the contractor was using a senior engineer to complete contract closeout functions. The government alleged that the labor involved was unreasonable because it was not ordinary for an engineer and could effectively be accomplished by a clerk. The ASBCA upheld the government's charge that this was an unreasonable cost. The contractor was also incurring a certain amount of cost associated with providing security to protect two huts at the contract work site. The government alleged that the costs were unreasonable, because the contract did not call for any such security measures and there was nothing extraordinary about the huts or their contents that would make such a cost necessary. The ASBCA, once again, agreed with the government.

Accepted Business Practices

Businesses operating in a competitive environment try to be cost-effective to maximize profits. Generally, if there is competition, the resulting increases paid are reasonable. The constraint on costs imposed by arm's-length bargaining can be troublesome. In particular, the government often questions dealings a contractor has with organizations that are related through common management or common ownership. The critical element is the extent of common control. Unfortunately, guidelines for determining this are not precise and have been established largely as the result of BCA decisions. Normally, an interest of 50 percent or more would be necessary to establish common control. However, as a practical matter, less than 50 percent ownership is needed to gain control if the remaining stock or ownership interest is dispersed among many owners.

In Brown Engineering Company (NASA BCA No. 31), the National Aeronautics and Space Administration Board of Contract Appeals (NASA BCA) concluded that common ownership of as little as 37 percent could result in a controlling interest. The NASA BCA was influenced by the fact that the two entities had a number of common directors and business facilities. Moreover, one entity owned all the stock of the other, and the actual nature of their business transactions implied common control.

In A.S. Thomas, Inc. (ASBCA No. 10745), however, the ASBCA found that common control did not exist even though one individual owned one of the firms outright and about 43 percent of the other company's stock. In Data Design Labs (ASBCA No. 26753), several executives of a publicly held contractor formed a leasing company to build office space and then lease it to the contractor. The same executives actually signed the lease on behalf of both the lessee contractor and the newly formed lessor company (although the lease had been approved in advance by the contractor's board of directors). The ASBCA held that, because of the approval of the lease by the contractor's board of directors and because the owners of the leasing company held less than 10 percent of the contractor's stock, no common control existed. The facts and circumstances of each case, in other words, determine whether common control exists.

If it is determined that common control exists, transfers of goods and services must be made at cost. This rule was established to avoid the pyramiding of profits that would be possible if profits were allowed on intracompany transfers. This issue is particularly critical for organizations that lease or rent buildings or equipment from related companies. Interorganizational transfers between such firms at other than cost, however, can be made under special circumstances.

Prudent Business Person
This criterion requires that management consider its responsibilities to the business owners, employees, customers, the government, and the public at large. Actions that may seem advantageous to employees may be at direct odds with responsibilities to shareholders, the government, and the public. For example, in the case of Digital Simulation Systems, Inc. (NASA BCA No. 975-8), the BCA stated that "the government properly disallowed a cost-plus-fixed-fee con-trac-tor's contribution to its employee's profit-sharing plan because the contractor's request for profit shares in excess of its net profits was unreasonable." Under the profit-sharing plan, the contractor was increasing the compensation paid to its officers beyond a reasonable profit level. The ASBCA noted that the owners of a business normally expect a return on their investment, and the contractor's method of distributing profits beyond the level of "net" profits was operating to deny such a return.

Significant Deviations
Any significant deviation from a contractor's established policies and practices will be examined closely by the government to determine if this action results in the incurrence of unallowable costs. Costs incurred through consistent application of contractor policies and procedures are more likely to be considered reasonable. Significant deviations raise government concerns regarding the allow-ability of costs. For example, in ARO, Inc. (ASBCA. 13623), a contractor granted several employees leave to participate in a golf tournament. The ASBCA ruled that the additional time off was contrary to the contractor's established practice and, therefore, the associated costs were unreasonable.

In comparison, in General Dynamics Electric Boat (ASBCA No. 18503), the government alleged that the contractor's B&P expenses were unreasonable because they differed significantly from B&P expenses in previous years. However, in ruling for the company, the ASBCA recognized that the significant difference in cost was reasonable given the contractor's declining government sales and resulting efforts to increase business.

Allocability
FAR 31.201-4 establishes the general criteria for determining cost allocability. A cost is allocable if it is assignable or chargeable to one or more cost objectives on the basis of relative benefits received or another equitable relationship. A cost is allocable to a government contract if it: (1) is incurred specifically for the contract; (2) benefits both the contract and other work, and can be distributed to them in reasonable relationship to the benefits received; or (3) is necessary to the overall operation of the business, although a direct relationship to any particular cost objective cannot be shown.

One of the underlying concepts of allocability is that of "full absorption." Full absorption refers to the allocation of all costs, variable and fixed, to final cost objectives. In contrast, "direct" or "marginal" costing methods apply only variable costs and treat fixed costs as period or sunk costs. This latter approach can be advantageous to management in controlling costs and in making decisions since only the variable costs are considered relevant. Notwithstanding this approach, only full absorption costing may be applied to the pricing and costing of government contracts.

The single most important body of knowledge relating to the allocation issues in government contract costing is the promulgations of the CASB. Because the various government regulations only provide an overview of allocation principles, allocability issues for contracts covered by the CAS are evaluated almost exclusively by the standards. The FAR recognizes and incorporates many of the standards. Even contractors that do not have any CAS-covered contracts feel the influence of the standards because government auditors frequently base their opinions regarding allocability issues on CAS concepts. (See Chapter 6 for further discussion of the CAS.)

Several Claims Court decisions and BCA cases have significantly influenced the development and application of the concept of allocability. These cases illustrate the basic arguments about allocability that often arise.

The proper allocation of costs that benefit several cost objectives has been the subject of a number of cases. In many of them, the government has attempted to establish that no government contracts benefited from, for example, marketing costs. Generally, decisions have held that identification of specific benefits is not necessary; it is sufficient to show that government contracts as a class benefit from the expense in question.

This was the finding in the ASBCA case involving Federal Electric Corporation (ASBCA No. 11324). Also, if the necessity of a cost for the overall operation of a business can

be established, then this fact alone usually provides sufficient justification for allocating the cost to government contracts. Patent costs were an example of this in a case involving TRW, Inc. (ASBCA No. 11499) decided by the ASBCA. Another case on costs that benefit the overall business involved General Dynamics Corporation (ASBCA No. 18503). In this case, the government objected to the company's allocation of commercial bid and proposal costs to government contracts, but the ASBCA allowed the allocations, holding that successful commercial bids would increase the overall business base and thus decrease the allocation of fixed expenses to government contracts. The government has also disputed the allocation of home office expenses.

In KMS Fusion, Inc. (24 CtCl 582), involving lobbying costs, which was decided before the specific cost principle that disallowed these costs, a contractor had maintained a Washington, D.C., office to keep in contact with government officials concerning programs of interest to the company, which was located in the midwest. The Claims Court ruled that benefits arising from a potential increase in business are sufficient to establish allocability of the cost, while observing that the whole government benefits, because the same cost base supports more productive activity.

Cases have clearly established that, even when GAAP addresses an issue that is disputed (though usually it does not), the specific contract's applicable provisions and government regulations will prevail. When one contractor contended, for example, that the appropriate allocation of a state tax refund was to the year in which the credit became available, the government claimed that the credit should instead be allocated to the year giving rise to the credit. Although the ASBCA acknowledged that the contractor's treatment of the credit was in accordance with GAAP, it concluded that compliance with GAAP was not the determining factor, since one of the clauses in the contract required the contractor to allocate the refund to the year in which the expense giving rise to the credit was originally incurred.

Costs Incurred Specifically for the Contract

A cost incurred specifically for the contract is usually a "direct cost." Direct costs normally include such items as direct labor, materials, and subcontracts. As defined by the FAR, a direct cost is "any cost that can be identified specifically with a cost objective."

Contractors have significant discretion in defining direct and indirect costs. In accordance with the CAS, contractors establish their definition of direct and indirect costs in the form of written policies and procedures and must apply them in a consistent manner. If a contractor does not have CAS-covered contracts, it should establish the same type of policies and procedures.

Both the FAR and the CAS require that: "No final cost objective shall have allocated to it as a direct cost any cost, if other costs incurred for the same purpose in like circumstances have been included in any indirect cost pool to be allocated to that or any other final cost objective. Costs identified specifically with the contract are direct costs of the contract and are to be charged directly to the contract. All costs specifically identified with other final cost objectives of the contractor are direct costs of those cost objectives and are not to be charged to the contract directly or indirectly."

For reasons of practicality, any direct cost of minor dollar amount may be treated as an indirect cost if the accounting treatment: (1) is consistently applied to all final cost objectives; and (2) produces substantially the same results as treating the cost as a direct cost.

Blanket costs are costs that are identifiable to cost objectives but are so numerous and minor in amount that such identification is impractical. For example, a blanket cost could be the supervision time used during a production process. This cost could be accumulated and for practical purposes be an "allocated" direct cost based on direct labor hours or dollars of the employees supervised.

Costs can only be treated as both direct and indirect if the costs are incurred for different purposes in different circumstances. An example is a contractor who incurs costs for fire fighting under two sets of conditions. One group of fire fighters is for general plant fire protection and another special group of fire fighters is for providing a 24-hour-a-day watch on inflammable material. The latter group has no responsibility for overall plant fire protection. This example illustrates costs incurred under "unlike circumstances."

Costs Benefiting Several Cost Objectives

FAR 31.203 defines an indirect cost as "any cost not directly identified with a single, final cost objective, but identified with two or more final cost objectives or an intermediate cost objective. It is not subject to treatment as a direct cost. After direct costs have been determined and charged directly to the contract or other work, indirect costs are those remaining to be allocated to the several cost objectives. An indirect cost shall not be allocated to a final cost objective if other costs incurred for the same purpose in like circumstances have been included as a direct cost of that or any other final cost objective."

The FAR further states that "indirect costs shall be accumulated by logical cost groupings with due consideration of the reasons for incurring such costs." Such costs are to be assigned on the basis of the relative benefits accruing to the several cost objectives. The government generally prefers the benefits-received criterion over other comparative factors (i.e., causal relationships generated by the base costs) because it considers benefits received to be more equitable and easier to administer. For example, if a government contract causes the contractor to build a fence around its facility, the cost is considered by the government to benefit the entire operation due to decreased employee pilferage, etc. Thus, the cost should be allocated to all work benefiting from the expenditure rather than just the work that actually caused the expenditure. Commonly, manufacturing overhead, selling expenses, and G&A expenses are grouped separately and allocated over different bases.

The accumulation and allocation of manufacturing costs based on beneficial/causal relationships is illustrated in the case of Ellis Machine Works (ASBCA No. 16135). In this case, the contractor wanted to allocate its manufacturing overhead over a base consisting of total labor and material costs.

The ASBCA stated that, given the wide variance in the amount of labor required on jobs having the same amount of total labor and material costs, "direct manufacturing labor is a more accurate measure of the extent of the use of the manufacturing plant." The ASBCA stated, in part, that the pertinent regulation ". . .states that a cost is allocable to a particular cost objective in accordance with the relative benefits received or other equitable relationship. A manufacturer's pool of manufacturing related overhead consists of those costs involved in owning and maintaining its manufacturing plant (buildings and machinery), such as taxes, depreciation, fire insurance, and maintenance. It also includes indirect expenses related to manufacturing labor, such as payroll taxes and insurance, vacations, welfare, pensions and other fringe benefits. Manufacturing overhead, which is the indirect expense of the manufacturing plant, should be allocated to the jobs that generate the need for the manufacturing plant and benefit from its use in the plant that each job generates the cost of and benefits from the manufacturing plant. It is obvious that a job which requires 1,000 hours of manufacturing labor benefits more from the manufacturing plant and should bear a larger share of the

manufacturing overhead than another job involving the same labor and material costs which requires only 100 hour of manufacturing labor."

Indirect cost pools are allocated either to other cost pools (intermediate cost objectives) or to final cost objectives (contracts). Sometimes the functions in a cost pool benefit only other cost pools. For example, occupancy costs could be allocated among cost pools on the basis of a facility measure, such as square footage. Intermediate cost pools are often treated as service centers. For example, computer, word processing, and relocation costs are often grouped in a service center pool and allocated on the basis of a resource usage measurement, such as associated equipment time by project. Costs in this category could ultimately be charged as other direct costs as well as indirect costs. For example, the cost of computer services may be charged to an indirect pool for work done in generating accounting records, whereas it will be charged as an other direct cost for output associated with a contract. No inconsistency in allocating costs is occurring here because the "circumstances" are not alike.

Finally, indirect cost pools might be allocated only to final cost objectives. Indirect costs associated with this category are generally grouped into manufacturing, engineering, and material overhead pools. Allocation of the costs is commonly over such bases as direct labor dollars or hours or material-dollars.

Costs Necessary to the Overall Operation of the Business

The FAR recognizes that this category of expenses cannot be allocated to cost objectives on any base reflecting cause or benefit but is allocable because it benefits the organization as a whole. The most common kinds of expenses in this category are general administration, marketing and sales, and legal and accounting. Because of the nature of these expenses, they must be allocated over a base representing the total activity of the business.

For CAS-covered contracts, CAS 410 requires such a base and provides three alternatives for allocation: (1) total cost input; (2) value-added (i.e., total cost input less materials and subcontracts); or (3) single-element (e.g., direct labor dollars). For modified CAS-covered contracts or non-CAS-covered contracts, as a practical matter, the choice of a total activity base should represent the cost input features of the CAS because government auditors will be applying these concepts in their evaluation of any G&A rate structure. Prior to CAS 410, contractors often used such activities as cost of goods sold or cost of sales as a representation of total activity. CAS 410 does not allow these methods and government auditors object to them as not being a true measure of total activity during a cost accounting period.

One of the more significant of the government's concerns in evaluating cost allocation relating to G&A expenses is the association of costs with commercial—that is, nongovernment—cost objectives. The allocation of selling and marketing expenses is a common area of controversy between government auditors and contractors.

Contract Terms/Advance Agreements

Contracting officers often use contract clauses to limit reimbursable costs. This can pose a problem, because improperly worded contract clauses (or contract clauses accepted carelessly) can lead to inequitable results. For example, a contract clause may not permit local travel mileage as a direct contract cost. If, however, the contractor's accounting system treats directly identifiable travel costs as direct costs that benefit specific cost objectives, the effect of such a clause is to make local mile-

age unallowable for contracts containing this clause. The unallowed costs would, nonetheless, have to be charged to specific contracts (even though they would not be reimbursed on a contract with this clause) and could not be treated as indirect costs. Contractors often assume that, under circumstances such as these, the unallowed costs could be charged to indirect cost pools. However, to be consistent with disclosed or established accounting practices, this cannot be done.

Contract clauses cannot be used to authorize or validate allocations that would conflict with cost principles in the CAS or the FAR. For example, assume that a contracting officer objects to the allocation of G&A to subcontracts on a contract requiring a large number of subcontracts. If the contractor's accounting system uses total cost input as the allocation base, the acceptance of a contract clause that limited the allocation of G&A only to costs not associated with subcontracts would result in noncompliance with both CAS and FAR consistency requirements (especially CAS 410). Consistency would require the contractor to allocate G&A based on total cost inputs, but because of the clause, the G&A thus allocated to this contract based on the subcontract costs could not be reimbursed. In fact, the government would be inconsistent in requiring a clause forbidding G&A allocations to subcontract costs in this case, because if total cost input is the most equitable allocation base, total cost input should be used as the allocation base for every contract. The G&A allocated as a result should, therefore, always be reimbursed by the government.

Contract clauses that establish ceilings on indirect cost rates are often included in cost-type contracts. Although allowable costs are by definition reimbursable, clauses of this type make indirect costs in excess of the ceiling unallowable even though they would otherwise be properly allocable and allowable.

The government believes that such clauses protect it from unexpected or "unreasonable" increases in indirect cost rates. Often, the existence of a sound budgeting and cost control system will convince the government that this clause is not necessary.

Other clauses may provide for postaward reviews (for the purposes of downward price adjustments only) of labor rates under time-and-materials, labor-hour, or fixed-price contracts. This type of clause produces a one-sided arrangement that should be avoided if at all possible. Often only a strong overall negotiating position can prevent the government's imposition of these contract clauses on a contractor.

FAR 31.109 encourages making advance agreements on the allowability of costs, particularly related to the reasonableness or allocability of costs, in an effort to avoid subsequent disputes. These advance agreements are not required, however, and the lack of an agreement does not create a presumption of unallowability either way. Advance agreements may be negotiated either before or during a contract's performance but should, in any case, be negotiated before the cost is incurred. The agreements between the government and the contractor must be in writing. Advance agreements may not be made to allow costs that would otherwise be unallowable under the FAR.

The FAR provides several examples of costs for which advance agreements may be particularly helpful, including: compensation for personal services; use charges for fully depreciated assets; deferred maintenance costs; precontract costs; IR&D expenses and B&P expenses; royalties and other costs for use of patents; selling and distribution costs; travel and relocation costs; costs of idle facilities/capacity; severance pay to employees on support service contracts; plant reconversion; professional services; G&A expenses; and construction plant and equipment costs.

Selling and product distribution costs are also frequently questioned and are thus also particularly suitable for advance agreements. The government contends that such costs have limited allocability to government contracts. However, certain case law has proven otherwise and the government has had to agree to the overall allocability of the selling and product distribution costs of contractors that have both government and commercial contracts.

Indirect Cost Pools

Indirect costs are classified as overhead or G&A expenses. Overhead includes all indirect costs incurred for the production of goods and services, while G&A expenses are the overall costs of running a business. Overhead would include, for example, the electricity used to operate a plant. G&A expenses, on the other hand, would include the costs of running the accounting department. Overhead is allocated to products or services, while G&A expenses are allocated to cost accounting periods. Overhead and G&A expenses are not considered homogeneous and therefore usually should not be accumulated in the same indirect cost pool.

Indirect cost pools should be designed to permit allocations on the basis of the benefits received by the cost objectives. They should consider the reasons for incurring the costs and the logical connection between the costs accumulated. In other words, cost pools should be homogeneous. The FAR does not specify the number of cost pools a contractor should have, although it does caution that the number and composition of the cost pools should be governed by practical considerations. If substantially the same results can be obtained by using fewer cost pools, fewer cost pools should be used.

Allocations of indirect costs should not be unduly complicated. An allocation that is theoretically more accurate is not necessarily better because the greater the number of cost pools, the more complicated the process of accumulating, allocating, and cross-allocating indirect costs becomes.

The most common types of cost pools in a manufacturing environment are manufacturing, engineering, and material-related cost pools. The types of pools established depend on the types and number of the contractor's organizational units and the kind of products or services provided. For example, if a contractor has several plants or business units with different indirect cost rates, separate pools may be established for each site. If, however, a contractor has several plants where the business mix is similar and a common manager is responsible for all of them, only one cost pool may be necessary. Other factors could influence this decision, such as the relative volume at each site and the materiality of the costs involved.

Once an allocation base for an indirect cost pool has been established, the base should be used consistently. All costs, including unallowable costs, should receive a pro rata allocation of the G&A expenses. So, if a contracting officer disallowed travel and per diem costs on a particular contract, a pro rata share of the G&A expenses is also unallowable.

Criteria for Establishing Cost Pools

The criteria for distinguishing between direct and indirect costs and for determining how many indirect cost pools to have are: (1) compliance with government procurement regulations; (2) maximization of cost recovery; (3) development of meaningful information for management decisions; and (4) achievement of precise yet practical allocations. These criteria often conflict, most apparently in the case of complying with procurement regulations while also maximizing recovery of costs.

Under fixed-price contracts, the amount the government reimburses is set by precontract negotiations, market prices, or catalog prices. Under cost-reimbursement contracts, the amount the government reimburses is less restricted. Therefore, contractors can maximize cost recovery by allocating as many indirect costs as are legitimate to cost-reimbursement contracts. Some contractors design their organizational structure to take maximum advantage of the different types of contracts they perform. For example, they might perform noncompetitive contracts in one business unit and competitive contracts in a different unit. In this way, they can develop costs and prices for each organizational unit and allocate indirect costs more advantageously.

Management officials need reliable data to conduct a business properly, and a contractor's cost accounting system should be designed with this in mind. If a contractor's cost structure is too complex or if it is overly responsive to other needs (e.g., the need to comply with government regulations or to maximize cost recovery), management may be left with little meaningful data on which to base day-to-day decisions. If, for example, a contractor segregates commercial and government contracts—both of which are profitable—into separate divisions and allocates a disproportionate share of costs to the government division, the commercial division may appear more profitable than it really is, and the government division may appear to be unprofitable.

The tradeoff that has to be considered in deciding how many indirect cost pools should be established is accuracy versus practicality. The greater the number of indirect cost pools, the greater the theoretical accuracy in identifying indirect costs with cost objectives. On the other hand, more indirect cost pools means having to collect and maintain additional cost accounting data; for each indirect cost pool established, the contractor must forecast indirect cost rates to use in pricing and negotiating contract prices. As cost pools proliferate, each pool collects a lesser share of total costs, and, as a result, forecasts of the indirect cost rates become increasingly unreliable.

Many government contractors progress from a simple cost accounting structure having only a single indirect cost pool to a much more elaborate cost accounting structure having many interrelated indirect cost pools. If all a contractor's final cost objectives are similar, a single indirect cost pool is likely to be the best structure. That is, if a contractor produces only one type of product or service and also uses only one type of contract, then the use of only one cost pool would probably be acceptable to the government. For contractors that produce more than one product or service under various types of contracts, however, the government usually requires at least a segregation of G&A expenses from all other indirect costs.

For contractors with several plants or business units, it is unlikely that each site would have identical indirect cost rates, so separate pools should usually be established for each site. If, however, the business mix is similar at all the sites and a common manager is responsible for them all, there may be no need for individual rates. Other factors could influence this decision, such as the relative volume at each site and the materiality of the costs involved.

However, separate pools might be needed even at a single site. This might especially be true if different products, product lines, services, or departments exist at one site and the allocation base (e.g., direct labor dollars) varies significantly among the products, product lines, services, or departments. For example, if one department incurs significantly higher occupancy costs than the other but incurs identical labor costs, then separate cost pools by department should probably be established. Otherwise, each department would receive the same utility allocation.

Contractors have considerable discretion in deciding how to allocate costs to contracts. In numerous cases (e.g., ASBCA No. 11050, NASA BCA No. 873-10), the Boards of Contract Appeals have established that a contractor-selected allocation method should not be altered by the government unless the method produces inequitable results. The contractor's method does not have to be the best alternative, but merely an equitable method.

Contractors should monitor the cost structure and periodically review conditions to ensure that the most advantageous cost structure is being used. Changed business conditions (e.g., replacement of manual labor with robotics, shift from a service to a product business line, opening of a new facility, changes in the competitive environment, development of new products, mergers and acquisitions) may demand a revised cost structure. Because of the CAS requirement to compute a cost impact statement for accounting changes, the timing of a cost structure change should consider the status of existing contracts, the fiscal period, and the expected date of significant new contracts.

Frequently, contractors seek to isolate all or a portion of government contract operations from commercial or other government operations to limit exposure to government reviews, to maximize cost recovery, or to achieve other business advantages. The organizational units created under these conditions are sometimes referred to as special business units. This approach receives considerable government scrutiny and is often not successful in achieving the desired results. The existence of separate legal entities does not have as much influence on the way the government reviews transactions as on the way costs are allocated or shared between those entities. The presence of shared facilities and services, common management, frequent transfer of personnel, intercompany projects, loaning of employees, etc., are all indicators of a single unit.

Often, to achieve adequate segregation of a special business unit, it is necessary to take actions that are not the most financially prudent. For example, avoiding the use of shared facilities and management might result in higher costs for the overall operation.

Accordingly, contractors would be wise to minimize the number of indirect cost pools. Usually, contractors find it much more difficult to convince the government to allow an indirect cost pool to be deleted than to add a new cost pool; the government usually assumes that the more cost pools a contractor has, the better.

Directly Associated Cost

The term "directly associated cost" refers to "any cost which is generated solely as a result of the incurrence of another cost, and which would not have been incurred had the other cost not been incurred." The term "directly associated cost" is used to identify incremental costs associated with specifically unallowable costs. CAS 405, Accounting for Unallowable Costs, uses it to establish a "but for" relationship between principal costs and associated costs. A principal cost is a cost that clearly results from an action that gives rise to unallowable costs (such as the salary of an employee engaged in an unallowable cost activity such as lobbying on a full-time basis). A directly associated cost is any incremental cost attributable to the unallowable activity (such as fringe benefits or office supplies for a full-time lobbyist). In short, a cost is considered to be directly associated with a principal cost if it would not have been incurred "but for" the incurrence of the principal cost.

If directly associated costs are included in a cost pool that is allocated using a base that includes the related unallowable cost, the directly associated costs should remain in the cost pool when calculating the amount of the directly associated costs to be disallowed. Keeping the unallowable costs in the base ensures that an allocable share of the directly associated costs will be disallowed.

For example:

Indirect cost pool expenses $1,200
Indirect cost pool allocation base
(direct labor dollars) $ 800
Indirect cost pool rate ($1,200/$800) 150%

Assume that, for some reason, $50 of direct labor is determined to be unallowable. Because the unallowed labor costs of $50 are included in the allocation base, the application of the indirect cost rate (150 percent) to the unallowed labor is sufficient to ensure that all directly associated costs are included in the unallowed costs. In this case, the total unallowed costs are $125 ($50 of direct labor plus 150 percent of $50, or $75, of indirect costs).

In all other cases, the directly associated costs, if material in amount, must be purged from the cost pool as unallowable costs. For example, assume that the unallowable activity is not direct labor, but some indirect cost (such as indirect labor). Assume also that the unallowable cost is $110 ($50 of principal costs plus $60 of directly associated costs). The recalculated indirect cost rate is then:

Indirect cost pool expenses
($1,200–$110) $1,090
Indirect cost pool allocation base $800
Indirect cost pool rate
($1,090/$800) 136.25%

In determining the materiality of directly associated costs, consideration should be given to the significance in dollars of the costs, the cumulative effect of the costs on cost pools, and the ultimate effect of the costs on government contracts. The salaries of employees who participate in activities that generate unallowable costs are treated as directly associated costs to the extent of time spent on the proscribed activity (if it is material). The time spent on such activities should be compared to total time spent on company activities to determine if the costs are material. Time spent by an employee outside normal working hours should not be considered unless the employee engages in company activities outside normal working hours so frequently that those activities are clearly part of the employee's regular duties. This might particularly be true of entertainment activities carried on outside normal working hours.

Cosmetically Low Rates

Sometimes a prime motivation in establishing direct versus indirect costs, groupings of indirect costs, and allocation bases for indirect costs is a desire to achieve low indirect cost rates. Even though reclassifying indirect costs as direct to obtain lower indirect cost rates does not change the total cost, unsophisticated buyers are frequently impressed by low individual cost rates, especially for cost-reimbursement contracts and T&M contracts in which the final price cannot be determined until the goods or services are actually delivered.

Customers offten complain that a particular indirect cost rate is "too high." This standalone statement is seldom warranted. For example, assume that a company has a single indirect cost rate of 180 percent:

Indirect Expenses	Allocation Base—Direct Labor Dollars	Rate
$1,800,000	$1,000,000	180%

That seems high, but is it? Let's change the accounting to segregate overhead and G&A:

Pool	Indirect Expenses	Allocation Base	Rate
Overhead	$1,200,000	$1,000,000 (Direct Labor Dollars)	120%
G&A	$ 600,000	$2,200,000 (Total Cost Input)	27%

That's better. But let's add a fringe benefit cost pool as well:

Pool	Indirect Expenses	Allocation Base	Rate
Fringe Benefits	$400,000	$1,000,000 (Direct Labor Dollars)	40%
Overhead	$800,000	$1,000,000 (Direct Labor Dollars)	80%
G&A	$600,000	$2,200,000 (Total Cost Input)	27%

That's even better. Now let's change the allocation base for overhead from direct labor dollars to direct labor costs, i.e., fringe benefits plus direct labor dollars:

Pool	Indirect Expenses	Allocation Base	Rate
Fringe Benefits	$400,000	$1,000,000 (Direct Labor Dollars)	40%
Overhead	$800,000	$1,400,000 (Direct Labor Dollars)	57%
G&A	$600,000	$2,200,000 (Total Cost Input)	27%

This is even better. However, this exercise only illustrates the dangers in reaching hasty conclusions on the propriety of an indirect cost rate. A better measure is the labor multiplier, i.e., the total indirect cost additives divided by the direct labor dollars. In practice, these additives include profit or markup, but for illustration purposes, markup is not included in the following discussion.

In this example, the multiplier is consistently 1.80 for each accounting variation. The multiplier negates most differences due to accounting structure. (It does not accommodate differences between classification of costs as direct versus indirect.) In addition, many companies compare their multiplier to others or to a perceived industry norm. For example, low-tech services where the customer provides facilities may result in a multiplier of only 1.30, whereas a high-tech business with elaborate facilities may result in a multiplier over 4.0

The use of automated production processes has a dual impact on indirect cost rates. First, the traditional allocation base of direct labor dollars is reduced. Second, the indirect costs related to equipment will likely increase because of the purchase of additional equipment. These conditions can have a dramatic impact on the rate, because the numerator increases and the denominator decreases. Some may simply interpret the resulting rate increase as a sign of inefficiency. This interpretation is shallow and erroneous, however, because the true measure of efficiency is total cost, not indirect rates.

Activity-based costing (ABC) has significantly affected traditional views of cost accounting and product costing. This approach does not focus on unit costs, but on costs of activities, and it acknowledges that not all costs are unit-dependent or fixed costs. For example, product costs are often influenced by a measure of activities such as number of units in a batch, physical measurements of the product, number of machine set-ups, number of parts involved, and number of engineering changes.

ABC does not use allocation bases consisting of noncost elements in lieu of costs, but first assigns costs to activities and then relates activities to products using measures of activity—termed cost drivers—that are not limited to allocations based on costs. The concept is useful in a competitive environment in which substantial data are available and multiple products are being manufactured.

The ABC application begins with matching costs to activities. Next, a cost driver is selected that best measures the activity and serves as the best allocation base for the cost of the activity. A schematic of the operations is helpful in identifying activities and the flow of product and cost.

Segregation of Unallowable Costs

Both CAS 405, Accounting for Unallowable Costs, and the FAR require the segregation of all expressly unallowable costs. Expressly unallowable costs include those specifically cited in the regulations or a contract as unal-lowable and those disputed cost determinations that have been upheld by a court or BCA. During an appeal process (i.e., after a DCAA determination or a contracting officer decision adverse to the contractor but before a court or BCA decision), these costs may be included in billings, claims, or proposals as long as they are identified in sufficient detail to provide adequate disclosure.

Because government cost principles may be revised from time to time, a contractor must keep abreast of developments to avoid allegations of not having properly segregated unallowable costs. Distinctions between allowable and unallowable costs are sometimes not easy to make. Areas that require careful review and documentation include congressional lobbying versus legislative liaison, executive branch lobbying based on merits versus liaison based on other than merits, B&P expenses versus marketing costs, and entertainment versus business conference and meeting expenses.

To screen unallowable costs, the contractor should establish policies to determine what costs will be excluded and how those costs will be removed from any claims or submissions to the government. Multi-di-vis-ion-al contractors must also consider the need for uniform policies and practices between organizational units. A vital step toward this effort is to involve the employees who incur the costs. These employees must have clear policies on entertainment costs, business conference costs, and travel costs. When claiming reimbursements from the company, the employees should be required to identify any costs that may be unallowable.

This policy alone is not sufficient. The company must also have procedures in place to routinely screen critical transactions as they occur and as they are recorded. It must have clear instructions for these procedures to ensure consistent application of common policies.

FAR 42.709 provides guidance for assessing penalties when contractors claim unallowable costs. The penalties cover final indirect cost rate proposals and the final statement of costs incurred or estimated to be incurred under a fixed-price incentive contract. The penalties pertain to all contracts in excess of $500,000, except fixed-price contracts without cost incentives or any firm-fixed-price contracts for the purchase of commercial items.

If the unallowable indirect cost claimed is expressly unallowable under a cost principle in the FAR or an executive agency supplement to the FAR, the penalty is equal to: (1) the amount of the disallowed costs allocated to contracts that are subject to this section for which an indirect cost proposal has been submitted; plus (2) interest on the paid portion, if any, of the disallowance. If the direct cost was determined to be unallowable for that contractor before proposal submission, the penalty is two times this amount. These penalties are in addition to other administrative, civil, and criminal penalties provided by law. It is not necessary for unallowable costs to have been paid to the con-tractor for a penalty to be assessed.

FAR 42.709-2 establishes responsibilities for penalty applications. The cognizant contracting officer is responsible for: (1) determining whether the penalties should be assessed; (2) determining whether such penalties should be waived; and (3) referring the matter to the appropriate criminal investigative organization for review and for appropriate coordination of remedies, if there is evidence that the contractor knowingly submitted unallowable costs. The contract auditor, in the review and/or the determination of final indirect cost proposals for contracts subject to this section, is responsible for: (1) recommending to the contracting officer which costs may be unallowable and subject to the penalties; (2) providing rationale and supporting documentation for any recommendation; and (3) referring the matter to the appropriate criminal investigative organization for review and

for appropriate coordination of remedies, if there is evidence that the contractor knowingly submitted unallowable costs.

Unless a waiver is granted, the cognizant contracting officer will assess the penalty when: (1) the submitted cost is expressly unallowable under a cost principle in the FAR or an executive agency supplement that defines the allowability of specific selected costs; or (2) the submitted cost was determined to be unallowable for that contractor prior to submission of the proposal. Prior determinations of unallowability may be evidenced by: (1) a DCAA Form 1 that the contractor did not appeal and that was not withdrawn by the issuing agency; (2) a contracting officer final decision that was not appealed; or (3) a prior BCA or court decision involving the contractor that upheld the cost disallowance.

The cognizant contracting officer is to waive the penalties at 42.709-1(a) when at least one of the following conditions exists:

1. The contractor withdraws the proposal before the government formally initiates an audit of the proposal and the contractor submits a revised proposal. (An audit will be deemed to be formally initiated when the government provides the contractor with written notice, or holds an entrance conference, indicating that audit work on a specific final indirect cost proposal has begun.)

2. The amount of the unallowable costs under the proposal that are subject to the penalty is $10,000 or less.

3. The contractor demonstrates, to the cognizant contracting officer's satisfaction, that it has established policies and personnel training and an internal control and review system that provide assurance that unallowable costs subject to penalties are precluded from being in-

cluded in the contractor's final indirect cost rate proposals, and the unallowable costs subject to the penalty were inadvertently incorporated into the proposal (i.e., their inclusion resulted from an unintentional error).

Penalties related to indirect cost rate proposals submitted before October 23, 1992, are assessed if the claimed costs were unallowable by "clear and convincing" evidence. On or after this date, penalties are assessed if the costs were "expressly unallowable," a less harsh, more objective standard.

Some government auditors have taken the position that penalties for claiming unallowable costs may be imposed even after an audit report is issued and the matter has been settled with the contracting officer. This guidance states that the penalty provision will be considered applicable even if a contracting officer has neglected to include the legislatively mandated clause in the contract. Until 1989, this guidance excluded issues of cost reasonableness and allocability as being subject to penalties. However, the most recent guidance is silent on these categories of cost disallowance.

CHAPTER 5

Principles— Selected Costs

Part 31 of the FAR states that costs shall be allowed to the extent that they are reasonable, allocable, and allowable under certain specific provisions. FAR Section 31.205 covers the allowability of 51 specific cost elements. This chapter focuses on those cost elements that involve complex ideas or are specific to government contracting, and are therefore most likely to need clarification.

GENERALLY UNALLOWABLE COSTS

The following categories of cost are generally unallowable under FAR 31.205.

Public Relations and Advertising Costs (31.205-1)

Generally, public relations and advertising costs relating to sales promotion are unallowable because the government procurement system generates sales through direct contacts and the solicitation of proposals.

Public relations activities consist of all undertakings designed to: (1) maintain, protect, and enhance the image of an organization or its products or services; or (2) maintain or promote reciprocal understandings and favorable relations with the general public or any segment thereof. Public relations activities include advertising and customer relations. Public relations costs include the costs of purchasing media time and space, engag-

ing the services of outside organizations, and paying the salaries, travel, and fringe benefits of employees engaged in public relations.

The FAR enumerates a nonexclusive list of allowable public relations costs, including: costs specifically required by the contract; costs incurred in responding to inquiries regarding the contractor's policies and activities; and costs associated with corresponding with the press, the public, customers, stockholders, and creditors. In addition, the list includes costs involved in conducting general liaison activities with the news media and government public relations officers that are necessary to inform the public on matters of public concern, such as notices of plant closings or openings, contract awards, financial information, and employee layoffs or rehirings. The list also includes: the costs of participation in such community service activities as blood banks, savings bond drives, charity drives, and disaster assistance; the costs of plant tours and open house functions; and the costs of ceremonies involving ship launchings, keel laying, commissioning, and rollout as provided specifically by the contract.

The provision generally prohibits public relations costs, not specifically allowed, that are incurred to promote the sale of products or services by stimulating interest, or by disseminating information calling favorable attention to the contractor for purposes of enhancing the company image to sell the company's products or services. Unallowable public relations costs include the costs of: sponsoring meetings, symposia, and seminars; and developing promotional material such as brochures, videotapes, magazines, handouts, and other media designed to call favorable attention to the contractor and its activities. (Also see 31.205-13, Employee Morale, Health, Welfare, Food Service, and Dormitory Costs and Credits; 31.205-21, Labor Relations Costs; 31.205-43, Trade, Business, Technical, and Professional Activity Costs; and 31.205-44, Training and Educational Costs.) Other unallowable costs include souvenirs, models, imprinted clothing, buttons, other mementos, and membership in civic and community organizations.

Product advertising refers to the use of any media forum to promote the products or services of the contractor where the advertiser has control over the content, manner, and printing of the advertisement. As listed in the FAR, advertising media include radio, television, newspapers, magazines, trade papers, direct mail, dealer cards, free goods, conventions, exhibits, window displays, and outdoor advertising.

Allowable advertising costs are those costs used to recruit the personnel necessary to fulfill contract obligations, as limited by FAR 31.205-34 (Recruitment Costs), acquire the scarce items required for contract performance, and dispose of scrap or surplus materials acquired for contract performance. Such costs must be specifically required by the contract or must arise from the contract requirements.

In addition to the flat statement of unallowability for all advertising costs except the three previously mentioned, the FAR cites the following advertising costs as explicitly unallowable: the costs of air shows and other special events, such as conventions and trade shows; and the costs of ceremonies, such as new product announcements.

Special rules cover costs incurred to promote American aerospace exports at domestic and international exhibits; reasonable costs are allowable, including transportation of the aircraft, parts, and equipment, and associated costs. However, some costs remain specifically unallowable, such as those for entertainment, hospitality suites/chalets, and other activities not necessary to establish and operate the exhibit.

Bad Debts (31.205-3)

The FAR provides that "debts, including actual or estimated losses arising from uncollectible accounts receivable due from customers and other claims, and any directly associated costs such as collection costs, and legal costs are unallowable." This provision is based on the premise that bad debt expenses are not allocable to government contracts because the government always pays its just debts. This provision has also been applied to situations such as when a terminated employee fails to reimburse the contractor for an outstanding cash advance.

Contributions or Donations (31.205-8)

Contributions and donations, which include cash, property, and service, are unallowable, regardless of the recipient. The stated rationale for this principle is that if contributions and donations were allowable, the government would be the actual maker of the gift to the recipient. This situation would permit contractors to make policy decisions regarding who received government support.

An exception is permitted in FAR 31.205-1(e)(1), Public Relations Costs, for costs pertaining to community service activities such as blood bank drives, charity drives, savings bond drives, and disaster assistance. For example, the time spent by employees in Red Cross blood drives either in-plant or recruiting vendors/subcontractors is allowable. However, membership in the Red Cross is not allowable.

Entertainment Costs (31.205-14)

Entertainment costs are unallowable. Unallowable entertainment costs are listed as the costs of amusement, diversion, and social activities as well as directly related costs, such as meals, lodging, gratuities, transportation, rentals, tickets to shows or sports events, and social club memberships.

In practice, most controversies involving entertainment costs arise because contractors classify an entertainment cost as proper. For example, a contractor may classify an entertainment cost as an employee morale cost or as a cost of professional meetings and conferences. The government will disagree, particularly if the cost relates to meals for employees not in travel status. Even when an activity is found to be calculated to improve employee morale for those in attendance, the ASBCA has found the cost to be unallowable when the event also had any aspects of amusement, diversion, and social activities.

Social club membership costs are specifically unallowable whether or not reported as taxable income by the employee enjoying membership privileges. Such costs include membership in social, dining, or country clubs or organizations having the same purpose.

Fines, Penalties, and Mischarging Costs (31.205-15)

Unless they are incurred to comply with specific contract terms and conditions or the written instructions of the contracting officer, fines and penalties are unallowable if they are the result of the contractor's violations of, or failure to comply with, federal, state, local, or foreign laws and regulations.

Costs incurred in connection with or related to the mischarging of costs on government contracts are unallowable. Such costs include those incurred to identify, measure, or otherwise determine the magnitude of the improper charging, and costs incurred to remedy or correct the mischarging, such as costs to rescreen and reconstruct records.

Interest and Other Financial Costs (31.205-20)

The FAR provides that "Interest on borrowings (however represented), bond discounts, costs of financing and refinancing capital (net worth plus long-term liabilities), legal and professional fees paid in connection with preparing prospectuses, costs of preparing and issuing stock rights, and directly associated costs are unallowable except for interest assessed by State or local taxing authorities under the conditions specified in FAR 31.205-41."

The government recognized interest expense as an unallowable cost as early as the 1940s. The government assumes that it is doing business with a properly capitalized organization—it does not wish to subsidize contractors who choose to use a high degree of leverage in their capital base. Since dividends are normally not allowable (because they are actually a distribution of profit rather than a cost), making interest expense reimbursable would encourage heavily leveraged firms.

Lobbying and Political Activity Costs (31.205-22)

Costs associated with the following activities are unallowable:

1. Attempts to influence the outcomes of any Federal, State or local election, referendum, initiative or similar procedure, through in kind or cash contributions, endorsements, publicity or similar activities;

2. Establishing, administering, contributing to or paying the expenses of a po-

litical party, campaign, political action committee, or other organization established for the purpose of influencing the outcomes of elections;

3. Any attempt to influence—(i) The introduction of Federal, state or local legislation, or (ii) The enactment or modification of any pending Federal, state or local legislation through communication with any member or employee of the Congress or state legislature (including efforts to influence state or local officials to engage in similar lobbying activity), or with any government official or employee in connection with a decision to sign or veto enrolled legislation;

4. Any attempt to influence—The introduction of Federal, state or local legislation, or the enactment or modification of any pending Federal, state or local legislation by preparing, distributing or using publicity or propaganda, or by urging members of the general public or any segment thereof to contribute to or participate in any mass demonstration, march, rally, fund raising drive, lobbying campaign or letter writing or telephone campaign,

5. Legislative liaison activities, including attendance at legislative sessions or committee hearings, gathering information regarding legislation, and analyzing the effect of legislation, when such activities are carried on in support of or in knowing preparation for an effort to engage in unallowable activities; or

6. Costs incurred in attempting to improperly influence (see 3.401), either directly or indirectly, an employee or officer of the Executive branch of the Federal Government to give consider-

ation to or act regarding a regulatory or contract matter.

The following activities are excepted from the coverage:

• Providing a technical and factual presentation of information on a topic directly related to the performance of a contract through hearing testimony, statements or letters to the Congress or a state legislature, or subdivision, member, or cognizant staff member thereof, in response to a documented request (including a Congressional Record notice requesting testimony or statements for the record at a regularly scheduled hearing) made by the recipient member, legislative body or subdivision, or a cognizant staff member thereof; provided such information is readily obtainable and can be readily put in deliverable form; and further provided that costs under this section for transportation, lodging or meals are unallowable unless incurred for the purpose of offering testimony at a regularly scheduled Congressional hearing pursuant to a written request for such presentation made by the Chairman or Ranking Minority Member of the Committee or Subcommittee conducting such hearing.
• Any lobbying to influence state or local legislation in order to directly reduce contract cost, or to avoid material impairment of the contractor's authority to perform the contract.
• Any activity specifically authorized by statute to be undertaken with funds from the contract.

"When a contractor seeks reimbursement for indirect costs, total lobbying costs shall be separately identified in the indirect cost rate proposal, and thereafter treated as other unallowable activity costs. Contractors shall maintain adequate records to demonstrate that the certification of costs as being allowable or unallowable (see 421.703-2) pursuant to this subsection complies with the requirements of this subsection. Existing procedures should be utilized to resolve in advance any significant questions or disagreements concerning the interpretation or application of this subsection."

Losses on Other Contracts (31.205-23)

The FAR provides that: "The excess of costs over income under any other contract (including the contractor's contributed portion under cost-sharing contracts) is unallowable." The concept behind this provision is that costs related to a specific contract should not be allocated to other work. Each contract should stand on its own in terms of profitability.

Improperly handled cost variances can lead government personnel to question costs on the grounds that the variances could be used as a way of recovering losses on unprofitable government contracts. Cost centers (e.g., wind tunnels, computer centers) are not considered to be contracts for purposes of this provision.

In a decision involving Unisys (ASBCA No. 41135), the contractor had incurred costs for technical efforts under a cost-reimbursement subcontract after all funds had been expended. The prime contractor was not required to make any payments beyond the amount in the subcontract. However, the subcontractor was also not required to perform beyond the efforts covered by the subcontract funding. The subcontract classified those costs that exceeded the fund limitation as IR&D costs. The government objected on the basis that the costs represented a loss on the subcontract and that costs in excess of the funding should have been charged to the subcontract.

The ASBCA disagreed with the government based on the opinion that the additional work was not required by the contract and was thus IR&D.

Organization Costs (31.205-27)

Expenditures in connection with (1) planning or executing the organization or reorganization of the corporate structure of a business, including mergers and acquisitions, (2) resisting or planning to resist the reorganization of the corporate structure of a business or a change in the controlling interest in the ownership of a business, and (3) raising capital (net worth plus long-term liabilities), are unallowable. Such expenditures include but are not limited to incorporation fees and the costs of attorneys, accountants, brokers, promoters and organizers, management consultants, and investment counselors, whether or not they are employees of the contractor. Unallowable "reorganization" costs include the cost of any change in the contractor's financial structure, excluding administrative costs for short-term borrowings for working capital, resulting in alterations in the rights and interests of security holders, whether or not additional capital is raised.

The costs of activities intended primarily to provide compensation are not considered organizational costs subject to this subsection, but are governed by 31.205-6. These activities include acquiring stock for executive bonuses, employee savings plans, and employee stock ownership plans.

The government formalized this cost principle in 1977 on the basis of considerations regarding allocability. The government is not concerned with the form of a con-trac-tor's organization and thus does not believe that organization costs are necessary for, or allocable to, government contracts.

Costs Related to Legal and Other Proceedings (31.205-47)

Costs incurred in connection with any proceedings brought by a federal, state, local, or foreign government for violation of, or a failure to comply with, a law or regulation by the contractor (including its agents or employees), or costs incurred in connection with any proceeding brought by a third party in the name of the United States under the False Claims Act, 31 U.S.C. 3730, are unallowable if the result is:

"(1) In a criminal proceeding, a conviction;

(2) In a civil or administrative proceeding, either a finding of contractor liability where the proceeding involves an allegation of fraud or similar misconduct or imposition of a monetary penalty where the proceeding does not involve an allegation of fraud or similar misconduct;

(3) A final decision by an appropriate official of an executive agency to debar or suspend a contractor, rescind or void a contract, or terminate a contract for default by reason of a violation or a failure to comply with a law or regulation;

(4) Disposition of the matter by consent or compromise if the proceeding could have led to outcomes listed in (1) through (3) above; or

(5) Not covered by paragraphs (1) through (4) above, but where the underlying alleged contractor misconduct was the same as that which led to a different proceeding whose costs are unallowable by reason of subparagraphs 1 through 4 above.

To the extent that they are not otherwise unallowable, costs incurred in connection with any proceeding under paragraph (b) above, commenced by the United States that is resolved by consent or compromise pursuant to an agreement entered into between the contractor and the United States, and which are unallowable solely because of paragraph (b) above, may be allowed to the extent specifically provided in such agreement.

In the event of a settlement of any proceeding brought by a third party under the False Claims Act in which the United States did not intervene, reasonable costs incurred by the contractor in connection with such a proceeding that are not otherwise unallowable by regulation or by separate agreement with the United States, may be allowed if the contracting officer, in consultation with his or her legal advisor, determines that there was very little likelihood that the third party would have been successful on the merits.

To the extent that they are not otherwise unallowable, costs incurred in connection with any proceeding under paragraph (b) above, commenced by a state, local, or foreign government, may be allowable when the contracting officer (or other official specified in agency procedures) determines that the costs were incurred either as a direct result of a specific term or condition of a federal contract or as a result of compliance with specific written direction of the cognizant contracting officer.

Costs incurred in connection with proceedings described in paragraph (b) above, but which are not made unallowable by that paragraph, may be allowable to the extent that: (1) the costs are reasonable in relation to the activities required to deal with the proceeding and the underlying cause of action; (2) the costs are not otherwise recovered from the federal government or a third party, either directly as a result of the proceeding or otherwise; and (3) the percentage of costs allowed does not exceed the percentage determined to be appropriate considering the complexity of procurement litigation, generally accepted principles govern-ing the award of legal fees in civil actions involving the United States as a party, and such other factors as may be appropriate. Such percentage shall not exceed 80 percent. Agreements shall be subject to this limitation. If, however, an agreement explicitly states the amount of otherwise allowable incurred legal fees and limits the allowable recovery to 80 percent or less of the stated legal fees, no additional limitation need be applied. The amount of reimbursement allowed for legal costs in connection with any proceeding, shall be determined by the cognizant contracting officer, but shall not exceed 80 percent of otherwise allowable legal costs incurred.

Costs not covered elsewhere in this subsection are unallowable if incurred in connection with:

1. Defense against federal government claims or appeals or the prosecution of claims or appeals against the federal government (see 33.201).

2. Organization, reorganization (including mergers and acquisitions) or resisting mergers and acquisitions (see also 31.205-27).

3. Defense of antitrust suits.

4. Defense of suits brought by employees or ex-employees of the contractor under section 2 of the Major Fraud Act of 1988 where the contractor was found liable or settled.

5. Costs of legal, accounting, and consultant services and directly associated costs incurred in connection with the defense or prosecution of lawsuits or appeals between contractors arising from either an agreement or contract concerning a teaming arrangement, a joint venture, or similar arrangement of shared interest or dual sourcing, coproduction, or similar programs, are unal-

lowable, except when (i) incurred as a result of compliance with specific terms and conditions of the contract or written instructions from the contracting officer, or (ii) when agreed to in writing by the contracting officer.

6. Patent infringement litigation, unless otherwise provided for in the contract.

7. Representation of, or assistance to, individuals, groups, or legal entities that the contractor is not legally bound to provide, arising from an action where the participant was convicted of violation of a law or regulation or was found liable in a civil or administrative proceeding.

8. Protests of federal government solicitations or contract awards, or the defense against protests of such solicitations or contract awards, unless the costs of defending against a protest are incurred pursuant to a written request from the cognizant contracting officer."

Costs that may be unallowable under 31.205-47, including directly associated costs, are to be segregated and accounted for by the contractor separately. While any proceeding is pending, the contracting officer will generally withhold payment of such costs. However, if in the best interests of the government, the contracting officer may provide for conditional payment upon provision of adequate security, or other adequate assurance, and agreement by the contractor to repay all unallowable costs, plus interest, if the costs are subsequently determined to be unallowable.

Goodwill (31.205-49)

When the price paid for a business by the acquiring company exceeds the sum of the identifiable individual assets acquired less liabilities assumed, based upon fair market values, the excess is commonly referred to as "goodwill." An intangible asset, goodwill may arise from the acquisition of a company as a whole or a portion thereof. Any costs for amortization, expensing, writeoff, or write-down of goodwill (however represented) are unallowable.

After losing a significant ASBCA decision over goodwill costs, the government formulated this principle to clearly establish goodwill as an unallowable cost. Purchased goodwill is the excess of the purchase price over the fair market value of the assets of an acquired business entity. The rationale for this cost principle is that the repeated sale of assets between contractors could increase contract costs to the government even though the same assets were used to provide goods or services to the government.

Costs of Alcoholic Beverages (31.205-51)

The costs of alcoholic beverages are unallowable. This provision was considered necessary to ensure that only reasonable and allocable costs are paid under government contracts.

Asset Valuations Resulting from Business Combinations (31.205-52)

For tangible capital assets, when the purchase method of accounting for a business combination is used, whether or not the contract or subcontract is subject to the CAS, the allowable depreciation and cost of money are based on the capitalized asset values measured and assigned in accordance with CAS 404, if allocable, reasonable, and not otherwise unallowable.

For intangible capital assets, when the purchase method of accounting for a business combination is used, allowable amortization and cost of money are limited to the total of

the amounts that would have been allowed had the combination not taken place.

Excessive Pass-Through Costs (31.203(i))

A specific provision on allowability of costs is set forth in FAR 31.203(i): "Indirect costs that meet the definition of 'excessive pass-through charge' are unallowable." The basic definition is an additive by an upper-tier contractor to a subcontractor's costs when the upper-tier contractor adds no or negligible value to the subcontracted work. An additive by the upper-tier contractor is applicable indirect costs such as G&A or subcontract administration overhead and profit or fee. No percentage reflecting excessive costs is cited in the regulation. In practice, some agencies use 8 percent as a limit. The onerous aspect of this rule is that a contractor may allocate indirect costs in accordance with its approved accounting system and negotiate a fixed-price contract, yet have the government retroactively deem a pass-through charge excessive. Contract clauses require specific disclosure of pass-through charges when subcontracting efforts exceed certain thresholds.

COSTS RELATED TO HUMAN RESOURCES

The allowability of the following costs related to human resources is addressed in FAR 31.205.

Compensation for Personal Services (31.205-6)

Compensation for personal services includes all remuneration, whether paid immediately or deferred, for services rendered by employees to the contractor during the period of contract performance. It includes, but is not limited to: salaries; wages; directors' and executive committee members' fees; bonuses (including stock bonuses); incentive awards; employee stock options and stock appreciation rights; employee stock ownership plans; employee insurance; fringe benefits; contributions to pension funds, other postretirement benefits, and annuity and employee incentive compensation plans; and allowances for off-site pay, incentive pay, location allowances, hardship pay, severance pay, and cost of living differential. Compensation for personal services is allowable subject to the following general criteria and additional requirements contained in other parts of this cost principle.

Bonuses and incentive compensation are allowable provided the awards are paid or accrued under an agreement entered into in good faith between the contractor and the employees before the services are rendered. They are also allowable pursuant to an established plan or policy followed by the contractor so consistently as to imply, in effect, an agreement to make such payment and that the basis for the award is supported.

Executive Compensation

Costs incurred after January 1, 1998, for compensation of a senior executive in excess of the benchmark compensation amount determined applicable for the calendar year by the Administrator of the Office of Federal Procurement Policy (OFPP) are unallowable. This limitation, which is generally not announced until May of the applicable year, is the sole statutory limitation on allowable senior executive compensation costs incurred after January 1, 1998, under new or previously existing contracts. This limitation applies whether or not the affected contracts were previously subject to a statutory limitation on such costs. The limit for the calendar year ending December 31, 2010, was $693,951. Since 1998 the average increase each year has been about 15 percent.

Compensation means the total amount of wages, salary, bonuses, deferred compensation, and employer contributions to defined contribution pension plans for the fiscal year, whether paid, earned, or otherwise accruing, as recorded in the contractor's cost accounting records for the fiscal year. The definition of "senior executive" has been changed for compensation costs incurred after January 1, 1999. Prior to January 2, 1999, senior executive means: (1) the Chief Executive Officer (CEO) or any individual acting in a similar capacity at the contractor's headquarters; (2) the four most highly compensated employees in management positions at the contractor's headquarters, other than the CEO, and (3) if the contractor has intermediate home offices or segments that report directly to the corporate office, the five senior executives at each such intermediate home office or segment. Effective January 2, 1999, senior executive includes the five most highly compensated employees in management positions at each home office and each segment of the contractor, whether or not the home office or segment reports directly to the contractor's headquarters.

Compensation Based on Changes in the Prices of Corporate Securities or Corporate Security Ownership

Any compensation that is calculated, or valued, based on changes in the price of corporate securities is unallowable. Any compensation represented by dividend payments or that is calculated based on dividend payments is unallowable. If a contractor pays an employee in lieu of the employee receiving or exercising a right, option, or benefit that would have been unallowable under this paragraph, such payments are also unallowable.

Pension Plans

The FAR defines pension plan as "a deferred compensation plan that is established and maintained by one or more employees to provide systematically for paying benefits to plan participants after their retirement, provided that the benefits are paid for life or are payable for life at the option of the employee."

Also treated as pension costs are expenditures such as permanent and total disability and death payments; survivorship payments to beneficiaries of deceased employees may be treated as pension costs provided that the benefits are an integral part of the pension plan and meet all the criteria pertaining to pension costs.

Generally, pension costs are allowable, subject to the cost limitations, standards, and exceptions set forth in the cost principle that limits cost allowability to the lesser costs, or to the amount deductible for the year's federal income tax. There are generally two types of pension plans: deferred benefit and defined-contribution benefit. Deferred benefit pension plan costs must be measured, allocated, and accounted for in accordance with CAS 412 (Composition and Measurement of Pension Costs) and CAS 413 (Adjustment and Allocation of Pension Costs). Defined-contribution benefit plan costs also must be measured, allocated, and accounted for in accordance with CAS 412 and CAS 413 provisions. Defined-contribution plans establish in advance, by the level of contributions, what benefits are to be paid, and contributions are made to provide the stated benefit.

One factor that might be used to determine whether pension costs are allowable is the IRS standards. In particular, Section 401 of the Internal Revenue Code requires that an employee's pension plan must be in writing and communicated to the employees, the employer's contributions must be irrevocably funded, and no discrimination may be made in favor of officers, supervisors, or highly compensated employees related to contributions or benefits. However, IRS approval of a pension plan does not mandate DCAA audit acceptance of the cost of the plan. Other considerations are the level of benefits under the plan and the time period for employment or membership before an employee's interest is vested under the plan.

Other Compensation

Fringe benefits are allowances and services provided by the contractor to its employees as compensation in addition to regular wages and salaries. Fringe benefits include, but are not limited to, the cost of holidays, vacation and sick leave, employee insurance, military leave, and supplemental unemployment benefit plans. To the extent that the costs of fringe benefits are reasonable and are required by law, employer-employee agreements, or established contractor policy, they are allowable.

That portion of the cost of company-furnished automobiles that relates to personal use by employees (including transportation to and from work) is unallowable regardless of whether or not the cost is reported as taxable income to the employees.

Although a government contract may provide that the costs of an employee's travel, relocation, wages, leave, and training are allowable, tuition costs at dependent schools abroad are not. While a contract may state that the government will provide access to schools on a space-available, tuition-paying basis to the contractor's employees, it may not require the government to pay tuition costs.

The ASBCA has allowed a contractor to be reimbursed for overtime compensation to employees required to travel outside working hours, even though the travel policy could be construed as an attempt to thwart the government's disallowance of first-class travel expenses.

Rebates and purchase discounts, regardless of form, granted to employees on products or services produced by the contractor or affiliates are unallowable. Both the Defense Acquisition Regulatory Council and the Civilian Agency Acquisition Council have indicated that such discounts and rebates are traditionally treated as reductions in profit margins or sales and, thus, are not costs and should not be allowable.

Compensation for severance pay, or dismissal wages, is allowable to the extent that it is: (1) required by law; (2) part of an employer-employee agreement; (3) established policy constituting, in effect, an implied agreement on the part of the contractor; or (4) the particular circumstances of the employment. Such compensation is made in addition to regular salaries and wages to terminated employees. Such compensation may be limited when paid in addition to early or normal retirement payments.

Backpay resulting from underpayment for work performed is allowable. Also, backpay to union employees for the difference in past and current wage rates for working during labor/management negotiations without a contract or labor agreement is allowable. For these costs to be allowable, management must have a formal agreement with the employees regarding such payments or the payments must be made pursuant to an established and consistently followed contractor policy or practice so as to allow the inference that the contractor agreed to make such payment.

Backpay awarded for violations of Federal Labor Laws or the Civil Rights Act of 1964 is unallowable. This latter category includes circumstances where backpay is not awarded as additional compensation for work that has been performed, such as where an employee was improperly discharged or discriminated against.

The compensation must be for work the employee provided in the current year; it may not constitute a retroactive adjustment of prior years' salaries or wages. Remuneration must be consistent with the terms and conditions of the contractor's established compensation plan or practices, thus implying an agreement to make the payments. Where the contractor makes major changes to the terms of existing or new compensation plans without informing the relevant contracting officer either before implementation of the revisions or within a reasonable time thereafter, and without allowing the government reasonable time to review the changes, the FAR directs that contracting officers will "normally challenge" the resultant increased costs.

Reasonableness of Compensation

The compensation in total must be reasonable. By the former standards, compensation was reasonable if the total paid to an employee was reasonable. Under the current FAR cost principle, compensation is reasonable if each of the allowable elements comprising the employee's compensation package is reasonable. The total reasonableness may still be challenged, however.

Factors used to determine reasonableness are general conformity with the compensation practices of similar-sized firms in the same industry, in the same geographic locale, and engaged in predominantly private sector work, and the cost of obtaining comparable services from other sources. The relative importance of these factors in determining reasonableness will vary according to the type of services generating the compensation.

Those elements of remuneration for which offsets will be considered are wages and salaries, incentive bonuses, deferred compensation, health insurance benefits, compensated personal absence benefits, pension and savings plan benefits, life insurance benefits, and compensated personal absence benefits. If any one element or the sum of all the elements comprising the compensation paid to an employee or class of employees is challenged by a contracting officer, the contractor must then demonstrate that the compensation was reasonable, and can show any circumstances surrounding the challenged item or that other compensation elements were lower than would be reasonable but for the challenged item. The contractor can only apply such an offset to allowable elements of compensation packages of employees in jobs within the same job grade or level.

Certain compensation costs are closely scrutinized. In instances of compensation to owners of closely held corporations, partnerships, sole proprietors, or members of their immediate family or persons contractually committed to acquiring a substantial financial interest in the contractor's enterprise, compensation costs are examined to determine whether the remuneration is reasonable for personal services rendered or whether the payment was a distribution of profits. Major revisions in existing compensation plans and new plans will be challenged by the contracting officer, particularly when insufficient or untimely notice is given to the government. If a contractor's business is not subject to normal competitive restraints on its compensation levels or if incurred compensation is above the amounts allowed as deductions by the Internal Revenue Code, these compensation costs will be scrutinized.

Deferred Compensation

Deferred compensation is payment made by an employer to compensate employees in the future for services rendered before receipt of the compensation. Deferred compensation is allowable when it is based on current or future services, but is not for work performed before the payment. It does not include payments of year-end accruals for salaries, wages, or bonuses paid within a reasonable time after the end of the cost accounting period.

Other Considerations

Two types of compensation associated with business acquisitions are unallowable. The first type is "golden parachutes," which are payments to employees under agreements in which they receive special compensation if their employment terminates following a change in the management or ownership of the business.

Likewise unallowable are "golden handcuffs." These are payments under plans introduced in connection with a change (whether actual or prospective) in management control of ownership; the employees receive special compensation payment for remaining with the contractor for a specified period of time.

The provision pertaining to labor/management agreements was not affected by the revisions to the FAR. Costs of compensation arising from labor/management agreements are not allowable if applied to government contracts, to the extent they are unreasonable, discriminatory against the government, or unwarranted by the character and circumstances involved.

A provision will be found to be discriminatory against the government where employee compensation is greater than amounts paid for comparable private sector work under similar circumstances. The application of special provisions of labor/management agreements (such as hazardous duty pay) is unwarranted if the provision is designed to apply to a specific set of circumstances that is significantly different from that arising under the government contract.

When personal services are performed in a foreign country, compensation may also include a differential that may properly consider all expenses associated with foreign employment, such as housing, cost of living adjustments, transportation, bonuses, additional federal, state, local, or foreign income taxes resulting from foreign assignment, and other related expenses.

Postretirement benefits (PRBs) cover all benefits, other than cash benefits and life insurance benefits paid by pension plans, provided to employees, their beneficiaries, and covered dependents during the period following the employee's retirement. Benefits encompassed include, but are not limited to, postretirement health care; life insurance provided outside a pension plan; and other welfare benefits such as tuition assistance, day care, legal services, and housing subsidies provided after retirement. To be allowable, PRB costs must be reasonable and incurred pursuant to law, employer-employee agreement, or an established policy of the contractor. In addition, to be allowable, PRB costs must also be calculated in accordance with the following:

1. Cost recognized as benefits when they are actually provided must be paid to an

insurer, provider, or other recipient for current year benefits or premiums.

2. If a contractor elects a terminal-funded plan, it does not accrue PRB costs during the working lives of employees. Instead, it accrues and pays the entire PRB liability to an insurer or trustee in a lump sum upon the termination of employees (or upon conversion to such a terminal-funded plan) to establish and maintain a fund or reserve for the sole purpose of providing PRB to retirees. The lump sum is allowable if amortized over a period of 15 years.

3. Accrual costing other than terminal funding must be measured and assigned according to generally accepted accounting principles and be paid to an insurer or trustee to establish and maintain a fund or reserve for the sole purpose of providing PRB to retirees. The accrual must also be calculated in accordance with generally accepted actuarial principles and practices as promulgated by the Actuarial Standards Board.

To be allowable, costs must be funded by the time set for filing the federal income tax return or any extension thereof. PRB costs assigned to the current year, but not funded or otherwise liquidated by the tax return time, will not be allowable in any subsequent year. Increased PRB costs caused by delay in funding beyond 30 days after each quarter of the year to which they are assignable are unallowable. Costs of post-retirement benefits attributable to past service ("transition obligation") as defined in Financial Accounting Standards Board Statement 106, paragraph 110, are allowable subject to the following limitation: "The allowable amount of such costs assignable to a contractor fiscal year cannot exceed the amount of such costs which would be assigned to that contractor fiscal year under the delayed recognition methodology described in paragraphs 112 and 113 of Statement 106."

The government is to receive an equitable share of any amount of previously funded PRB costs that revert or inure to the contractor. Such equitable share is to reflect the government's previous participation in PRB costs through those contracts for which certified cost or pricing data were required or that were subject to subpart 31.2.

Employee Stock Ownership Plans (ESOPs) (31.205-6(q))

Costs of ESOPs are allowable as deferred compensation under Cost Accounting Standard 415. For example, a contractor's contributions in any one year may not exceed the deductibility limits of the Internal Revenue Code for that year. Also, when the contribution is in the form of stock, the value of the stock contribution is limited to the fair market value of the stock on the date that title is effectively transferred to the trust. When the contribution is in the form of cash, stock purchases by the ESOP in excess of fair market value are unallowable. When the fair market value of unissued stock or stock of a closely held corporation is not readily determinable, the valuation will be made on a case-by-case basis taking into consideration the guidelines for valuation used by the IRS.

Employee Morale, Health, Welfare, Food Service, and Dormitory Costs and Credits (31.205-13)

Aggregate costs incurred on activities designed to improve working conditions, employer-employee relations, employee morale, and employee performance (less income generated by these activities) are allowable except as specifically limited. Some examples of allowable activities are house publications, health clinics, wellness/fitness centers, employee counseling services, and food and dormitory services, which include operating or furnishing facilities for dining rooms, cafeterias, canteens, vending machines, lunch wagons, living accommodations, and similar types of services for the contractor's employees at or near the contractor's facilities.

The cost of gifts is unallowable. Gifts do not include awards for performance or awards made in recognition of employee achievements pursuant to an established contractor plan or policy. Costs of recreation are unallowable, except for the costs of employees' participation in company-sponsored sports teams or employee organizations designed to improve company loyalty, teamwork, or physical fitness.

Losses from operating food and dormitory services may be included as costs only if the contractor's objective is to operate such services on a break-even basis. Losses sustained because food services or lodging accommodations are furnished without charge or at prices or rates that obviously would not be conducive to the accomplishment of such an objective are not allowable. A loss may be allowed however, if the contractor can demonstrate that unusual circumstances exist (e.g., the contractor must provide food or dormitory services at remote locations where adequate commercial facilities are not reasonably available; or charged but unproductive labor costs would be excessive but for the services provided or where cessation or reduction of food or dormitory operations will not otherwise yield cost savings) such that even with efficient management, operating the services on a break-even basis would require charging inordinately high prices, or prices or rates higher than those charged by commercial establishments offering the same services in the same geographical areas. Costs of food and dormitory services are to include an allocable share of indirect expenses pertaining to these activities.

When the contractor has an arrangement authorizing an employee association to provide or operate a service, such as vending machines in the contractor's plant, and retain the profits, such profits are to be treated in the same manner as if the contractor were providing the service. Contributions by the contractor to an employee organization, including funds from vending machine receipts or similar sources, may be included as costs incurred only to the extent that the contractor demonstrates that an equivalent amount of the costs incurred by the employee organization would be allowable if directly incurred by the contractor.

Professional and Consulting Costs (31.205-33)

Professional and consulting services are services rendered by persons who are members of a particular profession or possess a special skill and who are not officers or employees of the contractor. Examples include services acquired by contractors or subcontractors to enhance their legal, economic, financial, or technical positions. Professional and consultant services are generally acquired to obtain information, advice, opinions, alternatives, conclusions, recommendations, training or direct services such as studies, analyses, evaluations, liaison with government officials, or other forms of representation.

The costs of professional and consultant services are allowable when reasonable in relation to the services rendered and when not contingent upon recovery of the costs from the government. The costs of professional and consultant services performed under any of the following circumstances are unallowable:

1. Services to improperly obtain, distribute, or use information or data protected by law or regulation

2. Services that are intended to improperly influence the contents of solicitations, the evaluation of proposals or quotations, or the selection of sources for con-

tract award, whether award is by the government or by a prime contractor or subcontractor

3. Any other services obtained, performed, or otherwise resulting in violation of any statute or regulation prohibiting improper business practices or conflicts of interest

4. Services performed that are not consistent with the purpose and scope of the services contracted for or otherwise agreed to.

In determining the allowability of costs (including retainer fees) in a particular case, no single factor or any special combination of factors is necessarily determinative. However, the contracting officer will consider the following factors, among others:

1. The nature and scope of the service rendered in relation to the service required

2. The necessity of contracting for the service, considering the contractor's capability in the particular area

3. The past pattern of acquiring such services and their costs, particularly in the years prior to the award of government contracts

4. The impact of government contracts on the contractor's business

5. Whether the proportion of government work to the contractor's total business is such as to influence the contractor in favor of incurring the cost, particularly when the services rendered are not of a continuing nature and have little relationship to work under government contracts

6. Whether the service can be performed more economically by employment rather than by contracting

7. The qualifications of the individual or concern rendering the service and the customary fee charged, especially on nongovernment contracts

8. The adequacy of the contractual agreement for the service (e.g., description of the service, estimate of time required, rate of compensation, termination provisions).

Retainer fees, to be allowable, must be supported by evidence that: (1) the services covered by the retainer agreement are necessary and customary; (2) the level of past services justifies the amount of the retainer fees (if no services were rendered, fees are not automatically unallowable); (3) the retainer fee is reasonable in comparison with maintaining an in-house capability to perform the covered services, when factors such as cost and level of expertise are considered; and (4) the actual services performed are documented.

Fees for services rendered are allowable only when supported by evidence of the nature and scope of the service furnished. However, retainer agreements generally are not based on specific statements of work. Evidence necessary to determine that work performed is proper and does not violate law or regulation is to include:

1. Details of all agreements (e.g., work requirements, rate of compensation, nature and amount of other expenses, if any) with the individuals or organizations providing the services and details of actual services performed

2. Invoices or billings submitted by consultants, including sufficient detail as to the time expended and the nature of the actual services provided

3. Consultants' work products and related documents, such as trip reports indicating persons visited and subjects discussed, minutes of meetings, and collateral memoranda and reports.

Not all items listed must be available. However, sufficient evidence must exist to determine that the cost is allowable.

Recruitment Costs (31.205-34)

The following recruitment costs are allowable: (1) costs of help-wanted advertising; (2) costs of operating an employment office needed to secure and maintain an adequate labor force; (3) costs of operating an aptitude and educational testing program; (4) travel costs of employees engaged in recruiting personnel; (5) travel costs of applicants for interviews; and (6) costs for employment agencies, not in excess of standard commercial rates.

Help-wanted advertising costs are unallowable if the advertising does not describe specific positions or classes of positions, or includes material that is not relevant for recruitment purposes, such as extensive illustrations or descriptions of the company's products or capabilities.

Relocation Costs (31.205-35)

The costs of the permanent relocation of new or existing employees are generally allowable subject to FAR ceilings based on time, percentages, and absolute dollar amounts. Relocation costs are the expenses incurred by an existing employee with a permanent change of duty assignment for at least 12 months or an indefinite period, or resulting from the recruitment of a new -employee.

Allowable relocation costs include: travel costs of the employee and members of his or her immediate family; the costs of transporting household furnishings and personal effects to the new location; the costs of finding a new home, such as advance trips to locate living quarters and temporary lodging; closing costs incident to disposition of the employee's actual residence; and other necessary and reasonable expenses associated with relocation. Allowable costs now include payments for employees' Social Security or income taxes that increased due to reimbursement of relocation costs.

For these costs to be allowable, they must also meet the following criteria: (1) the move must be for the benefit of the employer; (2) reimbursement must be in accordance with an established policy or practice that is consistently followed by the employer and is designed to motivate employees to relocate promptly and economically; (3) the costs must not otherwise be unallowable under Subpart 31.2; and (4) amounts to be reimbursed cannot exceed the em-ploy-ee's actual expenses, except that, for miscellaneous costs of the type discussed above, a flat amount, not to exceed $5,000, may be allowed in lieu of actual costs.

Specific types of relocation costs are unallowable, such as a loss on the sale of a home; costs incident to acquiring the new home, such as real estate brokers' fees, property taxes, and property and mortgage life insurance; cost of litigation; and continuing payments of the mortgage principal on the residence being sold.

Trade, Business, Technical and Professional Activity Costs (31.205-43)

FAR 31.205-43 provides that three types of trade, business, technical, and professional activities are allowable: (1) memberships in trade, business, technical, and professional organizations; (2) subscriptions to trade, business, professional, or other technical periodicals; and (3) meetings and conferences, which includes the costs of meals, transportation, rental of meeting facilities, and other incidentals (provided that the primary purpose of incurring such costs is the dissemination of trade, business, technical, or professional information or the stimulation of production or improved productivity).

Training and Educational Costs (31.205-44)

Training and educational costs include the costs of training materials, textbooks, tuition, fees, compensation paid to employees while they are in training, and similar costs. The allowability of such costs depends on the type of training provided. Contractor expenses for maintenance, depreciation, and rental of training facilities are allowable to the extent that such costs are otherwise allowable under the contract.

Vocational training costs include costs for such programs below the college level as on-the-job, classroom, and apprentice programs designed to increase the vocational effectiveness of employees. These costs include compensation for trainees (but not overtime), the salaries of the training staff, training materials and textbooks, and tuition and fees for outside courses.

Allowable education costs for part-time instruction at the college level are limited to: (1) tuition and fees charged by the educational institution (or a special session), the institution's salaries, and related costs (which, however, cannot exceed the normal tuition payment); (2) salaries and related costs of instructors who are employees of the contractor; (3) training materials and textbooks; and (4) straight-time compensation for employees for time spent attending classes during working hours not in excess of 156 classroom hours per year where circumstances do not permit class attendance after normal working hours. This requirement may be modified by negotiation of an advance agreement.

The cost of full-time education at the post-graduate level is covered to the extent of tuition and fees. Costs are allowable if the course or degree pursued is related to the employee's field of work or expected work and the course or degree pursued is for a period of not longer than two school years or the length of the degree program, whichever is less. Subsistence and salaries and any other payments are unallowable.

Advance agreements may be negotiated to extend the limit of 156 hours per year per employee for part-time training at the college level or the two-year limit on full-time postgraduate study. Subsistence, salaries, or any other payments may also be allowed to the extent set forth in an advance agreement. The contractor must demonstrate that the costs are consistently incurred under an established program and that the course of study is related to the employee's current or reasonably foreseeable work.

Specialized training programs are those designed to enhance the effectiveness of managers or to prepare employees for management positions; they exclude courses that are part of a degree program. Costs of specialized training include enrollment fees and employee salaries, subsistence pay, training materials, and travel costs. Costs of attendance at such programs are allowable for up to 16 weeks per employee per year.

Certain training and educational costs are expressly unallowable. Grants made in any form to educational or training institutions are considered contributions and are, thus, unallowable.

Generally, educational costs are allowable only for employees. However, pay differentials may be provided for the education (at the primary and secondary levels only) of dependents of an employee who is working in a foreign country. To qualify, suitable education in the foreign country must be inordinately expensive, and these costs may be included in an overseas differential.

Travel Costs (31.205-46)

Travel costs incurred by employees in travel status while on company business are generally allowable. Travel costs include transportation, lodging, subsistence, and incidental expenses. Calculation of these costs may be based on the actual cost incurred, per diem or mileage costs, or a combination of these two methods to determine a reasonable charge.

Both direct and indirect travel costs are allowable under this cost principle. Travel costs directly attributable to a specific contract's performance are treated as direct costs under FAR 31.202. The costs incurred in the normal course of the overall administration of the business are treated as indirect costs.

The criteria for allowing corporate aircraft costs require that a flight manifest be maintained and made available for all such flights. The flight manifest, or log, must at a minimum contain the dates, times, and points of departure and arrival; the name of each passenger and his or her relationship to the contractor; the purpose of the trip; and authorization for the trip. Costs include those of charter, lease, operation, personnel, maintenance, depreciation, and insurance.

When the use of corporate aircraft is not required for contract performance, the allowability of flight costs is limited to the standard commercial fare unless the contracting officer specifically approves the extra cost. Under special circumstances, the contracting officer may agree to reimbursement greater than the standard airfare costs for the costs of corporate aircraft.

Costs related to personal use of company-owned or -leased automobiles are dealt with in the section dealing with compensation. These costs, including those of leasing, operating, maintaining, depreciating, and insuring the vehicles, are allowable, if reasonable, to the extent the automobiles are used for company business.

According to the DCAA Contract Audit Manual, advanced planning of travel should be an integral part of the contractor's internal travel policy. Such planning to combine visits to the same geographical area into a single trip would minimize the use of above-standard fares and accommodations and minimize the number of trips to the same location by multiple segments of the company.

In 1985, legislation revised the cost allowability criteria from reasonable meals and lodging to use of government employee per diem rates. The act creates parity between the allowable transportation, relocation, and travel expenses for contractor's employees and government reimbursement rates. The result is that contractor costs for travel, including lodging, other subsistence, and incidentals will only be allowable if reasonable and to the extent permitted for federal employees. This act authorizes the General Services Administration to establish reimbursement allowances for each locality for federal employees.

This principle was established to equalize the travel cost reimbursements of government and contractor employees. These per diem rates limit daily reimbursement on a location-by-location basis.

The rules in the government's Joint Travel Regulation (JTR), Federal Travel Regulation (FTR), and the Standardized Regulations are extensive. However, only three provisions apply to contractors. First, the definition of what constitutes meals, lodging, and incidental expenses contained in the per diem reimbursement also applies to contractor payments. Second, the daily limits for lodging and per diem also apply to contractor payments. However, contractor payment limitations are based on combined lodging and per diem each day whereas government employee limitations are based on individual lodging and per diem each day. Third, the unusual circumstances that permit reimbursement greater than the established limits also apply to contractor payments.

The FAR permits a deviation from this provision in special and unusual circumstances. Generally, it allows travel costs for lodging, meals, and incidental expenses up to a ceiling of 300 percent of the maximum per diem rates if certain conditions are met. Some of these conditions are: (1) the employee attends a meeting, conference, or training session where the lodging and meals must be incurred at a prearranged place and the lodging costs absorb all or practically all of the applicable maximum per diem rate; (2) the employee travels to a location where a special event or function has caused subsistence costs to increase temporarily during the period of the event or function; or (3) the employee incurs unusually high expenses because of special duties connected with the assignment, such as procuring a suite or other extraordinary accommodations.

The travel reimbursement regulations have removed taxes from being included in the published per diem lodging rates. This has the effect of lowering the amount allowable for per diem lodging. In late May 1999, a proposed rule was issued to remove the limitations on lodging and per diem costs levied by the Joint Travel Regulations (JTR) for contractors. Congress removed the JTR requirement for contractors in 1995. The proposed rule is unlikely to be put into effect because some rule writers believe that this action is not appropriate.

The costs of first-class air travel above the standard commercial fare are unallowable unless traveling by the lowest customary standard, coach, or equivalent airfare would necessitate circuitous routing, require travel during unreasonable hours, result in excessively long travel, cause increased overall travel costs, not adequately meet the physical or medical needs of the person traveling, or not be reasonably available to satisfy mission requirements. For airfare in excess of the normal standard commercial fare to be allowable, the contractor must document and justify these conditions supporting the use of the higher fares. The cost of these types of airfare tickets could be lowered if the contractor could use an advance ticket purchase system, which most airlines offer, if an itinerary is known a certain number of days in advance.

The ASBCA has disallowed the costs of first-class airfare where the company's policy was to permit first-class air accommodations when its employees scheduled their travel outside of normal working hours to the fullest extent possible. The contractor argued that the government benefited from such a policy because the employees traveled on their own time in order to fly first class. Additionally, the contractor asserted that these costs were necessary to provide its executives better and more secure working conditions and, alternatively, that they were allowable as additional compensation to corporate officers. However, the ASBCA rejected these arguments as not among the exceptions to the general rule disallowing airfare costs greater than the standard commercial rate. Additionally, the ASBCA noted that the employees receiving the benefit did not report the first-class differential as income in their individual income tax returns, and the contractor did not enter the amount as additional compensation.

COSTS RELATED TO PHYSICAL RESOURCES

The allowability of costs related to physical resources is addressed in FAR 31.205.

Cost of Money (31.205-10)

The cost of capital committed to facilities is an imputed cost calculated by applying a cost-of-money rate to the facilities capital employed in contract performance. The cost-of-money rate is the rate established by the Treasury Department for this purpose. The assets can be funded by either equity or debt, but since facilities capital includes all assets—not just assets purchased by issuing debt—the facilities capital cost is not considered a form of interest. CAS 414, Cost of Money as an Element of the Cost of Facilities Capital, establishes the basic ground rules for calculating the cost of facilities capital.

The cost-of-money factors should be computed to the fifth decimal place. They are to be applied in the same manner as indirect cost rates to recover the cost of money committed to facilities. They should be included on all contract proposals, public vouchers, and progress payment requests, as applicable. Regardless of the applicability of CAS 414, facilities capital costs are allowable if: (1) capital investment is measured, allocated, and costed in accordance with CAS 414; (2) adequate records are maintained to demonstrate compliance with CAS 414; (3) the cost is specifically identified in cost proposals for contracts on which it is claimed; and (4) requirements of 31.205-52 on asset write-ups are observed.

Inclusion of contract clause 52.215-30, Facilities Capital Cost of Money, specifically establishes the allowability of the cost of facilities capital for a specific contract (if the contractor computes such costs). If the cost is not proposed or if the contractor elects not to claim the cost, contract clause 52.215-31, Waiver of Facilities Capital Cost of Money, is included in the contract. Although the costs of facilities capital need not be recorded in the contractor's books and records, memorandum records kept in sufficient detail to be verified do have to be maintained. When allowable, the costs are considered "incurred" for purposes of reimbursements and progress payments.

The cost of capital assets under construction is a cost imputed by applying a cost-of-money rate to the costs incurred for capital assets under construction. As with the cost of capital committed to facilities, the cost-of-money rate is established by the Treasury Department and the resulting cost is not considered a form of interest. CAS 417, Cost of Money as an Element of the Cost of Capital Assets Under Construction, establishes criteria for measuring and allocating this cost.

Regardless of the applicability of CAS 417, fabrication or development is allowable if: (1) the cost of money is calculated and allocated in accordance with CAS 417; (2) adequate records demonstrate compliance with CAS 417; and (3) the costs are included in the capitalized costs that form the basis for depreciation or amortization.

Actual interest costs cannot be used in lieu of the facilities cost of capital assets under construction. The imputed cost need not be recorded in the books and records, although memorandum entries have to be maintained to permit verification of relevant supporting data. If the imputed cost is allowable, it is considered incurred for purposes of reimbursements and progress payments. Specifically, the cost-of-money factor, which is expressed in terms of a rate per unit of allocation base, is applied to payment requests as the applicable allocation base is incurred and billed.

Depreciation (31.205-11)

If a contractor shows that depreciation is reasonable and allocable as normal depreciation on a contractor's plant, equipment, and other capital facilities, it is an allowable contract cost. According to FAR 31.205-11, depreciation is "a charge to current operations which distributes the cost of a tangible capital asset, less estimated residual value, over the estimated useful life of the asset in a systematic and logical manner." Useful life relates to the economic usefulness, as opposed to the physical life of an asset in the contractor's operations. Economic usefulness is determined by the contractor's retirement and replacement practices.

Depreciation will be considered reasonable if the contractor's method of depreciation is: (1) consistent with the policies and procedures followed in the same cost center for private sector business; (2) reflected in the contractor's financial statements and books of account; and (3) both used and acceptable for federal income tax purposes. While depreciation costs are calculated differently for financial statements and tax purposes, allowable depreciation is limited to the amounts acceptable for federal income tax purposes and consistent with the depreciation procedures used on nongovernment business.

If a contractor has contracts subject to CAS 409, Depreciation of Tangible Capital Assets, the contractor must adhere to these standards for the CAS-covered contracts and may elect to use that provision for non-CAS contracts. If such an election is made, the contractor must apply all the requirements of CAS 409, ignoring any conflicting language in the FAR depreciation cost principle.

The FAR makes special provision for assets acquired before the effective date of CAS 409. Where the undepreciated asset amount of an asset (as a result of depreciation policies and procedures used previously for government contracts and subcontracts) is different from the undepreciated balance on the books of accounts and financial statements, for contract cost purposes, the allowable depreciated balance will be depreciated over the remaining life of the asset using the methods and useful lives followed for book purposes.

When property is acquired at no cost from the government, no depreciation is allowed. If an asset has been fully depreciated by the contractor or any division, subsidiary, or affiliate of the contractor under common control, no depreciation is allowed. However, if agreed upon, a reasonable charge for the use of such property is permitted. In calculating such a charge, consideration is given to costs, total estimated useful life at the time of negotiations, the effect of any increase in maintenance costs or decreased efficiency caused by age, and the amount of depreciation previously charged to government contracts or subcontracts.

The FAR applies the provision of CAS 404, Capitalization of Tangible Assets, to items acquired by users of a capital lease. Under Statement of Financial Accounting Standard No. 13, a lease must be classified as a capital lease for financial reporting purposes if any one of four stated criteria is present: (1) an automatic transfer of title; (2) a bargain purchase option; (3) lease terms that equal or exceed 75 percent of the total estimated economic life of the leased property; and (4) a situation in which the present value of the minimum lease payments is equal to or more than 90 percent of the excess of the fair value

of the property over any related investment tax credit retained by the lessor.

In the case of a sale and leaseback arrangement, rental costs are limited to the amount the contractor would have been allowed had it retained title to the property. In the event of a write-down from carrying value to fair value as a result of impairments caused by events or changes in circumstances, allowable depreciation of the impaired assets is limited to the amounts that would have been allowed had the assets not been written down. However, this does not preclude a change in depreciation resulting from other causes, such as permissible changes in estimates of service life, consumption of services, or residual value.

Gains and Losses on Disposition of Depreciable Property or Other Assets (31.205-16)

Gains and losses on the disposition of depreciable assets are generally recognized in the year they occur and are charged or credited to the cost pool that received the related depreciation amortization charges. Gains or losses are considered adjustments of prior depreciation or amortization charges. Thus, the amount of a gain or loss is the difference between the net proceeds (including insurance proceeds) and the book value of the asset. Gains are generally limited to the difference between the original cost capitalized and the undepreciated or unamortized value, except in the special case of involuntary conversions.

For example, assume that an asset was purchased for $1,100, the current unde-preciated value is $400, and the asset is sold for $1,500. The book gain is $1,100 ($1,500-$400), but the gain for government contracts purposes is limited to $700 ($1,100-$400). No gains or losses are recognized on the disposition of nondepreciable property. In one case, the ASBCA determined that the government was not entitled to share in the gain on sale of an asset when the original depreciation charges were not charged to government contracts.

Involuntary conversions occur as a result of events beyond the owner's control (e.g., fires, windstorms, floods, accidents, theft). When a cash insurance award is received and the asset is not replaced, the gain or loss is recognized in the period when the conversion takes place, and the gain is limited to the difference between the original cost and the book value of the asset at the time of the conversion. If the asset is replaced, however, the depreciable basis of the new asset can be adjusted by the amount of the gain or loss.

For example, assume that an asset had an original cost of $1,000 and a book value of $200, and was insured for $300. Assume that $3,000 is the cost of replacing the asset. Assume that the asset is destroyed by a hurricane. The contractor can elect to recognize a gain of $800 ($1,000-$200) and capitalize the asset at $3000 (therefore, the gain for government contract purposes is limited to the difference between the book value and the original cost). Alternatively, the contractor can elect simply to capitalize the difference between the replacement cost and the gain, $2,200 ($3,000–$800).

Idle Facilities and Idle Capacity Costs (31.205-17)

Costs arising from idle facilities are unallowable unless they meet one of the two following criteria: (1) the facilities are necessary to meet fluctuations in workload; or (2) the facilities were necessary when acquired and are now idle because of changes in requirements, production economies, reorganization, termination, or other causes that could not reasonably have been foreseen.

Idle facilities are normally allowable for a reasonable period of time (usually one year), depending on the actions taken to avoid the costs. In one case, the ASBCA held that idle facilities costs were allowable for a period of more than one year because: (1) the decrease

in business had not been foreseeable; and (2) the contractor had made efforts to reduce the costs.

Another issue in the same case was allocating the costs. Idle facilities, obviously, had no "total business" activity, the basis often used for making such allocations. The ASBCA, therefore, determined that the G&A costs of the division level that included the idle plant were the appropriate basis for making such an allocation. The ASBCA reached a similar conclusion in another case. Although the one-year limit was not strictly applied, the allocation base was not limited to the G&A pool of the idle plant. In general, the appropriate pool for allocation of such costs is the G&A pool that most closely relates to the overall business pertinent to the idled plant.

Maintenance and Repair Costs

This cost principle has been removed from the FAR (31.205-24); however, the concepts are still applicable and were not overcome by removal of the provision.

Maintenance and repair costs are incurred to keep property in efficient operating condition and are expensed in the year they are incurred. Normal maintenance and repair costs are allowable. Extraordinary maintenance and repair costs are allowable provided that those costs are allocated to the applicable periods for purposes of determining contract costs. Costs that are incurred to add permanent value to property or to prolong property's life appreciably, on the other hand, are classified as capital costs and cannot be expensed in the period incurred, but must instead be capitalized and allocated over the periods benefiting from the costs.

Manufacturing and Production Engineering Costs (31.205-25)

Manufacturing and production engineering costs are allowable. They include the costs of developing new or improved materials, systems, processes, methods, equipment, tools, and techniques to be used in the production process; deploying pilot production lines; improving current production facilities; and analyzing material and manufacturing producibility. These costs do not include basic and applied research, development effort created for sale, and costs subject to capitalization and amortization.

Plant Reconversion Costs (31.205-31)

Plant reconversion costs are incurred to restore or rehabilitate the contractor's facilities to approximately the condition they were in before the start of a government contract. These costs are unallowable except when incident to the removal of government-furnished property. Contracting officers are authorized to allow such additional contract costs when dictated by considerations of equity and when agreed to in advance.

Rental Costs (31.205-36)

Rental and lease costs of real and personal property are allowable to the extent reasonable, subject to two caveats: (1) rental cost under a sale and leaseback arrangement is limited to amounts that would have been allowable if title to the property had been retained; and (2) rental costs under leases between entities under common control are limited generally to normal ownership costs.

An additional caveat within this cost principle restricts the application of the principle to operating leases. Assets acquired under capital leases, defined in FAS-13, are leases that: (1) transfer ownership; (2) grant bargain purchase options; (3) cover the majority of the assets' remaining useful life; or (4) cover the difference between the value of the asset and the lessor's investment tax credit for the asset. These leases are treated as if purchased, and the costs are capitalized and depreciated over their useful lives.

The FAR provides that the reasonableness of rental costs of property acquired under operating leases will be determined by reference to rental costs of comparable property, if any; market conditions in the area; the type, life expectancy, condition, and value of the property; alternatives available; and other terms of the agreement.

The ASBCA has considered the subject of what constitutes a "sale and leaseback" under this FAR cost principle on several occasions. These decisions establish that a sale and leaseback of property that: (1) has never been the subject of depreciation charges; and (2) was not made for the purpose of raising capital, is not a "sale and leaseback" within the meaning of the cost principle.

Similarly, the ASBCA has considered the subject of "common control" of business entities for the purpose of this cost principle. The decisions hold that the contractor can rebut the potential for common control based upon interlocking officers and ownership interest—which would otherwise limit allowability of rental costs to the costs of ownership—by submitting evidence that common control was in fact exercised. Thus, if the contractor can establish that, despite appearances, separate management exists for the lessor and lessee and no one person or group actually controls both entities, rental costs payable under the lease, if reasonable, are allowable.

Special Tooling and Special Test Equipment Costs (31.205-40)

The costs of special tooling and test equipment are allowable and, usually, are clearly allocable to specific contracts. They are not allocable, however, if the tooling or equipment was acquired before the effective contract date (whether or not the tooling or equipment is subsequently altered or adapted for use in performance of the contract). Also, if the contract specifically excludes the tooling or equipment costs in question, the costs must be amortized or depreciated.

Some costs for special tooling or equipment are disallowed because the contractor could, with relatively minimal expense, make the tooling or equipment suitable for general use. The costs of adapting tooling or equipment for use on a government contract—and the costs of returning them to their prior configuration or condition after use—are allowable.

NEW BUSINESS-RELATED COSTS

The allowability of the following costs is addressed in FAR 31.205.

Independent Research and Development and Bid and Proposal Costs (31.205-18)

IR&D costs are the costs of a contractor's technical efforts sponsored by, or required in, performance of a contract or grant. Such activity is directed toward the conduct of basic or applied research, development, or systems and other concept simulation studies.

The goal of basic research is increasing knowledge of science and gaining a deeper understanding of the subject under study. Applied research is the practical application following basic research, although it may not be severable from the related basic research. Applied research also includes attempts to advance the state of the art and to determine and exploit the potential scientific discoveries or improvements in technology, materials, processes, methods, devices, or techniques.

Development consists of the systematic use of scientific and technical knowledge for the design, development, testing, or evaluation of a potential new product or service, or improvement of an existing product or service, to accomplish specific performance requirements or objectives. It specifically excludes subcontracted technical efforts undertaken solely to develop additional services for existing products and efforts to develop manufacturing, production materials, systems,

processes, methods, equipment, tools, and techniques not intended for sale.

Systems and other concept formulations are analyses to study efforts concerning particular IR&D efforts or aimed at identifying new or modifying and improving existing systems, equipment, or components. IR&D costs do not include technical efforts used to develop and prepare data specifically to support a bid and proposal submission.

Many issues arise over whether IR&D costs are proper indirect costs or the direct costs of a particular cost objective. The government prefers such costs to be direct under most circumstances. However, court and board decisions make it clear that unless the work is specifically required for contract performance, the costs are allowable IR&D costs.

B&P costs consist of the expenditures to prepare, submit, and support solicited or unsolicited bids and proposals for potential government or nongovernment contracts. These costs exclude the costs arising from grant or cooperative agreement special efforts or contract performance requirements.

The FAR incorporates CAS 420, Accounting for Independent Research and Development Costs and Bid and Proposal Costs. This provision establishes the requirements for the measurement, assignment, and allocation of IR&D and B&P costs. CAS 420 requires that IR&D and B&P costs be segregated and allocated on the same basis used for allocating G&A expenses.

Selling Costs (31.205-38)

This principle identifies the elements of selling that are covered by other cost principles, such as advertising costs. The cost elements are governed by the more specific principles.

"Selling" is defined by the regulation to encompass all efforts to market the contractor's products or services. It includes activities such as advertising, corporate image enhancement, market planning, direct selling, and bid and proposal expense. The costs of advertising and corporate image enhancement are covered more specifically in FAR 31.205-1, Public Relations and Advertising Costs. Corporate image enhancement also is covered by FAR 31.205-14, Entertainment Costs. Long-range market planning costs are controlled by FAR 31.205-12, Economic Planning Costs. Other market planning costs defined by this principle, such as market research and analysis and generalized management planning related to the development of the contractor's business, are allowable to the extent that they are reasonable.

Costs associated with direct selling efforts are allowable if they are reasonable in amount. Direct selling efforts consist of activities undertaken to convince particular prospective customers to purchase particular goods or services. These efforts are conducted by means of person-to-person contact and involve familiarization of potential customers with the offered products or services, terms of sale, and service conditions. Other forms of direct selling include individual demonstrations, consultations, provision of technical advice, and discussion of the adaptation of the contractor's products or services to meet the needs of the particular customer. Selling costs not specifically provided for are unallowable.

Brokerage or retainer fees, commissions, percentages, sellers' or agents' compensation, and similar payments are allowable only when paid to employees or established commercial or selling organizations maintained by the contractor for the purpose of securing business.

MISCELLANEOUS COSTS

The allowability of the following costs is addressed in FAR 31.205.

Contingencies (31.205-7)

A contingency is a possible future event or condition arising from presently known or unknown causes, the outcome of which is indeterminable at the present time. According to the FAR, the costs of contingencies are generally unallowable for historical costing purposes (i.e., for costs already incurred and recorded on the contractor's books). In some rare cases, a contingency may be recognized when it is applicable to a past period to give recognition to unsettled factors in the interest of expediting settlement.

For purposes of developing cost estimates, contingencies fall into two categories. The first category consists of contingencies that arise from presently known and existing conditions whose effects are reasonably foreseeable (e.g., anticipated costs of rejects and scrap). The costs of these contingencies are included as part of the cost estimate (e.g., as part of the cost of rejects or of rework material in the total estimated contract price). Historical data are usually relied on to establish the fact that rejects have occurred on a consistent basis and are used as a basis for estimating the cost of rejects in the current contract. Such data are necessary to support cost estimates because nomenclature reviews of contingent costs in price proposals usually lead the government to view such costs as contingent and, thus, unallowable.

The second category consists of contingencies that arise from conditions either known or unknown, but whose effect cannot be sufficiently measured to provide equitable results to either the contractor or the government (e.g., lawsuits). These contingencies are excluded from routine cost estimates, but may be estimated separately (if the basis upon which the cost is computed is also disclosed) to facilitate the negotiation of appropriate contractual coverage of the costs. In practice, however, these costs are difficult to support.

Economic Planning Costs (31.205-12)

Costs of corporate planning efforts, including long-range business activity, are generally allowable. This activity may include future changes in the contractor's markets, which may cause a possible reduction or increase of the products or services offered. This market change could have a significant effect on the contractor's operation, to the extent that plant expansion or relocation may ensue. It also may lead to an expansion in the form of a merger or acquisition of another business. This latter category of planning costs is allowable up to the point of acceptance by a board of directors. After acceptance, the costs fall under Part 27, Organization Costs.

Conversely, the long-range plan may envision a need to downsize or compress company operations. The planning cost for this size reduction is still an allowable cost under this part. The government is currently taking steps to address the allowability of the cost of downsizing or compression of operations and the resulting benefits.

Research and development and engineering costs designed to lead to new products for sale to the general public are not allowable under this principle.

Insurance and Indemnification (31.205-19)

The costs of insurance coverage that is maintained in connection with the general conduct of the contractor's business or is required or approved pursuant to contract terms are generally allowable.

To establish a program of self-insurance, contractors subject to CAS 416, Accounting for Insurance Cost, must follow the stated insurance requirements of that standard and Part 28 of the FAR. Also, the contractor must provide the contracting officer with such information as current financial statements, loss history, and formulas for establishing reserves.

If purchased insurance is available, the charge for any self-insurance coverage plus insurance administration expenses may not exceed the cost of comparable purchased insurance plus associated insurance administration expenses. Also, self-insurance charges for risk of loss from catastrophic losses are unallowable.

Insurance provided by captive insurers (i.e., insurers owned by or under the control of the contractor) is considered self-insurance, and charges for it must comply with the self-insurance provisions of CAS 416. However, if the captive insurer also sells insurance to the general public in substantial quantities and it can be demonstrated that the charge to the contractor is based on competitive market forces, the insurance will be considered purchased insurance.

CAS 416 requires that the allocation of insurance costs to cost objectives must be based on the beneficial or causal relationship between insurance costs and the cost objectives. The amount of insurance cost that may be assigned to a cost accounting period consists of the projected average loss for the period plus insurance administration expenses incurred during the same period.

Material Costs (31.205-26)

Generally, material costs are allowable. These include such items as raw materials, parts, subassemblies, components, and manufacturing supplies. Material costs must be adjusted for income or credits, including trade discounts, refunds, rebates, and returned materials. A contractor must establish that any failure to take cash discounts was reasonable.

Cost transfers between organizations under common control must be at a cost basis unless the contractor's established practice is to transfer at other-than-cost for nongovernment products and services and either an established catalog price or a price set by adequate price competition exists. Even then, the government may reject the other-than-cost price if that price is unreasonable.

Other Business Expenses (31.205-28)

When allocated on an equitable basis, the following other business expenses are allowable: (1) registry and transfer charges resulting from changes in the ownership of securities issued by the contractor; (2) the costs of shareholder meetings; (3) the costs of normal proxy solicitations; (4) the costs of preparing and publishing reports to shareholders; (5) the costs of preparing and submitting required reports and forms to taxing and other regulatory bodies; (6) incidental costs of directors' meetings; and (7) other similar costs.

Patent Costs (31.205-30)

Patent costs are incurred to protect rights to an invention and include the costs of preparing, filing, and prosecuting an application for a U.S. patent (when title or royalty-free license is to be conveyed to the government). These costs are often incurred by contractors who develop products or processes that they want to protect from uncompensated public use. The costs of general counseling services (including the fees of attorneys, engineers, and architects) on patents are allowable provided that the costs meet the requirements for professional and consulting costs.

Other patent costs are allowable only if incurred because of a specific contractual requirement. Such a requirement might exist if the government acknowledges that an item it needs cannot be produced without the contractor obtaining patent rights. In this case, however, the government must obtain the title or royalty for use of the patent before the costs are allowable. No costs related to foreign patents are allowable.

Precontract Costs (31.205-32)

Precontract costs are costs that are incurred before the effective date of a contract. These costs may include labor and special material costs incurred in contemplation of contract signing. The costs must result directly from contract negotiations, and they must be determined necessary to meet proposed delivery schedules. Precontract costs are allowable to the same extent, and on the same basis, as if they had been incurred after contract award.

The ASBCA has permitted precontract costs upon finding that the activity giving rise to those costs was necessary to meet delivery schedules several years in advance. Precontract costs can be addressed in an advance agreement.

Royalties and Other Costs for Use of Patents (31.205-37)

Royalties on a patent or amortization of the purchase price of a patent are allowable if necessary for contract performance unless: (1) the government has a license for the patent; or (2) the right to free use of the patent exists or the patent is invalid, unenforceable, or expired. If a patent was formerly owned by the contractor (i.e., owned, sold, and subsequently repurchased), costs are limited to the cost that would have been allowed had the contractor never sold the patent.

Government contracting personnel closely review the reasonableness of royalty costs when the recipient of royalty payments is affiliated with the contractor, the agreement was made in contemplation of award of the contract, or the agreement was made after the contract was awarded. If a contractor's capitalized value for a patent is low, for example (consisting, perhaps, of minor costs of researching and obtaining the patent), the contractor might decide to sell the patent to another party (sometimes related) and later either pay royalties on the patent or repurchase it and then amortize the costs. However, the mere fact that royalties are being paid to an affiliated party does not preclude the allowability of the payments, according to the ASBCA.

Some contemplated royalty payments are never actually paid because the government is successful in an antitrust suit or because the contractor is able to discontinue payments by mutual agreement. Government concern in such situations arises when a fixed-price contract has been negotiated on the basis of expected royalty payments and the costs are not subsequently incurred. The government may allege that the contractor has received a windfall profit and could lodge a defective pricing allegation if the contractor knew the royalty payments would never be made.

Taxes (31.205-41)

Taxes not declared unallowable by the FAR are allowable if recorded in accordance with GAAP. If otherwise allowable taxes are disputed by a contractor as being illegal or erroneous, the contractor must request and follow instructions from the contracting officer before paying the taxes. Any interest or penalty costs incurred as a result of following the contracting officer's instructions or incurred for lack of prompt response from the contracting officer are allowable.

Sometimes disputes arise over the applicability of state or local taxes levied on inventory in the contractor's possession to which the government has legal title because state and local taxes cannot be levied on the federal government. However, the government's title to property that is obviously in the possession of the contractor may be disputed by the local taxing authorities. In such cases, the

contractor should not pay the tax before asking the contracting officer's advice.

Refunds of allowable taxes, fines, or penalties have to be credited ratably to the government (as directed by the contracting officer) to the extent that the government participated in the original cost. Refunds are carefully reviewed to ensure that adequate credit is given to the government. Normally, refunds such as for any carryback loss provision can be credited in the year the refund is received. On the other hand, if the mix of contractor business has changed from the time when the tax was charged, the government may seek an alternative allocation of the credit.

The following taxes are unallowable contract costs: (1) federal income and excess profits taxes; (2) taxes related to financing, refinancing, or refunding operations or reorganizations; (3) taxes for which exemptions are directly or indirectly available (see below); (4) special tax assessments on land that represents capital improvements; (5) taxes on real and personal property not used in connection with government contracts; (6) taxes related to funding deficiencies and related transactions under deferred compensation plans; and (7) tax accruals to recognize the difference between taxable income and pretax income as recognized in the financial statements.

The indirect tax exemptions are available not to the contractor but to the federal government. For example, a contractor might claim an indirect tax exemption from property owned by the government but actually in the contractor's possession. Because the federal government is exempt from state and local taxes, it considers inventory on government contracts—even when still in the contractor's possession—to be exempt from state and local taxes. If the contracting officer determines that obtaining such an exemption is too great an administrative burden, however, the tax is allowable. Any partial tax exemption attributable to the government renders any remaining portion of the tax unallowable.

Because tax exemptions might exist for government-owned inventory held by the contractor, special rules on the allocation of taxes have been developed. Taxes on property used solely for government work must be allocated only to government contracts, and taxes on property used solely for nongovernment work must be allocated only to nongovernment contracts. If property taxes are insignificant, however, separate allocations are not necessary. Similarly, if separate allocations do not differ significantly from a combined allocation, separate allocations are not required. If property is used for both government and nongovernment work, taxes should be allocated to all work based on the relative use of the property.

Tax accruals arising from differences between state and local taxable income and the income reported for financial purposes are not allowable. The government, in other words, accepts only the taxes reflected on the tax return (i.e., taxes actually paid).

After considerable governmental review and discussion covering a period of years, the environmental tax found at section 59A of the Internal Revenue Code, also called the "Superfund Tax," has been included as an allowable tax cost.

Termination Costs (31.205-42)

The termination of a contract creates different circumstances and permits deviation from many of the cost principles and the CAS. Upon notification of a termination, the contractor should segregate costs related to the termination settlement. Generally, costs that cannot be avoided, costs that would have been amortized in future periods, and settlement expenses are allowed as part of the claim under a terminated contract.

The costs of common items reasonably usable on the contractor's other work are not allowable unless the contractor submits evidence that the items could not be retained at cost without sustaining a loss. (For example, a common item such as welding rod cannot be included in termination costs because it can be used elsewhere. However, if the contract required purchasing more welding rod than the company could use in 50 years on other work, the costs may still be claimed on the termination.)

Costs that cannot be discontinued immediately after the effective date of termination, despite all reasonable efforts by the contractor, are generally allowable. However, any costs continuing after the effective date of the termination due to the negligent or willful failure of the contractor to discontinue the costs are unallowable.

Initial costs, which include the following, are allowable: starting load and preparatory costs; excessive spoilage due to inexperienced labor; idle time and subnormal production due to testing and changing production methods; training; and lack of familiarity or experience with the product or process.

Loss of useful value of special tooling, and special machinery and equipment, are generally allowable, as are rental costs under unexpired leases, less the residual value of such leases, if shown to have been reasonably necessary for the performance of the terminated contract.

Settlement expenses, which include accounting, legal, and clerical expenses necessary for preparing, assembling, and presenting the claim, are generally allowable. These costs, usually considered indirect, are charged direct to a termination claim, and are not included in their usual indirect cost pools.

Subcontractor claims are treated with the same type of review and scrutiny as the contractor's claims. These costs, including the allocable portion of the claims common to the contract, are generally allowable. A prime concern should be a review to ensure no duplication of costs claimed.

Environmental Cleanup Costs

No cost principle has been published on environmental costs. However, the decision not to promulgate such a regulation did not come easily. A draft cost principle on environmental costs was prepared to address the allowability of environmental cleanup costs. The first version would have rendered most of those costs unallowable except for contractors operating government-owned facilities. The next version has been opposed by certain government agencies, because it would make most of those costs allowable. The Department of Defense (DOD) opinion was that perhaps no specific coverage is necessary, because the principles of allocability could resolve any disputes.

Allocability cannot satisfactorily resolve all potential issues, however. If costs are incurred now (i.e., when the contractor has all government business) based on a liability that arose years ago (i.e., when the contractor had substantially all commercial business), the costs would be considered unallocable, because the costs should be allocated to commercial business. On the other hand, if costs are incurred now (i.e., when the contractor has all commercial business) based on a liability that arose years ago (i.e., when the contractor had substantially all government business), the costs may be allocable to government contracts, but no government contracts exist. In any event, the costs could not be recovered.

From 1992 to 1997, a draft cost principle was coordinated within the government, but publication has been delayed. However, the DOD contract auditors and contract administrators are applying the concepts through an audit guidance document. Although the guidance states that environmental costs are normal costs of doing business and are gener-

ally allowable if reasonable and allowable, the detailed discussions behind this statement disclose numerous conditions in which the government might consider the costs to be unallowable. For example, for these costs to be allowable, a contractor must have taken prompt and prudent actions to minimize damages. Some costs may have to be capitalized as an improvement to land and thus become unallowable as a cost related to nondepreciable assets.

Another implementation guide suggests that contractors should not be reimbursed for costs if contamination could have been avoided. Increased costs resulting from the contractor not taking immediate action after a contamination is discovered are unallowable under this guidance. Any recoveries through insurance and other sources must be credited to the government. If the contamination is at a closed segment, the costs should be assigned to the segment that assumed the work of the closed segment. If no segment presently has that work, the guidance states that this cost is not directly allocable to any other segment. In the case of a closed segment in which the property has been sold, the auditors are advised to consider whether the sales price of the land was higher due to the contractor's agreement to clean up the facility. Therefore, the costs are considered part of the gain or loss on the sale of the land and not an allowable contract cost. Finally, under most conditions, each contaminator is legally responsible for the entire cost of a cleanup. According to the audit guidance, if the contractor is required to pay for any portion of another firm's liability, those costs are unallowable as bad debt expense unless the firm is no longer in existence.

In subsequent clarification of this guidance, the determination of "environmental wrongdoing" was specifically stated to include incidents regardless of whether any formal charges were made against the contractor. If no other reasonable means of allocating cleanup costs can be established, the period of time that the facilities were occupied should be used according to this guidance. Cost allocations should be included as part of a G&A cost pool rather than an overhead pool.

During 1993, DOD began collecting data on about two dozen contractors who had incurred significant environmental cleanup costs. The data will be analyzed to develop policies that ensure consistent treatment of the costs. The draft cost principle will then be revised for further consideration.

In 1991, DOD and Lockheed entered into an agreement whereby DOD would reimburse most of the cost of environmental cleanup activities at a location that had been used predominantly for defense contracts for many years. Advance agreements are desirable in this area in view of the amount of dollars involved and the concern that, for lack of specific coverage in the FAR, an agency may allege the costs to be unallowable.

The American Institute of Certified Public Accountants issued Statement of Position 96-1 on "Environmental Remediation Liabilities" in 1996. This pronouncement provides for accrual of costs, including legal fees, at the point in time that a liability is known to exist.

Restructuring Costs (DFARS 231.205.70)

The increasing significance of downsizing and restructuring, particularly in the defense and aerospace industries, requires that special attention be paid to cost allowability. DOD has established a policy to accommodate downsizing efforts that reduce costs or maintain unique capabilities needed by the government. This policy relates to novation agreements that permit a contract to be transferred to a new party. Such agreements are needed when a business combination occurs. The government will generally not agree to a transfer unless the new parties agree that the contract price will be no greater than the

price that would have been charged had the transfer not occurred. DOD policy is to accept novations without restrictions on price increases as long as costs will be lower in the long term or a capability vital to the government will be retained because of the business combination.

The implementation of this policy requires that an advance agreement be negotiated before any restructuring costs are allowable. A contractor must submit a detailed proposal of estimated costs and savings resulting from the restructuring. The auditor may recommend that certain costs be amortized over a period of up to five years. Any capitalized costs will be excluded from the cost-of-money calculation according to DOD policy; however, the basis for this is not likely to be supported by a Board of Contracts Appeals or the courts. Any accounting for restructuring costs is not likely to be considered an accounting change because restructuring is a new cost.

A restructuring cost is considered external if it involves two or more separate entities. A restructuring cost is internal if it involves only one entity. External costs are allowable based on the considerations noted. Costs that are specifically unallowable (e.g., incorporation fees, depreciation on the basis of asset valuations) will not be allowable under restructuring cost provisions. The comparison of savings and costs will be made using present value techniques. In 1995, the Cost Accounting Standards Board issued a retroactive interpretation of numerous standards that echoed the DOD guidance on external restructuring.

In 1995 and 1996, Congress enacted legislation that resulted in cost principle revisions to the DOD FAR Supplement. External restructuring costs are the nonroutine, nonrecurring costs after a business combination that affect the operations of entities not previously under common control. Normally these costs are considered to be incurred within three years of the business combination. Restructuring costs of $2.5 million or less are considered immaterial and not subject to the cost limitations related to restructuring costs.

Restructuring costs related to business combinations that occurred on or before September 30, 1996, or not using FY 1997 funds, are allowable if the audited savings meet or exceed the amount of the restructuring costs. For business combinations after September 30, 1996, and if FY 1997 funds were used, the restructuring costs are allowable if: (1) the savings exceed the restructuring costs by a ratio of at least 2 to 1; or (2) the savings exceed the costs by a ratio of less than 2 to 1 but the Secretary of Defense determines that the business combination resulted in the preservation of a critical defense capability.

Cost of Government Shutdowns

The federal budget process caused several agencies to shut down operations during late 1995 and early 1996. Under some circumstances, contractor costs associated with these shutdowns may be allowable. Some agencies, particularly the Environmental Protection Agency, have expressed a policy of denying most claims, especially those for direct labor costs.

If a contracting officer issued a stop work order, the contractor will have an excellent chance of cost recovery. The contractor should have taken reasonable steps to limit the cost impact. If employees can be furloughed based on company policies, this should be done. If no stop order was issued, the chances of recovery are less, but must be evaluated on a case-by-case basis. For stop work orders and resulting delay periods, for years, contractors have been able to recover unabsorbed overhead based on formulas accepted in previous court and Board of Contract Appeals decisions.

CHAPTER 6

Cost Accounting Standards

The Cost Accounting Standards Board (CASB) was established by law on August 15, 1970. When Congress did not appropriate funds for the CASB in 1980, the CASB ceased to exist on September 30, 1980. During its ten-year life, the CASB promulgated 19 individual cost accounting standards that will influence government contracting for many years to come. Legislation was passed in the late 1980s to authorize a new CASB under the authority of the Office of Federal Procurement Policy.

ORIGINAL CAS LEGISLATION

The original CASB was created for a variety of reasons and conditions that existed in the 1960s: (1) contractors had inconsistent accounting practices; (2) generally accepted accounting practices (GAAP) and the then-applicable procurement regulations (Armed Services Procurement Regulation, or ASPR) permitted too much perceived flexibility in cost accounting; (3) negotiated contracts were at a high volume; (4) defense spending was at a high volume; (5) the General Accounting Office (GAO) said that cost accounting standards were feasible; and (6) government agencies agreed on the need for cost standards. Industry disagreed.

At the 1968 congressional hearings on the Defense Production Act, witnesses testified that ascertaining the profit on a particular contract was nearly impossible because of the absence of consistent accounting practices by defense contractors. As a result, the development of uniform accounting standards for defense contractors was proposed. In May 1968, the House passed legislation that included a new requirement that GAO develop uniform accounting procedures for negotiated defense contracts and subcontracts of over $100,000. GAO found the terms and concepts to be unclear and suggested that a study be undertaken.

Congress was influenced heavily by two factors: (1) the large proportion (86 percent) of defense procurements entered into on a negotiated basis; and (2) testimony that different cost accounting practices followed by defense contractors could result in a lack of adequate cost information that would impair comparability among bidders. The estimate of a contractor's cost plays an important role in establishing price.

The House Report noted that uniform cost principles were necessary because of substantially increased costs of procurement and to help prevent excessive profits. The Senate Banking and Currency Committee held hearings on the bill in June 1968. The Committee heard testimony that the essential function of cost accounting is to allocate direct and overhead costs to individual orders. The cost accounting principles followed have a significant impact on determining contractor costs. As examples, various cost items, such as depreciation and research and development, can be determined and allocated in different ways. Without uniform cost principles, a large burden is placed on procurement officials to evaluate a contractor's accounting practices without the guidance of authoritative support for using alternatives in specific circumstances. As a result, more work by auditors and procurement officials is required, and procurement costs are excessive.

Responding to these views, Congress, in PL 90-370, provided for GAO, in cooperation with the Department of Defense (DOD) and the Bureau of the Budget (now the Office of Management and Budget) and in consultation with the accounting profession and the defense industry, to "undertake a study to determine the feasibility of applying uniform cost accounting standards to be used in all negotiated prime and subcontract defense procurements of $100,000 or more."

In conducting the feasibility study, GAO did its own research, receiving studies and comments from various government agencies, industry associations, and accounting organizations. GAO used a questionnaire that sought information on the nature of CAS and current accounting practices and on the types of uniform standards that might be feasible.

In the Comptroller General's Report to Congress (January 19, 1970), GAO concluded that, while establishing cost accounting standards to attain a higher degree of consistency and uniformity among government contractors in cost accounting matters was appropriate, establishing standards in such detail that would result in precisely mandated methods of computing costs for each different kind of cost under all circumstances in government contracting was not feasible. Further, GAO found that CAS should apply to all negotiated contracts, both defense and nondefense, since the same kind of potential benefits would accrue to government agencies negotiating these contracts. GAO observed that even though the subject of costs versus benefits is highly controversial, and industry strongly believed that the costs outweigh the benefits, the cumulative benefit to the federal government should exceed the implementation costs of the proposed CAS.

As a result of GAO recommendations, the proposal to create the CASB and develop CAS was included in proposed legislation. During the public hearings on the bill, representatives of the accounting profession expressed mixed feelings on the proposal. The American Institute of Certified Public Accountants maintained a rather neutral position, and government representatives strongly advocated the legislation.

Industry generally opposed the legislation for the following reasons: (1) the concepts and real objectives and methods of attaining uniform CAS had not been sufficiently described by GAO or in the proposed legislation; (2) a significant enough need for the use of CAS had not been demonstrated; (3) having to comply with standards was expected to be costly (especially in view of the lack of specific benefits that might flow from their use); and (4) congressional desires and objectives could be accomplished through appropriate modification of existing regulations.

Despite industry's objections, the Defense Production Act Amendments of 1970 included congressional intent to establish the CASB, which became law by enactment of PL 91-379 on August 15, 1970.

BASICS OF PUBLIC LAW 91-379

Under its legal mandate, the CASB, which consisted of a five-person board headed by the Comptroller General, issued standards to achieve uniformity and consistency in cost accounting, provided certain statutory exemptions, provided for contractors to disclose existing cost accounting practices, and issued rules and regulations covering implementation.

The legislation stipulated that the CASB answer to Congress. In this connection, it paralleled GAO reporting responsibilities. The law further required that the U.S. Comptroller General serve as chairman of the CASB and be responsible for appointing four members to terms of four years each. It prescribed certain criteria that the four additional members must meet: (1) two must be from the accounting profession, one of whom is to be knowledgeable about cost accounting problems in the small business community; (2) one must be from industry; and (3) one must be from a federal agency.

The law was Congress' attempt to capture some of the concepts described in the GAO report. Specifically: (1) the standards should achieve consistency and uniformity in cost accounting principles; and (2) the principles must be followed by prime contractors and subcontractors involved in negotiated defense contracts during the several phases of contract pricing, including the estimating, accumulation, and reporting of costs.

The law exempted contracts from coverage if the price is based on catalog or market prices of commercial items sold in quantities to the public or if the price was set by either regulation or law. In addition, the legislation granted the CASB rather broad responsibility in amending its regulations and permitting exemptions from its standards for certain classes of contracts.

The legislation required contractors to disclose to the government in writing their cost accounting practices, including a detailed explanation of their methods of cost accounting. In addition, contractors must agree that the contract price can be adjusted downward for higher costs charged against government contracts because of the contractors' failure to comply with the CAS or with their own cost accounting practices, as described in the disclosure statement.

CASB OPERATING POLICIES

In a March 1973 document entitled *Statement of Operating Policies, Procedures and Objectives*, the CASB described the framework of its operation, including how it formulated the CAS and its rules and regulations. In this document, the CASB stressed objectives like uniformity and consistency, and explained the process of developing standards. The CASB believed that this statement should present the fundamental objectives of its operation, thus setting the stage for future productive dialogue with interested parties concerned with its work.

In May 1977, the CASB published a *Restatement of Objectives, Policies and Concepts*, based on its experience to date. The CASB stated that this document was meant to publicize its current views so that interested members of the public could better understand the complex and difficult issues the CASB faced, as well as its philosophy.

In developing a standard, the CASB used as a starting point a myriad of information gathered from a variety of sources, mostly based on potential problems in the broad area of cost accounting. The CASB screened these problems, retaining for extensive research those it believed demanded the most attention. It involved itself in a detailed investigation of prior authoritative statements. It analyzed information developed from the disclosure statements filed by contractors, and it visited a number of contractors' offices and plants to obtain additional information on the particular cost accounting subject under scrutiny.

After having developed its own thought processes to the point where it recognized some of the existing problems associated with a potential standard, the CASB prepared a discussion paper. It circulated this paper for comment to a wide range of interested parties, including government agencies, contractors, professional groups, and trade associations. On the basis of the responses, the CASB would either abandon a project, perform additional research, or prepare a draft standard to be distributed for comments. The CASB evaluated the responses to a draft standard and appropriately modified the draft.

As required by Congress, the CASB published the draft standards in the *Federal Register* so that the public had at least 30 days during which it could submit comments, criticisms, and suggestions. After comments were received, the CASB evaluated them and revised the standard accordingly. Then, the CASB published the final standard in the *Federal Register* and submitted it to Congress for approval. No congressional objection to the standard was raised during a period of 60 continuous days of congressional session, so the standard automatically became law, effective at the beginning of the second fiscal quarter after 30 days from final publication.

AFTER THE DEMISE OF THE ORIGINAL CASB

When the CASB went out of existence in 1980, it left a void. There were 19 standards but no authoritative government agency to interpret, amend, or grant waivers to them or to promulgate new standards. In 1984, DOD decided to fill that void by establishing the CAS as regulations, which were included in the FAR, and by establishing a CAS Policy Group as a separate committee under the FAR regulatory structure to administer and provide means for changing the CAS.

The CAS Policy Group functioned within the Defense Acquisition Regulation (DAR) Council and was staffed with members of each of the Services, the Office of the Secretary of Defense, Defense Logistics Agency, National Aeronautics and Space Administration, General Services Administration, and DCAA. All members except the chairman served on a part-time basis. The CAS Policy Group did not issue any additional standards. Its efforts were directed primarily at administering the current standards and making modifications as required by the changing business environment.

Objections arose from some in industry that the government had total control of the

CAS. While the CASB had representation from public accounting, academia, and industry, the CAS Policy Group had only government members. Congress believed these objections were valid. On November 17, 1988, Congress passed Public Law 100-679 to recreate the CASB as an independent unit of the Office of Federal Procurement Policy. It would consist of five members: the OFPP administrator as chairman, one each from DOD and GSA, and two from the private sector.

BASIC CAS REQUIREMENTS

Contracts subject to the CAS are required by law to include a clause fully describing compliance obligations. The clause covers a number of issues. The contractor must: (1) complete a disclosure statement describing its cost accounting practices and follow these consistently in estimating, accumulating, and reporting costs; (2) comply with the CASB's standards; and (3) adjust the contract price on the basis of failure to comply with disclosed cost accounting practices or the CASB standards.

Price Adjustments

Because changes in CAS applicability or the contractor's disclosed cost accounting practices may have an impact on contract pricing, paragraph (a)(4) of the CAS clause provides that the contractor shall:

> (4)(i) Agree to an equitable adjustment as provided in the Changes clause of this contract if the contract cost is affected by a change which, pursuant to (3) above, the Contractor is required to make to the Contractor's established cost accounting practices.
>
> (ii) Negotiate with the Contracting Officer to determine the terms and

conditions under which a change may be made to a cost accounting practice other than a change made under other provisions of this paragraph 4; *provided,* that no agreement may be made under this provision that will increase costs paid by the United States.

(iii) When the parties agree to a change to a cost accounting practice, other than a change (4)(i) above, negotiate an equitable adjustment as provided in the Changes clause of this contract.

However, a contractor's or subcontractor's failure to comply with the CAS or disclosed cost accounting practices may also have an impact on contract pricing. Paragraph (a) (5) of the clause provides that the contractor shall:

(5) Agree to an adjustment of the contract price or cost allowance, as appropriate, if the Contractor or a subcontractor fails to comply with an applicable Cost Accounting Standard or to follow any cost accounting practice consistently and such failure results in any increased costs paid by the United States. Such adjustment shall provide for recovery of the increased costs to the United States together with interest thereon computed at the rate determined by the Secretary of the Treasury pursuant to Pub, L. 92-41, 85 Stat. 97, or 7 percent per annum, whichever is less, from the time the payment by the United States was made to the time the adjustment is effected.

These provisions of the CAS clause provide for price adjustments in three different situations: (1) initial compliance with a standard; (2) "voluntary" changes; and (3) noncompliance. Because the factors involved in each situation are significantly different, the regulations provide separate treatment. However, price adjustments to contracts for a new standard, "voluntary" changes, or noncompliance are required only if the amounts involved are material.

The CASB promulgated general criteria for determining materiality. The FAR provides that the administrative contracting officer (ACO), who is given the responsibility for CAS administration, has the right to forgo action to adjust contracts if the amount involved is not considered material. However, in the case of noncompliance, this section requires the ACO to inform the contractor that the government reserves the right and is required to make appropriate contract adjustments if, in the future, the ACO determines that the cost impact has become material and the contractor is not excused from the obligation to comply with the applicable standard or rules and regulations involved.

Covered Contracts

The cost accounting standards apply to negotiated contracts and subcontracts in excess of $650,000.[1] Explicitly excepted from the statutory coverage are contracts and subcontracts for the acquisition of commercial items and those in which the price is set by law or regulation. The term "subcontract," as used within the statutory paragraph on the applicability of the CAS, is defined to include transfers of commercial items between divisions, subsidiaries, or affiliates of a contractor or subcontractor. As implemented in the CAS Board's regulations, the commercial-item exemption covers firm fixed-price contracts and subcontracts, and fixed-price contracts and subcontracts with economic price adjustments, provided that such price adjustments are not based on actual costs incurred.

---

[1]As of early 2010, this threshold was not consistent with the threshold for submission of cost or pricing data. In the future an attempt may be made to set these thresholds on a consistent basis.

Before the commercial item exception was enacted in 1996, contracts in which the price was based on "established catalog or market prices of commercial items sold in substantial quantities to the general public" were excepted. The definition of established catalog or market prices and related terms was tied by CASB regulation to definitions used in the procurement regulations. The FAR provided the definitions in its coverage of cost and pricing data requirements.

A business unit that receives a covered contract of less than $50 million may elect modified CAS coverage if the covered contracts that it was awarded in the immediately preceding cost accounting period totaled less than $50 million. Modified coverage requires only that the business unit comply with: CAS 401, Consistency in Estimating, Accumulating, and Reporting Costs; CAS 402, Consistency in Allocating Costs Incurred for the Same Purpose; CAS 405, Accounting for Unallowable Costs; and CAS 406, Cost Accounting Period. Once an election for modified coverage is made during a cost accounting period, it has to be applied to all covered contracts received during that period. Award of a single covered contract of $50 million or more, however, requires compliance with all the standards.

Exempt Contracts

Contracts and subcontracts entered into under sealed bidding procedures are exempt, as are those awarded to small businesses concerns. Firm-fixed-price contracts and subcontracts awarded without submission of any cost data are exempt also. Until the early 2000s, this exemption was for situations where *no* cost data are submitted as opposed to where no *certified* cost data are submitted. However, currently, submission of uncertified data (data termed "other than cost or pricing data") will not cause a contract or subcontract to be CAS-covered.

Exempt from CAS coverage are any contracts or subcontracts of less than $7.5 million, provided that, at the time of award, the business unit of the contractor or subcontractor is not performing any CAS-covered contracts or subcontracts valued at $7.5 million or greater. This is a significant exemption for many companies.

Prior to the statutory exemption for contracts for commercial items, procuring agencies were permitted to waive the application of the CAS to individual firm fixed-price contracts for commercial items when cost or pricing data were not obtained. The Board decided to delegate this authority in December 1995, after considering industry concerns that contractors submitting limited cost data for the purposes of cost realism evaluation or the like would subject themselves to CAS coverage. Additionally, commercial time-and-material and labor-hour contracts are exempt from all CAS requirements

Contracts and subcontracts with foreign governments are categorically exempt, and those awarded to foreign concerns are subject only to CAS 401, Consistency in Estimating, Accumulating, and Reporting Costs, and CAS 402, Consistency in Allocating Costs Incurred for the Same Purpose. An additional exemption existed for contracts and subcontracts executed and performed entirely outside the United States in late 2010; however, a proposed rule will likely eliminate this exemption. An exemption also exists for contracts and subcontracts performed in the United Kingdom by a U.K. contractor that has filed the appropriate disclosure statement in the U.K., and for certain subcontracts under the NATO Plastic Hull Minesweeper (PHM) Ship program.

Waivers of CAS Coverage

The CAS Board may waive all or part of the requirements in the CAS clauses when a contractor refuses to accept those requirements and no other source is available to meet the contracting agency's needs.

The FAR describes the circumstances under which agencies may waive CAS coverage. Contractors or subcontractors may refuse to accept all or part of the requirements of the CAS clauses. If the contracting officer determines that it is impractical to obtain the materials, supplies, or services from any other source, the contracting officer can prepare a request for waiver describing the proposed contract or subcontract and containing:

1. An unequivocal statement that the proposed contractor or subcontractor refuses to accept a contract containing all or a specified part of a CAS clause and specific reason for that refusal

2. A statement as to whether the proposed contractor or subcontractor has accepted any prime contract or subcontract containing a CAS clause

3. The amount of the proposed award and the sum of all awards by the agency requesting the waiver to the proposed contractor or subcontractor in each of the preceding three years

4. A statement that no other source is available to satisfy the agency's needs on a timely basis

5. A statement of alternative methods considered for fulfilling the need and the agency's reasons for rejecting them

6. A statement of steps being taken by the agency to establish other sources of supply for future contracts for the products or services for which a waiver is being requested

7. Any other information that may be useful in evaluating the requests.

CAS STEERING COMMITTEE AND WORKING GROUP

DOD chartered the CAS Steering Committee and Working Group in August 1975 to overcome problems and delays in administration of the CAS. As described in the charter, the Working Group was intended to: (1) monitor CAS field administration; (2) identify CAS problems; (3) provide immediate reaction when appropriate, through informal or written provisional guidance; (4) determine underlying causes of CAS-related problems; and (5) initiate corrective action.

The actual functions of the Working Group included coordinating information on questions and papers submitted through the members, recommending revisions to procurement regulations when appropriate, and preparing formal interim guidance papers, after Steering Committee approval, on subjects of widespread interest. The guidance served as implementing instructions. The effort included interpreting elements of the CASB rules and regulations that needed clarification and helping ensure consistency in the implementation process.

The Working Group functioned for six years. During that time, it issued 25 working papers and one amendment on the following subjects:

Working Item No.	Group Subject
76-1	Interim guidance for implementing CAS 412
76-2	Application of the CAS to contract modifications and to orders placed under basic agreements.
76-3	Interim policy for application of the CAS to subcontracts

76-4   Interim guidance on determining increased costs to the government for "CAS-covered" FFP contracts

76-5   Interim guidance on treatment of implementation costs related to changes in cost accounting practices

76-6   Interim guidance on application of the CAS clause to changes in contractor's established practices when a disclosure statement has been submitted

76-7   Interim guidance on the significance of "effective" and "applicability" dates included in the CAS

76-8   Interim guidance on use of the offset principle in contract price adjustments resulting from accounting changes

76-9   Interim guidance for measurement of cost impact on FFP contracts

77-10   Retroactive implementation of the CAS when timely compliance is not feasible

77-11   Interim guidance for the implementation of CAS 410, Allocation of Business Unit G&A Expenses to Final Cost Objectives

77-12   Interim guidance on deliberate noncompliance and inadvertent noncompliance

77-13   Interim guidance on the applicability of CAS 405 to costs determined unallowable on the basis of allocability

77-14   Interim guidance on early implementation of new CAS issued by the CASB

77-15   Interim guidance on the influence of the CAS regulations on contract terminations

77-16   Interim guidance on applicability of the CAS to letter contracts

77-17   Identification of the CAS contract universe at a contractor's plant

77-18   Interim guidance for implementation of CAS 414, Cost of Money as an Element of the Cost of Facilities Capital and DPC 76-3

77-19   Administration of leased facilities under CAS 414

77-20   Policy for withdrawing determination of adequacy of disclosure statement

78-21   Allocation of business unit G&A expenses to final cost objectives

78-21   Amendment 1

78-22   Development of asset service lives

79-23   Administration of equitable adjustments for accounting changes not required by new CAS

79-24   Allocation of business unit G&A expenses to facilities contracts

81-25   Change in cost accounting practice for state income and franchise taxes as a result of change in method of reporting income from long-term contracts

THE STANDARDS

The Cost Accounting Standards Board issued 19 standards. Each standard is highlighted below.

Standard 401: Consistency in Estimating, Accumulating, and Reporting Costs

This standard requires consistency in classifying elements of costs as direct versus indirect, describing the types of costs included in indirect cost pools, and allocating indirect costs.

Because of the absence of specific criteria in the cost principles, contractors historically had considerable latitude in changing their cost accounting practices. In fact, contractors could change from one acceptable practice to another to increase the amount of costs recoverable from the government in negotiated contracts. For example, under a negotiated cost-plus-fixed-fee (CPFF) contract, contractors could use one cost accounting practice for the contract proposal and another practice after contract award, resulting in a change of costs allowable. Under these circumstances, for non-CPFF work, such as commercial or fixed-price government work, contractors would charge fewer costs (and hence earn greater profit) than originally anticipated, solely as a result of the change in cost accounting practice.

The CASB has stated that:

> The purpose of this Cost Accounting Standard is to insure that each contractor's practices used in estimating costs for a proposal are consistent with cost accounting practices used by him in accumulating and reporting costs. Consistency in the application of cost accounting practices is necessary to enhance the likelihood that comparable transactions are treated alike. With respect to individual contracts, the consistent application of cost accounting practices will facilitate the preparation of reliable cost estimates used in pricing a proposal and their comparison with the costs of performance of the resulting contract. Such comparisons provide one important basis for financial control over costs during contract performance and aid in establishing accountability for costs in the manner agreed to by both parties at the time of contracting. The comparisons also provide an improved basis for evaluating estimating capabilities.

A contractor is restricted in several ways in classifying costs. If the contractor designates a cost as direct at the cost proposal stage, the contractor must charge it as direct during contract performance. For the composition of indirect cost pools, when a contractor has two overhead pools each consisting of different types of cost at the cost proposal stage, the contractor cannot remove certain costs from one pool and place them in the other pool during contract performance. For allocating indirect costs, if a contractor -proposed that a single overhead pool be -allocated on the basis of direct labor dollars, the contractor cannot change that basis to direct labor hours during contract performance.

This standard permits the grouping of like costs where it is not practical to estimate contract costs by individual cost element or function. However, it demands that costs estimated for proposals be presented in such a manner and in sufficient detail that any significant cost can be compared with the actual cost accumulated and reported.

Standard 402: Consistency in Allocating Costs Incurred for the Same Purposes

This standard covers equitably allocating costs to cost objectives, charging costs consistently as direct versus indirect, establishing criteria to avoid charging similar costs in like circumstances as both direct and indirect, and charging similar costs as direct versus indirect under different circumstances.

This standard also stipulates that each type of cost be allocated "only once and on only one basis to any contract or other cost objective." It intends to "guard against the overcharging of some cost objectives and to prevent double counting. Double counting occurs most commonly when cost items are allocated indirectly to a cost objective without eliminating like cost items from indirect cost pools which are allocated to that cost objective."

Double counting is charging any kind of cost (e.g., travel, supervision, quality control) directly to a contract without removing similar costs from an overhead pool, a portion of which is being allocated to the same cost objectives as the direct cost charges.

This standard clearly points out the government's objective when it states:

> No final cost objective shall have allocated to it as an indirect cost any cost, if other costs incurred for the same purposes, in like circumstances, have been included as a direct cost of that or any other final cost objective. Further no final cost objective shall have allocated to it as a direct cost any cost, if other costs incurred for the same purpose, in like circumstances, have been included in any indirect cost pool to be allocated to that or any other final cost objective.

In other words, the government is willing to absorb its fair share of any cost, whether direct or indirect, but not more than its fair share in those circumstances when the same cost is charged directly and indirectly to its contract through overhead allocations. Contractors would be well advised to plan very carefully their decisions on charging costs incurred in similar circumstances as either direct or indirect. Once these decisions are made, contractors are precluded from altering the accounting practice without becoming involved in potential price adjustments to existing contracts.

Standard 403: Allocation of Home Office Expenses to Segments

The purpose of this standard is to establish criteria for allocating the expenses of a home office to the segments of the organization based on the beneficial or causal relationship between such expenses and the receiving segments.

This standard provides for: (1) identifying expenses for direct allocations to segments; (2) accumulating expenses into separate pools to be allocated to segments on various bases; and (3) allocating to all segments any remaining or "residual" home office expenses required to manage the entire organization. The appropriate implementation of this standard will limit the amount of home office expense classified as residual. The standard seeks to decrease broad allocations and advocates charging costs directly to the segments on a beneficial/causal basis as much as possible.

Expenses incurred by a home office should be divided into the three broad categories. Expenses incurred on behalf of particular segments—central payments or accruals for pension costs, group insurance, state and local income tax, and franchise tax—should be allocated only to those segments. The direct charging of costs to benefiting segments carries out the CAS concept of beneficial or causal relationships. Under it, if the expenses are incurred specifically for a segment, they should be allocated only to that segment, and not to other segments that neither received the benefit nor caused the expense.

This standard points out that if the beneficial or causal relationship cannot be specifically identified, costs should be grouped in homogeneous pools and allocated to segments on the basis of the various services furnished to the segments. For example, various centralized service functions performed by the home office may include personnel administration and centralized data processing. In addition, there may be staff management or policy guidance to segments, such as manufacturing, accounting, and engineering.

The various bases over which these expenses should be allocated are not dictated or required specifically by this standard, but rather are left to the contractor's judgment. The base selected must be one that appropriately measures the flow of benefits from these functions to the segments.

To help the contractor choose a base, the standard offers some valuable insight into preferred techniques; that is, using a hierarchy for cost allocations. For example, in allocating centralized service, the preferred allocation is the actual activity of the organization providing the service, such as labor hours or machine hours. If these data are unavailable, an alternative technique is measuring the output of the supporting functions, such as units or end products produced.

According to this standard, where neither activity nor output can be measured, a surrogate should be chosen to represent the activity of the segment receiving the benefit. As long as the surrogate represents a reasonable measure of the services received by the segment, it should result in varying the cost allocation in proportion to the services actually received.

This standard also deals with those broad staff management functions that are not identifiable with any segment or specific activity in the segments, but that represent costs necessary to the conduct of all segments. Called residual expenses, they should be a minimal amount after all the allocations required in the first two categories of cost and expenses have been performed. As anticipated by this standard, typical residual expenses are those of top management and their related corporate expenses. They should be allocated to the segments using a base representing the total activity of such segments.

When residual expenses amount to 3.35 percent of the first $100 million in sales and various lower percentages on higher volume, the standard calls for a three-part formula to allocate them to segments. The three-part formula encompasses payroll dollars, operating revenue, and tangible capital assets plus inventory. If inequities result from using this type of formula, the government and the contractor should agree on a special allocation of residual expenses to segments on a basis more commensurate with the benefits received, according to the standard.

An example of possible inequity in allocating residual expenses may be where one segment performs considerable functions for itself but other segments rely on the home office for those functions. This inequity might exist in foreign subsidiaries; government-owned, company-operated plants; domestic subsidiaries with less than a majority ownership; and joint ventures.

Standard 404: Capitalization of Tangible Assets

This standard requires written minimum policies for asset capitalization, requires a service life of two years or shorter and an acquisition cost criterion of $5,000, permits higher minimum dollars for original asset complement and for improvements, and requires that assets constructed for own use must absorb a full share of G&A and full indirect costs if similar to the contractor's normal product line.

According to the CASB, this standard requires establishing and adhering to policies governing the capitalization of tangible assets on the basis of the concept of enterprise continuity; that is, tangible assets will benefit future periods of time. Asset acquisitions should be capitalized and the cost allocated to current and future accounting periods so that cost objectives in those periods bear their fair share of the asset cost.

Furthermore, capitalization should be based on a policy that is applied consistently. Certain capitalization standards are required: a service life of two years (which can be shorter) and an acquisition cost criterion of $5,000 (which can be less). Contractors also are allowed to designate higher minimum dollar amounts for original installation of low-cost equipment and for betterments and improvements, on the basis that higher limitations must be reasonable in the particular circumstances.

The standard says that when costs are incurred to extend the asset's life or increase its productivity, and the costs exceed the capitalization criteria established by the contractor, the costs must be capitalized.

This standard includes provisions for determining the types of costs that should be capitalized. These costs include the asset's purchase price, all costs necessary to prepare the asset for use (installation and transportation, for example), and any adjustments for discounts and premiums.

If contractors construct their own tangible assets, this standard has criteria for determining the amounts to be capitalized. It requires capitalization of amounts that take in all indirect costs properly allocable to these assets, including a full share of G&A expenses if the asset is identical or similar to the contractor's regular product line. If the item is not similar to the contractor's normal product, all allocable indirect costs are to be capitalized, except that G&A expenses are limited to those identifiable with the self-constructed asset. This concept is a marked departure from the actual practice of many contractors, who mostly write off indirect and G&A expenses as period costs, with no identification with the constructed asset.

For financial accounting under the purchase method of accounting for business combinations, capital assets are assigned a portion of the costs not to exceed the fair value at date of acquisition. Further, when the fair value of identifiable assets minus the liabilities assumed exceeds the purchase price of the acquired company, the value otherwise assignable to capital assets must be reduced proportionately. For government contract accounting, both asset writeups and write-downs are ignored.

In contrast, under the pooling of interest method of accounting for business combinations, amounts established for capital assets for financial statement purposes must be the values used in determining the cost of the assets.

Standard 405: Accounting for Unallowable Costs

This standard requires that unallowable costs be segregated to prevent them from being charged to the government, be nevertheless allocable to the cost objectives on the usual beneficial or causal basis, and be determined by procurement regulations rather than by the CASB.

This standard eases contract administration by establishing guidelines for identifying unallowable costs and their cost accounting treatment. It requires specific identification in the accounting records (or memo records) of costs that a procurement agency has determined to be unallowable, for the purpose of keeping those costs out of any billing, claim, or cost proposal applying to a government contract.

Costs that are "directly associated" with unallowable costs may also be disallowed by a contracting officer and, hence, be subject to the standard. For example, travel expenses incurred in connection with entertainment expenses would be "directly associated" costs, since they would not have been incurred but for the unallowable entertainment expenses.

The determination of costs as unallowable can be either a mutually agreeable issue between the contracting parties or a unilateral decision by the contracting officer. Once the decision is made, however, any cost incurred for the same purpose under similar circumstances will also be unallowable.

If any work performed is identified as not contractually authorized, and the costs associated with that work are determined to be unallowable, those costs must be segregated like any other unallowable costs and continue to bear their fair share of any indirect cost allocations.

Unallowable costs need not be identified in the formal accounting records. They must at least be maintained in informal or memorandum records, however, so that they are appropriately considered in any cost accounting determinations.

Standard 406: Cost Accounting Period

This standard requires that the cost accounting period usually be the same as the fiscal year, the same cost accounting period be used for both pool and base determination, and the following exceptions be considered: (1) an indirect function in existence for partial year; (2) a mutual agreement of contracting parties; and (3) in transitional periods, a change in fiscal year.

Because the flow of both direct and indirect costs during any 12-month cost accounting period can be erratic in terms of amounts for each month or quarter, allocating only the indirect costs that happen to occur during the few months of contract performance is not proper cost accounting. A variety of costs are properly stated only annually. Use of interim estimates for these costs, then, can produce an estimate over or under the amount of costs applicable to the contract. The example shows an improper overallocation in the shorter period, which resulted from application of an overstated overhead rate.

The standard recognizes that certain indirect cost functions may actually exist for just part of a year and so should be allocated to cost objectives only during that period. In that case, indirect costs can apply solely to contracts performed during that portion of the year. Included might be reorganizations within the company, resulting in the elimination of certain supervisory levels; marketing changes; or the installation of a data processing system.

Standard 406 also permits the use of a 12-month period other than the fiscal year as the cost accounting period if its use is an established practice. In addition, it permits the use of a transitional cost period, limited to a total of 15 months, whenever there is a change of fiscal year. Such a "change in accounting practice" is, of course, subject to that portion of the regulations.

The standard does not require that the indirect cost rates used to expedite the closing of contracts be based on the actual data for the 12-month cost accounting period. It points out that indirect rates developed for that purpose can be used as long as they represent estimates for the full 12-month cost accounting period.

Standard 407: Use of Standard Costs For Direct Material and Direct Labor

This standard deals with written policy for establishing standard costs, standard costs recorded in formal accounts, standard costs and variances booked at production unit level, criteria for labor standards, criteria for material standards, material price and quantity variance from standard, and labor cost rate and time variance from standard.

Standard 407 designates the following standard costs: labor rate, labor time, material price, and material quantity standards. It requires that:

1. Criteria for standard setting and revision be written and followed consistently.

2. Cost standards and variances be entered in the books at the production unit level.

3. Material price variances be recognized at the time purchases of material are entered into the books of account or at the time material cost is allocated to production units. (If these variances are recognized at the time purchases of material are entered into the books of account, they must be accumulated separately by homogeneous groupings of material. If they are recognized at the time material cost is allocated to production units, they may be combined with material quantity variances to form a single material cost variance account.)

4. Labor cost variances be recognized at the time labor cost is incurred in producing units. Similar to material variances, labor rate variances and labor time variances may be combined into one labor cost variance account.

5. Annual allocation of all variances to cost objectives, including ending in-process inventory, be based on various criteria described in the standard.

Standard 408: Accounting for Costs of Compensated Personal Absences

This standard covers: (1) vacation, sick leave, and holiday costs; (2) establishment of cost incurred when liability occurs (i.e., the accrual basis of accounting); and (3) method of determining amounts.

This standard is intended to improve the way in which the costs of compensated personal absence, such as vacation, sick leave, and holidays are determined, and to increase the probability that the costs will be allocated to the proper cost objectives and to the ap-

propriate cost accounting period. Basically, it requires that these costs be assigned to the cost accounting period when the employee earns the right to be paid for the absences. Standard 408 also notes the 406 requirement that costs of compensated personal absences for the entire cost accounting period (usually 12 months) be allocated among final cost objectives during that entire period.

This standard has significant implications for those companies that are either growing or shrinking markedly, because of the lag between the time employees earn certain compensated personal absences (such as vacation) and the actual payment. Since the standard requires the accrual method of accounting, it can make a considerable difference for some companies in determining costs by accounting periods.

Determination of the cost coincides with the time the contractor becomes liable for eventual payment to the employee. Compensated personal absences will be considered as earned and, therefore, a cost to the company, only in the cost accounting period when it is paid—which is equivalent to the cash basis of accounting—as long as no outstanding liability is due the employee.

In determining the amount for the period, a company should take into account the anticipated nonuse of compensated personal absence. In other words, a company should not include as a cost an amount for compensated personal absences that is due but will, in all probability, never be paid. For example, when a company grants vacation periods, but for one reason or another the employee cannot take the vacation, the company never actually incurs the cost.

For determining the amount of cost, a company can use either the current or anticipated wage rates that will be in effect when the liability is paid. For example, if a group of employees is presently being paid an average of $10 an hour when vacation is earned but will be paid $11 per hour in the future when the vacation is actually taken, then either of these rates can be used in determining the cost for the period when the vacation is earned.

The adoption of a new plan or a change to an existing plan may increase the liability at the beginning of the first cost accounting period for which that new plan or change is effective. In that event, the excess costs may not be recognized as costs for the period in which the recognition of the greater liability occurs. The excess costs should be held in a "suspense account" and charged as a contract cost when the amount of the total suspense account is greater than the liability for a future period.

Standard 409: Depreciation of Tangible Capital Assets

This standard addresses: (1) service lives based on records of past retirements; (2) grouping of assets; (3) two-year period to develop records of past retirements; (4) modification of depreciation life for expected physical economic changes; (5) no experience with similar equipment (IRS guideline data); (6) sampling of asset lives; (7) method of depreciation as a reflection of consumption of services (financial statement basis ordinarily acceptable); and (8) gains and losses on disposition of assets.

This standard furnishes guidelines for determining the cost of tangible capital assets assignable to the several cost accounting periods over which the assets are used and provides criteria for allocating depreciation costs to the various cost objectives within the accounting periods. It states that annual depreciation costs should be a financial measure of the use of the tangible assets and, as a result, those costs should flow systematically and rationally to the various accounting periods over which the assets are used.

The total cost of the asset subject to depreciation is the amount of the capitalized cost less its estimated residual value. The method of depreciation to be used—straight-line,

sum-of-the-years-digits, declining-balance, etc.—should be based on the pattern of consumption of services furnished by the asset over its entire life. For example, if a significant amount of a particular asset is consumed in its early stages, a depreciation method that results in higher amounts in the earlier years should be used. In contrast, if an asset is used up in equal annual amounts over its service life, the straight-line method of depreciation would more accurately reflect its use pattern. This standard describes a variety of criteria to help determine the asset consumption by accounting periods.

Depreciation may be charged directly to cost objectives under certain circumstances, but it should be allocated to appropriate indirect cost pools in other circumstances. If depreciation costs are charged directly to cost objectives rather than to indirect cost pools, the contractor must consistently charge depreciation costs of all similar assets used for similar purposes in the same manner. The years of service life for assets must be based on the contractor's actual experience with the retirement of similar assets.

This standard describes some of the techniques for its application by giving background on the nature of depreciation charges. These charges basically consist of two factors: (1) the number of years the asset will be used (i.e., its service life); and (2) the likely pattern of the consumption or use of the asset for each year of its useful life, commonly defined as the depreciation method.

In determining these factors, the standard considers both physical and economic aspects, including the quantity and quality of expected use of the asset in terms of its output, the amount of repair and maintenance, the particular cost accounting periods during which such costs would be incurred, and technical or economic obsolescence (which can be substantial depending on the industry).

This standard requires that a consistent policy—which recognizes that assets are acquired during the year, not just at the beginning—be followed for determining the beginning and ending cost accounting periods of asset use. Assets need not be dealt with individually under the standard if a combination of assets is simpler and more practical for the contractor. Again, consistency is important in making the decision. Under this standard, the estimated years of usefulness, or service life, must be based on the contractor's actual experience with similar assets and must be supported adequately by records maintained for retirements or withdrawal from active use.

For determining the number of years an asset will be used, the standard permits a modification based on changes that might be expected in the future. For example, a replacement asset for a piece of equipment that lasted 10 years in the past may not last 10 years in the future. The contractor must fully demonstrate that the future life of the replacement equipment is less than 10 years, for reasons such as changes in the quality or quantity of expected output of the newly acquired asset or changes related to its economic usefulness, influenced by technical or economic obsolescence of the asset prospectively.

If the contractor has had no experience with a particular type of asset, he can estimate the future service life of newly acquired assets on the basis of the Internal Revenue Code guideline period (mid-range). However, once the contractor has acquired sufficient experience, he must use the data based on that experience. This standard also permits the contracting parties to agree on shorter estimated service lives if the equipment is being acquired or used for unique purposes.

Standard 409 specifically points out that the depreciation method used for financial accounting purposes (not federal income tax purposes) must be used for contract costing purposes, unless it does not reflect the expected consumption of asset services or is unacceptable for federal income tax purposes. This provision is important because

it focuses on the depreciation method. For this reason, a contractor's choice of a method can be significant in relation to government costing purposes; it should be very carefully thought out.

If a contractor decides to change the method of depreciation for newly acquired assets from the one used for like assets under similar conditions, he must document that decision by projecting the expected consumption of services of those new assets. To change a depreciation method for newly acquired assets, the contractor should develop the proper technical support to justify the change, using the criteria described in the standard.

This standard points out that an amount should be determined and considered in arriving at the total cost subject to depreciation, as long as the estimated residual value is greater than 10 percent of the asset cost. In this case, the standard seems to have adopted a practical threshold that precludes taking into account residual values less than 10 percent of the asset cost. The standard also says that the residual value need not be deducted from capitalized costs in determining depreciable costs when the depreciation method used is either the declining-balance or the class-life asset method.

A contractor may revise the estimated service life or depreciation method, as well as the residual value, during the life of the asset when its operational circumstances or other outside factors change so significantly that distortions would result if modifications were not made.

Gains and losses when assets are sold must be allocated to the cost accounting period when the disposition is actually made. When assets combined or grouped along with other assets for service life and depreciation purposes are disposed of, gains or losses are not to be recognized but must be processed through the accumulated depreciation reserve account. In addition, if an asset is traded in on a new asset, gains or losses are included in computing the depreciable cost of the new asset.

Industry objected to this standard primarily because it believed recognition of cost (via longer service life) would be delayed and, hence, significantly decrease cash flow to the contractor from depreciation costs included in contract pricing. Industry's objections were so strong that the CASB departed from its usual promulgation process and republished the proposed standard for a second round of comments.

In addition, congressional hearings were held in response to the strong opposition. The CASB stated, in its testimony, that it intended to issue another standard that would tend to offset some of the claims of negative effects raised by contractors. This standard became 414, Cost of Money as an Element of the Cost of Facilities Capital.

Standard 410: Allocation of Business Unit General and Administrative Expenses to Final Cost Objectives

This standard deals with: (1) the definition of G&A expenses; (2) the allocation of G&A expenses only to final cost objectives; and (3) the use of cost input base (sales/cost of sales not acceptable) to allocate G&A expenses, including total production cost, value added (labor and overhead but excluding material and subcontract cost), single-element cost input (such as labor cost), and special allocations.

This standard provides criteria for allocating G&A expenses on the basis of their beneficial/causal relationship to final cost objectives. It intends to achieve a higher degree of objectivity as well as a higher degree of comparability among contractors in such allocations.

G&A expense as included in this standard is: "Any management, financial and other expense which is incurred by or allocated to a business unit and which is for the general management and administration of the business unit as a whole. G&A expense does not include those management expenses whose beneficial or causal relationship to cost objectives can be more directly measured by a base other than a cost input base representing the total activity of a business unit during a cost accounting period."

Several fundamental requirements are described in this standard:

1. G&A expenses should be accumulated in a single indirect, cost pool and allocated only to final cost objectives.

2. The G&A expense pool should generally be allocated via a cost input base representing the total activity of the business unit.

3. If G&A expenses have a particular beneficial/causal relationship to a particular cost objective that is not reflected in the amounts allocated on a cost input basis, special allocations must be made.

4. If the contractor includes costs that do not now satisfy the definition of G&A expenses but have historically been classified as G&A expenses, these expenses can remain in the pool unless they can be allocated to cost objectives on a beneficial or causal relationship measured by a base other than cost input.

Various techniques may be used to apply these requirements. Where one segment of a contractor's operation incurs G&A expenses that benefit another segment, these expenses must be removed from the pool of the incurring segment and allocated to the benefiting segment on a beneficial or causal relationship basis. The G&A expense pool may be combined with other non-G&A expenses for allocation to final cost objectives only if the combined pool is appropriate for allocation under the standard.

The cost input base required in the standard for allocating G&A expenses basically underlines the premise that G&A costs incurred in any cost accounting period are related to the total activity during that period as measured by costs incurred. Although, historically, many companies allocated G&A expenses on the basis of cost of goods sold, the CASB concluded that this base is not indicative of the total activity carried out during the period since the cost of goods sold is merely an accounting reflection of the items sold during the period without taking into account increases or decreases in inventory levels, which is a measure of plant/company activity.

Although the standard favors the total cost input as the generally acceptable measure of the total activity of a business unit, it permits several alternatives, such as value-added and single-element cost input. The standard points out that the value-added cost input, which excludes material and subcontract costs, may be appropriate when the inclusion of these costs would distort the allocation of G&A expenses in proportion to the benefits received. While the standard permits the use of a single-element cost input base, such as direct labor hours or dollars, it points out that this base may not produce equitable results when that single element does not really indicate the total activity of the cost objectives involved or is an insignificant part of the total cost of at least some of the final cost objectives.

CAS 9904.410-40(b)(1) prohibits cost of sales/services as an allocation base for G&A and requires a cost input base (but not necessarily *total* cost): "The G&A expense pool of a business unit for a cost accounting period shall be allocated to final cost objectives of that cost accounting period by means of *a* cost input base representing the total activity of the business unit....The cost input base selected shall be the one which best represents the total activity of a typical cost accounting period." (Emphasis added)

CAS 9904.410.50(d) expands on the different cost input base alternatives. "The cost in-put base selected to represent the total activity of a business unit during a cost accounting period may be: Total cost input; *value-added cost input*; or single element cost input. The determination of which cost input base best represents the total activity of a business unit must be judged on the basis of the circumstances of each business unit." (Emphasis added) Furthermore, this CAS citation states: "Value-added cost input *shall* be used as an allocation base where inclusion of material and subcontract costs would significantly distort the allocation of the G&A expense pool in relation to the benefits received, and where costs other than direct labor are significant measures of total activity. A value-added cost input base is total cost input less material and subcontract costs."

Some have mistakenly interpreted the CAS provisions to state a preference for a total cost input base. This CAS citation should be sufficient to reject this misconception. The DOD CAS Working Group attempted to clarify this in Working Group Item 78-21 (Amendment 1): "There is no specific statement of preference in the standard." In addition, this item states: "The existence of a wide range of material and subcontract content among contracts may signal the precondition for a potential significant distortion."

The DCAA Contract Audit Manual at DCAM 8-410.1 expands on these points: "The selection of the best base [for G&A] involves judgments on whether inclusion of certain base costs cause 'distortions' in allocating G&A to some contracts....The ASBCA, in essence, ruled that there is no preferred allocation base to distribute G&A expenses other than the one which best represents total activity (Ford Aerospace and Communications Corporation, Aeronutronic Division, ASBCA No. 23833). The following are some examples where the value-added or single-element base may be appropriate: ...Contractors whose business activity is clearly labor intensive, but have contracts that include major purchasing and subcontracting responsibility on a 'pass-through' basis which causes significant distortions in allocated G&A. Consideration should be given to a value-added or single element base."

This standard describes how the cost allocations received from a home office should usually be included in the receiving segment's G&A expense pool. These costs would consist of various line management costs of particular segments or groups, any residual expenses allocated from the home office, and any directly allocated expense related to the general management and administration of the receiving segment as a whole.

Separate allocations from the home office related to such specialized functions as centralized services, staff management of specific activities (e.g., engineering, manufacturing), or central payments or accruals received by a segment (e.g., taxes), however, should not be allocated to the receiving segment's G&A expense pool. These various techniques may be used to apply these requirements. Where one segment of a contractor's operation incurs G&A expenses that benefit another segment, these expenses must be removed from the pool of the incurring segment and allocated to the benefiting segment on a beneficial or causal relationship basis. The G&A expense pool may be combined with other non-G&A expenses for allocation to final cost objectives only if the combined pool is appropriate for allocation under the standard.

This standard recognizes that, in certain companies, a home office segment might perform the home office functions and also be responsible for an operating segment that has its own final cost objectives. In these circumstances, the expenses of the home office functions should be segregated from those of the operating segment.

While this standard requires that G&A expenses be allocated to items produced or worked on for stock (since those costs represent part of the cost input base), it recognizes that some contractors do not charge G&A expenses to inventory in their account-

ing records. Therefore, this standard permits contractors to use the G&A rate of the cost accounting period in which the items are issued to final cost objectives in determining the G&A expense applicable to those issues of stock.

In addition, this standard also realizes that a certain final cost objective, in relation to other cost objectives, may receive significantly more or less benefit from G&A expenses than would ordinarily be recognized by the allocation methods described. In those circumstances, the standard permits special agreements between the contracting parties to allocate the expenses in different amounts to more appropriately accomplish its beneficial/causal objectives. The cost objectives and amounts of G&A expenses subject to special allocations should be excluded from base and pool before the rest of the G&A expenses are allocated to all other cost objectives.

Standard 411: Accounting for Acquisition Costs of Materials

This standard: (1) requires policies and practices in writing; (2) permits costing methods, such as first-in, first-out (FIFO), last-in, first-out (LIFO), weighted/moving average, and standard costs; (3) rejects annual LIFO adjustment method; (4) requires consistency for similar material; (5) charges material to cost objectives; and (6) provides for allocating cost of materials to indirect functions.

Generally, this standard provides criteria for determining the cost of materials, including the inventory costing method to be used. According to the CASB, it should improve the measurement and assignment of costs to cost objectives as well as to cost accounting periods.

CAS 411 contains a few fundamental requirements, such as written statements of accounting policies and practices for material costs and the methods to be used in allocating such costs to cost objectives. In addition, while it permits a contractor to allocate the costs of material used directly in production directly to an indirect cost pool, if those costs are not consumed in a particular cost accounting period, the standard requires that the amount not used up, when significant, be established as an asset at the end of the period.

The standard also seeks to achieve uniformity in a contractor's methods by requiring that the same costing method be used within the same business unit for similar categories of materials. This standard includes in its definition of material costs the acquisition costs of the material, properly adjusted for any extra charges, discounts, or credits that might have been earned. That inclusion does not mean, however, that the contractor is prevented from accumulating net adjustments in appropriate overhead pools and allocating them in some consistent fashion to cost objectives.

This standard permits the several conventional inventory costing methods to be used when materials are issued from company-owned inventory, such as (1) FIFO, (2) LIFO, (3) weighted/average cost, (4) moving/average cost, or (5) standard cost. It precludes, however, the use of the annual LIFO adjustment method of determining inventory costs. According to the CASB, this method of inventory valuation violates the "systematic and rational costing of issues of materials to cost objectives." To offset this prohibition, however, the standard permits direct charging of materials to contracts where the materials are appropriately identified.

Standard 412: Composition and Measurement of Pension Cost

The following key issues are covered in this standard: (1) components of pension costs, including defined-contribution plans and defined-benefit plans; (2) handling of unfunded actuarial liabilities; (3) methods of measuring pension costs, including accrued benefit cost method and projected benefit cost method; (4) actuarial assumptions; and (5) assignment of pension costs to periods on the basis of liability that has to be liquidated or compelled.

This standard contains criteria for determining the amount of pension costs that is applicable to particular cost accounting periods as well as guidelines for calculating the essential elements of pension costs. The standard deals broadly with two types of pension plans: defined-benefit and defined-contribution. A defined-benefit plan is one in which the benefits to be paid in the future are firmly established in the present. Contributions paid by the employer are the pension costs, which are intended to pay benefits to employees in some future period. By contrast, a defined-contribution plan is one in which the ultimate benefits are unknown. Only the employer's contributions are known.

Under each plan, different elements contribute to the total pension costs paid. Under a defined-benefit pension plan, several specific elements constitute the total cost: (1) the normal cost for the period; (2) part of any unfunded actuarial liability; (3) an interest equivalent on the unamortized portion of any unfunded actuarial liability; and (4) an adjustment for any actuarial gain or loss that might be present. In the defined-contribution pension plan, on the other hand, the amount of the net contribution required for that particular cost accounting period, after dividends and other credits where applicable, determines the total cost.

For defined-benefit pension plans accounted for under the pay-as-you-go cost method, the components of pension cost for a cost accounting period are: (1) the net amount of periodic benefits paid for that period; and (2) an amortization installment, including an interest equivalent on the unamortized settlement amount, attributable to amounts paid to irrevocably settle an obligation for periodic benefits due in current and future cost accounting periods.

For defined-benefit pension plans other than those accounted for under the pay-as-you-go cost method, the amount of pension costs of a cost accounting period must be determined by use of an immediate-gain actuarial cost method. Each actuarial assumption used to measure pension cost is to be identified separately and is to represent the contractor's best estimates of anticipated experience under the plan, taking into account past experience and reasonable expectations. The validity of each assumption used should be evaluated solely with respect to that assumption. Actual assumptions used in calculating the amount of an unfunded liability should be the same as those used for other components of pension cost.

Except for costs assignable to future periods, the amount of pension cost computed for a cost accounting period is assignable only to that period. For defined-benefit pension plans other than those accounted for under the pay-as-you-go cost method, the pension cost is assignable only if the sum of (1) the unamortized portions of assignable unfunded actuarial liability and (2) the unassignable portions of unfunded actuarial liability separately identified and maintained equals the total unfunded actuarial liability. Pension costs assigned to a cost accounting period are allocable to intermediate and final cost objectives only if they meet the requirements for allocation. Pension costs not meeting these requirements may not be reassigned to any future cost accounting period.

A liability is considered liquidated during a period if funding actually occurs by the time the federal income tax return is filed. The standard defines "actuarial liability" as "Pension cost attributable, under the actuarial cost method in use, to years prior to the date of a particular evaluation. As of such date the actuarial liability represents the excess of the present value of the future benefits and administrative expenses over the present value of future contributions for the normal cost for all plan participants and beneficiaries. The excess of the actuarial liability over the value of the assets of a pension plan is the unfunded actuarial liability."

Since many pension plans carry a certain amount of unfunded actuarial liability, the standard addresses the required cost accounting for that amount. When part of any unfunded liability is included in pension costs, it must be separately identified and included in equal annual installments. Further, the annual installments must include two elements: an amortized portion of the liability plus an interest equivalent on the unamortized portion of that liability.

If the contractor has already begun amortizing the unfunded actuarial liability, this standard requires no change in the amortization period adopted by the contractor. If, on the other hand, the contractor had not yet started amortization when this standard was issued, the amortization period could be no more than 30 years or less than 10 years, except if the plan was in existence on January 1, 1974. In that case, the amortization period cannot exceed 40 years or be less than 10.

This standard requires that pension cost applying to prior years that was specifically unallowable then under existing government contract provisions must be separately identified and eliminated from any unfunded actuarial liability being amortized. The standard also stipulates that when a defined-benefit pension plan is funded exclusively with individual or group permanent insurance or annuity contracts, the plan be treated as a defined-contribution plan even though it may, in fact, be called a defined-benefit pension plan.

Under those plans where the benefits that ultimately flow to the employees are a function of salaries and wages, the calculation of "normal cost" for the year must be based on a percentage of the payroll. On the other hand, where the pension benefit is not a function of salaries and wages, the calculation is based on employee service.

To avoid any short-term fluctuations, this standard proposes that actuarial assumptions reflect long-term rather than short-term trends. This standard requires that any pension costs funded in excess of amounts computed as applying to a cost accounting period consistent with the criteria in the standard be applied to pension costs of future cost accounting periods, not the current cost accounting period.

Standard 413: Adjustment and Allocation of Pension Cost

Standard 413 covers the following issues: (1) annual actuarial gains and losses, including immediate-gain actuarial method and spread-gain actuarial method; (2) circumstances requiring separate calculation of pension cost by segment, including termination gain or loss, different level of benefits/eligibility/age, different assumptions, and merged plans; and (3) actuarial value of fund assets.

This standard, like 412, Composition and Measurement of Pension Cost, is quite complex. Fundamentally, it requires that: (1) actuarial gains and losses be calculated annually and be assigned to the cost accounting period for which the actuarial valuation is made and to subsequent periods; (2) the value of all pension fund assets be determined under an asset valuation method that accounts for unrealized appreciation and depreciation of pension fund assets; and (3) pension costs be allocated to each segment having participants in a pension plan.

A separate calculation of pension costs for a segment is required when these three conditions are present. When these three conditions are not present, allocations may be made by calculating a composite pension cost for two or more segments and allocating this cost to these segments by means of an allocation base. When pension costs are computed separately for a segment or segments, the assignable cost limitation is based on their as-

sets and liabilities. In addition, the amount of pension cost assignable to a segment or segments may not exceed the maximum tax-deductible amount computed for the plan as a whole and apportioned among the segments.

For contractors who compute a composite pension cost covering plan participants in two or more segments, the base used for allocating such costs must be representative of the factors on which the pension benefits are based. For example, a base consisting of salaries and wages should be used for pension costs that are calculated as a percentage of salaries and wages; a base consisting of the number of participants should be used for pension costs that are calculated as an amount per participant. If pension costs are calculated separately for one or more segments, the contractor should make a distribution among the segments for the maximum tax-deductible amount and the contribution to the funding agency.

When apportioning the maximum tax-deductible amount (which is determined for a qualified defined-benefit pension plan as a whole pursuant to the Employee Retirement Income Security Act of 1974—ERISA) to segments, the contractor must use a base that considers the otherwise assignable pension costs or the funding levels of the individual segments. When apportioning amounts deposited to a funding agency to segments, the contractor must use a base that is representative of the assignable pension costs, determined in accordance with the CAS for the individual segments. However, for qualified defined-benefit pension plans, the contractor may first apportion amounts funded to the segment or segments subject to this standard.

Pension cost for a segment should be calculated separately whenever any of the following conditions materially affect the amount of pension cost allocated to the segment:

1. A material termination of employment gain or loss is attributable to the segment.

2. The level of benefits, eligibility for benefits, or age distribution is materially different for the segment than for the average of all segments.

3. The appropriate actuarial assumptions are, in the aggregate, materially different for the segment than for the average of all segments.

Calculations of termination of employment gains and losses should take into account factors such as unexpected early retirements, benefits becoming fully vested, and reinstatements or transfers without loss of benefits. An amount may be estimated for future reemployments.

Pension cost should also be calculated separately for a segment when: (1) the pension plan for that segment becomes merged with that of another segment, or the pension plan is divided into two or more pension plans; and, in either case, (2) the ratios of market value of the assets to actuarial accrued liabilities for each of the merged or separated plans are materially different from one another after applying the benefits in effect after the pension plan merger or division.

For a segment whose pension costs are required to be calculated separately, such calculations are to be prospective only; pension costs need not be redetermined for prior years. For a segment whose pension costs are required to be calculated separately, an initial allocation of a share in the undivided market value of the assets of the pension plan to that segment should be made as follows:

1. If the necessary data are readily determinable, the funding agency balance to be allocated to the segment should be the amount contributed by, or on behalf of, the segment, increased by income received on such assets and decreased by benefits and expenses paid from such assets. Likewise, the accumulated value of permitted unfunded accruals to be allocated to the segment should be the amount of permitted unfunded accruals assigned to the segment, increased by interest imputed to such assets and decreased by benefits paid from sources other than the funding agency.

2. If the data are not readily determinable for certain prior periods, the market value of the assets of the pension plan should be allocated to the segment as of the earliest date such data are available. This allocation should be based on the ratio of the actuarial accrued liability of the segment to the plan as a whole, determined in a manner consistent with the immediate-gain actuarial cost method or methods used to compute pension cost.

The actuarial value of the assets of the pension plan are to be allocated to the segment in the same proportion as the market value of the assets. If, prior to the time a contractor is required to use this standard, it has been calculating pension cost separately for individual segments, the amount of assets previously allocated to those segments need not be changed. After the initial allocation of assets, the contractor should maintain a record of the portion of subsequent contributions, permitted unfunded accruals, income, benefit payments, and expenses attributable to the segment and paid from the assets of the pension plan. Income and expenses should include a portion of any investment gains and losses attributable to the assets of the pension plan. Income and expenses of the pension plan assets should be allocated to the segment in the same proportion that the average value of assets allocated to the segment bears to the average value of total pension plan assets for the period for which income and expenses are being allocated.

In late 2010 the CASB was in the process of harmonizing the requirements of CAS 412 and 413 with the Pension Protection Act. The latter legislation significantly accelerated payments to defined-benefit pension plans beyond the cost that is allowable per CAS. The proposed CAS revisions would close the gap between the amount required by the Pension Act and the amount allowable per CAS.

Standard 414: Cost of Money As an Element of the Cost of Facilities Capital

This standard deals with measuring the cost of facilities capital, determining "imputed" interest rates, and identifying facilities capital. This standard is an outgrowth of CAS 409, which addresses depreciation, in response to contractors' strong objections that CAS 409 tends to minimize cost recovery related to use of assets.

The CASB recognized an imputed cost of capital for facilities used in performing government contracts. Even though government contract costing does not generally allow interest costs and conventional accounting practice does not permit recording imputed cost of capital, the CASB acknowledged that fixed assets and other facilities used in conducting government business require investment by the contractor. Through this standard, the CASB attempted to recognize and quantify the amount of imputed interest on these investments. The CASB intended to put all contractors on an equal footing as far as recovering the financing costs of facilities, regardless of the extent of debt or equity financing used.

According to this standard, the cost of capital must be computed separately for each contract by identifying those facilities that will be used on the contract and calculating the cost of money in relation to those facilities. The amount so determined is then included as a separate line item of cost in negotiating the contract price.

The investment in capital assets used for computing the cost of money should be based on the accounting information used for contract cost purposes. This information basically includes the fixed assets giving rise to depreciation costs (plus cost of land) that are included in overhead costs applying to government contracts. The net amount of the assets, or depreciated value—rather than the gross—is the base. Any accumulated depreciation incurred by the contractor to date has been recovered in contract pricing and, hence, should not be part of the base for computing the imputed cost of capital on the unrecovered investment in those assets.

The rate to be used is published semiannually by the Secretary of the Treasury under PL 92-41. The cost of capital must be determined for facilities whose related depreciation has been included in each indirect cost pool. In this manner, the cost of capital within each overhead pool can be calculated as part of the overhead rate, and each contract share can be calculated on the basis of the portion of the base contributed by each contract. Basically, if a contractor has only a single government contract for the full year and the facilities' net book value amounted to $1 million, recovery under this standard (assuming an 8 percent rate) would amount to $80,000.

Standard 415: Accounting for the Cost of Deferred Compensation

This standard deals with: (1) cost to be assigned to the period when the obligation is incurred (accrual accounting), including conditions of "obligations incurred"; (2) cost amount as present value of future benefits, including how to determine "future benefits" in the form of money, stock, or options; and (3) forfeitures (cost reduction) in period of occurrence.

This standard applies to the cost of all deferred compensation plans except those dealt with specifically in other standards (i.e., pension plans). It provides criteria for determining the cost of the various deferred compensation plans that companies adopt and for assigning those costs to the appropriate cost accounting periods.

Deferred compensation is an award given for services rendered in one or more cost accounting periods before the date the employee actually receives the award. (Deferred compensation does not include year-end accruals for salaries, wages, or bonuses that are generally paid within a short period of time after the close of the year.) This standard attempts to inject the accrual accounting concept into that of deferred compensation by requiring that the benefits eventually to be paid be assigned to the period when the entitlement was earned. If the benefits are not firmly obligated, however, and thus do not occur in the year the services were rendered, they should be dealt with on a cash basis of accounting when payment is made.

Recognizing that future payments to employees are worth less at the present time than they will be in the future (because of the time value of money), the standard establishes appropriate criteria for discounting the future amounts to be paid in determining present costs.

The firmness of an obligation before it qualifies as a cost in the current accounting period is an important consideration. The future payment of money, other assets, shares of stock, or other items of value must be required so that the contractor cannot unilaterally avoid this payment. Further, the amount of the future payment must be measurable with reasonable accuracy and the recipient of the award must be known. If the terms of the deferred compensation agreement call for certain events, it must be reasonably probable that those events will occur. If these conditions are not met, the cost of the deferred compensation must be included as a cost only in the accounting period when the compensation is actually paid to the employee.

The eventual amount of deferred compensation, when it includes principal plus interest as a fixed rate, must include the interest in the computation. When no interest is included in the award, the compensation is limited to the amount of the award itself.

In calculating the present value of the future award, the amount to be paid has to be discounted to its present value using the Secretary of the Treasury's semiannually published interest rate under PL 92-41.

Forfeitures sometimes occur in deferred compensation plans. When they do, they reduce the amount of the award originally assigned to a prior period plus the same rate of interest described above, compounded annually. The forfeiture calculated in this manner is dealt with as a reduction of the contract cost in the period when the forfeiture occurs.

Logical and reasonable rules apply to determining awards of deferred compensation that are made in other than money. For example, in the case of stock, its market value on the day the award is made is a proper basis for valuation. For stock options, the amount by which the stock's market value exceeds the option price on the measurement date is the proper basis for valuation. For valuing other types of assets, an orientation toward market value is appropriate.

Standard 416: Accounting for Insurance Costs

This standard addresses: (1) calculating the amount of cost for premium payments, including accounting for deposits, reserves and funds, prefunding of retired workers and terminally funded plans, and self-insurance, including purchasing coverage and measuring loss or cost when amounts are paid and unpaid; and (2) allocating cost on the basis of the beneficial/causal relationship, including segment identification and catastrophic losses.

Fundamentally, this standard requires that: (1) the amount of insurance cost be equal to the "projected average loss" for the period plus related administration expenses; and (2) the allocation of insurance costs to cost objectives be based on the beneficial or causal relationship with cost objectives.

The projected average loss can be based on the amount of premium paid, less dividends received, allocated among the cost accounting periods covered by the policy term. Where insurance applies only to a single, final cost objective, the premium need not be prorated among cost accounting periods.

When any part of a premium can be included as a deposit in published financial statements, it should be accounted for as a deposit in determining insurance costs. Deposits include amounts retained by the insurer for inclusion in a reserve (or fund) for the insured's benefit, unless: (1) the reserve objectives are stated in writing; (2) the required reserve amounts are determined actuarially; (3) additions to the reserve are made systematically; and (4) if payments to attain reserve objectives are made from a source other than the reserve, the payments into the reserve are reduced accordingly.

If an insurance program is designed to prefund coverage on retired persons, the following four criteria need to be met: (1) payments must be made to an insurer to establish a reserve specifically for that purpose; (2) the policyholder must have no right of recapture of the reserve as long as any active or retired participant remains alive, unless the financial interests of the remaining participants are satisfied through other means; (3) the annual amount added to the reserve cannot be greater than would be required to apportion the cost of the insurance over the working lives of the active employees; and (4) in a terminally funded plan, the actuarial present value of benefits applying to retired employees must be amortized over 15 years.

In addition to these "funded" types of insurance expenses, this standard recognizes that projected average loss may be based on a program of "self-insurance." If insurance could be purchased against the self-insured risk, its cost could be used as the amount of the projected average loss, adjusted in the future for actual loss experience the same way that purchased insurance would be. On the other hand, if insurance cannot be bought, the amount of projected average loss must be based on the contractor's experience, relevant industry experience, and -anticipated conditions in accordance with accepted actuarial principles. In these cir-cum-stances, the amount of actual losses may be used as costs for the period only if they are expected to approximate the projected average loss. However, any actual losses arising under self-insurance programs for retired persons should be allowed as costs for the period unless a reserve is established.

Under a self-insurance plan, actual losses are measured by: (1) the actual cash value of property destroyed (not depreciated book value); and (2) amounts actually paid to repair damaged estates, to beneficiaries, or to claimants. If claims are not yet paid, they should be estimated in an amount that could be included as an accrued liability in financial statements prepared in accordance with GAAP. If the liability will not be disbursed for more than one year, it should be discounted to its present value.

Standard 417: Cost of Money As an Element of the Cost of Capital Assets Under Construction

This standard establishes criteria for measuring the cost of money attributable to tangible or intangible capital assets under construction as an element of the cost of those assets.

Fundamentally, this standard requires that interest be capitalized by applying an interest rate, determined by the Secretary of the Treasury under PL 92-41, to the construction costs incurred in each accounting period, after appropriately considering the rate at which the construction costs are incurred. For example, if all construction costs of $1 million were made equally during an accounting period, the average construction costs during the period would amount to $500,000. Using an 8 percent interest rate, this means that $40,000 of interest would have to be capitalized.

This standard also states that other methods (Financial Accounting Standard No. 34: Capitalization of Interest Cost) for calculating the cost of money to be capitalized may be used as long as the resulting amount does not differ materially from the one above.

Standard 418: Allocation of Direct and Indirect Costs

This standard addresses: (1) consistent determination of direct and indirect costs; (2) criteria for accumulating indirect costs in cost pools; and (3) guidelines for selecting an allocation measure on the basis of the beneficial or causal relationship between an indirect cost pool and cost objectives.

Each business unit must have a written statement of accounting policies and practices for classifying costs as either direct or indirect. In this connection, the CASB defines a direct cost as one that can be identified specifically with a particular final cost objective, and an indirect cost as one with two or more final cost objectives or one or more intermediate cost objectives.

Actual or standard costs may be used in determining direct labor and material costs. In addition, an average cost or preestablished rates for labor may be used for groups of employees performing interchangeable functions or for groups performing their functions as an integrated team. Significant cost variances should be allocated, at least annually, to cost objectives in proportion to costs previously allocated.

Indirect costs must be accumulated in homogenous cost pools, that is, pools in which all significant costs have similar beneficial or causal relationships to cost objectives.

Each separate cost pool must be allocated to cost objectives in reasonable proportion

to the beneficial or causal relationship of the pooled cost to cost objectives. To comply, the basis used for allocation depends on the type of costs included in the pool. For example, if the cost pool consists primarily of managing direct labor activities, a direct labor hour or dollar base is appropriate. Similarly, if pool costs are primarily facility-related, such as depreciation, maintenance, or utilities, a machine hour base is appropriate.

If overhead pool costs are allocated over a base such as direct labor, those costs are charged to all appropriate direct labor, including final cost objectives (such as contracts), goods produced for inventory, IR&D and B&P projects, process cost centers under a process cost system, intra- or inter-company work, and self-construction of tangible capital assets.

On the other hand, if the pool costs consist primarily of costs other than direct labor management, such as those for occupancy, a service center, or the company aircraft, resource consumption can be specifically identified with cost objectives and the following hierarchy for cost allocation should be followed: (1) a measure of the resource consumption of the cost-pool activities; (2) an output measure of the cost-pool activities; or (3) a surrogate representative of resources consumed, which varies in proportion to the services received.

Indirect cost pools that benefit one another may be allocated using such methods as cross-allocation (reciprocal) or sequential. On the other hand, an indirect cost pool may be allocated using a different base if that base better represents the benefits received by the cost objective.

Standard 420: Accounting for Independent Research And Development (IR&D) and Bid and Proposal (B&P) Costs

This standard covers: (1) types of costs to be included; (2) level of cost accumulation;

(3) method of allocating costs incurred at business unit and home office levels; (4) possible difference in assigning costs to cost accounting periods between IR&D and B&P expenses; and (5) accounting for costs incurred by one segment that benefit other segments.

Some of the standard's more significant fundamental requirements are:

- IR&D and B&P costs are to be accumulated at the individual project level, unless the amounts are not material. If they are not, the costs may be combined into one or more projects, separately identified in cost pools.
- The individual project costs are to include all allocable costs, both direct and indirect, except G&A expenses, and are to be accumulated in cost pools.
- Allocation from cost pools, both at the business unit and home office level, is to be on the basis of the beneficial or causal relationship.

In its promulgation comments, the CASB stated that G&A expenses should not be allocated to IR&D and B&P project costs because these costs are of general benefit and, as such, resemble G&A expenses. Although B&P costs incurred in a cost accounting period may not be assigned to any other period, IR&D costs may be assigned to some other period if permitted under existing laws and regulations or by other controlling factors.

The cost of IR&D and B&P projects performed by one segment for another segment should be considered IR&D and B&P work of the receiving segment, not of the performing segment. The performing segment should allocate G&A expenses to those project costs. Further, where costs of projects incurred at a segment benefit more than one segment of the business unit, they should be allocated as home office projects in accordance with certain criteria. Specifically, contractors first must allocate the costs of projects accumulated at the home office to its segments on a direct basis if such projects can be identified with specific segments. They must then allocate the costs of remaining or residual projects among all segments on the same basis.

DISCLOSURE STATEMENT

The disclosure statement satisfies statutory requirements, establishes a company's cost accounting practices for determining costs under affected government contracts, and provides a data bank of a company's cost accounting practices to be used by the CASB in researching and developing proposed standards.

Dollar Threshold of Contract Awards For Determining Filing Requirements

A disclosure statement is required for any business unit selected to receive a CAS-covered contract or subcontract of $50 million or more. The statement must be submitted prior to contract award. Moreover, any company that, together with all its segments, received net awards of negotiated prime contracts and subcontracts subject to the CAS totaling more than $50 million in its most recent cost accounting period, must submit a disclosure statement before award of its first CAS-covered contract in the immediately following cost accounting period. If the first CAS-covered contract is received within 90 days of the start of the cost accounting period, the contractor is not required to file until the end of 90 days.

When a disclosure statement is required for a company, a separate statement must be submitted for each segment whose costs included in the total price of any CAS-covered contract or subcontract exceed $650,000 unless: (1) the contract or subcontract is of the type or value exempted by the rules; or (2) in the most recently completed cost accounting period, the segment's CAS-covered awards were less than 30 percent of total segment sales for the period *and* less than $10 million.

Each corporate or other home office that allocates costs to one or more disclosing segments performing CAS-covered contracts must submit Part VIII of the disclosure statement. Foreign contractors and subcontractors who are required to submit a disclosure statement may, in lieu of filing a Form No. CASB-DS-1, make disclosure by using a disclosure form prescribed by an agency of their government, provided that the CASB determines that the information disclosed will satisfy the objectives of Public Law 100-679. The use of alternative forms has been approved for contractors in Canada and the Federal Republic of Germany. The submission of a new or revised disclosure statement is not required for any non-CAS-covered contract or from any small business.

For educational institutions, the disclosure requirements are similar to those for commercial organizations. Educational institutions are required to submit disclosure statements for any unit that is part of a college or university location identified in Exhibit A of OMB Circular A-21 that is selected to receive a CAS-covered contract or subcontract in excess of $650,000. This submission must be made prior to contract award. A disclosure statement is not required, however, if the listed entity can demonstrate that the net amount of federal contract and financial assistance awards received during its immediately preceding cost accounting period was less than $25 million.

Any educational institution unit that is selected to receive a CAS-covered contract or subcontract of $25 million or more must submit a disclosure statement before award. Also, any education institution that, together with its segments, received net awards or negotiated prime contracts and subcontracts subject to the CAS totaling $25 million or more in its most recent cost accounting period, of which at least one award exceeded $1 million, must submit a disclosure statement before award

of its first CAS-covered contract in the immediately following cost accounting period. However, if the first CAS-covered contract is received within 90 days of the start of the cost accounting period, the institution is not required to file until the end of 90 days.

Revisions to Disclosure Statements

A disclosure statement must be revised to implement requirements of new standards, to correct noncompliance practices, and to reflect changes in cost accounting practices agreed to by the contracting parties. Equitable adjustments of contract prices apply to these changes.

The CASB defined "cost accounting practice" as any accounting method or technique that is used to measure cost, assign cost to cost accounting periods, or allocate cost to cost objectives.

Measurement of cost encompasses accounting methods and techniques used in defining the components of cost, determining the basis for cost measurement, and establishing criteria for using alternative cost measurement techniques. Determination of the amount paid or a change in the amount paid for a unit of goods and services is not a cost accounting practice. Examples of costs are: (1) the use of historical cost, market value, or present value; (2) the use of standard cost or actual cost; and (3) the designation of those items of cost that must be included or excluded from tangible capital assets or pension cost.

Assignment of cost to cost accounting periods refers to a method or technique used in determining the amount of cost to be assigned to individual cost accounting periods. Examples of cost accounting practices that involve the assignment of cost to cost accounting periods are requirements for the use of specific accrual basis accounting or cash accounting for a cost element.

Allocation of cost to cost objectives includes both direct and indirect allocation of cost.

Examples of cost accounting practices involving allocation of cost to cost objectives are the accounting methods or techniques used to accumulate cost, to determine whether a cost is to be directly or indirectly allocated, to determine the composition of cost pools, and to determine the selection and composition of the appropriate allocation base.

A "change to either a disclosed cost accounting practice" or an established cost accounting practice is any alteration in a cost accounting practice, whether or not such practices are covered by a disclosure statement. However, the initial adoption of a cost accounting practice for the first time a cost is incurred, or a function is created, is not a change in cost accounting practice. Also, the partial or total elimination of a cost or the cost of a function is not a change in cost accounting practice. (Function is an activity or group of activities that is identifiable in scope and has a purpose or end to be accomplished.) Finally, the revision of a cost accounting practice for a cost that previously has been immaterial is not a change in cost accounting practice.

Exemptions

In addition to the CASB's authority to exempt contractors from all or part of its regulations and standards, the only other exemption from filing a disclosure statement for a company otherwise required to do so is allowed when an agency head decides that securing the statement is impractical. In this event, the agency head may authorize award of a contract or subcontract.

Review and Approval of Disclosure Statement

The FAR provides for review and approval of the disclosure statement by the responsible ACO, based on DCAA advice. The auditor's review is confined to determining whether or not the statement adequately describes the cost accounting practices and is current, accurate, and complete.

Ordinarily, the disclosure statement as submitted by the contractor is presumed to be adequate. A disclosure statement is only an expression of a contractor's cost accounting practices and in no way represents approval of such practices by the contracting agency, the CASB, or DCAA.

When a cost accounting practice is changed, the disclosure statement must also be changed. The revised statement is subject to a review similar to the one described above to judge whether the change complies with CASB promulgations and FAR Part 31.

Detailed Requirements of Disclosure Statement

The disclosure statement is quite detailed; it calls for the following data: (1) general information and certification; (2) direct costs; (3) direct versus indirect costs; (4) indirect costs; (5) depreciation and capitalization practices; (5) other costs and credits; (6) pension costs, deferred compensation, and insurance costs; and (6) corporate and/or group expenses.

General Information and Certification

Required data include name of the company and designation of the type of reporting unit (i.e., corporate home office, group, division, or subsidiary). The required certificate states ". . .this statement is the complete and accurate disclosure. . .of its cost accounting practices, as required by the disclosure regulation of the [CASB]."

The general type of information required includes, for the most recently completed fiscal year, amounts of government prime contracts and subcontracts and commercial sales and principal products sold to the government (by SIC code). More detailed information is called for to explain the nature of the cost accounting system (standard job order, process, or average) and the extent of integration of the cost accounting system with financial accounting records.

Direct Costs

Direct costs are materials, labor, and other costs charged as direct (rather than as indirect via overhead) to government or commercial contracts. For material costs, information is requested regarding whether the charge is through an inventory account or directly from purchases. If through an inventory account, the method should be described (i.e., standard or average costs, FIFO, or LIFO). Other information asked for includes the method of accumulating variances from standard (plantwide, by product, by department, etc.), disposition of variances (prorated between inventories and cost of goods sold or charged or credited to overhead), and frequency of standards revisions.

For direct labor costs, information is needed for categories of labor (manufacturing and engineering); classes of labor included in each category; and whether actual or average rates are used, as opposed to standard rates. If standard costs are used, considerable data on variances are required, including type of variance (rate or efficiency) and method of accumulating and disposing of variances, similar to material variances.

Regarding interorganizational transfers of materials and labor costs, information is requested on the calculation of amounts (i.e., at fully absorbed costs, including G&A expenses, full cost plus an arbitrary markup, or catalog/market price).

Direct versus Indirect Costs

A narrative is required to describe when costs are charged as direct versus indirect. In addition, treatment code data need to be completed for direct materials, labor, and miscellaneous costs involved, with appropriate designation of direct versus indirect and related overhead pools where those costs would be charged.

Indirect Costs

Allocation base codes are provided to describe how various indirect, G&A, and service center cost pools are allocated to government contracts. Each of the overhead pools described should be assigned the proper allocation base code to designate how those costs are allocated to government contracts. G&A expenses are handled in a similar manner, by designating how the costs accumulated in these pools are allocated to government contracts.

The disclosure statement describes service centers and departments or functions that perform services for others in the reporting unit. In addition to the allocation base code, the category code and rate code are required to be designated for the various service centers if applicable:

- **Category code.** Generally, costs incurred by service centers are, or can be, charged or allocated: (1) partially to specific final cost objectives as direct costs and partially to other indirect cost pools (such as a manufacturing overhead pool) for subsequent reallocation to several final cost objectives, referred to as Category "A"; and (2) only to several other indirect cost pools (such as manufacturing overhead pool, engineering overhead pool, and G&A expense pool) for later reallocation to several final cost objectives, referred to as Category "B."
- **Rate code.** Some service centers may use predetermined billing or costing rates to charge or allocate the costs (Rate Code A), while others may charge or allocate on an actual basis (Rate Code B).

The disclosure statement requests information about those circumstances when overhead and G&A rates are allocated at less than full rate. For example, subcontract costs may not carry a full G&A allocation or purchased labor may not carry a full overhead allocation.

For IR&D and B&P costs, disclosure must be made for the method of allocation, such as part of G&A pool, as a separate rate, or transferred to corporate or home office level (and subsequently reallocated to all segments on some basis).

Depreciation and Capitalization Practices

For each category of asset (e.g., land improvement, buildings, machinery), a designation is required for cost accounting under government contracts regarding depreciation methods, such as straight-line or declining-balance; method of determining useful life, such as IRS guidelines, replacement experience, or engineering estimate; and treatment of residual value. These methods must then be compared with accounting for financial and tax purposes, and differences must be noted.

Additional questions relate to use charges for fully depreciated assets; gains and losses on disposition of depreciable property; capitalization or expensing of specific costs, such as freight-in installation costs; and minimum dollar and useful life criteria for capitalization.

Other Costs and Credits

The accounting must be explained for miscellaneous costs and credits, such as vacation, holiday, and sick pay; supplemental unemployment benefits; severance pay; miscellaneous receipts (property rental and selling services); and proceeds from employee welfare activities.

Pension Costs, Deferred Compensation, and Insurance Costs

Considerable detailed information regarding pension costs of the three largest plans is required in the following areas: extent of funding; actuarial cost method; frequency of actuarial computations and assumptions; amortization of prior service costs; adjustment for actuarial gains or losses; unrealized gains and losses; and amortization of actuarial gains or losses.

The questions on deferred compensation, like profit-sharing or stock bonus plans, relate to whether or not the plan is qualified under Section 401(a) of the Internal Revenue Code and the method of charging costs to government contracts (i.e., when accrued as a cost, when contributions are made to a trust fund, or when paid to employees).

Insurance questions relate to: method of providing insurance; type of purchased insurance plans; accounting for earned refunds and dividends; employee contributions; employee sharing in refunds and dividends; and self-insured and purchased workers' compensation, liability, and casualty insurance.

Corporate and/or Group Expenses

The disclosure statement segregates these expenses into three categories: directly chargeable to corporate segments for centrally performed services or purchase; separately allocated to a limited group of corporate segments; and residual expenses allocated to all corporate segments.

For each of these three categories, the statement requires an identification of the costs allocated and the method of allocation, using the allocation base previously described. In addition, it questions the circumstances under which segment expenses are transferred to the corporate or group office, whether or not fixed management charges are made to segments in lieu of pro rata or allocation basis, and the extent to which government-owned, company-operated plants are allocated corporate expenses.

CHAPTER 7

Developing Cost Estimates for Proposals

In preparing to negotiate reasonable contract prices, contractors will need to estimate costs. These cost estimates must be developed using good techniques and, when available, sound historical data. In addition, contractors must comply with unique government rules and regulations.

THE ESTIMATING PROCESS

The development of a cost proposal is usually a team effort, with staff from various disciplines such as marketing, engineering, manufacturing, quality control, and finance collaborating. If a proposed product or service is similar or identical to other products or services the company has produced, historical cost data may be valuable in developing the proposed cost.

Cost estimating techniques can vary for products versus services. The guidance in this chapter is intended for both circumstances. For specific techniques, the guidance may have more or less significance for products or for services.

In addition, changes over time in both the nature and amount of costs as well as the method of production should be considered in developing cost estimates. For example, pay rates for direct labor might change, overhead rates might be higher or lower depending on the company's overall business volume, and G&A rates might be substantially different from those actually incurred in performing the prior work. These basic data need to be adjusted and updated to reflect what can reasonably be expected to occur during performance of the contract. An estimate should not be blindly based on historical cost data; in fact, forecast data are more relevant than historical data. On the other hand, for government reviews, historical data are easier to validate than forecasts.

In developing cost estimates for products with which the company has had little experience, individuals in the various functional areas, such as engineering and manufacturing, will usually be responsible for developing estimated hours of production and material as well as subcontractor costs. Estimated hours should be priced at the various labor rates expected to be incurred while working on the contract, and overhead rates should be developed to represent anticipated overhead costs during performance of the contract.

Development of a cost estimate is a very important and complicated part of the proposal. A contractor must be concerned with maintaining a competitive posture but at the same time realizing a fair profit. A contractor is also concerned with responding to the government in a timely fashion while making sure that the estimate is accurate and well-supported to minimize costs questioned by the auditors. During this process, a contractor must recognize and adhere to applicable government cost regulations.

Because this important task is so difficult, the value of a comprehensive set of written policies and procedures defining the requirements of cost estimating cannot be overstated. The following considerations should be included in the written procedures:

- Describe the method for developing pricing rates for both direct and indirect costs.
- Base rates on current, accurate, and complete data as developed from the accounting records.
- Anticipate changes in the size and character of the work force.
- Define the method for computing labor rates (e. g., average versus actual rates).
- Provide for periodic review of established bidding rates to compare actual rates and budgeted amounts.
- Define the method used for computing cost escalation.
- Set timelines and number of quotations and subcontracts needed for procuring material and subcontracts.
- Develop support needed for decrement factors (e.g., experienced reductions in price).
- Set basis for source selection.
- Determine emphasis on the use of quantity discounts for purchases of material items.

Quantity Estimates

Several elements need to be established in the written policies and procedures regarding the development of quantity estimates. Important characteristics include: (1) timeliness of quantitative estimates based on current designs, drawings, and specifications; (2) flexibility of the estimating system to reflect changes (e.g., in manufacturing process and tooling escalation); (3) definition of the steps necessary to develop a basic unit estimate and application of attrition/scrap factors; (4) identification of sources available for determining basic material type and quantity

requirements; (5) application of parametric estimating tools (e.g., learning curve); and (6) application of manufacturing labor standards (e.g., work measurement standards).

Make-or-Buy Decisions

The determination of whether to make or buy an item is very important within the framework of proposal estimating. A "make" item is an item or work effort to be produced by the prime contractor or its affiliates, subsidiaries, or divisions. A "buy" item is an item or work effort to be produced or performed by a subcontractor. The FAR requires prospective contractors to submit make-or-buy programs for all negotiated acquisitions whose estimated value is $10 million or more except when: (1) the proposed contract is for research or development and, if prototypes or hardware are involved, no significant follow-on production is anticipated; or (2) the price is adequately competed or established by catalog or market. The government reserves the right to review and agree on the contractor's make-or-buy program whenever it deems appropriate to ensure a fair and reasonable contract price.

Direct Labor Costs

Direct labor costs are determined by multiplying direct labor hours by direct labor rates.

Direct Labor Hours

Direct labor cost estimates may be grouped according to the two methods used in developing the cost estimates: (1) those developed primarily from the application of technical data; and (2) those developed primarily from recorded direct labor costs. The method used in arriving at an estimate will depend on the nature of the procurement and the extent of the contractor's experience making the item—and thus the associated labor requirements. When the proposal contemplates a research and development contract or a production contract for which the contractor has had no prior cost experience, the labor estimate should be based on technical data. When the contract is a follow-on contract, the labor estimate should be based on prior labor experience, adjusted for expected changes for future work.

For goods and products, the labor hour estimates are more dependent on analysis of the product specifications, historical production experience, learning curves application, work measurement standards, and production routings. For services, the labor hour estimates are more dependent on analysis of the statement of work and may not be critical if the level of effort is established in the Request for Proposals or if the contract type is other than fixed price. The use of historical data has much less relevance when estimating labor hours for service contracts.

When historical cost data are available, the estimated direct labor cost probably will be a projection of those data. Such a direct labor cost projection should not be made on the assumption that the cost pattern or trend will continue unchanged during the period of the proposed contract; it should consider other related factors.

Factors that affect the productivity of labor normally will not be the same today as they were last week or last month. Therefore, labor costs accumulated in the past, adjusted only for changes in the labor rate, or labor costs for the last job lots produced, are not sufficient data on which to base an estimate. Rather, current experience, adjusted for anticipated reductions or other variations, should be used.

An estimate for unusual or "nonrecurring" costs may need to be included. Such costs are not normally disclosed by a routine review of labor because they are usually treated and charged as direct labor costs without further identification or segregation. Nonrecurring costs may be revealed through a review of labor costs for selected tasks, jobs, or cost centers not associated with a normal job or process and a review of job lot records for unusual jobs.

Setup time costs also need to be considered. These are the costs required for changing over a machine or method of production from one job to another; they include the time for tearing down the previous setup and preparing the machine or process for the new operation. Setup may also include the time for the production and inspection of the first acceptable piece or test group of pieces. It does not include the time required to clean up the work area during or at the end of a production period unless regular readjustments need to be made during the production cycle. This readjustment time may be charged either as production or setup time, depending on the contractor's accounting policy and the extent of the readjustment. When the setup for a process job is recorded as the first operation on an operation sheet, the time and cost may be similarly charged.

Other conditions influencing an estimate for labor hours include: (1) supplementary assembly lines established to accommodate temporarily accelerated production schedules or other emergency measures; (2) the introduction of more efficient and cost-effective material issuing and handling procedures to eliminate or prevent bottlenecks and reduce work stoppage; (3) training of employees; (4) transfers of employees between assembly lines, work areas, departments, shifts, and jobs; and (5) special tooling. To determine whether labor hour estimates reflect recent improved conditions, current labor operation sheets must be compared with those in prior periods and with those reflecting advance production schedules.

Direct Labor Rates

In addition to the labor hour estimates, direct labor rates need to be projected. Direct labor rates used to estimate direct labor costs may be at expected individual rates or expected average rates. The latter rates may be either estimated separately for each proposal or preestablished for pricing many proposals submitted over a given period of time.

Contractors may use a variety of methods to combine the various direct labor grades and functions, and the associated pay rates for estimating costs. Methods should take into account: (1) differences in the type, size, and importance of labor operations; (2) the type and arrangement of production facilities; (3) the manner and extent of departmentalization; and (4) the type and dollar values of government and commercial contracts and products.

Individual employee rates may be used when the persons who will perform the work under the proposed contract are known. A determining factor in the award of a contract may be the "know-how" of specific individuals, and their agreement to perform the work under the contract. In other cases, individual rates may be used when the contract requires a caliber of employees whose pay rates do not represent the average rates paid within their labor classifications.

While the use of individual rates in cost estimating will produce precise results, average rates within labor classifications are generally developed and employed for practical purposes. Either approach may result in reasonable estimates provided that a consistent practice is followed and deviations will not affect the proper recovery of anticipated costs.

The development of average rates may include a single plantwide average or a separate average rate for a function, grade, class of labor, cost center, department, or production process. The use of average rates is generally warranted because within each unit of an operating plant, each production situation and associated group of workers usually has a labor norm and cost pattern. Average rates, properly computed and applied, will express the labor norm and equalize the effect of indeterminable factors usually associated with other methods. The use of average rates is preferable, for example, when a contractor is unable to project with any degree of reliance the: (1) identity of those who will perform each operation and, correspondingly, the individual rates of pay; (2) exact production processes to be used, particularly when the contractor has no applicable experience; and (3) precise labor requirements.

Direct Material Costs

Direct material costs include costs of raw materials, purchased parts, subcontracted parts and components, and other material directly identified with the engineering effort or the manufacture of a product. Costs of spoilage, obsolescence, and similar conditions involving losses of direct material associated with production are generally considered loading factors and may be included in indirect costs.

The method of estimating direct material costs depends on the type of accounting and adjunct statistical data available. The data may include directly applicable experience for an entire product, as in the case of a follow-on procurement, or certain parts and components comprising a product, as in the case of an estimate for an item substantially similar or related to an item previously produced. The data also may include general or indirectly applicable experience for factors such as direct material cost per pound of product and ratios of direct material to direct labor for similar products.

Information on which to base estimates for direct material costs usually may be obtained from one or a combination of the following sources: (1) cost records for the last completed contract (appropriately adjusted); (2) cost records for the last lot or a selected number of lots of the last completed contract; (3) experienced direct material costs plotted on an improvement curve relating to the same or similar product or components; (4) priced bills of material; (5) a priced bill of material for a related product (appropriately adjusted);

(6) direct material costs included in a pilot run of a prototype model; (7) a prior cost estimate adjusted to reflect current needs; (8) a budget prepared for the period during which the same or similar item was produced; and (9) experience factors and ratios established for related or unrelated products of similar size and complexity.

A properly prepared bill of material generally will provide a sound basis for estimating direct material cost. The document will contain a detailed listing of the types and quantities required for raw material and for each component and part. It may also include allowances for: (1) expected losses; (2) defects; (3) spoilage during processing; (4) scrap generated; (5) common supply type items, such as welding rods, nuts, bolts, and washers; or (6) other additives to the basic material requirements. When the bill of material contains only the basic material requirements, loading factors stated in the form of percentage of material costs may be applied to provide for expected losses of materials and common supply type items.

When the estimate relates to a follow-on procurement and prior experience exists, the bill of material should be current and should reflect all anticipated changes in the unit quantitative requirements. Current and prior bills of material for the same product should be compared. When the estimate relates to a completely new product, only rough sketches or prints of design may be available for a prototype. The types and quantities of required materials may be developed primarily on the basis of personal experience and judgment. Estimates for completely new products usually involve significant technical determinations.

Sources for pricing components include standard costs, previous purchase order prices adjusted for quantity differences, current vendor quotations, and current order placement prices. When the source is standard costs, the variance factor should be realistic in relation to past, current, and probable future experience. When prices are developed from previous purchases, the prices (stock record cards or purchase orders) should be current and appropriate for the estimated quantity required. When prices are developed from current vendor quotations, sufficient bid solicitations should be obtained.

Contractors may use prices paid for the same items in previous purchases in estimating the material cost of follow-on procurement when current vendor bids have not been obtained. However, they must make sure that: (1) recent purchase orders were selected to obtain applicable prices and adjusted, where necessary, to reflect current and future price trends; (2) prices for purchase orders selected are for comparable quantities required in the follow-on procurement; (3) quantity discounts were taken into consideration when increased quantities are to be purchased; and (4) consideration has been given to reduction in vendors' prices when follow-on purchases reflect the elimination of high start-up costs. When pricing a follow-on contract, contractors should consider the ownership and value of materials that are residual from a preceding government contract and usable on the proposed contract.

Where the preceding contract is cost-type, the residual materials normally will be government-owned; accordingly, if those materials can be used, the contractor should include them in the proposal at no cost. Where the preceding contract was of a fixed-price type subject to price adjustment, the contractor should review the terms of the settlement to determine ownership. If the materials are government-owned, the contractor should include them in the proposal at no cost. If the materials are contractor-owned, the contractor should include them at their original cost, the market price, or the value assigned in negotiating the price of the preceding contract.

The estimated cost of scrap and spoilage may be included in proposals as direct cost, as a percentage factor applied to some other base cost, or as part of indirect cost. However, the method of estimating such cost must be consistent with the accounting method for the proposed contract and the accounting procedures should give proper recognition to any salvageable material generated. When previous procurements for the same or related products are available, these estimates can be based on historical data.

Graphic analyses can be very useful for this purpose. A time series chart can be used to plot the movement of these costs or the percentage relationship to a volume base, such as direct material cost, on a monthly or less frequent interval. A scatter chart can likewise show groups of units produced. Since scrap, spoilage, and rework costs generally are higher during the early stages of a contract and diminish progressively as production techniques improve, plot points that indicate abnormally high costs should be highlighted. The reasons for high costs should then be analyzed, and the likelihood of their recurrence should be assessed.

Provisions for obsolescence and inventory adjustments may be included in cost estimates as percentage factors applied to a cost base or as a part of indirect cost. Percentage factors derived from past experience should be considered. Adjustments for the exclusion of nonrecurring and abnormal writeoff and transfers-back of obsolete material to productive inventory should be made. Commercial companies should ensure that material variance and similar costs are not excluded from cost estimates because the costs may be recorded directly against cost of sales without being charged to production costs.

Other Direct Costs

Other direct costs are costs that by their nature can be considered indirect costs but that, under some circumstances, can be identified specifically with a particular cost objective such as a product, service, program, function, or project. Costs classified as other direct costs vary in accordance with the treatment prescribed by the accounting system and estimating procedures, and often include overtime premium, special tooling, travel and subsistence, computer services, reproduction, and overnight mailings. Various types of other direct costs may be estimated by applying percentage or conversion factors (such as number of staff hours per month) to some other basic cost or to basic estimates of required staff months of effort.

Data accumulated in the accounting system or adjunct statistical records that may be helpful in estimating design engineering include: (1) the total number of basic design hours expended on previous contracts of similar complexity; (2) the number of various types of drawings required and the average number of hours expended by type of drawing for prior contracts of varying degrees of complexity; (3) the percentage factors for support engineering (the direct engineering effort other than that expended by detailed designers working the design department); and (4) percentage factors for engineering effort incidental to changes made during production that represent refinements of the product to attain improved performance.

Production engineering generally represents engineering effort expended during the life of a contract and commences with the completion of the initial design. Initial design is usually segregated from other engineering effort in the accounting or statistical records.

Special tooling is designed to reduce the requirements for direct labor hours and costs, speed production, and improve techniques, tolerances, and finished parts. The term includes jigs, dies, fixtures, molds, patterns, special gauges, and special test equipment used in the production of end items. The term does not include general purpose tools, capital equipment, expendable tools, small hand tools, tools acquired before the contract, replacement tools, and items of tooling that are usable for the production of items not required under the contract.

Special test equipment includes either single or multipurpose integrated test units engineered, designed, fabricated, or modified to accomplish special purpose testing in the performance of the contract. Such testing units comprise electrical, electronic, hydraulic, pneumatic, mechanical, or other items or assemblies of equipment that are mechanically, electrically, or electronically interconnected so as to become a new functional entity, causing the individual item or items to become interdependent and essential for testing the development or production of particular supplies or services. The term "special test equipment" does not include material, special tooling, buildings, and nonseverable structures (except foundations and similar improvements necessary for the installation of special test equipment), and plant equipment items used for general plant testing purposes.

Travel and subsistence costs usually include the costs of transportation, lodging, meals, and incidental expenses incurred by personnel while in travel status. When included as other direct costs, the estimate usually is based on the contemplated number of trips, places to be visited, length of stay, transportation costs, and estimated per diem allowance. Estimates for this cost should consider government Joint Travel Regulation (JTR) per diem rates, transportation rates based on the use of less than first class service, projected transportation costs for personnel, mileage allowances, and a comparison of the current estimate with experienced costs of prior procurements of a similar nature.

The cost for provisions requiring contractor engineering personnel to service delivered equipment, usually referred to as field service expense, may be included in the estimate as a separately identifiable item under other direct costs or as a part of indirect cost. It must com-

ply, however, with the proposed accounting system to be used in costing the contract as well as all applicable CAS.

The cost of installation, maintenance, and repair, and the development of operating instructions may be identified in the records as field service expense, guarantee expense, warranty expense, or reserve for guarantee. The cost estimate may include provision for royalties as a separate identifiable item under other direct costs or as part of indirect costs. Proposals that include such costs should identify preproduction, start-up, and other nonrecurring costs, including such elements as preproduction engineering, special tooling, special plant rearrangement, training programs, initial rework or spoilage, and pilot runs.

Indirect Costs

The estimation of indirect costs and rates requires an understanding of evaluation techniques and insight into to what reasonably may be expected to occur in future operations. The impact of these occurrences and their influence on projected indirect costs and overhead rates must be projected. Knowledge of the accounting policies, particularly those for distinguishing direct costs from indirect costs and the basis for allocating indirect costs to contracts, is necessary for to the development of accurate expense forecasts.

Graphic analyses and statistical techniques can be helpful in evaluating estimated indirect costs. While these techniques alone do not provide a basis for firm forecasts of costs, in appropriate circumstances, they can provide a basis for ascertaining whether estimated costs are within a cost range of what can reasonably be expected in the future.

Indirect cost estimates require consideration of anticipated future operations. They can be based on analyses and projections of historical cost patterns and related data, but they must contemplate changes that may influence the projections.

For example, the accounting policies governing the treatment of certain indirect expenses may change. Such policies may reclassify an expense from direct to indirect or introduce a new method of accumulating and allocating indirect cost. Changes of this nature may affect the estimates for indirect costs and the computation of indirect cost rates.

Management objectives may change as a result of economic conditions and increased competition. For example, in the past management may have emphasized a program to increase sales, while now management is emphasizing a program to reduce costs.

Indirect labor usually represents a substantial portion of indirect costs. Estimates for indirect labor should include analyses of variable, semivariable, and nonvariable classifications in a current representative period. The ratios of each category to direct labor should be computed and compared with similar ratios for estimated cost. Projections of indirect labor requirements and the related costs can also be compared with manpower budgets. Indirect labor wage rates can be determined by reviewing personnel or payroll records. When projected costs include wage increases, the proposed increases must have been approved by management and be in accordance with applicable agreements.

Differentiation should be made in the treatment of the nonvariable, semivariable, and variable components of indirect material cost. Ratios of these expense classifications to appropriate bases should be computed and compared with similar ratios for estimated cost. Projections of indirect labor requirements and the related costs also can be compared with manpower budgets. Indirect labor wage rates can be determined by reviewing personnel or payroll records. Again, when projected costs include wage increases, the proposed increases must have been approved by management and be in accordance with applicable agreements.

Overhead rates can be very difficult to estimate for future periods because a number of factors can influence either the base or overhead pool, both of which influence the rate. As noted, the rate is determined by dividing the overhead cost pool by the base costs, such as direct labor, over which overhead costs are to be allocated.

An overhead pool can consist of a variety of costs incurred by the company to support direct labor actually performing work under the contract. Some overhead costs, such as rent, depreciation, and supervision, are relatively fixed and will continue at substantially the same level regardless of whether direct labor increases or decreases. Other overhead costs, such as supplies, tooling, and fringe benefits of direct labor personnel, tend to vary somewhat in proportion to the amount of direct labor.

As the contractor's direct labor rises and falls in relation to business volume, the overhead rate will change, but not necessarily in the same magnitude. For example, assume that a contractor has sales of $100 million a year and is operating at only 70 percent of capacity with an overhead rate of 200 percent. If sales increase by 25 percent, to $125 million, the overhead rate will probably decrease, for example, to 175 percent because certain fixed costs will not go up proportionately to the higher sales.

In developing cost proposals, the contractor needs to determine, prospectively, the level of sales volume as well as the level of production volume to be able to forecast the labor base. Since prices are based heavily on estimated costs, a lower cost structure will produce lower prices, and vice versa. The contractor should, of course, always project realistic forecasts for overhead rates.

How important is the accuracy of overhead rate forecasts? The answer varies depending on the nature of the contracts. If the contractor is overly optimistic in forecasting overhead rates in an FFP contract, the result may be lower profits or even a loss on the contract if higher overhead rates are incurred when the contract is being performed. Conversely, in a cost-reimbursement contract, the contractor is not nearly as financially exposed by an inaccurate forecasting of overhead rates (or any other cost for that matter) since the contractor is entitled to be reimbursed for actual costs incurred up to the ceiling in the contract (or any ceiling rates specified in the contract). For example, a contractor may forecast a 150 percent overhead rate during contract negotiations and incur a 200 percent overhead rate during contract performance. Under these circumstances, the contractor is entitled to reimbursement of actual costs, which reflect the 200 percent overhead rate.

The same principle applies to G&A expenses. A contractor must look into the future period of contract performance and: (1) forecast, as accurately as possible, the costs that will be included in the G&A pool; (2) properly relate the G&A cost pool to the base costs estimated to be incurred during that period; and (3) develop a rate that will be applied to the estimated costs of the base.

Frequent audit issues address proper indirect cost rates for proposals. Some government auditors rely exclusively on historical indirect cost rates to the exclusion of all facts relevant to the period of time when the priced work will be performed. Estimating indirect cost rates in this manner is a dangerous practice. Budgets are vital, yet many companies do not have budgets covering the entire period of a prospective contract. For example, for a five-year contract, a contractor may have budgets for two years and simply use the year 2 indirect cost rate for the remaining three years in the proposal. Some government auditors demand a budget for each of the five years.

INDIRECT COST ESTIMATING WORKSHEET

Figures 22 and 23 present worksheets to assist in estimating indirect costs. Figure 22 is the employee worksheet, which requires input for either individual employees or groups of employees. Required information includes salary level, planned or targeted utilization (i.e., the percentage of time other than indirect), and incentive compensation. Figure 23 is the fringe benefit worksheet, which consists of statutory benefits, paid absences, and other benefits. Estimates may be in lump-sum amounts or rates per person per year, per total compensation, etc.

Figure 24 is the overhead worksheet (one worksheet per cost pool). This worksheet consists of indirect labor, building facilities, equipment facilities, and miscellaneous costs. Inputs are either lump-sum amounts or rates per employee, etc. Figure 25 is the worksheet for G&A costs, which include indirect labor (executive and administrative), fringe benefits on indirect labor, building facilities, equipment facilities, business development (sales, marketing, bid and proposal, and independent research and development), miscellaneous costs, unallowable costs, and corporate allocations.

SUBMITTING PRICE PROPOSALS

The instructions for submitting price proposals when cost or pricing data are required are contained in FAR Table 15-2, and are essentially carryovers from those formerly used in conjunction with the Standard Form 1411, Price Proposal Cover Sheet, which is now obsolete.

General Instructions

Note 1 to FAR Table 15-2 describes the requirement for submitting cost or pricing data that are derived from FAR Part 15 and the Truth in Negotiations Act. Offerors are reminded that a distinction exists between submitting cost or pricing data and merely making available books, records, and other documents without identification or elaboration. The offeror's requirement for submission of cost or pricing data is met when

Figure 22
EMPLOYEE WORKSHEET

Employee	Average Salary	Total Salaries	Utilization Target	Incentive Compensation	Direct Labor	Paid Absences	Training & Meetings	Other Indirect	B&P	IR&D	Total	Direct Labor	Paid Absences	Training & Meetings	Other Indirect	B&P	IR&D	Incentive Compensation	Total Labor $
Direct																			
20 Systems Analyst I	$50,000	$1,000,000	90.00%	5.00%	77.45%	12.98%	0.96%	8.61%	0.00%	0.00%	100.00%	$774,519	$129,808	$9,615	$86,058	$0	$0	$50,000	$1,050,000
10 Systems Analyst II	60,000	600,000	85.00%	5.00%	73.15%	12.98%	0.96%	12.91%	0.00%	0.00%	100.00%	438,894	77,885	5,769	77,452	0	0	30,000	630,000
5 Systems Analyst III	70,000	350,000	90.00%	5.00%	77.45%	12.98%	0.96%	8.61%	0.00%	0.00%	100.00%	271,082	45,433	3,365	30,120	0	0	17,500	367,500
35 Programmer I	40,000	1,400,000	90.00%	5.00%	77.45%	12.98%	0.96%	8.61%	0.00%	0.00%	100.00%	1,084,327	181,731	13,462	120,481	0	0	70,000	1,470,000
18 Programmer II	50,000	900,000	90.00%	5.00%	77.45%	12.98%	0.96%	8.61%	0.00%	0.00%	100.00%	697,067	116,827	8,654	77,452	0	0	45,000	945,000
7 Programmer III	60,000	420,000	90.00%	5.00%	77.45%	12.98%	0.96%	8.61%	0.00%	0.00%	100.00%	325,298	54,519	4,038	36,144	0	0	21,000	441,000
5 Quality Control	80,000	400,000	80.00%	5.00%	68.85%	12.98%	0.96%	17.21%	0.00%	0.00%	100.00%	275,385	51,923	3,846	68,846	0	0	20,000	420,000
90 Other Employees	65,000	5,850,000	90.00%	5.00%	59.45%	12.98%	0.96%	6.61%	5.00%	15.00%	100.00%	3,477,938	759,375	56,250	386,438	292,500	877,500	292,500	6,142,500
190 (Employees) Subtotal		$10,920,000		5.00%	67.26%	12.98%	0.96%	8.09%	2.68%	8.04%	100.00%	$7,344,510	$1,417,500	$105,000	$882,990	$292,500	$877,500	$546,000	$11,466,000
Overhead																			
1 Manager	$150,000	$150,000	10.00%	5.00%	8.61%	12.98%	0.96%	77.45%	0.00%	0.00%	100.00%	$12,909	$19,471	$1,442	$116,178	$0	$0	$7,500	$157,500
1 Administrative Assistant	35,000	35,000	15.00%	0.00%	12.91%	12.98%	0.96%	73.15%	0.00%	0.00%	100.00%	4,518	4,543	337	25,602	0	0	0	35,000
1 Project Accountant	45,000	45,000	80.00%	0.00%	68.85%	12.98%	0.96%	17.21%	0.00%	0.00%	100.00%	30,981	5,841	433	7,745	0	0	0	45,000
3 (Employees) Subtotal		$230,000		3.26%	21.05%	12.98%	0.96%	65.01%	0.00%	0.00%	100.00%	$48,407	$29,856	$2,212	$149,525	$0	$0	$7,500	$237,500
Total		$11,150,000		4.96%	66.30%	12.98%	0.96%	9.26%	2.62%	7.87%	100.00%	$7,392,917	$1,447,356	$107,212	$1,032,516	$292,500	$877,500	$553,500	$11,703,500
General and Administrative																			
Executives																			
1 President		$200,000		10.00%		12.98%		87.02%			100.00%		$25,962		$174,038			$20,000	$220,000
1 Vice President		150,000		5.00%		12.98%		87.02%			100.00%		19,471		130,529			7,500	157,500
1 CFO		120,000		5.00%		12.98%		87.02%			100.00%		15,577		104,423			6,000	126,000
3 (Employees) Subtotal		$470,000		7.13%		12.98%		87.02%			100.00%		$61,010		$408,990			$33,500	$503,500
Administrative																			
1 Accounting		$45,000		5.00%		12.98%		87.02%			100.00%		$5,841		$39,159			$2,250	$47,250
1 Human Resources		60,000		5.00%		12.98%		87.02%			100.00%		7,788		52,212			3,000	63,000
1 Information Technology		80,000		5.00%		12.98%		87.02%			100.00%		10,385		69,615			4,000	84,000
1 Purchasing		50,000		5.00%		12.98%		87.02%			100.00%		6,490		43,510			2,500	52,500
4 (Employees) Subtotal		$235,000		5.00%		12.98%		87.02%			100.00%		$30,505		$204,495			$11,750	$246,750
Total General and Administrative		$705,000		6.42%		12.98%		87.02%			100.00%		$91,514		$613,486			$45,250	$750,250
200 Employees		$11,855,000		5.05%	62.36%	12.98%	0.90%	13.88%	2.47%	7.40%	100.00%	$7,392,917	$1,538,870	$107,212	$1,646,001	$292,500	$877,500	$598,750	$12,453,750

Figure 23
FRINGE BENEFIT CALCULATION WORKSHEET

Fringe Benefits	Dollars	Base Amt.	Base Name	Rate			Source/Assumption
Statutory							
Social Security Taxes	$774,123	12,485,850	Salary, Incentive Comp., Severance, OT Premium	6.20%			Rate per IRS
Medicare Taxes	181,045	12,485,850	Salary, Incentive Comp., Severance, OT Premium	1.45%			Rate per IRS
Federal Unemployment Tax	0	1,600,000	Tax Base	0.00%			Rate Estimate
State Unemployment Tax	16,000	1,600,000	Tax Base in VA	1.00%			Rate Estimate
Subtotal Statutory	$971,168			8.65%			
Paid Absences							
Vacation	$683,942	11,855,000	Salary	5.77%		3	Weeks
Holidays	364,769	11,855,000	Salary	3.08%		8	Days
Sick Leave	136,788	11,855,000	Salary	1.15%		3	Days
Bereavement Leave	91,192	11,855,000	Salary	0.77%		2	Days
Military Duty	45,596	11,855,000	Salary	0.38%			Estimate
Jury Duty	11,399	11,855,000	Salary	0.10%			Estimate
Maternity/Paternity Leave	205,183	11,855,000	Salary	1.73%			Estimate
Subtotal Paid Absences	$1,538,870			12.98%			
Other Benefits							
Health Insurance	$480,000	200	Person/Year	$2,400			Estimate
Dental Insurance	240,000	200	Person/Year	$1,200			
Vision Insurance	120,000	200	Person/Year	$600			
Short Term Disability	100,000	200	Person/Year	$500			Estimate
Long Term Disability	200,000	200	Person/Year	$1,000			Estimate
Retirement Plan—401k	300,000	200	Salary	$6,000	50.00%	50.00%	50% participation/ 50% match
Retirement Plan—Other	0	200	Person/Year	$0			
Life Insurance	20,000	200	Person/Year	$100			
Workman's Compensation	40,000	200	Person/Year	$200			
Transportation	0	200	Person/Year	$0			
Education Benefits	100,000	200	Person/Year	$500			
Clothing	16,000	200	Person/Year	$80			
Subtotal Other Benefits	$1,616,000						
Total Fringe Benefits	$4,126,038						
Total Labor Dollars							
Direct Labor	$7,392,917						
Overhead Labor	1,139,727						
General and Administrative Labor	613,486						
Bid and Proposal Labor	292,500						
Independent Research and Development Labor	877,500						
Total Labor Dollars	$10,316,130						
Fringe Benefit Rate	**40.00%**						

all accurate cost or pricing data reasonably available to the offeror have been submitted, either actually or by specific identification, to the contracting officer or an authorized representative of the contracting officer.

Data not reasonably available are not required to be submitted and an offeror is not obligated to recast existing data into any particular format to meet this disclosure requirement. The reference to "actual submission or specific identification" is an option. An offeror's obligation is not to submit and specifically identify cost or pricing data. The purpose of this optional means of compliance is to accommodate situations where voluminous data make it impractical to actually submit all cost and pricing data. However, the ability to satisfy the requirements by specific

Figure 24
OVERHEAD CALCULATION WORKSHEET

Overhead	Dollars	Base Amt.	Base Name	Rate			Source/Assumption
Indirect Labor							
Management and Supervision							
Manager	$116,178						Employee Worksheet
Administrative Assistant	25,602						Employee Worksheet
Project Accountant	7,745						Employee Worksheet
Meetings	64,327	$11,150,000	Salary	0.58%	1	1	1 Meeting for 1 Hr/Month
Training Time	42,885	$11,150,000	Salary	0.38%	1	2	1 two hr. Session per Quarter
Incentive Compensation	553,500						Employee Worksheet
Severance Pay	20,000						Estimate
Overtime Premium	10,000						Estimate
Other Non-Chargeable Time	$882,990						Employee Worksheet
Subtotal Indirect Labor	$1,723,227						
Fringe Benefits on Overhead Labor	$455,845	$1,139,727		40.00%			Indirect Labor x FB Rate
Facilities							
Building							
Rent or Depreciation	$900,000						Estimate
Electric	90,000						Estimate
Water	30,000						Estimate
Gas	50,000						Estimate
Telephone	120,000						Estimate
Other Utilities	10,000						Estimate
Janitorial Services	60,000						Estimate
Security	100,000						Estimate
Maintenance	60,000						Estimate
Subtotal Building	$1,420,000						
Equipment							
Computer Equipment— Rent or Depreciation	$500,000						Estimate
Internet Access	20,000						Estimate
Intranet	50,000						Estimate
Office Furniture and Equipment— Rent or Depr.	125,000						Estimate
Maintenance	40,000						
Subtotal Equipment	$735,000						
Subtotal Facilities	$2,155,000						
Miscellaneous							
Shipping	$1,000						Estimate
Small Tools, Equipment and Supplies	1,000						Estimate
Safety Supplies	2,000						Estimate
Subscriptions	2,000						Estimate
Professional Dues	1,000						Estimate
Training	5,000						Estimate
Travel							Estimate
Transportation	30,000						Estimate
Meals and Lodging	7,500						Estimate
Automobile Mileage	400						Estimate
Car Rentals	5,000						Estimate
Parking	1,000						Estimate
Miscellaneous	1,000						Estimate
Business Meals	20,000						Estimate
Overhead							
Postage and Courier Services	5,000						Estimate
Printing and Reproduction	5,000						Estimate
Recruiting	30,000						Estimate

continues

Figure 24
OVERHEAD CALCULATION WORKSHEET (continued)

Overhead (cont.)	Dollars	Base Amt.	Base Name	Rate			Source/Assumption
Office Supplies	50,000						Estimate
Publications	5,000						Estimate
Conferences and Seminars	10,000						Estimate
Software	350,000						Estimate
Vehicle Expenses	100,000						Estimate
Property Taxes	10,000						Estimate
General Insurance	10,000						Estimate
Property Insurance	5,500						Estimate
Outside Services	50,000						Estimate
Consultants	96,000						Estimate
Subtotal Miscellaneous	$803,400						
Total Overhead	$5,137,472						
Total Labor Dollars							
Direct Labor Dollars—Defense Division	$7,392,917						
Bid and Proposal Labor	292,500						
Independent Research and Development Labor	877,500						
Total Labor Dollars	$8,562,917						
Overhead Rate	60.00%						

identification is not a license to simply list data without explaining their relevance to the price proposal.

Offerors are further reminded that any subsequently obtained relevant cost or pricing data should be submitted promptly to the contracting officer in a manner that clearly shows how the information relates to the offeror's price proposal. These data should be submitted directly to the contracting officer, not to the government auditor. The requirement for submission of cost or pricing data continues up to the time of agreement on price, or an earlier date agreed upon between the parties if applicable. In practice, the contracting officer seldom agrees to an earlier cutoff date.

Note 2 to Table 15-2 informs offerors that by submitting the proposal, the offeror grants the contracting officer or an authorized representative the right to examine the records that formed the basis for the pricing proposal. The authorized representative is generally a contract auditor, but may also be a contract administrator or price analyst. The government examination can take place at any time before award and in some rare instances has actually occurred after contract award. The examination may include review of those books, records, documents, and other types of factual information (regardless of form or whether the information is specifically referenced or included in the proposal as the basis for pricing) that will permit an adequate evaluation of the proposed price. This is an open-ended and extremely subjective condition.

The more mundane items required by Table 15-2 include: (1) solicitation, contract, and/or modification number; (2) name and address of offeror; (3) name and telephone number of point of contact; (4) name of contract administration office (if available); (5) type of contract action (i.e., new contract, change order, price revision/redetermination, letter contract, unpriced order, or other); (6) proposed cost, profit or fee, and total; (7) whether the use of government property will be required in the performance of the contract, and, if so, what property; (8) date of submission; and (9) name, title, and signature of authorized representative.

Exhibit 25
GENERAL AND ADMINISTRATIVE CALCULATION WORKSHEET

General and Administrative (G&A)	Dollars	Base $	Base Name	Rate			Source/Assumption
Indirect Labor							
Executives							
President	$174,038						Employee Worksheet
Vice President	130,529						Employee Worksheet
CFO	104,423						Employee Worksheet
Incentive Compensation	33,500						Employee Worksheet
Subtotal Executive	$442,490						
Administrative							
Accounting	$39,159						Employee Worksheet
Human Resources	52,212						Employee Worksheet
Information Technology	69,615						Employee Worksheet
Purchasing	43,510						Employee Worksheet
Contract Hires (Temporary Services)	0						
Incentive Compensation	11,750						Employee Worksheet
Subtotal Administrative	$216,245						
Miscellaneous							
Severance Pay	2,000						Estimate
Overtime Premium	100						Estimate
Subtotal Miscellaneous	$2,100						
Subtotal Indirect Labor	$660,836						
Fringe Benefits on Indirect Labor	$245,370	$613,486		40.00%			Indirect Labor x FB Rate
Facilities							
Building							
Rent or Depreciation	$150,000						Estimate
Electric	1,000						Estimate
Water	200						Estimate
Gas	300						Estimate
Telephone	12,000						Estimate
Other Utilities	1,000						Estimate
Janitorial Services	2,000						Estimate
Security	5,000						Estimate
Maintenance	5,000						Estimate
Subtotal Building	$176,500						
Equipment							
Computer Equipment— Rent or Depreciation	$10,000						Estimate
Internet Access	2,000						Estimate
Intranet	2,000						Estimate
Office Furniture and Equipment— Rent or Depr.	10,000						Estimate
Maintenance	5,000						Estimate
Subtotal Equipment	29,000						
Subtotal Facilities	$58,000						
Business Development							
Sales and Marketing							
Consultants	$10,000						Estimate
Commissions	0						Estimate
GSA Industrial Funding Fees	0						Estimate
Travel	4,000						Estimate
Printing Costs	1,000						Estimate
Outside Services	500						Estimate
Subtotal Sales and Marketing	$15,500						

continues

Exhibit 25
GENERAL AND ADMINISTRATIVE CALCULATION WORKSHEET (continued)

Bid and Proposal							
Salaries	$292,500						Employee Worksheet
Fringe Benefits	116,988	$292,500		40.00%			Salaries x FB Rate
Overhead	175,491	$292,500		60.00%			Salaries x OH Rate
Consultants	10,000						Estimate
Travel	2,000						Estimate
Outside Services	1,000						Estimate
Subtotal Bid and Proposal	$597,979						
Subtotal Sales and Marketing							
Independent Research and Development							
Salaries	$877,500						Employee Worksheet
Fringe Benefits	350,965	$877,500		40.00%			Salaries x FB Rate
Overhead	526,472	$877,500		60.00%			Salaries x OH Rate
Consultants	10,000						Estimate
Travel	2,000						Estimate
Outside Services	1,000						Estimate
Subtotal Independent Research and Development	$1,767,936						
Subtotal Business Development	$2,365,915						
Miscellaneous							
Subscriptions	$5,000						Estimate
Professional Dues	5,000						Estimate
Training	20,000						Estimate
Travel							
Transportation	40,000						Estimate
Meals and Lodging	20,000						Estimate
Automobile Mileage	1,900						Estimate
Car Rentals	6,000						Estimate
Parking	2,000						Estimate
Miscellaneous	5,000						Estimate
Business Meals	20,000						Estimate
Postage and Courier Services	10,000						Estimate
Printing and Reproduction	6,000						Estimate
Recruiting	30,000						Estimate
Bank Charges	5,000						Estimate
Office Supplies	20,000						Estimate
Publications	5,000						Estimate
Conferences and Seminars	10,000						Estimate
Software	25,000						Estimate
Vehicle Expenses	6,000						Estimate
State and Local Taxes	10,000						Estimate
Property Taxes	1,000						Estimate
General Insurance	20,000						Estimate
Property Insurance	20,000						Estimate
Business Licenses	10,000						Estimate
Legal Consultants	20,000						Estimate
Patent and Copyright Consultants	10,000						Estimate
Business Consultants	50,000						Estimate
Other Consultants	10,000						Estimate
Directors and Officers Insurance	50,000						Estimate
Gain/Loss on Disposition of Assets	10,000						Estimate
Subtotal Miscellaneous	$452,900						
Unallowable Costs							
Bad Debts	$1,000						Estimate
Interest Expense	5,000						Estimate
Advertising	1,000						Estimate

continues

Exhibit 25
GENERAL AND ADMINISTRATIVE CALCULATION WORKSHEET (continued)

Trade Shows	2,000						Estimate
Gifts	500						Estimate
Contributions and Donations	1,000						Estimate
Goodwill	0						Estimate
Asset Write-ups	0						Estimate
Entertainment	1,000						Estimate
Federal Income Taxes	2,000						Estimate
Per Diem Over Government Rates	1,000						Estimate
Alcoholic Beverages	160						Estimate
Fines and Penalties	200						Estimate
Key Man Life Insurance	1,000						Estimate
Subtotal Unallowable Costs	$15,860						
Corporate Allocations							
Executives	$230,000						Estimate
Information Services	10,000						Estimate
Accounting	10,000						Estimate
Human Relations	10,000						Estimate
Residual Expenses	17,000						Estimate
Subtotal Corporate Allocations	$277,000						
Total General and Administrative	$4,060,020						
Total Cost Input							
Direct Labor	$7,392,917						Employee Worksheet
Fringe Benefits	2,956,870		$7,392,917			40.00%	Direct Labor x FB Rate
Overhead	5,137,472						Overhead Worksheet
Materials and Subcontracts	700,000						Estimate
Other Direct Costs	50,000						Estimate
Total Cost Input	$16,237,259						
General and Administrative	25.00%						

Other questions to be answered include: (1) whether the offeror's organization is subject to the CAS; (2) whether the offeror's organization has submitted a CAS Board disclosure statement; (3) whether the offeror's disclosure statement has been determined to be adequate; (4) whether the offeror has been notified that it is or may be in noncompliance with the disclosure statement or the CAS, and, if so, an explanation; (5) whether any aspect of this proposal is inconsistent with the offeror's disclosed practices or applicable CAS, and, if so, an explanation; and (6) whether the proposal is consistent with established estimating and accounting principles and procedures and FAR Part 31, Cost Principles, and, if not, an explanation.

The answers to these questions are crucial. If an offeror is not subject to the CAS because it is a small business (or any other exemption), this fact should be included in the response to the questions. An offeror should also indicate whether or not it is subject to full or modified CAS coverage. If no disclosure statement has been submitted, the offeror should either: (1) state that no disclosure statement is required; or (2) indicate the status of any disclosure statement submission. If any aspect of the price proposal is not consistent with the CAS or FAR Part 31, an offeror should review the circumstances carefully to determine if the proposal should be revised to be consistent. An answer that the proposal is not consistent with either regulation will undoubtedly cause potential significant problems in obtaining contract award or in negotiating a price.

The instructions require the following statement: "This proposal reflects our estimates and/or actual costs as of this date and conforms with the instructions in FAR 15.403-5 (b)(1) and Table 15-2. By submitting this proposal, we grant the contracting officer and authorized representative(s) the right to examine, at any time before award, those records, which include books, documents, accounting procedures and practices, and other data, regardless of type and form or whether such supporting information is specifically referenced or included in the proposal as the basis for pricing, that will permit an adequate evaluation of the proposed price."

This statement is the certification that appeared on the now defunct SF 1411. The reference to FAR provisions obligates the offeror to be responsive to any requirements in that portion of the FAR. Finally, the provision regarding access to records is necessary because of the absence of a contract clause (and contract) providing for any access to the offeror's books and records.

The instructions further request the offeror to include an index, appropriately referenced, of all the cost or pricing data and information accompanying or identified in the proposal. The format provided by offerors and accepted by the government is not fixed and in practice may vary substantially. In addition, an offeror should annotate any future additions and/or revisions on a supplemental index. This requirement is a good idea from a contractor perspective because documentation of what data have been submitted to the government could be a critical issue in any allegation of violations of the Truth in Negotiations Act.

The instructions state that an ". . .offeror must clearly identify that cost or pricing data are included as part of the proposal." The need for the statement is questionable because the instructions are only applicable where cost or pricing data are required and the offeror is responding to this requirement.

In addition, the offeror must submit with the proposal any information reasonably required to explain its estimating process, in-

cluding the judgmental factors applied and the mathematical or other methods used in the estimate, including those used in projecting from known data and the nature and amount of any contingencies included in the proposed price. Judgmental factors include describing what or how specific historical data were selected for estimating purposes. This might include describing learning curve applications, average hour calculations based on selected historical data, etc. For materials, this might involve describing how material prices were estimated—recent prices (and how recent), quotes, moving average of recent prices, etc.

Contingencies must be identified—not because contingencies are unallowable, but because the government seeks to ensure that contingencies are considered only once in any price negotiation. If contingencies are specifically priced in the proposal, then the risk (and thus margin or profit) might be less.

Offerors must show the relationship between contract line item prices and the total contract price. Offerors must attach cost element breakdowns for each proposed line item, using the appropriate format prescribed in the "Formats for Submission of Line Item Summaries" section of Table 15-2. Supporting breakdowns for each cost element, consistent with the offeror's cost accounting system, must be provided. The cost elements are essentially direct labor, materials and subcontracts, other direct costs, overhead, and G&A expense plus cost of money.

When more than one contract line item is proposed, a summary total amount covering all line items for each cost element must be included in the proposal support. Whenever an offeror has incurred costs for work performed before submission of a proposal, the offeror must identify those costs in the price proposal. If the offeror has reached an agreement with government representatives on use of forward pricing rates and factors, the agreement should be identified, a copy included, and its nature described.

Offerors are informed that as soon as practicable after final agreement on price or an earlier date agreed to by the parties, but before the award resulting from the proposal, the offeror must, under the conditions stated in FAR 15.406-2, submit a Certificate of Current Cost or Pricing Data. In practice, this date could be as long as several months after completion of negotiations.

Required Breakdowns

Depending on an offeror's accounting system, an offeror must provide breakdowns for the following basic cost elements, if applicable:

- Materials and services
- Direct labor
- Indirect costs
- Other costs
- Royalties
- Facilities capital cost of money
- Profit.

Materials and Services

Offerors should provide a consolidated, priced summary of individual material quantities included in the various tasks, orders, or contract line items being proposed and the basis for pricing (e.g., vendor quotes, invoice prices). Not only must each contract line item be priced, but a summary of materials for all items in the proposal must be provided. The purpose of this summary is to assist in the evaluation of material unit prices based on quantities expected to be used for the entire contract.

An offeror is to include raw materials, parts, components, assemblies, and services to be produced or performed by others. The specific contractor terminology is not important; the items to be included are any direct costs incurred by others. For all items proposed, the offeror should identify the item and show the source, quantity, and price. If these three

factors cannot be determined, they must be estimated. For example, the planned source may be known, but this could change by the time the materials are actually purchased. The quantity should be known—including an estimate for material attrition. The price will most likely have to be based on an estimate. It is often difficult to obtain quotes unless the supplier is assured of the possibility of a subsequent order. All this assumes that the product is sufficiently designed to permit development of a bill of material.

Offerors are expected to conduct price analyses of all subcontractor proposals. This may involve a variety of techniques, including comparison of prior prices, prices from competitors, and in-house cost estimates.

In addition, offerors should conduct cost analyses for all subcontracts when cost or pricing data are submitted by the subcontractor. *A cost analysis cannot be conducted unless the potential subcontractor has submitted cost or pricing data.* When these cost or pricing data and analyses exist, an offeror is expected to include these analyses as part of its own cost or pricing data submissions for subcontracts expected to exceed $700,000. The subcontractor's cost or pricing data should be submitted as part of the offeror's cost or pricing data. These requirements also apply to all subcontractors who are required to submit cost or pricing data.

Regarding materials, offerors are expected to provide data showing the degree of competition and the basis for establishing the source and reasonableness of price for those acquisitions exceeding, or expected to exceed, $700,000 that are priced on the basis of adequate price competition. For interorganizational transfers priced at other than the cost of comparable competitive commercial work of the division, subsidiary, or affiliate of the contractor, an offeror must explain the pricing method.

Offerors should obtain cost or pricing data from prospective sources for those acquisitions exceeding $700,000 and not otherwise exempt (i.e., adequate price competition, commercial items, prices set by law or regulation, or waiver). An offeror must provide data showing the basis for establishing source and reasonableness of price. These requirements mean that the source selection should be described in terms of competitive prices, market prices, catalog prices, commercial items, intercompany transfers, unique technical capabilities, sole source, direct source, etc., and whether reasonableness was established by competition, market conditions, price analysis, or cost analysis.

In addition, an offeror is requested to provide a summary of its cost analysis and a copy of cost or pricing data submitted by a prospective source in support of each subcontract, or purchase order that is the lower of either: (1) $10,000,000 or more; or (2) both more than $550,000 and more than 10 percent of the offeror's proposed price. The contracting officer may require cost or pricing data in support of proposals in lower amounts. Remember, if no cost or pricing data have been submitted to the offeror, none can be submitted to the government. Offerors may have little leverage to demand cost or pricing data from a potential subcontractor who does not think it has a chance for subcontract award or who simply declines to provide any data until an actual prime contract exists.

Subcontractor cost or pricing data must be accurate, complete, and current as of the date of final price agreement on the subcontract (not the date of price agreement on the prime contract), or an earlier date agreed upon by the parties. The prime contractor is responsible for updating a prospective subcontractor's data. In recent years, court decisions have made this a more proactive requirement on the part of a prime contractor. Specifically, recent decisions have suggested that prime contractors should actively seek updated data rather than merely ensure that subcontractor cost or pricing data are current, accurate, and complete as of the date of the subcontract price agreement.

For standard commercial items fabricated by the offeror that are generally stocked in inventory, the offeror should provide a separate cost breakdown, if priced based on cost. For interorganizational transfers priced at cost, an offeror must provide a separate breakdown of cost elements. In other words, for transfers at cost, the same data are required as if the offeror's organization were proposing to perform the work. Providing these data can be difficult for decentralized organizations that do not normally provide each other with cost data.

An offeror is requested to analyze the cost or pricing data and submit the results of its analysis of a prospective source's proposal. When submission of a prospective source's cost or pricing data is required, it must be included along with the offeror's cost or pricing data submission. An offeror must also submit any other cost or pricing data obtained from a subcontractor, either actually or by specific identification, along with the results of any analysis performed on those data. These stated requirements are frequently not achieved in practice. If prospective subcontractors refuse to submit such data before assurances of award or a perception of reasonable award potential, there may be no subcontractor information to provide to the government. What does not exist cannot be provided!

Direct Labor

An offeror is to provide a time-phased breakdown of labor hours, rates, and cost by appropriate category, and furnish bases for estimates. The time-phased requirement means that direct labor hours should be estimated by month, quarter, or year. Direct labor rates should likewise be identified by time period. Labor categories are those established by the offeror. However, an offeror should use categories that exist in its cost accounting system. Frequently, a request for proposals may require categories that are not consistent with the offeror's accounting system. Care needs to be taken to ensure that a reconciliation of the categories is documented.

Finally, the basis for the hours and rates should be provided. Typical bases for hours include historical average hours, application of learning curves, work measurement standards, and engineering estimates. Typical bases for rates include historical rates adjusted for various escalation factors, area/industry rates, and letters documenting offers of employment.

Indirect Costs

An offeror should indicate how it computed and applied indirect costs, including cost breakdowns. This includes showing trends and budgetary data to provide a basis for government evaluation of the reasonableness of proposed rates. Offerors should indicate the rates used and provide an appropriate explanation. This means that historical data and/or budgets should be used to support proposed rates. Elimination of any unallowable costs from historical data or budgets should be evident in the supporting data.

Other Costs

An offeror must list all other costs not otherwise included in the categories described above. These might include special tooling, travel, computer and consultant services, preservation, packaging and packing, spoilage and rework, and federal excise tax on finished articles. The basis for pricing these items should be provided.

Royalties

At one time, royalties were a significant cost element. The FAR instructions require that if royalties exceed $1,500, an offeror must provide the following information on a separate page for each separate royalty or license fee: (1) name and address of licensor; (2) date of license agreement; (3) patent numbers; (4) patent application serial numbers, or other basis on which the royalty is payable; (5) brief description (including any part or model numbers of each contract item or component on which the royalty is payable); (6) percentage or dollar rate of royalty per unit; (7) unit price of contract item; (8) number of units; (9) total dollar amount of royalties; and (10) if specifically requested by the contracting officer, a copy of the current license agreement and identification of applicable claims of specific patents.

Facilities Capital Cost of Money

If an offeror elects to claim facilities capital cost of money as an allowable cost, it must submit Form CASB-CMF and show the calculation of the proposed amount. Service contractors or others with few assets often do not claim this cost because it is insignificant for them and requires additional administrative efforts to claim.

Profit

Chapter 8 describes profit and fee guidelines.

CHAPTER 8 Contract Price Negotiation and Profit Guidelines

In late 2010 the Defense Contract Audit Agency (DCAA) greatly reduced the number of price proposal reviews and increased the intensity of the reviews performed. Price proposals for fixed-price type contracts under $10 million and for cost-type contract proposals under $100 million will seldom be reviewed. However, for fixed-price proposals over $100 million and cost-type proposals over $250 million, the audit will be much more in-depth than previously. For these significant proposals, DCAA will conduct a detailed "walk-through" of each proposal before an audit begins. This process can take as much as a full week and may involve the contracting officer and every contractor employee who participated in proposal preparation.

After an auditor has submitted a report on a price proposal evaluation to the contracting officer, price negotiation will take place if the contractor is selected to be a potential candidate for the contract. Since this phase of the procurement process is a "negotiation," each party will have to give and take on the final price. The contractor must realize that the contracting officer is going to question certain costs going into the total proposed price, based on advice furnished by the auditor or other technical advisors. In the price negotiation, the contractor should be fully alert to the implications of that price on the company.

Price is composed of two elements: cost and markup. Although cost represents the larger portion of price, markup (profit or fee) is at least as important to the contractor in negotiations. The more accurate term for what the government regulations refer to as "profit" on fixed-price type contracts and "fee" on cost type contracts is "markup."

Despite the regulatory use of the terms "profit" and "fee" in casual government contracting jargon, the terms are used somewhat interchangeably. The true "profit" or net income for a contractor is what the business earns after deductions for unallowable costs and taxes and is usually referred to as "net after taxes." Profit or fee prenegotiation objectives do not necessarily represent net income to contractors. Rather, they represent that element of the potential total remuneration that contractors may receive for contract performance over and above allowable costs.

How much profit should a contractor seek and how can a certain level of profit be justified? Contractors are not required to submit details of their profit or fee objectives or to follow a particular format or rationale in their profit calculations; government agencies, however, usually must follow structured procedures in evaluating proposed profit levels. Contractors may use the government procedures, and many, in fact, do. But even those who use a different technique would be wise to become familiar with the government's procedures in preparation for negotiations.

Contractors also should be aware of statutory limitations on profit. A contracting officer may not negotiate a price or fee that exceeds the following statutory limitations, imposed by 10 U.S.C. 2306(e) and 41 U.S.C. 254(b):

- For experimental, developmental, or research work performed under a cost-plus-fixed-fee contract, the fee may not exceed 15 percent of the contract's estimated cost, excluding fee.
- For architect-engineer services for public works or utilities, the contract price or the estimated cost and fee for production and delivery of designs, plans, drawings, and specifications may not exceed 6 percent of the estimated cost of construction of the public work or utility, excluding fees.
- For other cost-plus-fixed-fee contracts, the fee may not exceed 10 percent of the contract's cost, excluding fee.

It is important to note that these limitations are based on estimated costs, not actual costs. The relationship of profit to estimated costs cannot exceed these amounts; however, the relationship of profit to the actual costs may result in a percentage greater than these amounts.

During World War II, Congress established the Renegotiation Board. The express purpose of this board was to review contracts, and the profit/fee each had earned. In particular, the board reviewed fixed-price contracts for "excessive" contractor profit. Needless to say, this board was not viewed fondly by the contractor community. The enabling legislation for the board finally lapsed and Congress did not renew it. Fortunately, no such legislation exists today. Unfortunately, some people still improperly refer to excess or windfall profits—a concept no longer supported by any regulatory basis.

Although the FAR does not elaborate on profit guidelines, each agency has the authority to do so in its supplement to the FAR. The Department of Defense (DOD) has established its own guidelines, as has the National Aeronautics and Space Administration (NASA). The former guidelines emphasize performance risk, contract risk, and contract financing. The latter guidelines are similar, but reduce profit objectives by the amount of cost of money claimed by the contractor. Most other agencies do not have formal profit guidelines. Unofficially, some agencies seek little or no profit on consultant costs, subcontract costs, and other selected cost items.

GOVERNMENT VS. COMMERCIAL PROFIT

A basic concept (which contractors hope is being addressed and possibly changed) is the fact that contracting with the government is usually driven by cost while commercial transactions are generally driven by price. The result of this business arrangement is that a considerably lower level of profit is derived from government contracts. That is not to say that as a buying public we are being overcharged. Conversely, it simply means that the government is not prone to use taxpayer-backed funds to provide a reasonable profit to contractors. Because of this fact in government contract transactions, some contractors refuse to do business with the government.

This reluctance has created two distinct industrial bases, one commercial and one governmental. Many companies are either 100 percent commercial or 100 percent government. There are instances where the product/service mix is both commercial and government. This has many times been the result of a company's ability to use some of its products that were originally designed or developed for the government in the commercial marketplace.

Despite the lower profits from government business, many companies remain contractors. The reasons vary from performing the work for the sake of national defense to being enmeshed in government business and unable to break out of it. Some others may be in the position of incurring related costs anyway so they might as well have some of the marginal costs absorbed by performing on contracts. Whatever the reason, contractors are many and varied, and have a variety of reasons, other than just being profitable, for conducting government business.

DEPARTMENT OF DEFENSE GUIDELINES

DOD has promulgated guidelines for evaluating a contractor's requests for profit or fee. The current version was established in 1987 as a result of a DOD profit survey, which recommended that the guidelines focus on performance rather than cost elements.

Several minor revisions have been made from time to time since 1987. Most significantly, for a period of time no markup was allowed on G&A costs—this no longer applies. During the time that G&A did not carry a markup, many contractors properly reclassified costs from G&A to overhead.

Weighted Guidelines Method

This method, which is found in DFARS 215.404-70, is DOD's structured approach for performing profit analysis in contract actions where the price is to be negotiated. For many years, the guidelines were based on the contract-estimated costs, often by cost element such as direct labor, direct materials, subcontracts, etc. In 1986, the DOD guidelines were revised in response to congressional concern that previous changes to the regulations had created profit beyond a level that was warranted under the circumstances. The goal of the new guidelines was to lower profit.

The guideline changes were significant and not merely a reshuffling of prior factors. First, guidelines for manufacturing, services, and research and development contracts are no longer separate. Second, the guidelines attempt to decrease the reliance on estimated costs and stress the technical aspects of the proposal when establishing the profit level.

Third, the guidelines integrate the financing considerations involved in the contractual terms into the calculation of profit. In other words, they make the extent of progress payments a factor in determining how much profit will be earned. Fourth, the guidelines place greater emphasis on facilities capital. This emphasis is selective in that certain assets will generate more potential profit than other assets.

An example of the DOD weighted guidelines method is presented in Figure 26.

Profit Objective Determination

The DOD contracting officer is required to use the weighted guidelines method or an alternate structured approach to determine the prenegotiation profit objective for any negotiated contract action that requires cost analysis, except on cost-plus-award-fee contracts. An alternate structured approach can be used for contracts under $700,000, architect-engineer contracts, construction contracts, contracts primarily requiring delivery of material supplied by subcontractors, termination settlements, and unusual situations. However, the alternate approach must specifically address the same four basic elements—performance risk, contract risk, working capital -adjustment, and facilities capital employed—used in the weighted guidelines method.

DD Form 1547, Record of Weighted Guidelines Method Application, implements DOD's structured approach for performing the profit analysis necessary to develop a prenegotiation profit objective. It focuses on four profit factors: (1) performance risk; (2) contract-type risk; (3) facilities capital employed; and (4) cost efficiency.

The contracting officer assigns a value to each profit factor; the value multiplied by the base results in the profit objective for that factor. Each profit factor has a normal value and a designated range of values. The normal value represents average conditions on the

Figure 26
EXAMPLE OF DOD WEIGHTED GUIDELINES METHOD

RECORD OF WEIGHTED GUIDLINES APPLICATION					REPORT CONTROL SYMBOL **DO-A&T(Q)1751**		

1. REPORT NO.	2. BASIC PROCUREMENT INSTRUMENT IDENTIFICATION NO.				3. SPIIN	4. DATE OF ACTION	
	a. PURCHASING OFFICE	b. FY	c. TYPE PROC INST CODE	d. PRISN		a. YEAR	b. MONTH

5. CONTRACTING OFFICE CODE				ITEM	COST CATEGORY		OBJECTIVE
6. NAME OF CONTRACTOR				13.	MATERIAL		$4,200,000
				14.	SUBCONTRACTS		2,300,000
7. DUNS NUMBER		8. FEDERAL SUPPLY CODE		15.	DIRECT LABOR		5,821,000
				16.	INDIRECT EXPENSES		6,071,000
9. DOD CLAIMANT PROGRAM		10. CONTRACT TYPE CODE		17.	OTHER DIRECT CHARGES		74,000
				18.	SUBTOTAL COSTS (13 thru 17)		$18,466,347
11. TYPE EFFORT		12. USE CODE		19.	GENERAL AND ADMINISTRATIVE		2,772,250
				20.	TOTAL COSTS (18 + 19)		$21,238,597

	WEIGHTED GUIDLINES PROFIT FACTORS						

	CONTRACTOR RISK FACTORS		ASSIGNED WEIGHTING	ASSIGNED VALUE	BASE (Item 18)	PROJECT OBJECTIVE
21.	TECHNICAL		30%	7.00%		
22.	MANAGEMENT/COST CONTROL		70%	7.00%		
23.	PERFORMANCE RISK (COMPOSITE)			7.00%	$21,238,597	$1,486,702
24.	CONTRACT TYPE RISK			1.00%	$21,238,597	$212,386
25.	WORKING CAPITAL	COSTS FINANCED	LENGTH FACTOR	INTEREST RATE		
		$0	1.15	4.250%		0

	CONTRACTOR FACILITIES CAPITAL EMPLOYED	ASSIGNED VALUE	AMOUNT EMPLOYED	
27.	LAND		$0	
28.	BUILDING		0	
29.	EQUIPMENT	35%	0	0
30.	COST EFFICIENCY FACTOR	ASSIGNED VALUE	BASE (Item 20)	
		1%	21,238,597	212,386
31.		TOTAL PROFIT OBJECTIVE		$1,911,474

	NEGOTIATED SUMMARY				
			PROPOSED	OBJECTIVE	NEGOTIATED
31.	TOTAL COSTS				$21,238,597
32.	FACILITIES CAPITAL COST OF MONEY (DD Form 1861)				0
33.	PROFIT				1,911,474
34.	TOTAL PRICE (LINE 31 + 32)				$23,150,071
35.	MARKUP RATE (Line 31 + 32 divided by 31)				9.00%

	CONTRACTING OFFICER APPROVAL			
36. TYPED/PRINTED NAME OF CONTRACTING OFFICER (Last, first, Middle Initial)	37. SIGNATURE OF CONTRACTING OFFICER	38. TELEPHONE NO.	39. DATE SUBMITTED	
96.	97.	98.	99.	

Form 1547, JUL 2002

	OPTIONAL USE	
	PREVIOUS EDITION IS OBSOLETE	

prospective contract when compared to all goods and services acquired by DOD. The designated range provides values based on above normal or below normal conditions. In the price negotiation documentation, the contracting officer need not explain assignment of the normal value, but should address conditions that justify assignment of other than the normal value.

Performance Risk

The performance risk profit factor addresses the contractor's degree of risk in fulfilling the contractual requirements. The factor consists of two parts: (1) technical—the technical uncertainties of performance; and (2) management—the degree of management effort necessary to ensure that contract requirements are met.

Each factor is an integral part of developing the composite profit value for performance risk. The contracting officer weights each factor according to the contractor's performance risk in providing the supplies or services required by the contract. While any value may be assigned within the designated range, the maximum and minimum values will be restricted to cases where performance risk is substantially above or below normal. The following example demonstrates how a composite profit value for performance risk is calculated.

	Assigned Weighting	*Assigned Value*	*Weighted Value*
Technical	60%	5.0%	3.0%
Management	40	4.0	1.6
Composite value	100%	4.6%	

The profit objective amount is computed by multiplying a composite profit value, assigned by the contracting officer (in this example 4.6%), times total contract costs, excluding facilities capital cost of money.

	Normal Value	*Designated Range*
Standard	5%	3% to 7%
Technology Incentive	9%	7% to 11%

Contracting officers may use the alternate designated range for research and development and service contractors when these contractors require relatively low capital investment in buildings and equipment compared to the defense industry overall. If the alternate designated range is used, no profit will be given for facilities capital employed.

Technical Risk. This criterion focuses on the contract requirements and the critical performance elements in the statement of work or specifications. Factors considered include the technology being applied or developed by the contractor, technical complexity, program maturity, performance specifications and tolerances, delivery schedule, and the extent of warranty or guarantee coverage.

A higher than normal value may be assigned where there is substantial technical risk, such as when the contractor is: (1) either developing or applying advanced technologies; (2) manufacturing items using specifications with stringent tolerance limits; (3) using highly skilled personnel or state-of-the-art machinery; (4) performing services and analytical efforts of utmost importance to the government and to exacting standards; (5) through independent development and investment, reducing the government's risk or cost; (6) accepting an accelerated delivery schedule to meet DOD requirements; or (7) assuming additional risk through warranty provisions.

Extremely complex, vital efforts to overcome difficult technical obstacles that require personnel with exceptional abilities, experience, and professional credentials may justify a value significantly above normal.

A maximum value may be assigned when there is development or initial production of a new item, particularly if performance or quality specifications are tight or there is a high degree of concurrent development or production.

A lower than normal value may be assigned in those cases where the technical risk is low, such as when the contractor is acquiring off-the-shelf items, specifying relatively simple requirements, applying little complex technology, performing efforts that do not require highly skilled personnel, performing routine efforts, performing on mature programs and procedures, or performing follow-on efforts or repetitive-type procurements. In addition, a significantly lower than normal value could be assigned for routine services, production of simple items, rote entry or routine integration of government-furnished information, or simple operations with government-furnished property.

Management Risk. This criterion considers the management effort involved on the part of the contractor to integrate the resources (including raw materials, labor, technology, information, and capital) necessary to meet contract requirements. The evaluation should: (1) assess the contractor's management and internal control systems using contracting office information and reviews made by field contract administration offices or other DOD field offices; (2) assess the management involvement expected on the individual contract action; (3) consider the degree of cost mix as an indication of the types of resources applied and value added by the contractor; and (4) consider the contractor's support of federal socioeconomic programs, such as small business concerns, and small business concerns owned and controlled by socially and economically disadvantaged individuals.

A higher than normal value may be assigned in those cases where the management effort is intense, such as when the value add-ed by the contractor is both considerable and reasonably difficult, the effort involves a high degree of integration or coordination, or the contractor has a substantial record of active participation in federal socioeconomic programs. A maximum value may be assigned when the effort requires large-scale integration of the most complex nature, involves major international activities with significant management coordination (e.g., offsets with foreign vendors), or has critically important milestones.

A lower than normal value may be assigned in those cases where the management effort is minimal, such as when, in a mature program, many end-item deliveries have been made, the contractor adds minimum value to an item, efforts are routine and require minimal supervision, the contractor provides poor quality, untimely proposals, the contractor fails to provide an adequate analysis of subcontractor costs, or the contractor does not cooperate in the evaluation and negotiation of the proposal.

A value significantly below normal may be justified when reviews performed by the field contract administration offices disclose unsatisfactory management and internal control systems (e.g., quality assurance, property control, safety or security) or the effort requires an unusually low degree of management involvement.

The technology factor is primarily applicable to acquisitions that include development, production, or application of innovative new technologies. The technology incentive range does not apply to efforts restricted to studies, analyses, or demonstrations that have a technical report as their primary deliverable. The technology incentive range should be used when contract performance includes the introduction of new, significant technological innovation. Innovation may be in the form of development or application of new technology that fundamentally changes the characteristics of an existing product or system and that results in increased technical performance, improved reliability, or reduced costs, or a new product or system that achieves significant technological advances over the product or system it is replacing.

Contract-Type Risk and Working Capital Adjustment

This factor focuses on the degree of cost risk accepted by the contractor under varying contract types. The working capital adjustment is an adjustment added to the profit objective for contract-type risk. It only applies to fixed-price contracts that provide for progress payments. Although it uses a formula approach, it is not intended to be an exact calculation of the cost of working capital. Its purpose is to give general recognition to the contractor's cost of working capital under varying contract circumstances, financing policies, and the economic environment.

The following extract from DD 1547 is annotated to explain the process.

Item	Contractor Risk Factors	Assigned Value	Base (Item 18)	Profit Objective		
24	Contract Type Risk	(1)	(2)	(3)		
	Cost Financed	Length Factor	Interest Rate			
25	Working Capital (4)	(5)	(6)	(7)	(8)

(1) Select a value from the list of contract types using the appropriate evaluation criteria.

(2) Insert the total allowable costs excluding the facilities capital cost of money.

(3) Multiply (1) by (2).

(4) Only complete this block when the prospective contract is a fixed-price contract containing provisions for progress payments.

(5) Insert the amount computed per the Costs Financed paragraph of this section.

(6) Insert the appropriate figure from the Contract Length paragraph of this section.

(7) Use the interest rate established by the Secretary of the Treasury (see DFARS 230.7101-1(a)). Do not use any other interest rate.

(8) Multiply (5) by (6) by (7). This is the working capital adjustment. It is not to exceed 4 percent of the allowable costs, excluding facilities capital cost of money.

Contract values for normal and designated ranges are:

Contract Type	Notes	Normal Value	Designated Range
Firm-fixed-price, no financing	(1)	5%	4% to 6%
Firm-fixed-price, with performance-based payments	(6)	4%	2.5% to 5.5%
Firm-fixed-price, with financing	(2)	3%	2% to 4%
Fixed-price-incentive, no financing	(1)	3%	2% to 4%
Firm-fixed-price, with performance-based payments	(6)	2%	0.5% to 3.5%

Contract Type	Notes	Normal Value	Designated Range
Fixed-price with redeterminable provision	(3)		
Fixed-price-incentive, with financing	(2)	1%	0% to 2%
Cost-plus-incentive-fee	(4)	1%	0% to 2%
Cost-plus-fixed-fee (4)		.5%	0% to 1%
Time-and-materials contracts (including overhaul contracts priced on time-and-material basis)	(5)	.5%	0% to 1%
Labor-hour contracts(5)		.5%	0% to 1%
Firm-fixed-price-level-of-effort-term	(5)	.5%	0% to 1%

(1) "No financing" means that the contract either does not provide progress payments, or provides them only on a limited basis, such as financing of first articles. A working capital adjustment is not computed.

(2) "With financing" means progress payments. When progress payments are present, compute a working capital adjustment.

(3) For the purpose of assigning profit values, treat a fixed-price contract with redeterminable provisions as if it were a fixed-price-incentive contract with below normal conditions.

(4) Cost-plus contracts do not receive the working capital adjustment.

(5) These types of contracts are considered cost-plus-fixed-fee contracts for the purposes of assigning profit values. They do not receive the working capital adjustment in Block 26. However, they may receive higher than normal values within the designated range to the extent that portions of cost are fixed.

(6) When the contract includes provisions for performance-based payments, do not compute a working capital adjustment.

The contracting officer should consider elements that affect contract-type risk, such as length of contract, adequacy of cost data for projections, economic environment, nature and extent of subcontracted activity, protection provided to the contractor under contract provisions (e.g., economic price adjustment clauses), ceilings and share lines contained in incentive provisions, and risks associated with contracts for foreign military sales (FMS) that are not funded by U.S. appropriations.

The contracting officer will assess the extent to which costs have been incurred prior to definitization of the contract action. The assessment will include any reduced contractor risk on both the contract before definitization and the remaining portion of the contract. When costs have been incurred prior to definitization, the contract-type risk is generally regarded to be in the low end of the designated range. If a substantial portion of the costs has been incurred prior to definitization, the contracting officer may assign a value as low as 0 percent, regardless of contract type.

A higher than normal value may be assigned in those cases where there is substantial contract-type risk, such as when the contract involves effort with minimal cost history, is long-term without provisions protecting the contractor (particularly when there is considerable economic uncertainty), includes incentive provisions (e.g., cost or performance incentives) that place a high degree of risk on the contractor, or has FMS sales (other than those under DOD cooperative logistics support arrangements or those made from government inventories or stocks) where the contractor can demonstrate that there are substantial risks above those normally present in DOD contracts for similar items.

A lower than normal value may be assigned in cases where contract risk is low, such as when the contract involves a very mature product line with extensive cost history, is relatively short-term, contains provisions that substantially reduce the contractor's risk, or includes incentive provisions that place a low degree of risk on the contractor.

The costs financed equal total costs multiplied by the portion (percent) of costs financed by the contractor. Total costs equal all allowable costs, excluding facilities capital cost of money, reduced as appropriate when: (1) the contractor has little cash investment (e.g., subcontractor progress payments liquidated late in the period of performance); (2) some costs are covered by special financing provisions, such as advance payments; or (3) the contract is multiyear and there are special funding arrangements.

The portion financed by the contractor is generally the portion not covered by progress payments (i.e., 100 percent minus the customary progress payment rate). For example, if a contractor receives progress payments at 75 percent, the portion financed by the contractor is 25 percent. On contracts that provide flexible progress payments or progress payments to small businesses, the customary progress payment rate for large businesses should be used.

The contract length factor is the period of time that the contractor has a working capital investment in the contract. The factor is based on the time necessary for the contractor to complete the substantive portion of the work, and is not necessarily the period of time between contract award and final delivery (or final payment). Periods of minimal effort should be excluded, should not include periods of performance contained in option provisions, and should not, for multiyear contracts, include periods of performance beyond those required to complete the initial program year's requirements.

The contracting officer should use the following table to select the contract length factor, should develop a weighted average contract length when the contract has multiple deliveries, and may use sampling techniques provided they produce a representative result.

Period to Perform Substantive Portion (in months)	Contract Length Factor
21 months or less	.40
22 to 27 months	.65
28 to 33 months	.90
34 to 39 months	1.15
40 to 45 months	1.40
46 to 51 months	1.65
52 to 57 months	1.90
58 to 63 months	2.15
64 to 69 months	2.40
70 to 75 months	2.65
76 months or more	2.90

For example, a contractor is to be awarded a negotiated contract for assembly work. The contracting officer's prenegotiation cost objective for each is $500,000. The period of performance is 40 months, with assemblies being delivered in the 34th, 36th, 38th, and 40th month of the contract (average period is 37 months). The contractor will receive progress payments at 75 percent (contractor portion is 25 percent), and the current interest rate is 8 percent.

Contractor Risk Factors	Assigned Value	Base	Profit Objective
Contract Type Risk	3%	$500,000	$15,000

	Cost Financed	Length Factor	Interest Rate	
Working Capital	$125,000	1.15	8%	$11,500*

*Working capital adjustment is appropriate as the adjustment does not exceed 4% of the contract costs ($500,000 × 4% = $20,000).

Facilities Capital Employed

This factor focuses on encouraging and rewarding aggressive capital investment in facilities that benefit DOD. It recognizes both the facilities capital that the contractor will employ in contract performance and the contractor's commitment to improving productivity.

The following extract from DD Form 1547 has been annotated to explain the process:

Item	Contractor Facilities Capital Employed	Assigned Value	Amount Employed	Profit Objective
26	Land	N/A	(2)	N/A
27	Buildings	N/A	(2)	N/A
28	Equipment	(1)	(2)	(3)

(1) Select a value from the list of Normal and Designated Ranges using criteria from the Evaluation section.

(2) Use the allocated facilities capital attributable to land, buildings, and equipment, as derived in DD 1861, Contract Facilities Capital Cost of Money (see Figure 27). This form can only be completed after application of the CAS form for computing the cost of money (see Figure 28).

In addition to the net book value of facilities capital employed, facilities capital that is part of a formal investment plan should be considered if the contractor submits reasonable evidence that achievable benefits to DOD will result from the investment, and the benefits of the investment are included in the forward pricing structure. If the value of intracompany transfers has been included at cost (i.e., excluding profit), the allocated facilities capital attributable to the buildings and equipment of those corporate divisions supplying the intracompany transfers should be added to contractor's allocated facilities capital. This addition should not be made if the value of intracompany transfers has been included at price (i.e., including profit).

Values: Normal and Designated Ranges

Asset Type	Normal Value	Designated Value
Land	0%	N/A
Buildings	0%	N/A
Equipment	17.5%	10% to 25%

In evaluating facilities capital employed, the contracting officer should relate the usefulness of the facilities capital to the goods or services being acquired under the particular contract. The contracting officer should also analyze the productivity improvements and other anticipated industrial base-enhancing benefits resulting from the facilities capital investment, including the economic value of the facilities capital (e.g., physical age, undepreciated value, idleness, expected contribution to future defense needs) and the contractor's level of investment in defense-related facilities as compared with the portion of the contractor's total business that is derived from DOD.

In addition, the contracting officer should consider any contractual provisions that reduce the contractor's risk of investment recovery, such as termination protection clauses and capital investment indemnification. Also, the contracting officer should ensure that increases in facilities capital investments are not merely asset revaluations attributable to mergers, stock transfers, takeovers, sales of corporate entities, or similar actions.

Figure 27
DD 1861—CONTRACT FACILITIES CAPITAL COST OF MONEY

CONTRACT FACILITIES COST OF MONEY	Form Approved OMB No. 0704-0267 Expires Feb 28, 1995

Public reporting burden for this collection of information is estimated to average 10 hours per response, including the time for reviewing instructions, searching existing data sources, gathering and maintaining the data needed, and completing and reviewing the collection of information. Send comments regarding this burden estimate or any other aspect of this collection of information, including suggestions for reducing this burden to Washington Headquarters Services, Directorate for Information Operations and Reports, 1215 Jefferson Davis Highway, Suite 1204, Arlington, VA 22202-4302, and to the Office of Management and Budget, Paperwork Reduction Project (0704-0267), Washington, DC 20503.

PLEASE DO NOT RETURN YOUR COMPLETED FORM TO EITHER OF THESE ADDRESSES.
RETURN COMPLETED FORM TO YOUR CONTRACTING OFFICIAL

1. CONTRACTOR NAME	2. CONTRACTOR ADDRESS
3. BUSINESS UNIT	
4. RFP/ CONTRACT PIIN NUMBER	5. PERFORMANCE PERIOD

6. DISTRIBUTION OF FACILITIES CAPITAL COST OF MONEY

POOL a.	ALLOCATION BASE b.	FACILITIES CAPITAL COST OF MONEY c.	
		FACTOR (1)	AMOUNT (2)
Manufacturing	$5,821,000	0.00825	$48,023
General and Administrative	18,466,000	0.00021	3,878
d. TOTAL			$51,901
e. TREASURY RATE			5.000%
f. FACILITIES CAPITAL EMPLOYED (TOTAL DIVIDED BY TREASURY RATE)			$1,038,022

7. DISTRIBUTION OF FACILITIES CAPITAL EMPLOYED

	PERCENTAGE a.	AMOUNT b.
(1) LAND	25.0%	$259,506
(2) BUILDINGS	30.0%	$311,407
(3) EQUIPMENT	45.0%	$467,110
	100.0%	$1,038,022

DD FORM 1861, MAR 93	PREVIOUS FORM IS OBSOLETE	DFA07

**Figure 28
FACTORS COMPUTATION FOR
FACILITIES CAPITAL COST OF MONEY**

Contractor: Address:
Business Unit:

COST ACCOUNTING PERIOD
1. Applicable Cost of Money Rate   5.00%

Business Unit / Facilities Capital	2 Accumulation and Direct Distribution of N.B.V.	3 Basis of Allocation	4 Total Net Book Value	5 Cost of Money for the Accounting Period	6 Allocation Base for the Period	7 Facilities Cost of Money Factor
Recorded	$6,588,000					
Leased Property	1,769,000					
Corporate and/or Group	293,000					
Total	$8,650,000					
Undistributed	240,000					
Distributed	$8,890,000					
Indirect Cost Pools						
Manufacturing	$8,027,000	$223,000	$8,250,000	$412,500	$50,000,000	0.00825
G&A	623,000	17,000	640,000	32,000	150,000,000	0.00021
Total	$8,650,000	$240,000	$8,890,000	$444,500		

A higher than normal value may be assigned if the facilities capital investment has direct, identifiable, and exceptional benefits. Indicators are: (1) new investments in state-of-the-art technology that reduce acquisition costs or yield other tangible benefits such as improved product quality or accelerated deliveries; (2) investments in new equipment for research and development applications; or (3) contractor demonstrates that the investments are over and above the normal capital investments necessary to support anticipated requirements of DOD programs.

A value significantly above normal may be assigned when there are direct and measurable benefits in efficiency and significantly reduced acquisition costs on the effort being priced. Maximum values apply only to those cases where the benefits of the facilities capital investment are substantially above normal. A lower than normal value may be assigned if the facilities capital investment has little benefit to DOD. Indicators are: (1) allocations of capital apply predominantly to commercial product item line items; (2) investments are for furniture and fixtures, home or group level administrative offices, corporate aircraft, hangars, or gymnasiums; or (3) the facilities are old or largely idle. A value significantly below normal may be assigned when a significant portion of defense manufacturing is performed in an environment characterized by outdated, inefficient, and labor-intensive capital equipment.

Cost Efficiency Factor

This special factor provides an incentive for contractors to reduce costs. To the extent that the contractor can demonstrate cost reduction efforts that benefit the pending contract, the contracting officer may increase the pre-negotiation profit objective by an amount not to exceed 4 percent of total objective cost. The following criteria are used to determine if using this factor is appropriate:

- The contractor's participation in single-process initiative improvements.
- Actual cost reductions achieved on prior contracts.
- Reduction or elimination of excess or idle facilities.
- The contractor's cost reduction initiatives (e.g., competition advocacy programs, technical insertion programs, obsolete parts control programs, spare parts pricing reform, value engineering, outsourcing of functions such as information technology). Metrics developed by the contractor such as fully loaded labor hours (i.e., cost per labor hour, including all direct and indirect costs) or other productivity measures may provide the basis for assessing the effectiveness of the contractor's cost reduction initiatives over time.
- The contractor's adoption of process improvements to reduce costs.
- Subcontractor cost reduction efforts.
- The contractor's effective incorporation of commercial items and processes.
- The contractor's investment in new facilities when such investments contribute to better asset utilization or improved productivity.

NASA GUIDELINES

Agencies other than DOD often follow different guidelines in addressing profit. NASA, in the NASA FAR Supplement, takes an approach similar to the DOD method for a structured profit or fee objective.

Of special interest to contractors is NASA's policy toward facilities capital cost of money. According to NASA regulations, when facilities capital cost of money is included as an item of cost in the contractor's proposal, it cannot be included in the cost base for calculating profit/fee. In addition, a reduction in the profit/fee objective will be made in the amount equal to the facilities capital cost of money allowed in accordance with FAR 31.205-10(a)(2). The regulations also state that CAS 417, Cost of Money As an Element of the Cost of Capital Assets Under Construction, should not appear in contract proposals. These costs are included in the initial value of a facility for purposes of calculating depreciation under CAS 414.

Figure 29 is an example of the application of NASA profit/fee guidelines. As of July 1999, NASA was considering adopting the DOD profit/fee guidelines.

OTHER AGENCIES' GUIDELINES

Other agencies address profit and facilities capital cost of money in varying ways. In some instances, they have incorporated a weighted guideline type of approach. In other cases, the subject of facilities capital cost of money is addressed in the supplemental regulation; however, it is seldom addressed in actual contract negotiation. Accordingly, a potential government contractor should either review the pertinent regulations of the agency he will be dealing with, or seek advice from a knowledgeable professional source.

The Department of Energy (DOE) does not have specific forms for profit/fee negotiations. However, in narrative form, the guidelines are very similar to the NASA guidelines. Figure 30 is an example of the application of DOE guidelines.

Figure 29
EXAMPLE OF APPLICATION OF NASA PROFIT/FEE GUIDELINES

<table>
<tr><td colspan="2">National
Aeronautics and
Space
Administration</td><td colspan="4">**Structured Approach**
Profit/Fee Objective</td></tr>
<tr><td colspan="3">1. CONTRACTOR</td><td colspan="3">4. RFP/ CONTRACT NO</td></tr>
<tr><td colspan="3">2. BUSINESS UNIT</td><td colspan="3">5. CONTRACT TYPE</td></tr>
<tr><td colspan="3">3. ADDRESS</td><td colspan="3"></td></tr>
<tr><td colspan="3" align="center">**CONTRACTOR EFFORT**</td><td colspan="3"></td></tr>
<tr><td colspan="5">6. MATERIAL</td><td>$4,200,000</td></tr>
<tr><td colspan="5">7. SUBCONTRACTORS</td><td>2,300,000</td></tr>
<tr><td colspan="5">8. DIRECT LABOR</td><td>5,821,000</td></tr>
<tr><td colspan="5">9. INDIRECT EXPENSES</td><td>6,071,347</td></tr>
<tr><td colspan="5">10. OTHER DIRECT COSTS</td><td>74,000</td></tr>
<tr><td colspan="5">11. SUBTOTAL COSTS</td><td>$18,466,347</td></tr>
<tr><td colspan="5">12. GENERAL AND ADMINISTRATIVE</td><td>2,772,250</td></tr>
<tr><td colspan="5">13. SUBTOTAL (Base used to calculate Profit/Fee)</td><td>$21,238,597</td></tr>
<tr><td colspan="5">14. COST OF MONEY</td><td>$2,527,833</td></tr>
<tr><td colspan="5">**15. TOTAL COST OBJECTIVE**</td><td>$23,766,430</td></tr>
<tr><td colspan="6" align="center">**WEIGHTED GUIDELINE PROFIT FACTORS**</td></tr>
<tr><td>PERFORMANCE
RISK FACTORS</td><td>ASSIGNED
WEIGHTING</td><td>ASSIGNED VALUE
(Range = 4% to 8%
normal = 6%)</td><td>CALCULATED %</td><td>BASE</td><td>PROFIT/FEE
OBJECTIVE</td></tr>
<tr><td></td><td>(a)</td><td>(b)</td><td>(c)</td><td>(d)</td><td>(e)</td></tr>
<tr><td>16. TECHNICAL</td><td>30.0%</td><td>6.0%</td><td>1.8%</td><td>$21,238,597</td><td>$382,295</td></tr>
<tr><td>17. MANAGEMENT</td><td>35.0%</td><td>6.0%</td><td>2.1%</td><td>21,238,597</td><td>446,011</td></tr>
<tr><td>18. COST CONTROL</td><td>35.0%</td><td>6.0%</td><td>2.1%</td><td>21,238,597</td><td>446,011</td></tr>
<tr><td>TOTAL ASSIGNED WEIGHT (100%)</td><td>100.0%</td><td></td><td></td><td></td><td></td></tr>
<tr><td>19. COMPOSITE PERFORMANCE RISK</td><td>Line above must
equal 100%</td><td></td><td></td><td></td><td>$1,274,316</td></tr>
<tr><td>20. CONTRACT TYPE RISK
(See Instructions for range)</td><td></td><td></td><td>ASSIGNED VALUE
4%</td><td>$21,238,597</td><td>849,544</td></tr>
<tr><td>21. WORKING CAPITAL
(See Instructions for range)</td><td>COSTS FINANCED
$5,309,649</td><td></td><td>LENGTH FACTOR
1.15</td><td>INTEREST FACTOR
4.250%</td><td>259,509</td></tr>
<tr><td>OTHER CONSIDERATIONS</td><td></td><td>WEIGHT RANGE
(Max of 5% Total)</td><td>WEIGHT
DESIGNATED</td><td>BASE</td><td></td></tr>
<tr><td>22. PAST PERFORMANCE</td><td></td><td>−1% TO +1%</td><td>0.20%</td><td>$21,238,597</td><td>42,477</td></tr>
<tr><td>23. SOCIO-ECONOMIC, ENVIRONMENTAL
PUBLIC POLICY IMPLEMENTATION</td><td></td><td>−.5% TO +.5%</td><td>0.20%</td><td>$21,238,597</td><td>42,477</td></tr>
<tr><td>24. CORPORATE CAPITAL INVESTMENT</td><td></td><td>0% TO +1%</td><td>0.28%</td><td>$21,238,597</td><td>59,468</td></tr>
<tr><td>25. UNUSUAL UNPLANNED GAP USEAGE</td><td></td><td>−1% TO 0%</td><td>0.00%</td><td>$21,238,597</td><td>0</td></tr>
<tr><td>26. OTHER INNOVATIONS & EFFICIENCIES</td><td></td><td>DISCRETIONARY</td><td>0.25%</td><td></td><td></td></tr>
<tr><td>SUBTOTAL OTHER CONSIDERATIONS</td><td></td><td>MAX TOTAL = 5%</td><td>0.93%</td><td>$21,238,597</td><td>197,519</td></tr>
<tr><td colspan="3" rowspan="3"></td><td rowspan="3"></td><td>27. SUBTOTAL PROFIT OBJ</td><td>$2,725,310</td></tr>
<tr><td>COST OF MONEY OFFSET</td><td>197,477</td></tr>
<tr><td>28. TOTAL PROFIT OBJECTIVE</td><td>2,527,833</td></tr>
<tr><td colspan="3" align="center">COMPOSITE OF COMPARISONS</td><td></td><td></td><td></td></tr>
<tr><td colspan="5">29. FEE % TOTAL COST (without COM offset—cost of money is not subtracted from fee)</td><td>12.83%</td></tr>
<tr><td colspan="5">30. (FEE less COM offset) % OF TOTAL COST OBJECTIVE (cost of money IS subtracted from fee)</td><td>11.90%</td></tr>
<tr><td colspan="6">**NASA FORM 634**   SEP 99 PREVIOUS EDITIONS ARE OBSOLETE</td></tr>
</table>

Figure 30
EXAMPLE OF APPLICATION OF DOE GUIDELINES

Department of Energy*				
Contractor Effort (Weight ranges (percent)	Range	Assigned Weight	Base	Amount
A. Material Acquisition:				
1. Purchased parts	1 to 3	3.00%	$1,250,000	$37,500
2. Subcontracted items	1 to 4	4.00%	4,000,000	160,000
3. Other materials	1 to 3	3.00%	1,250,000	37,500
B. Labor skills:				
1. Technical and managerial				
a. Scientific	10 to 20	20.00%	1,164,200	232,840
b. Project management/administration	8 to 20	20.00%	1,164,200	232,840
c. Engineering	8 to 14	14.00%	1,164,200	162,988
2. Manufacturing	4 to 8	8.00%	1,164,200	93,136
3. Support services	4 to 14	14.00%	1,164,200	162,988
C. Overhead:				
1. Technical and managerial	5 to 8	8.00%	2,023,667	161,893
2. Manufacturing	3 to 6	6.00%	2,023,667	121,420
3. Support services	3 to 7	7.00%	2,023,667	141,657
D. Other direct costs	3 to 8	8.00%	74,000	5,920
E. G&A (General Management)	5 to 7	7.00%	2,772,000	194,040
II. Contract Risk (type of contrast weights applied to total cost of items 1A thru E)	0 to 8	8.00%	21,238,000	1,699,040
				$3,443,762
III. Capital Investment (Weights applied to the net book value of allocable facilities)	5 to 20	20.00%	778,517	155,703
IV. Independent Research				
A. Investment in IR&D program (Weights applied to allocable IR&D costs)	5 to 7	7.00%	550,000	38,500
B. Developed items employed (Weights applied to total profit for items 1A thru E)	0 to 20	20.00%	3,443,762	688,752
V. Special Program Participation (Weights applied to total of profit for items 1A thru E)	−5 to 5	5.00%	3,443,762	172,188
VI. Other Considerations (Weights applied to profits for items 1A thru E)	−5 to 5	5.00%	3,443,762	172,188
Total				$4,671,094
Percentage				21.99%

*Not a DOE form

CHAPTER 9   Truth in Negotiations

Congress passed the Truth in Negotiations Act (TINA) on December 1, 1962, as Public Law 87-653. TINA requires that contractors disclose to the government details about costs they expect to incur during the performance of a contract awarded through negotiated procurement. This disclosure—and the sanctions that can be imposed if disclosure is not made—are intended to enable the government to negotiate a price based on a realistic and fully knowledgeable assessment of a contractor's cost expectations.

Violations of the Truth in Negotiations Act are commonly referred to as "defective pricing." The act is an important device to guard against profiteering by contractors by means of nondisclosure of cost or pricing data. However, an "excessive profit" is not necessarily evidence of a defective pricing, and a contract loss does not mean that defective pricing did not occur.

The TINA and FAR provisions on defective pricing have been strengthened over the years. Fundamentally, TINA requires contractors to disclose their cost or pricing data and to certify that the data are current, accurate, and complete as of the date of agreement on contract price. To the extent that this certification is erroneous, the government, under a price reduction clause, is entitled to a lower contract price even on firm-fixed-price contracts subject to TINA.

The objective of TINA is to place government price negotiators on equal grounds with contractors by requiring disclosure of cost and pricing data. However, while the contractor is required to disclose data, the contractor is not required to use the disclosed data in developing its price proposal. A contractor may select from available data and exercise judgment in estimating costs and developing a proposed price. However, the nondisclosure of relevant data that were reasonably available, even if the contractor did not consider them in the pricing, is defective pricing.

APPLICABILITY OF THE LAW

Originally, the Truth in Negotiations Act covered only contracts entered into by the Department of Defense and the National Aeronautics and Space Administration. Civil agencies eventually implemented the statutory provisions by procurement regulation. Thus, civilian agencies and military agencies have had similar provisions on defective pricing for many years. The disparity between military and civilian agencies in terms of statutory coverage was removed when the Competition in Contracting Act was passed in 1984. This legislation applied the provisions of TINA to civilian agencies as well as the military.

In 1993, the administration initiated an acquisition reform movement known as the National Performance Review (NPR). Two of the goals of the NPR were to streamline the acquisition process and to adopt commercial best practices. The NPR initiative was the precursor to two significant laws subsequently passed by Congress: the Federal Acquisition Streamlining Act of 1994 (FASA) and the Federal Acquisition Reform Act of 1996 (FARA). These three efforts by the administration and Congress all sought to have the government procure products and services from more suppliers, preferably commercial contractors.

At the outset, it was apparent that all the procurement legislation—particularly TINA and the CAS, which are the biggest impediments to commercial producers—could not be nullified or changed. Thus, the next approach was to exempt as much procurement as possible from this onerous legislation. This objective was accomplished by broadening the definition of what constituted "commercial" products and services. These acts touched upon virtually every aspect of the solicitation and award process, and changed the requirement for submitting cost or pricing data (the trigger point for virtually every TINA violation allegation). Because of the dire consequences attached to defective data, all government contractors need to understand when cost and pricing data are truly required.

BASIC COVERAGE

Contractors need to be aware of how TINA addresses certain key aspects of their negotiated procurements; in other words, what contracts—or, more appropriately, what contract actions—are covered by TINA. Specifically, contractors should be aware of the dollar threshold, the limitation of TINA to negotiated contracts, and how the requirements are passed down from a prime contractor. The treatment of contract changes or modifications is also significant.

Covered Contracts

TINA's defective pricing provisions apply to the following pricing actions:

1. Negotiated prime contracts over $700,000[1]

2. Prime contract modifications or changes over $700,000

3. Negotiated subcontracts over $700,000 at any tier, if the prime contractor and each higher-tier subcontractor have been required to furnish cost and pricing data (unless waived)

4. Subcontract modifications or changes over $700,000 at any tier, if the prime contractor and each higher-tier subcontractor have been required to furnish cost and pricing data.

For contract and subcontract modifications or changes over $700,000, the provisions apply not only to negotiated contracts, but also to contracts that were initially the result of sealed-bid procedures. This is necessary because the government does not have adequate assurance that competitive forces will generate a reasonable price for a contract modification under sealed-bid conditions. When a contractor is undertaking a contract modification, no real competitive forces can be brought to bear, so the government seeks the additional assurance of price reasonableness provided through the disclosure of cost or pricing data.

The $700,000 threshold for contract modifications is determined by adding the upward price adjustments and the downward price adjustments. For example, if a contract modification consists of a downward price adjustment of $400,000 and an upward price adjustment of $400,000, the total modification amounts to $800,000; thus, the modification is subject to the provisions of the act.

Some contracting officers request certification for awards of less than $700,000; however, there is no legal requirement to do so and the regulations discourage this practice. A contracting officer may not require the submission of cost or pricing data to support any action (contracts, subcontracts, or modifications), but may require information *other than cost or pricing data* to support a determination of price reasonableness or cost realism. However, any contractor who *certifies* to cost and pricing data for such awards is covered by the same provisions and is liable for the same price adjustments as required by law. Thus, the watchword is: If certification is not required, don't certify!

Prohibitions on Obtaining Cost or Pricing Data

Cost or pricing data may not be obtained for acquisitions at or below the simplified acquisition threshold, which is currently $100,000.[2] A contracting officer may not require submission of cost or pricing data to support any action (contracts, subcontracts or modifications), but may require information *other than cost or pricing data* to support a determination of price reasonableness or cost realism under the following conditions:

1. When the contracting officer determines that prices agreed upon are based on adequate price competition

2. When the contracting officer determines that prices agreed upon are based on prices set by law or regulation

3. When a commercial item is being acquired

4. When a waiver has been granted

5. When a contract or subcontract is being modified for commercial items.

Adequate Price Competition

A price is based on adequate price competition if two or more responsible offerors, competing independently, submit priced offers that satisfy the government's expressed requirement and if: (1) award will be made to the offeror whose proposal represents the best value where price is a substantial factor in source selection; and (2) there is no finding that the price of the otherwise successful offeror is unreasonable.

Adequate price competition also exists when there was a reasonable expectation that two or more responsible offerors, competing independently, would submit priced offers in response to the solicitation's expressed requirement, even though only one offer is received from a responsible offeror. In addition, the acquisition must also meet the following criteria:

1. The contracting officer can reasonably conclude that the offer was submitted with the expectation of competition (i.e., circumstances indicate that the offeror believed that at least one other offeror was capable of submitting a meaningful offer and the offeror had no reason to believe that other potential offerors did not intend to submit an offer).

2. The determination that the proposed price is based on adequate price competition is reasonable, and is approved at a level above the contracting officer.

A price is also based on adequate price competition if price analysis demonstrates that the proposed price is reasonable in comparison with current or recent prices for the same or similar items.

Consideration must also be given to reflect changes in market conditions, economic conditions, quantities, or terms and conditions under contracts that resulted from adequate price competition. For example, if cost or pricing data were furnished on previous production buys and the contracting officer determines that those data—when combined with updated information—are sufficient, an exception may be granted.

Commercial Items

An acquisition for an item that meets the commercial item definition is exempt from the requirement for cost or pricing data. According to FAR 2.101, "commercial item" means any item, other than real property, that is of a type customarily used for nongovernmental purposes and that: (1) has been sold, leased, or licensed to the general public; or (2) has been offered for sale, lease, or license to the general public. A commercial item is also any item that evolved from and through advances in technology or performance and that is not yet available in the commercial marketplace, but will be available in the commercial marketplace in time to satisfy the delivery requirements under a government solicitation.

Furthermore, commercial items include any item that would satisfy this definition, except for: (1) modifications of a type customarily available in the commercial marketplace; or (2) minor modifications of a type not customarily available in the commercial marketplace made to meet federal government requirements. "Minor" modifications means modifications that do not significantly alter the nongovernmental function or essential physical characteristics of an item or component, or change the purpose of a process. Factors to be considered in determining whether a modification is minor include the value and size of the modification and the comparative value and size of the final product. Dollar values and percentages may be used as guideposts, but are not conclusive evidence that a modification is minor.

Installation services, maintenance services, repair services, training services, and other services also can meet this definition. These services are considered commercial items if they are procured for support of a commercial item, if the source of such services: (1) offers such services to the general public and the federal government contemporaneously and under similar terms and conditions; and

(2) offers to use the same work force to provide such services to the federal government as is used to provide such services to the general public.

Commercial items include services of a type offered and sold competitively in substantial quantities in the commercial marketplace based on established catalog or market prices for specific tasks performed under standard commercial terms and conditions. This includes services that are sold based on hourly rates.

Waivers

The head of the contracting activity may waive the requirement for submission of cost or pricing data in exceptional cases. This official may consider waiving the requirement if the price can be determined to be fair and reasonable without submission of cost or pricing data.

If the head of the contracting activity has waived the requirement for submission of cost or pricing data, the contractor or higher-tier subcontractor to whom the waiver relates is considered as having been required to provide cost or pricing data. Consequently, award of any lower-tier subcontract expected to exceed the cost or pricing data threshold requires the submission of cost or pricing data unless an exception otherwise applies to the subcontract or the waiver specifically includes the subcontract and the rationale supporting the waiver for that subcontract.

Other circumstances where cost or pricing data are not required include: (1) the exercise of an option at the price established at contract award or initial negotiation; and (2) the evaluation of proposals used solely for overrun funding or interim billing price adjustments.

Requiring Information Other Than Cost or Pricing Data

The contracting officer should not obtain more information than is necessary for determining price reasonableness or evaluating cost realism. The contracting officer should require submission of information from the offeror only to the extent necessary to determine the reasonableness of the price.

Unless an exception exists for adequate price competition or the prices are set by law or regulation, the information submitted by the offeror must include, at a minimum, appropriate price information on the same or similar items sold. The contractor's format should be used for submittal of the information. The contracting officer will ensure that the information is sufficiently current to permit negotiation of a fair and reasonable price. Requests for updated information should be limited to information that affects the adequacy of the proposal. Such data *should not be certified.*

If adequate price competition exists but unusual circumstances make it necessary for the contracting officer to acquire additional information to ascertain price reasonableness, the contracting officer should, to the maximum extent practicable, obtain additional information from sources other than the offeror. In addition, the contracting officer should request information to determine the cost realism of competing offers or to evaluate competing approaches.

Limitations relating to commercial items include: (1) requests for sales data should be limited to data for the same or similar items during a relevant time period; and (2) information should be requested in the form regularly maintained by the offeror as part of its commercial operations. This commercial item information is exempt from the Freedom of Information Act and may not be disclosed outside the government.

PRICE REDUCTIONS

To enforce the contractor's obligations to disclose cost or pricing data, the Truth in Negotiations Act provides for a price reduction for defective pricing as follows:

A prime contract or change or modification thereto under which such a certificate is required shall contain a provision that the price to the government, including profit or fee, shall be adjusted to exclude any significant sums by which it may be determined by the head of the agency that such price was increased because the contractor or any subcontractor required to furnish such a certificate, furnished cost or pricing data which, as of the date agreed upon between the parties (which date shall be as close to the date of the agreement on the negotiated price as it is practical), was inaccurate, incomplete, or noncurrent.

This statutory provision and its regulatory implementation have been the subject of many decisions by the Claims Court and Boards of Contract Appeals. These must be examined to understand the full magnitude of a contractor's responsibility for disclosure of cost or pricing data.

SPECIAL SUBCONTRACT CONSIDERATIONS

The government's right to lower a prime contract price extends to where it had been increased because a subcontractor furnished defective cost or pricing data. The FAR rules governing submission of data require the prime contractor to submit cost or pricing data for subcontracts that are: (1) $12,500,000 or more; or (2) both more than $700,000 and more than 10 percent of the prime con-trac-tor's proposed price, unless the contracting officer believes such submission is unnecessary.

A contracting officer may request that the contractor or subcontractor submit to the government, or cause submission of, subcontractor cost or pricing data for subcontracts between $100,000 and $700,000 that the contracting officer considers necessary

When a subcontract exceeds the $700,000 threshold, subcontractor cost or pricing data are to be current, accurate, and complete as of the date of price agreement, or, if applicable, an earlier date agreed upon by the parties and specified on the contractor's Certificate of Current Cost or Pricing Data. The contractor will update the subcontractor's data, as appropriate, during source selection and negotiations.

If there is more than one prospective subcontractor for any given work, the contractor need only submit to the government cost or pricing data for the prospective subcontractor most likely to receive the award.

The same exemptions that apply to prime contractors also apply to prospective and actual subcontractors. Data are required only from the most likely subcontractor for each component, as long as the prime's subcontract estimate is based on that sub-con-tractor's data. These requirements flow down to all tiers; that is, the data of a first-tier prospective subcontractor must include data from the most likely second-tier subcontractors who are: (1) over $10 million; or (2) over $700,000 and over 10 percent of the first-tier subcontract's price.

The prime contractor and the higher-tier subcontractors all have a responsibility to review and evaluate the prospective and actual subcontractors' cost or pricing data that they send to the government as part of the prime contractor's cost or pricing data submission.

The FAR requires a prime contractor to "flow down" this standard contract clause in its subcontracts to obtain cost or pricing data from all actual subcontractors: (1) before any subcontract expected to exceed $700,000 is awarded; and (2) before the pricing of any subcontract modification involving aggregate increases or decreases in costs (plus applicable markup or fee) expected to exceed $700,000, except where an exemption exists. Under the FAR, a prime contractor is responsible for defective data submitted by a subcontractor. To protect itself, a prime contractor may want to include an indemnification clause for defective pricing in its subcontracts. The inclusion of such a clause is a matter of negotiation between a prime contractor and a subcontractor.

What happens when a prime contract is negotiated before the subcontract price is negotiated? Under a flexibly priced prime contract, the government has a continuing and direct financial interest in subcontractor prices that is unaffected by the agreement on the prime contract price. However, when the prime contract is firm-fixed-price, defective data in an actual subcontract submitted and negotiated after the prime contract price has been finalized have no effect on the prime contract price. No audit recommendation for price reduction is appropriate.

A different question arises when subcontracts are awarded before prime contracts. Examples are letter contracts and unpriced change orders. Then, the contract clause requires the subcontractor's data to be complete, accurate, and current as of the date of the subcontractor's price agreement rather than the prime's certification date.

The law grants agency representatives access to subcontractor records. Prime contractors have no extracontractual right to audit a subcontractor's books and records. It is only through an audit clause in the subcontract that this right can arise. Many subcontractors will submit to government audit but, for competitive reasons, refuse the same access to prime contractors. In these cases, the government is obligated to give a prime all the information necessary to support a prime contract price reduction for defective subcontractor data, which should help the prime to some extent in any action against the subcontractor. Confidential business information can be made available, however, "only under conditions that will fully protect it from improper disclosure."

GOVERNMENT BURDEN OF PROOF

The government has the burden of proof to show entitlement to a price cut under the price reduction for defective pricing clause of the contract. In Singer Co., Librascope Division (ASBCA No. 17604), the Court of Federal Claims stated: "There is no question that the government has the burden of proof of all elements of defective pricing cases."

Basically, the government must prove five elements:

1. The information provided by the contractor fits the definition of cost or pricing data and it existed before the agreement on price.

2. Current, accurate, and complete data were reasonably available to the contractor before the agreement on price.

3. Current, accurate, and complete data were not submitted to the contracting officer or one of his or her authorized representatives and the government did not have actual knowledge of the data.

4. The government relied on the defective data in its negotiations with the contractor.

5. Defective data caused an increase in the contract price.

Each of the burden-of-proof areas has evolved over time, primarily from interpretation in the case law. Relevant cases are primarily Board of Contract Appeals and Court of Federal Claims decisions. Much of the discussion in this section refers to decisions that have had a significant impact on the interpretation and development of the Truth in Negotiations Act.

Cost or Pricing Data

The government must prove that the alleged defective data submitted are, in fact, "cost or pricing data" before their lack of disclosure can be used to require a price reduction. FAR 15.401 defines cost or pricing data as:

> . . .all facts that, as of the date of price agreement or, if applicable, an earlier date agreed upon between the parties that is as close as practicable to the date of agreement on price, prudent buyers and sellers would reasonably expect to affect price negotiations significantly. Cost or pricing data are data requiring certification in accordance with 15.406-2. Cost or pricing data are factual, not judgmental, and are verifiable. While they do not indicate the accuracy of the prospective contractor's judgment about estimated future costs or projections, they do include the data forming the basis for that judgment. Cost or pricing data are more than historical accounting data; they are all the facts that can be reasonably expected to contribute to the soundness of estimates of future costs and to the validity of determinations of costs already incurred. They also include such factors as: vendor quotations; nonrecurring costs; information on changes in production methods and in production or purchasing volume; data supporting projections of business prospects and objectives and related operations costs; unit-cost trends such as those associated with labor efficiency; make-or-buy decisions; estimated resources to attain business goals; and information on management decisions that could have a significant bearing on costs.

Although the FAR definition of cost or pricing data relates to factual information rather than to contractor estimates and judgment, factual data are broadly interpreted, and the distinction between facts and judgments may at times be difficult to determine. For example, a contractor's judgmental analysis involving estimates is factual, and while the government cannot allege defective pricing based on the accuracy of these estimates, it can do so based on the concealment or misrepresentation of judgments. In Aerojet-General Corporation (ASBCA No. 12264), internal engineering analyses, which were reasonably available within the company before negotiations with the government, concluded that a subcontractor's proposal was substantially overstated. The contractor argued that as of the date of its certificate with the government, a final agreement on any price reduction had not been reached with the subcontractor (Straza).

In resolving this issue, the Board observed: "The above argument misses the point. The appellant's obligation under the contract was to furnish accurate, complete, and current cost and pricing data. This the appellant did not do. Appellant's engineering analyses, cost estimates or other data which revealed that some elements of Straza's quotation were significantly overstated are in themselves significant cost and pricing data, which appellant relied on in its negotiations with Straza. We hold that the failure to disclose these analyses, cost estimates or other data was sufficient to justify a finding, which we hereby make, that the appellant did not furnish accurate, complete, and current cost or pricing data."

The definition of cost or pricing data also states that the data must be material enough to affect price negotiations significantly. The question has often been asked, What is "significant"? Significance is not necessarily based on relative value. In Sylvania Electric Products, Inc. v. U.S. (202 Ct. Cl. 16, 479 F.2d 1342), the court said that significance is to be defined in terms of any "logical nexus between the nondisclosed pricing data and the possibility of lower negotiated contract price." In American Bosch Arma Corporation (ASBCA No. 10305), the Board found that approxi-

mately $21,000 on a $15 million contract was significant. The Board stated that whether or not the undisclosed data were significant depended on their effect upon the negotiation of a fair price, and not upon their percentage dollar effect on the whole contract.

The statutory definition of cost or pricing data was codified for the first time in the FY 1987 DOD authorization bill. This definition provided that cost or pricing data include only data that are factual and verifiable and do not include judgmental data. However, the data do include the factual information from which a judgment was derived. House and Senate conferees were very concerned with clarifying the definition of cost or pricing data that "a contractor is not required to provide and certify to data relating to judgments, strategies, plans for the future, or estimates. A contractor is required, on the other hand, to disclose any information relating to execution or implementation of any such strategies or plans."

The conferees provided the following example. A corporate decision to attempt to negotiate a new labor wage rate structure with its employee union, although verifiable, is not considered cost or pricing data. If the company liaison made an offer to the union, the fact that an offer has been made, and the details and status of the offer, on the other hand, are information that should be conveyed to the government.

The Conference Report accompanying the 1988 TINA amendments reversed this position by noting: ". . .the conferees believe that a contractor should disclose a decision to act or judgmental data, even though is has not been implemented."

The statutory definition, combined with the conferee language, should assist contractors in determining what are cost or pricing data. Consequently, a contractor is not required to disclose judgments as long as the underlying facts are disclosed. Further, strategies and plans need not be disclosed until the contractor has taken steps to execute or implement them.

Consider the following example as a more practical illustration of what is and isn't defective pricing.

First, assume that a contractor tells the government that last year's direct labor rate was $10.00 per hour. This is a fact; if incorrect, this is defective pricing. Second, assume that a contractor tells the government that the estimate for the direct labor rate for next year is $11.00 per hour. This is a judgment; if the eventual rate is $10.80, this is not defective pricing.

Third, assume that the contractor tells the government that the estimated direct labor rate for next year is $11.000 based on last year's rate of $10.00 and planned escalation of 10 percent. The $10.00 per hour rate is a fact that could be subject to defective pricing. The 10 percent is a judgment; if the eventual escalation is only 5 percent, this is not defective pricing. Fourth, assume that a contractor tells the government the same statement as in the third scenario but has budgetary data, board of director minutes, or other documents that indicate that the planned escalation is 5 percent. The 10 percent is judgment; however, if there are additional data that are not disclosed that would have influenced the government acceptance of the 10 percent, this is defective pricing.

Fifth, assume the same facts as in scenario four, but the contractor tells the government that the 5 percent is an objective that may not be attained. This disclosure obviates any defective pricing.

The concept of cost or pricing data is comprehensive in scope. The FAR identifies a number of factors that are generally viewed as cost or pricing data. However, which data are cost or pricing data requiring disclosure to the government and which data are not are issues that often depend on the factual circumstances of a given case. Numerous judicial decisions over the years have dealt with these issues.

Vendor/Subcontractor Quotes

Vendor quotations and subcontractor proposals obtained by prime contractors are specifically included in the FAR's definition of cost or pricing data. Frequent questions in this area include: What is the prime contractor's responsibility to require submittal of, and actually review the adequacy of, cost or pricing data submitted by subcontractors? What if the prime or higher-tier subcontractor did not rely on quotes in pricing its data? Do subcontractor prices settled after the prime has certified its data and negotiated with the government have to be disclosed? Each of these areas is discussed in the following paragraphs.

Subcontractor Data and Prime Contractor's Responsibilities. Prime contractors are responsible for obtaining and reviewing cost or pricing data from subcontractors. FAR 15.404-3 states that the prime contractor or subcontractor is to: (1) conduct appropriate cost or price analyses to establish the reasonableness of proposed subcontract prices; (2) include the results of these analyses in the price proposal; and (3) when required, submit subcontractor cost or pricing data to the government as part of its own cost or pricing data. Any contractor or subcontractor that is required to submit cost or pricing data must also obtain and analyze cost or pricing data before awarding any subcontract, purchase order, or modification expected to exceed $700,000, unless an exception applies to that action.

Specifically, the FAR states:

> The contractor shall submit, or cause to be submitted by the subcontractor(s), cost or pricing data to the Government for subcontracts that are the lower of either (i) $12,500,000 or more or (ii) both more than the pertinent cost or pricing data threshold and more than 10 percent of the prime contractor's

proposed price, unless the contracting officer believes such submission is unnecessary. The contracting officer may require the contractor or subcontractor to submit to the Government, or cause submission of, subcontractor cost or pricing data below the thresholds covered in (i) and (ii) that the contracting officer considers necessary for adequately pricing the prime contract.

Subcontractor cost or pricing data shall be submitted in the format provided in Table 15-2 of 15.408 or the alternate format specified in the solicitation. Subcontractor cost or pricing data shall be current, accurate, and complete as of the date of price agreement, or, if applicable, an earlier date agreed upon by the parties and specified on the contractor's Certificate of Current Cost or Pricing Data. The contractor shall update subcontractor's data, as appropriate, during source selection and negotiations. If there is more than one prospective subcontractor for any given work, the contractor need only submit to the Government cost or pricing data for the prospective subcontractor most likely to receive the award.

Depending on the circumstances, the prime contractor and higher-tier subcontractors may conduct these cost or price reviews in a number of ways, ranging from simple desk reviews (particularly in situations involving relatively low dollar value combined with high reliance on the subcontractor's data) to comprehensive analyses and audits of subcontractor's cost or pricing data. For example, the prime or higher-tier subcontractor may have a significant amount of current cost information about the subcontractor in its files that history shows to be highly accurate.

Often, the government's contracting officer and the prime or higher-tier subcontractor request an assist audit from a government audit agency such as the Defense Contract Audit Agency (DCAA). The contracting officer conducts these reviews if he or she believes that doing so is necessary to ensure reasonableness of the total proposed price. Also, a prime contractor or higher-tier subcontractor may request that an assist audit be conducted, especially if the contractor cannot conduct these reviews or the subcontractor refuses access to its books and records. Procedurally, the request for an assist audit should be made to the requesting contractor's administrative contracting officer (ACO) who, in turn, will contact the subcontractor's ACO, who will issue the request to the cognizant audit agency.

When it comes to the prime or higher-tier subcontractor's responsibilities for subcontract cost or pricing data, the question often arises of what types of information must be disclosed to the government. When dealing with identifiable, actual subcontractors (i.e., the price has been negotiated before the prime's certification with the government), the prime must disclose all cost or pricing data and related results of cost/price analysis to the government, and flow down (i.e, pass on or include in the subcontract provisions) the subcontract cost or pricing data contract clause. The FAR requires that for prospective subcontractors, actual data obtained from the prospective subcontractor need not be submitted to the government unless certain dollar and other threshold criteria are met. However, the prime contractor still must disclose to the government "the results of subcontract reviews and evaluations as part of their own cost or pricing data submission."

What constitutes "results" of subcontract reviews? Disclosure is a double-edged sword for contractors. Too much disclosure may be construed as negatively affecting the contractor's negotiating ability with the government. However, too little disclosure may end in defective pricing. Generally, a contractor must disclose to the government any factual data that are significant in determining price. This includes the results of fact-findings, audits, and miscellaneous analyses. In ensuring compliance with TINA, however, the government does not require that the contractor use all, or any, of the data in determining its cost or price.

Disclosure to the government of a range of possible subcontract prices or costs by element, based on analysis, is necessary for complying with the Truth in Negotiations Act. The contractor may state, if applicable, that it does not rely on certain areas of that range in developing its price. In this way, some of the prime contractor's negotiating strategy may be salvaged and compliance maintained; that is, disclosure is accomplished, but judgment is maintained in the estimation process.

A contractor is also responsible for updating the cost or pricing data of its prospective subcontractor. Any subcontractor data that a prime contractor submits to the government must be current, accurate, and complete as of the final price agreement—that is, the date specified on the prime contractor's certificate of current cost or pricing.

Contractor Reliance on Quotes. Questions about the need for disclosing data relating to vendor quotes or subcontractor proposals often arise if the prime contractor or higher-tier subcontractor does not rely on the quote/proposal at all in its pricing. In other words, would the data qualify as cost or pricing data? The safest rule is to make full disclosure and identify the degree of reliance placed on the data. Anything short of this runs the risk of defective pricing.

Judicial decisions in this area have been somewhat inconsistent, and the resolution of the cases has truly been based on the facts and circumstances of each case. By and large, the facts must be clear enough to show that the data in question were in no way considered by the contractor in developing its price. Further, there should be evidence that the

government would not have relied on the data either.

This element of contractor nonreliance has to be something more than non-an-ti-ci-pa-tion of award. For example, in Chu Associates, Inc. (ASBCA No. 15004), the Board ruled that a subcontractor's quotation, received before the prime's signing of its certificate with the government, but not intended to be used, did not constitute cost or pricing data, and Chu's failure to disclose it therefore was not defective pricing.

In the Board's decision, it described the distinction between the facts and circumstances in this case (and another, decided the other way!) as follows:

> This case represents a variation of the Luneberg Lens issue decided by the Court of Claims (Cutler-Hammer, Inc. v. United States, 189 Ct. Cl. 76). In that case the contractor failed to disclose a quotation it had received from a potential supplier. Although that contractor regarded the non-disclosed quotation as being unreasonably low, and hence not to be taken seriously, it was interested enough to follow it up with a request for a technical proposal, which it received two days before it executed its Certificate of Current Cost or Pricing Data.
>
> The Court held that such a quotation, which was under active consideration prior to the date on which the Certificate was executed, was cost or pricing data that should have been disclosed. By contrast, although appellant here received the Geonautics quote well before the date on which it executed its Certificate of Current Cost or Pricing Data, it gave no consideration before that date to the use of Geo-nautics as a source of supply, nor did it make so much as a casual investigation of its capabilities

of performing the work. Under such circumstances, we conclude that the cost or pricing data furnished by appellant were accurate, complete, and current as of the date its Certificate was executed.

Subsequent decisions have apparently taken a more stringent view. For example, in Bell & Howell Co. (ASBCA 11999), the Board said, "The vendor quotes themselves were cost or pricing data; the contractor's judgmental decision not to base its proposal price on such quotations was not cost or pricing data."

Subcontract Prices Negotiated After Prime's Price Agreement with the Government. The Truth in Negotiations Act requires that all cost or pricing data be current, accurate, and complete as of the "price agreement date" between the prime contractor and the government. As a practical matter, the contract execution date is often some time later than the price agreement date. The question then arises: "Are updated data such as negotiated subcontract prices received after price agreement date but before contract execution date cost or pricing data that should be disclosed?" The answer is no. In Paceco, Inc. (ASBCA No. 16548), the Board ruled that the government's right of recovery to overstatements is limited to ". . .data not current as certified on the contractor's certificate of current cost or pricing data (that is, effective as of the price agreement date)."

Notwithstanding the nonapplicability of the Truth in Negotiations Act to data updated after the price agreement date, other problems may come up. For example, if government auditors determine that a contractor is regularly delaying its finalization of price with subcontractors until after price agreement with the government, they may decide that the contractor's estimating system is inadequate. This is especially true if the prime contractor consistently negotiates a

lower price with the subcontractor than was initially proposed to the government. Trying to resolve this perceived problem, auditors will often develop a decrement factor to apply to proposed subcontract costs, resulting in audit-recommended cost questions. The decrement factor is based on historical trends of average lower negotiated subcontract prices realized by the prime. Often referred to as price-reduction techniques by contractors, auditors use the concept to question costs in their proposal recommendation to contracting officers.

Nonrecurring Costs

Nonrecurring costs generally involve specific start-up activity and materials that are required on a one-time basis. The FAR recognizes nonrecurring costs as cost or pricing data needing disclosure to the government. Such costs are often developed on the basis of engineering estimates. These estimates and related analysis constitute factual data, and therefore must be disclosed to the government. Engineering estimates should be well-documented on a rational and overall judgmental basis. In addition, contractors must be careful to identify and disclose any updates to the nonrecurring costs before the price agreement date with the government (e.g., due to changes in scope of work or engineering adjustments to estimating rationale).

Changes in Production Methods or Purchasing Volume

Changes in production methods used or purchasing volume are factual data that could potentially affect a negotiated price, and the FAR thus classifies them as cost or pricing data. However, when does the change become cost or pricing data, and therefore disclosable in forward-pricing proposals? Is it when management makes the decision to change or when the change actually goes into effect? The answer depends largely on the individual facts and circumstances. Generally speaking, whenever management has finalized its decision to initiate a change, that change becomes cost or pricing data as long as the change could reasonably affect price negotiations.

For example, assume that management finalizes a decision to switch its existing manual engineering drawing system over to an automated computer-aided design system. Expected labor productivity improvement is 4 to 1, but the equipment will not be obtained until approximately one year later. When should this information be disclosed to the government? At a minimum, the contractor would be obliged to disclose its anticipated change on any proposals involving length of performance extending beyond the equipment's anticipated acquisition date. In addition, the potential productivity improvement factor is a critical factual item that must be disclosed.

Another example might involve a contractor's decision to alter purchase volumes, perhaps purchasing common parts on an overall requirement basis rather than on a project-by-project basis. Such requirement buys will undoubtedly lead to higher volume purchases and result in increased quantity discounts. Since the decision will affect the price, it is necessary to disclose it as cost or pricing data.

Data Supporting Projections

Factual data supporting projections are defined as cost or pricing data. Assuming that the data are reasonably available to a contractor and are significant enough to affect price, the data must be disclosed to the government. In reviewing cost rates, government auditors and contracting officers often want to review the build-up of supporting data. Information such as budgets, accounting records documenting historical material costs, and cost accounting methods used in estimating, accumulating, and recording costs are commonly requested. For forward-pricing rate agreements (FPRAs), the current regulations require that an FPRA be identified each time a new proposal is certified. In addition, the contractor must disclose any change in circumstances or any new data that affect the accuracy of the previously established rate. A contractor's failure to disclose such changes may constitute defective pricing.

Controversy occasionally arises between the government and contractors in determining the level of detail and type of data that must be disclosed as cost or pricing data supporting projections. For example, government auditors often want to obtain all budgetary information at all levels within a contractor's organization, including data referred to as motivational budgets or profit plans. Contractors often take exception to releasing overly detailed information to auditors on the basis that such data are not necessary for the auditor's review of rates.

For example, formalized budgetary data modified and consolidated at a higher organizational level represent the basis for the forward-pricing rates on which the company relies. Whether it is necessary to disclose to the government lower-level detailed budgetary data as well as motivational budget information is a question that can be addressed only after considering the unique circumstances of a given case. The issue often revolves around the manner in which the data are used in conjunction with their causal relationship to the proposed price.

The form of data usage and association with the proposed price were addressed in E-Systems (ASBCA No. 17557), a major Board decision dealing with defective pricing. The unique facts of this case, which are essential to the accurate application of the legal principles involved, are succinctly stated in the opening paragraph of the decision: "This dispute involves a Government action to recover $445,684 because of claimed defects in the cost and pricing data submitted by the appellant during the negotiation of a contract. The alleged defective data consists of a profit plan, which admittedly was not provided to the government by the appellant.

It is the Government's position that the profit plan included information concerning future work which justified projecting substantially lower overhead rates than those accepted by the Government on the basis of other data provided by the appellant."

The profit plan included information that was not consistent with the formal budget management used in projecting forward-pricing rates. If certain assumptions in the profit plan were included in the forward-pricing computation, they could have altered the rates significantly. To what extent does the variant information in the profit plan have to be disclosed as cost or pricing data? In finding for the contractor in its nondisclosure of the profit plan data, the Board focused its decision on a number of apparently critical factual elements.

The basic underlying firm data upon which the appellant's profit plan was based were known by the government auditors and negotiators. The appellant's profit plan included inaccuracies because it was not prepared in accordance with the appellant's normal accounting methods. Specifically, the profit plan did not indicate the high- and low-volume overhead rates or research and engineering charges. The plan included an arbitrary addition of $3 million of forecast future work. The plan was prepared primarily for training purposes and was not used as the basis for any significant management decisions.

Unit-Cost Trends

Unit-cost trends are included in the FAR definition of cost or pricing data. Common examples of these trends are experienced labor and material costs incurred on previous buys or similar contracts. Such historical data need to be disclosed to the government, notwithstanding actual reliance by the contractor in pricing the proposal.

In Lambert Engineering Company (ASBCA No. 13338), the contractor's accounting records of direct manufacturing labor were kept in dollars. Government auditors (here,

the General Accounting Office) conducting a postaward review identified a period, between the contractor's initial submission of its proposal and price negotiation, when costs were incurred on a similar-to contract. The auditors alleged that incurrence of these costs during the interim period constituted cost or pricing data that should have been disclosed as updated data. Much of the controversy in this case involved the method the auditors used to derive the alleged updated labor hours.

The hours were determined by dividing the recorded manufacturing labor hours by a composite hourly labor rate. Lambert Engineering rebutted by stating that even if the "labor-hour data is the best obtainable, it is not good enough." Lambert Engineering argued that it was charged with misrepresenting facts; however, since the alleged facts were nonexistent and the government's contentions were based strictly on estimates, the charge was legally invalid.

The Board rejected Lambert Engineering's arguments and its concept of cost or pricing data. Regarding the labor-hour data, the Board stated:

> . . .while admittedly not "actuals," [the labor-hour data] were the sort of data which prudent buyers and sellers would reasonably expect to have significant effect on the price negotiations. . .the data were verifiable in the sense that they could be checked out against the cost data from which they were derived. They showed unit cost trends associated with labor efficiency since they were calculated in a consistent manner. Appellant submitted such data with the proposal. Having done so, it had an obligation, we think, to keep the data current at least to the time of price negotiation.
>
> In short, we consider that the labor hour estimates submitted by ap-

pellant with its proposal were facts which could reasonably be considered by a prudent negotiator to have a significant bearing on the contract price, notwithstanding the element of approximation introduced by the use of the composite labor rate. Therefore, we hold that these facts, that is, the estimates derived from appellant's historical cost data, are themselves cost or pricing data within the meaning of this term as used in appellant's certificate and the "Price Reduction for Defective Cost or Pricing Data" clause.

A contractor need not use a learning curve to prepare an estimate. If a learning curve is used, it should be disclosed. If data for construction of a learning curve are not disclosed, this could be defective pricing. However, a contractor is not obligated to perform a learning curve analysis to avoid defective pricing. Board decisions stress that the Truth in Negotiations Act requires disclosure of existing data but not creation of analyses or formats that the government would like to see.

Make-or-Buy Decisions

Make-or-buy decisions qualify as cost or pricing data as they relate to forward pricing on proposals. Such decisions may be made informally or formally, in accordance with the requirements of the FAR. One of the common problems in determining what decisions are cost or pricing data has to do with the contractor's categorization of the decision as a "must make," "must buy," or "can either make or buy" decision. For example, if a contractor proposes that an item is a "must buy," yet there is information reasonably available within the organization that a make is possible, and such data are not disclosed, the contractor could be faced with defective pricing.

In FMC Corporation (ASBCA Nos. 10095 and 11113), FMC bid a *purchase* for certain components, but in performing the contract,

it *manufactured* the items. The government alleged that FMC knew, prior to price negotiation, that it could manufacture the items but did not disclose such data. Based on the facts, the Board found, however, that even though FMC had then been engaged in experiments that ultimately led the company to manufacture the items, the results were not reasonably available to FMC at the price negotiation date.

Management Decisions Affecting Costs

Management decisions affecting costs could qualify as cost or pricing data. Such circumstances can arise in numerous ways. A proposed change in an accounting practice is a common example. Clearly, once management has decided to make the change—for example, alter an allocation method or redefine a cost as direct or indirect—such data must be disclosed to the government. The impact of the change must be reflected in pricing the proposal from the anticipated change date forward.

Available Data

The regulations require data to be accurate, complete, and current on the date of agreement on price. The terms "accurate" and "complete" are reasonably self-evident. The meaning of "current," however, raises questions of lag time in corporate communications and the reasonable availability of certain types of data. The regulations say that the contractor must disclose all significant and relevant data reasonably available at the time of negotiations. Unfortunately, there are no formula rules that can be applied to the definition of "significant and relevant."

The contractor's responsibility is not limited by the personal knowledge of its negotiator if the undisclosed facts were known at a reasonably high level in the company. In the Aerojet General decision, the fact that neither the contractor's negotiators nor the person who signed the certificate was aware of the engineering analysis of the subcontractor was not important. The Board determined that the data were reasonably available because some Aerojet management executives, including negotiators of the subcontract, were aware that the sub-con-trac-tor's proposal was excessive. The Board stated: "The appellant is obligated to furnish accurate, complete, and current cost and pricing data to the extent that the data are significant and reasonably available. This obligation cannot be reduced either by the lack of administrative effort to see that all significant data are gathered and furnished the government, or by the subjective lack of knowledge of such data on the part of appellant's negotiators or the person who signed the certificate."

Lag-time problems can occur in any procurement in which significant amounts of data must be disclosed and then analyzed. The first lag-time problem occurs in any large organization in which pricing information takes some time to process through the accounting system. In Sylvania Electric Products, Inc. (ASBCA No. 13622), the Board held that because the contractor had no established procedures for channeling revised vendor quotes to the proposal manager, it had the duty to take the initiative and recheck for later quotes up to the time of agreement on price. On appeal, the Court of Claims took a harsher position, stating that a one-week delay in communicating the vendor data was ". . .untenable, even ludicrous. A simple telephone call could have obviated the situation."

Contrasted with the Sylvania case, in the American Bosch Arma Co. case, the contractor had a more formalized procedure for channeling data through the accounting system. Under that procedure, the Board found that a posting time of two weeks to a month was not unreasonable. In part, the Board said: "The contracting officer found that in appellant's organization the time lag from receipt of a vendor's quotation and its posting or recording was two weeks to a month. The record indicates that the recognized method of checking prices under the make-buy structure was to examine 'buy-cards' in the Purchasing Department and extract from them the latest purchase order prices or vendor's quotations. Thus a new price or quotation would not be available on the buy-card until two weeks to a month after the date of purchase order or quotation. . . .We find that pricing data. . .was not reasonably available."

One of the major differences is that in Sylvania Electric Products the contractor was found lacking in applicable established policies and procedures, while just the opposite was true in American Bosch Arma. In defining "reasonable availability," it appears beneficial for contractors to establish and document their general practices for processing cost or pricing data. An established practice, consistently applied, can go a long way in defining what is reasonable and effectively decrease the amount of government subjectivity in reviewing a contractor's system. Government auditors often view weaknesses in documenting established policies and procedures in this area as indicators of potential problems—such as defective pricing. With such risk indicators, additional audit effort is commonly exerted to ferret out expected problems.

A second major lag-time problem concerns updating cost or pricing data at the price agreement date with the government. It is vitally important for a contractor to establish a procedure to update data right up to the point of a negotiated agreement. To ensure that this happens, some contractors have an internal certification process. After agreement on price but before signing the government's certificate of current cost or pricing data, a contractor would routinely have established key individuals within the estimating system conduct an update analysis, commonly referred to as a "sweep," and certify that all information was current, accurate, and complete. If new data were found, those data would be disclosed to the government. Only then would the certificate be signed.

Given the significance of a defective pricing allegation, the contractor should have an ironclad system of written policies and procedures and associated internal controls so that cost or pricing data can be updated properly. A contractor's procedure should cover such subjects as changes in make-or-buy decisions, submission of updated forward-pricing rates, changes in escalation factors, updated vendor quotes or purchase orders, anticipated alterations in production methods, and availability of residual materials from previous contracts.

A practical illustration of available data is presented in the following situation. A contractor was awarded a contract for fueling hoses. The materials expected to be used were expensive and therefore influential in negotiating the contract price. After the contract was signed, the contractor's engineers discovered a means to reduce the material content of the hose and increase profits. What is the key issue in determining if this is defective pricing? The key issue is when did the company (not the company negotiators) know that the material could be reduced. If this happened before the date of price agreement, this is defective pricing. If this happened after the date of price agreement, this is not defective pricing.

Submission of Data

The FAR formerly required that cost or pricing data be submitted on a Standard Form 1411. While this is no longer required, the same information must still be submitted in accordance with FAR 15.408. During negotiations, the contractor must submit all documents with a possible bearing on those overall costs—actually, by physical delivery to the government, or through written identification. The mere availability of these records to the government is not sufficient. At the very least, specific identification and an indication of availability are required.

This concept is illustrated in M-R-S Manufacturing Company (ASBCA No. 14825). The contractor's accounting system accumulated information by parts and production runs. In submitting the proposal, M-R-S apparently used the unit costs from the highest cost production runs. Data from other production runs were available for government audit review, but the contractor did not affirmatively disclose, nor did the auditor review, the data.

In ruling that the contractor's disclosure was inadequate, the Board noted:

> We disagree. The data which appellant furnished were neither complete nor current. At the time when the priced bill of materials was given the auditor, other production orders representing production runs with significantly lower labor costs occurring at a later date than the one cited and furnished were in possession of appellant. These data were not furnished or otherwise disclosed to representatives of the Government. But appellant views the facts as establishing that all cost and pricing data were actually and physically submitted to the Government together with the advice and information as to variances in and between costs proposed and other experienced costs, since a complete audit could be performed from the priced bill of materials in the data referenced in the bill of materials to which the auditor had access.
>
> We think appellant misconstrues its obligations with respect to the furnishing of data. Whether the auditor was familiar with appellant's accounting system or not, or whether a complete price analysis could have been conducted from the materials furnished the auditor, together with the other materials the auditor had at hand, makes little difference.

Appellant may quote its prices on any basis it wishes, it may formulate its profit factor on any basis it wishes, and it may use any fair accounting system it wishes. However, when it chooses to furnish cost factors on which to base its prices, it must also disclose variances it knows it has currently experienced in the application of those same factors when the costs quoted are, in relation to the other currently experienced costs, significantly overstated. If a cost is known when the contract price is being negotiated it must be furnished accurately, completely, and on a current cost basis.

Significant cost differences among production runs were known to appellant at the time the contract was negotiated. This information was readily extractable from its accounting records. Appellant did not disclose the costs and pricing data to the Government by calling to anyone's attention the cost variances in the production runs or by physically handing over to the auditor, as it might easily have done, other material production order documents. Lambert Engineering Company (ASBCA No. 13338). We find, therefore, that the Government was not furnished complete and current cost and pricing data pertaining to the four manufactured parts and the lack of such data resulted in significant overstatement of the contract price.

A similar decision was made in McDonnell Douglas Corporation (ABSCA No. 12786). The Board held that information on Kardex files that was available to the government, but not specifically called to its attention, was not reasonably furnished, and a price reduction was therefore granted. The concept of disclosure was defined as physical delivery and actual knowledge by the government. The Board stated: "The contractor satisfies the requirements of the Truth in Negotiations Act so as to be immune from any claim for price reduction if he makes a full disclosure of all pertinent cost and pricing data, and there is a disclosure for the purposes of the Act, not only when the contractor furnishes the data to the contracting officer in a physical sense, but also when the contracting officer or the persons who represent the Government in negotiating the price have actual knowledge of the specific data."

In Sylvania Electric Products, Inc. (ASBCA No. 13622), the Board extended its definition of disclosure by suggesting that, in some instances, mere identification and submission are not sufficient, but rather that the contractor must specifically explain the significance of the data for the government. Here, the government alleged that the contractor had failed to furnish accurate, complete, and current data. The contractor countered with the argument that "by furnishing the government data (documents) from which the government could have discovered the materials cost errors in the proposal, by checking the data furnished against documents in the proposal, it thereby disclosed the materials cost errors, even though the government did not check such data against the proposal, hence did not in fact discover the materials cost errors in the proposal."

Although there was some confusion over which documents were actually furnished, the Board proceeded as if all the data, as claimed by the contractor, were submitted to the price analyst. However, the Board reasoned that the data were not adequate, because none of the documents "actually showed that the material costs in the proposal were in error." On that basis, the Board ruled that disclosure might include more than physical delivery of the data to the government; in fact, it might even be necessary to inform the government of the 'form and content' of the data."

The Board summarized its position this way:

> In order that there be effective disclosure of cost and pricing data by the prospective contractor, either the Government must be clearly advised of the relevant cost and pricing data or it must have actual (rather than imputed) knowledge thereof. It does not suffice to make available or physically hand over for government inspection files which, if examined, would disclose differences between proposal costs and lower historical costs. It is also necessary in order to make a disclosure, to advise the Government representatives involved in the proposed procurement of the kind and content of the cost or pricing data and their bearing on the prospective contractor's proposal which examination of the files would disclose. Our decisions in McDonnell Douglas Corp., supra, Lambert Engineering Company (ASBCA No. 13338) and Aerojet-General Corp. (ASBCA No. 12264) point in this direction. The decision herein follows the path which they blazed. In this light, even if appellant's exhibits had all been disclosed to the price analyst or any other cognizant Government representative, such mere transmission of documents without informing the Government representatives of the current cost or pricing data which they contain is not a "disclosure" within the meaning of GP 48 and the underlying statute (10 USC 2306(f)).

The disclosure of cost or pricing data begins with the initial submittal of information required by FAR 15.408, Table 15-2, Contract Pricing Proposal Cover Sheet. Cost element breakdowns are required. Also attached to the cost proposal is the con-tractor's rationale used in developing costs (e.g., forward-pricing rates, labor hours, material units, factors).

After the initial submission of cost data, formal revised submissions may be required. However, the next major disclosure point is at, or immediately preceding, negotiations. Here, a contractor must be certain to update its cost or pricing data from initial submission to price agreement date. The contractor may issue new cost or pricing data in accordance with FAR 15.408 or, more likely, notify the contracting officer in writing that certain items have been updated accordingly. Updating is a critical phase of the proposal process since the contractor certifies that its data are current, accurate, and complete.

In disclosing cost or pricing data, this question is often asked: To whom must the disclosure be made? The FAR states that "when certified cost or pricing data are required, the contracting officer shall require the contractor or prospective contractor to submit to the contracting officer the data." To maximize protection against defective pricing, the best approach is to specifically disclose the data directly to the contracting officer. However, several judicial decisions have established the principle that adequate submission is made by disclosing the data to the contracting officer or to his or her representative.

For example, in Whittaker Corporation (ASBCA No. 17267), the Board determined that certain data updated between the time the pricing proposal had been prepared and the time it had been certified, had been properly disclosed. The disclosure was made to the government auditor who reviewed the pricing proposal as well as to the ACO's technical specialist. However, no disclosure was made to the contracting officer during negotiation. In this regard, the Board concluded:

> The Government has the burden of proving that its personnel who participated in the proposal evaluation or the negotiation of the contract were not clearly advised of the rel-

evant cost or pricing data and that they lack actual knowledge thereof (Norris Industries, Inc. (ASBCA No. 15442). Physical delivery of the data to the government's agents is not required. The disclosure obligation is satisfied by making them aware of the significance of undelivered data to the negotiation process. M-R-S Manufacturing Company v. United States (203 Ct. Cl. 551, 492 F.2d 835). The Board has held that the obligation is met by furnishing the data to the Government auditor who audits the proposal. Defense Electronics, Inc. (ASBCA No. 11127). The government appears to rest its claim on the fact that the relevant orders were not disclosed at the time of negotiations. Compliance with the disclosure obligation, however, is not limited to the negotiations (Norris Industries, Inc. and Defense Electronics, Inc.). Under the facts established here, the Government's burden of proof is not satisfied merely by showing that disclosure was not made during negotiations. It must also show that the disclosure was not made to other Government personnel to whom disclosure can effectively be made. It has failed to do so as to Item 1.

A contractor's sole reliance on disclosing certain data to contracting officer representatives or auditors, for example, instead of directly to the contracting officer, is risky business. Introducing another link into the chain multiplies the chances for a communication mishap. Cases have gone just as easily against contractors in this area. For example, in American Machine & Foundry Co. (ASBCA No. 15037), three purchase orders were at issue. The contractor claimed that it had disclosed them to the government auditor. However, the Board found that the contractor's negotiator had informed the contracting officer that there were only two orders. The Board concluded that the contractor had misrepresented the facts.

Submission or disclosure of cost or pricing data is at the heart of the Truth in Negotiations Act. Compliance with its requirements represents an arduous task for most contractors. The major hurdle to overcome is communication within the estimating system. Communication means that estimating personnel know the act's requirements and their assigned responsibilities. The estimating system must provide for established communication channels that operate on request on a timely basis.

It is important to recognize that disclosure and contractor reliance on the data in its pricing are two completely different issues. A contractor has an affirmative duty to disclose accurate, current, and complete data (Sylvania and M-R-S). But the contractor has no obligation under the act to use the information in its pricing. To fully disclose data, the contractor need only inform the contracting officer that certain elements are not relied on for pricing purposes. For example, in Bell & Howell Co. (ASBCA No. 11999), the contractor failed to disclose a number of price quotes, for several reasons. Most concerned anticipated problems with those vendors, and so the contractor did not rely on them in its pricing and claimed that these quotes were not cost or pricing data.

The Board, disagreeing, observed: "We find no merit in the contractor's contention that the six undisclosed low quotes were not 'cost or pricing data' as defined in ASPR 3-807.3(e), which defines cost or pricing data as including such factual matters as vendor's quotations. The vendor quotations themselves were cost or pricing data; the contractor's judgmental decision not to base its proposed price on such quotations was not cost or pricing data. Appellant could have complied with the Truth in Negotiations Act by submitting the same proposed price that it did, but disclosing the low quotes and explaining why it was not using them for pricing purposes."

Reliance

As a condition of its application, the defective pricing clause requires that the contractor's submission of defective data caused an overstated price. This requirement depends on proving that in negotiating the contract price, the government relied on the defective data. And so, had it known the data were defective, the government would have negotiated a lower price. In asserting that the defective data caused a higher contract price, the government need not reconstruct specific amounts attributable to the defective data. Even if the government shows its right to a presumption of reliance, this presumption is not irrefutable. In Universal Restoration, Inc. v. U.S. (798 E2d 1400 (CA-FC)), a sole-source contractor would accept nothing less than its standard overhead markup under a contract for emergency repair work.

Several factors worked in the contractor's favor sufficient to rebut a presumption of reliance by the government. The majority noted that: "Universal was the only source available to perform the original emergency repair work; that it would have been impracticable to allow another contractor to perform any of the contract work; that Universal's prices were found by the government to be fair and reasonable; that Universal would accept nothing less than its established overhead markup; and that the government made no attempt to negotiate with Universal for a reduction in any part of its proposals."

The FY 87 DOD Authorization Act maintains the nonreliance defense for contractors, notwithstanding that the proposed language is aimed to eliminate it. However, many of the individual elements of defense cannot any longer be used as the "sole" basis for defending a defective pricing claim. In this regard, a contractor cannot depend exclusively on the basis that: (1) it was a sole-source supplier; (2) it was in a superior bargaining position; (3) the contracting officer should have known that the data were defective; (4) the agreement was based on total cost and not individual cost elements; or (5) the contractor or subcontractor did not submit a cost and pricing certificate.

In determining reliance, or its lack, a critical document that may offer valuable information is a price negotiation memorandum (PNM). The PNM, as used by government contracting officers, summarizes the results of negotiations between the government and the contractor. The contracting officer is required to prepare a PNM at the conclusion of each negotiation. The memorandum is then included in the contract file. The FAR requires that the PNM contain the following elements:

1. Purpose of the negotiation

2. Description of the acquisition

3. Name, position, and organization of each person representing the contractor and the government in negotiation

4. Current status of the contractor's purchasing system when material is a significant cost element

5. If certified cost or pricing data were required, the extent to which the contracting officer relied on the cost or pricing data submitted and used them in negotiating the price and recognized as inaccurate, incomplete, or noncurrent any cost or pricing data submitted; the action taken by the contracting officer and the contractor as a result; and the effect of the defective data on the price negotiated

6. If cost or pricing data were not required for price negotiations over $700,000,

the exemption or waiver used and the basis for claiming or granting it

7. If certified cost or pricing data were required for price negotiations under $700,000, the rationale for such requirement

8. Summary of the contractor's proposal, the field-pricing-report recommendations, and the reasons for any substantial variances from them

9. Most significant facts or considerations controlling the establishment of the prenegotiation price objective and the negotiated price, including an explanation of any significant differences between the two positions

10. Basis for determining the profit or fee prenegotiation objective and the profit or fee negotiated.

A contractor should have its negotiators take sufficient notes, similar to the PNM, during negotiations with the government. Negotiation participants should be instructed in the key types of information requiring special attention, such as updated information disclosed, statements by government negotiators pertaining to reliance or its lack, and disclosed data not relied on by the contractor in cost estimating. As a practical matter, it may be beneficial to consolidate the notes taken by contractor participants into a single document to avoid confusion in the future; the PNM is a good information source that contractors can use to establish the basis for their compliance with the Truth in Negotiations Act.

Many government contracting officers include a statement in each PNM that declares that the government relied on all information provided by the contractor. The intent of this statement is to establish reliance on any data that are subsequently found to be defective. However, a mere statement to this effect may not be sufficient to establish that the government relied on the data. The Board and courts tend to look at the facts, such as in the following decision (ASBCA No. 32660).

A contractor had proposed a scrap factor based on a prior production model. The contractor disclosed the limited scrap data for the model being priced. However, because the scrap data for the new model were considered limited and not reliable, the contractor elected to price scrap based on a prior production model. The government audit would not use the data on the prior model, but instead used the limited data despite the contractor's objections. Negotiations were held on this basis. Subsequently, defective pricing was found in the scrap data for the prior model. The government demanded a price adjustment, but the Board concluded that the government pricing position did not rely on the defective data.

Price Increase

The government has the burden of proving that the defective data actually increased the contract price and what the dollar impact is. However, court and Board decisions have effectively shifted this burden to where there is now a rebuttable presumption that the defective data increased the contract price (Sylvania Electric Products, Inc. v. U.S., 202 Ct. Cl. 16). The principle of natural and probable consequence was established in American Bosch Arma Corporation (ASBCA No. 10305). The Board concluded, without any specific evidence about the effect of nondisclosure on the negotiated target cost, that it must "adopt the natural and probable consequences of the disclosure as representing its effect." The Board then computed the price reduction on the basis of the overestimates not disclosed plus related burden and profit.

In the absence of any strong evidence to the contrary, the contract price is generally reduced dollar for dollar according to the natural-and-probable-consequences doctrine. Where a contractor can show some evidence that the government did not rely on defective data or can otherwise prove that negotiations significantly diminished the impact of the defective data, the Board has been more likely to reduce the contractor's liability. To avoid liability altogether, a contractor must generally furnish overwhelming evidence against reliance and significant impact.

In determining a price reduction, the government must assume a baseline for price comparison. In determining an audit baseline for postaward reviews, DCAA focuses on the cost data provided by the contractor with its last formal cost submission, plus any additional cost or pricing data subsequently submitted to the contracting officer or representative before agreement on price. Any price decreases for defective data are calculated based on this baseline amount.

For example, assume that the total contract cost proposed and certified was $800,000, no additional cost or pricing data were submitted by the contractor, and $750,000 was the negotiated price. DCAA's postaward audit finds the data defectively priced and determines the appropriate price to be $725,000. The baseline for audit is $800,000, and the adjustment for defective pricing is $75,000, not $50,000. Why isn't the baseline $750,000, the negotiated price? DCAA views the downward negotiation of costs, either in total or by individual element, as related to judgmental factors inherent in the contractor's certified proposal and not to factual cost or pricing data because, as in this case, no additional data were submitted.

Assume that in this example, DCAA had questioned $25,000 in its preaward proposal review. DCAA's approach during a post-award review to determine the impact of any defective pricing is to decrease the baseline by the amount of original cost questioned. In this example, the new baseline is $475,000 and the defective pricing impact is $50,000.

These examples are consistent with the concept of natural and probable consequences established in case law. In other words, without evidence to the contrary, the natural and probable consequence of defective data is a contract price increase due to the defect. In establishing that the defective data caused a higher contract price, the contracting officer is not expected to reconstruct the negotiation by speculating on what the mental attitudes of the negotiating parties would have been had the correct data been submitted when the agreement on price was made.

Setoffs

In the context of defective pricing, setoff means that a contractor's monetary liability for the defective data that increased the contract price may be decreased or set off by the amount that other defective data decreased the contract price. In 1969, the Federal Court of Claims, in Cutler Hammer, Inc. v. U.S. (189 Ct. Cl. 76, 416 R 2d 1306), overturned the previous Board decision (Cutler-Hammer, Inc., ASBCA No. 10900) and allowed setoffs. Cutler-Hammer was a landmark case in what had been a hotly disputed area.

The decision was not easy because neither the law nor the legislative history offered definitive guidance. The court's decision to allow setoffs was based in part on the following reasoning:

> It is clear that when only overstatements are included in estimates, the Government has the right to reduce the contract price. In such a situation, a downward revision of the price is mandated. Whether offsets in favor of the contractor are to be allowed presents a more difficult question, the answer to which is not so readily apparent. The legislative history of the Act does indicate that efforts were made to have the language of

P.L. 87-653 cover situations where errors in favor of the Government would cancel out errors in favor of the contractor, but these efforts were to no avail. Plaintiff contends that the literal language of the statute allows setoffs; defendant argues that the language of the statute in the legislative history dictates against allowing understatements to be set off against overstatements. In our view, neither the statute nor the legislative history is clear-cut. In the absence of concise guidelines, we must resort to finding the legislative intent.

It is argued that since the statute talks in terms of "reducing" the contract price, and the contract clause speaks in terms of "excluding" defective prices, there can only be a downward revision of price. With this we agree, but we interpret these words to mean that where overstatements exceed understatements, the price is not raised. Data revealing understated costs must meet the same criteria as those showing overstated costs. In other words, the setoffs must be facts rather than judgments (1) existing at the time of agreement on price, (2) not disclosed to, or not actually known by the government, (3) in data relied on by the government, and (4) presumed to have a dollar impact.

The application of setoffs is guided by many parameters:

1. Setoffs apply only within the same "pricing action" (that is, contract or its modification) and cannot be offset between different pricing actions even on the same contract.

2. Within the same pricing action, setoffs are allowable within the various line items of the cost or pricing data as certified. For example, understated labor can be set off against overstated labor, material, indirect cost, etc.

3. Setoffs can be applied only against overstated defective data and cannot exceed that overstated amount. A contractor cannot increase the price of the contract through the use of setoffs.

It is generally recognized that the defective pricing clause is not a vehicle for repricing proposed cost elements. The Board has generally held that setoffs were allowed only when the omission was unintentional. However, in Rogerson Aircraft Controls (ASBCA No. 27954), the Board ruled that intentional understatements do not, as a matter of law, disqualify the setoff. Here, the contractor submitted defective data overstating its raw material costs.

However, no significant change was made in the final price because the contractor had unintentionally understated its overhead rate. In finding for the contractor on this issue, the Board stated:

> In Cutler-Hammer, Inc. v. United States (189 Ct. Cl. 76, 416 F.2d 1306), where the Court first allowed the setoff of understatements in a defective pricing action, it made no distinction between intentional and unintentional understatements when it rejected the argument that allowance of setoffs would encourage "buying-in." The Court's discussion of "buying-in" was unnecessary if it believed that intentional understatements should not be eligible for setoffs.
>
> Moreover, in subsequently reversing on factual grounds the Board's decision in Lockheed Aircraft Corp. (ASBCA No. 10453), that an intentional understatement was not eli-

gible for setoff, the Court expressed skepticism as to the Board's legal conclusion. Lockheed Aircraft Corp. v. United States (202 Ct. Cl. 787, 790-91, 485 F. 2d 584, 586). We hold that the intentional nature of an understatement does not, as a matter of law, disqualify that understatement as a setoff against an overstatement. Whether an intentional understatement would have been raised as a setoff in a negotiation depends on the particular facts of each case. On the facts of Rogerson's case we have found that the understatement would have been raised, and that the price would not have been reduced.

The rule established in Rogerson Aircraft regarding the allowance of intentional offsets under certain circumstances appears to be moot since Congress amended the Truth in Negotiations Act in the FY 1987 DOD Authorization Act. The amendment establishes by statute a contractor's right to offset; however, it prohibits an offset if "the contractor intentionally withheld from the government information that would indicate a higher cost for an item or service and, thus, certified that the cost or pricing data it submitted was accurate, complete and current when, in fact, the contractor knew it to be false." It is possible, however, that the Rogerson case may still prove useful in supporting an agreement for "nonreliance" when an intentional understatement is known to both parties.

The Role of a Certificate

A certificate of current cost or pricing data has in the past been a prerequisite to establishing liability under the Truth in Negotiations Act regardless of the form of the contract clause (Libby Welding Corp., ASBCA No. 15084). Under this ruling, there could be no defective pricing adjustment unless there was a certificate at the prime contractor level. However, this rule does not apply to subcontracts. The lack of a subcontractor certificate, if otherwise appropriate, is not a bar to recovery by the government against the prime for defective data submitted by the subcontractor.

Despite the Libby Welding rule, recent case law states that a certificate at the prime level may in fact not be necessary for defective pricing liability under the act. In Beech Aircraft Corporation (ASBCA No. 25388), a certificate at the prime level was not obtained and yet the contractor was found subject to the Truth in Negotiations Act. The basic premise was that the contracting officer did not have the authority to waive the data requirement since, according to regulation, only the agency head has that power.

In Beech, when the government issued an unpriced delivery order directing a contractor to purchase filter kits from a subcontractor who refused to supply cost or pricing data, the government did not waive the data requirement and was not stopped from establishing a lower price for the filter kits than that quoted by the subcontractor prior to delivery. The subcontractor, who was the sole source of the kits, had a standing policy not to supply cost or pricing data, even though it was required to do so by the Truth in Negotiations Act. Since the government urgently needed the filter kits to resolve a stalling problem in aircraft engines it had purchased from the contractor, the contracting officer ordered the contractor to procure them without having obtained the cost or pricing data. This action could not constitute a waiver of the data requirement inasmuch as the contracting officer was without authority to waive a statutory requirement. Nor did the contracting officer by his action acquiesce in the price quoted by the subcontractor, since the contracting officer issued an unpriced delivery order and had persisted in his attempts to obtain the data.

CHAPTER 10

Contract Administration

Individuals involved in the administration of contracts need to have an awareness of potential issues. A basic understanding of problems that may arise will help limit the impact on contractor operations.

RESPONSIBILITY FOR CONTRACT ADMINISTRATION AND AUDITS

The administration of government contracts may either be carried out by the contracting officer (CO) responsible for contract award or be delegated to an administrative contracting officer (ACO). In agencies other than DOD, contract administration generally is not delegated. Within DOD, most contracts are assigned to an ACO who is with the Defense Logistics Agency (DLA) within the organizational unit identified as the Defense Contract Management Agency (DCMA).

The DCMA maintains and distributes the *Federal Directory of Contract Administration Services Components*. This directory lists the names and telephone numbers of those DCMA and other agency offices that offer contract administration services within designated geographic areas and at specified contractor plants. The directory is available at www.dcma.mil/. Contractors often need to know who their ACO is to be able to respond fully to RFPs.

Contract Administration Duties

Government contract administration functions encompass a long list of duties. In any one circumstance, all or some of these functions may be delegated to an ACO. Not all functions are applicable for each contract.

Functions include reviewing the contractor's compensation structure, reviewing the contractor's insurance plans, conducting postaward orientation conferences, reviewing and evaluating contractors' proposals, negotiating forward-pricing rate agreements, negotiating advance agreements applicable to treatment of costs, and determining the allowability of costs.

Duties also include issuing Notices of Intent to Disallow or Not Recognize Costs, establishing final indirect cost rates and interim billing rates, resolving issues in controversy, preparing findings of fact, and issuing decisions under the disputes clause. In connection with the CAS, duties include determining the adequacy of a contractor's disclosure statements, determining whether disclosure statements are in compliance with the CAS and FAR Part 31, determining a contractor's compliance with the CAS and disclosure statements, negotiating price adjustments, and executing supplemental agreements under the CAS clauses.

Other functions include reviewing and approving or disapproving the contractor's requests for payments under the progress payments or performance-based payments clauses, managing special bank accounts, ensuring timely notification by the contractor of any anticipated overrun or underrun of the estimated cost under cost-reimbursement contracts, monitoring the contractor's financial condition and advising the contracting officer when that financial condition jeopardizes contract performance, analyzing the quarterly limitation on payments statements, and recovering overpayments from the contractor.

Additional responsibilities include issuing tax exemption forms, ensuring that duty-free entry certificates are processed and executed, negotiating and executing contractual documents for settlement of partial and complete contract terminations for convenience, processing and executing novation and change of name agreements, performing property administration, and performing necessary screening, redistribution, and disposal of contractor inventory.

Contract administration also includes providing production support, conducting surveillance, and performing status reporting, including the timely reporting of potential and actual slippages in contract delivery schedules. In addition, responsibilities include: conducting preaward surveys; ensuring contractor compliance with contractual quality assurance requirements; ensuring contractor compliance with contractual safety requirements; performing engineering surveillance to assess compliance with contractual terms for schedule, cost, and technical performance in the areas of design, development, and production; and evaluating for adequacy and performing surveillance of contractor engineering efforts and management systems that relate to design, development, production, engineering changes, subcontractors, tests, management of engineering resources, reliability and maintainability, data control systems, configuration management, and independent research and development.

Contract administration also involves: performing engineering analyses of contractor cost proposals; reviewing engineering change proposals for proper classification; monitoring a contractor's value engineering program;

reviewing the contractor's purchasing system; consenting to the placement of subcontracts; reviewing small, small-disadvantaged, and women-owned small business master subcontracting plans; ensuring a contractor's compliance with small, small-disadvantaged, and women-owned small business subcontracting plans; and determining that the contractor has a drug-free workplace program and a drug-free awareness program.

Contract Audits

Government contractors (other than educational institutions and nonprofit organizations) are normally audited by what is known as the "cognizant federal agency," which is generally the agency with the largest dollar amount of negotiated contracts. For educational institutions and nonprofit organizations, the cognizant federal agency is determined in accordance with OMB Circular A-21, Cost Principles for Educational Institutions, and OMB Circular A-122, Cost Principles for Nonprofit Organizations. Once a federal agency assumes cognizance for a contractor, it is expected that the agency will remain cognizant for at least five years to ensure continuity and ease of administration.

The Department of Defense contract audit organization is the Defense Contract Audit Agency (DCAA), which is by far the most significant contract audit agency in the federal government. Other departments and agencies have three sources of audit services when they have audit cognizance. First, they may contract for audit services with DCAA. NASA relies on DCAA for essentially all its contract audits. Second, the agency may contract with a public accounting firm for these services. DOE and the Environmental Protection Agency (EPA) often use this approach. Third, the agency may have a limited staff of contract auditors within the Office of the Inspector General (IG) or other organization. EPA has some contract auditors assigned to the IG office. The Department of Health and Human Services has an organization outside the IG's office to conduct certain indirect cost audits.

A contract auditor is responsible for submitting information and advice to a contracting office based on analysis of the contractor's financial and accounting records or other data related to the contractor's incurred and estimated costs. An auditor also reviews the financial and accounting aspects of the contractor's cost control systems and performs other analyses and reviews that require access to the contractor's financial and accounting records supporting proposed and incurred costs.

Contracting officers request audit services directly from the responsible audit agency designated in the *Directory of Federal Contract Audit Offices*. DCAA maintains and distributes this directory, which identifies cognizant audit offices and the contractors over which they have cognizance. The directory is also available at the DCAA website: www.dcaa. mil/. The responsible audit agency may decline requests for services if its resources are inadequate to accomplish the required tasks.

FINANCIAL ASPECTS

The following sections address some of the most common issues encountered in contract administration. Contract payments are significant because of their impact on the financial condition of the company. If a company has cost-reimbursement contracts, it must be aware of its responsibilities for submitting an annual indirect cost rate proposal. Contractors should also be aware of cost-sharing arrangements and indirect cost rate ceilings, and how these affect profits. Some contractors may be requested to propose forward-pricing rate agreements. Another financial aspect relates to closing out cost-reimbursement contracts. Finally, this section addresses the issue of government retroactive disallowance of incurred costs.

Contract Payments

The federal government uses several methods of contract payment. The simplest is payment on delivered goods or services under firm-fixed-price contracts and labor under time-and-materials and labor-hour contracts. The contractor delivers the goods or services at an agreed-to price and payment is made.

However, many government contracts are not completed for a significant time period. Thus, the government offers interim payments under the two basic contract types—cost-reimbursement and fixed-price. For cost-reimbursement contracts, interim payments are considered reimbursement of costs rather than contract financing. This distinction is important for provisions of the Prompt Payment Act, which applies only to payments for completed goods and services under fixed-price contracts (i.e., not to interim progress payments).

Provisional or Interim Billing Rates

The contracting officer or auditor responsible for establishing the final indirect cost rates is also responsible for determining the billing rates applicable to both cost-reimbursement and fixed-price contracts. The contracting officer or auditor establishes billing rates on the basis of information obtained from recent reviews, previous rate audits or experience, or budgetary data. Billing rates should be set as close as possible to the final indirect cost rates anticipated for the contractor's fiscal period, as adjusted for any unallowable costs. The most important data for establishing these rates are the expected cost levels for the period covered by the rates. Unfortunately, many government auditors hesitate to accept estimates and rely solely on the rate for the most recent year.

Once established, billing rates may be revised—either prospectively or retroactively—by mutual agreement to prevent substantial overpayment or underpayment. When agreement cannot be reached, the contracting officer may unilaterally determine the billing rates. A contractor should monitor rates during the year and request revisions wherever appropriate. Both overbilling and underbilling should be avoided. Overbilling means that the contractor will have to return substantial funds to the government. Underbilling means that the contractor does not have full use of the funds it has earned.

The elements of indirect cost and the base or bases used in computing billing rates should not be considered determinative of the indirect costs to be distributed or of the bases of distribution to be used in the final settlement. In other words, the govern-ment's approval of indirect cost rates does not necessarily commit the government to accept, for final rate purposes, the cost allocations used in preparing those rates.

When a contractor submits a certified final indirect cost rate proposal for the conclusion of a year, the contractor and the government may mutually agree to revise billing rates to reflect the proposed indirect cost rates until that proposal has been audited and settled. This approach has become more common in recent years. Previously, no adjustments were permitted until a government final audit had been performed. However, problems resulted because funds were often no longer available when the final audit was completed years later.

Final Indirect Cost Rates

Final indirect cost rates are established on the basis of either contracting officer determination or auditor determination. Within 120 days after settlement of the final indirect cost rates, a contractor should submit a completion invoice or voucher reflecting the settled amounts and rates on all contracts physically completed in the year covered by the proposal. As of late 2010 the submission has no FAR-mandated format. However, the FAR does suggest a format such as the DCAA-developed ICE (indirect cost electronically) Excel workbook format. While this format is not mandatory, some of the schedules are advisable. Certain schedules are redundant and reflect obsolete FAR requirements; these should not be submitted. A FAR revision is being considered to make this format a requirement.

Figure 31 (see page 211) contains a "cleaned up" version of the DCAA ICE. The color-coded links have been eliminated, links have been minimized, redundant and obsolete schedules have been removed, and proper borders have been added.

Contracting Officer Determination

A contracting officer determination basis is used for business units of a multidivisional corporation under the cognizance of a corporate ACO, with that officer responsible for the determination. Negotiations are conducted on a coordinated or centralized basis, depending on the degree of centralization within the contractor's organization. Contracting officer determination is also used for business units that are not under the cognizance of a corporate ACO, but that have a resident ACO. (An ACO is considered resident if at least 75 percent of his or her time is devoted to a single contractor.)

In accordance with the Allowable Cost and Payment clause at FAR 52.216-7 or 52.216-13, the contractor submits a final indirect cost rate proposal to the contracting officer and to the cognizant auditor. A proposal should be submitted within six months following the expiration of the contractor's fiscal year. Extensions are commonly granted. Audits are often not initiated within one year of submission. (Although a contractor must meet the six-month limit, the audits are typically conducted later.)

The required content of the proposal and supporting data will vary depending on such factors as business type, size, and accounting system capabilities. DCAA has prepared a model indirect cost submission that covers all required information and additional data that are not required but that facilitate an audit. DCAA also has prepared spreadsheets in Excel workbook format for submission of the information. The Model Incurred Cost Proposal is published in Chapter 5 of DCAA Pamphlet (DCAAP) No. 7641.90, Information for Contractors. The model is available at www.dcaa.mil/.

The auditor submits an advisory audit report to the contracting officer identifying any relevant advance agreements or restrictive terms of specific contracts. The contracting officer heads the government negotiating team, which includes the cognizant auditor and technical or functional personnel as required. The government negotiating team develops a negotiation position. The contracting officer may not resolve any questioned costs until obtaining: (1) adequate documentation on the costs; and (2) the contract auditor's opinion on the allowability of the costs.

The cognizant contracting officer: conducts negotiations; prepares a written indirect cost rate agreement; prepares a negotiation memorandum covering the disposition of significant matters in the advisory audit report; reconciles all costs questioned, identifying items and amounts allowed or disallowed in the final settlement as well as the disposition of period costing or allocability issues; presents reasons why any of the auditor's recommendations were not followed; and identifies cost or pricing data submitted during the negotiations and relied on in reaching a settlement. The contracting officer also notifies the contractor of the individual costs that were considered unallowable and the respective amounts of the disallowance.

Auditor Determination Procedure

The cognizant government auditor establishes final indirect cost rates for business units not established by the contracting officer. The contractor submits the indirect cost rate proposal to the contracting officer and auditor. The auditor audits the proposal and seeks agreement on indirect costs rates with the contractor. The auditor then prepares an indirect cost rate agreement, which is signed by the contractor and the auditor. If agreement cannot be reached, the auditor forwards the audit report to the contracting officer, who will then resolve the disagreement.

Cost-Sharing Rates and Ceilings on Indirect Cost Rates

Cost-sharing arrangements may call for the contractor to participate in the costs of the contract by accepting indirect cost rates lower than the anticipated actual rates. In such cases, a negotiated indirect cost rate ceiling may be incorporated into the contract. These techniques are sometimes used for cost-sharing under research and development contracts where it is prudent to provide a final indirect cost rate ceiling in a contract. Examples of such circumstances are when the proposed contractor: (1) is a new or recently reorganized company, and thus has no past or recent record of incurred indirect costs; (2) has a recent record of a rapidly increasing indirect cost rate due to a declining volume of sales without a commensurate decline in indirect expenses; or (3) seeks to enhance its competitive position in a particular circumstance by basing its proposal on indirect cost rates lower than those that may reasonably be expected to occur during contract performance, thereby causing a cost overrun.

Forward-Pricing Rate Agreements

Forward-pricing rates are agreements to use specified indirect cost rates in pricing contract modifications and small dollar contracts. Agreements are generally used only for high dollar-value contractors. Negotiation of forward-pricing rate agreements (FPRAs) may be requested by the contracting officer or the contractor, or initiated by the ACO. In determining whether or not to establish such an agreement, the ACO should consider whether the benefits to be derived from the agreement are commensurate with the effort of establishing and monitoring it. Normally, FPRAs should be negotiated only with contractors that have a significant volume of government contract proposals. The cognizant contract administration agency determines whether an FPRA will be established.

An ACO obtains a contractor's forward-pricing rate proposal, which requires cost or pricing data that are accurate, complete, and current as of the date of submission. Upon completing negotiations, the ACO prepares a price negotiation memorandum (PNM) and forwards copies of the PNM and the FPRA to the cognizant auditor and to all contracting offices that are known to be affected by the FPRA. A Certificate of Current Cost or Pricing Data is not required at this time.

The FPRA provides specific terms and conditions covering expiration, application, and data requirements for systematic monitoring to ensure the validity of the rates. The agreement provides for cancellation at the option of either party and requires the contractor to submit to the ACO and to the cognizant contract auditor any significant change in cost or pricing data.

When an FPRA is invalid, the contractor should submit and negotiate a new proposal to reflect the changed conditions. If an FPRA has not been established or has been invalidated, the ACO will issue a forward-pricing rate recommendation (FPRR) to buying activities, with documentation to assist negotiators. In the absence of an FPRA or FPRR, the ACO must include support for the rates used. The contractor and the ACO may negotiate continuous updates to the FPRA.

DCAA auditors often encourage even the smallest contractors to seek forward-pricing rate agreements. Small contractors are not expected to have these agreements per the FAR. The forward-pricing rate agreement pro-

cess has become somewhat convoluted in practice. When DCAA makes recommendations to a contracting officer for such rates, if the contracting officer (the FAR-designated official for setting such rates) deviates significantly from the DCAA recommended rates, DCAA will not accept the contracting officer-approved rates in its audit recommendations. Instead, DCAA will use its own recommended rates.

Quick-Closeout Procedure

Normally, flexibly priced contracts are closed after completion of the final indirect cost rate audit. This sometimes occurs several years after completion of the contract. As an alternative, a quick-closeout procedure may be used. The contracting officer may negotiate the settlement of indirect costs for a specific contract in advance of the determination of final indirect cost rates, if:

1. The contract is physically complete.

2. The amount of unsettled indirect cost to be allocated to the contract is relatively insignificant. (Indirect cost amounts will be considered insignificant when the total unsettled indirect cost to be allocated to any one contract does not exceed $1,000,000 and the cumulative unsettled indirect costs to be allocated to one or more contracts in a single fiscal year do not exceed 15 percent of the estimated, total unsettled indirect costs allocable to cost-type contracts for that fiscal year.)

3. Agreement can be reached on a reasonable estimate of allocable dollars.

Determinations of final indirect costs under the quick-closeout procedure provided for by the Allowable Cost and Payment clause at FAR 52.216-7 or 52.216-13 are final for the contract covered by the agreement, and no adjustment is made to other contracts for over- or underrecoveries of costs allocated or allocable to that contract. Indirect cost rates used in the quick closeout of a contract are not considered a binding precedent when establishing the final indirect cost rates for other contracts.

Disallowing Costs After Incurrence

Cost-reimbursement contracts, the cost-reimbursement portion of fixed-price contracts, letter contracts that provide for reimbursement of costs, and time-and-materials and labor-hour contracts provide for disallowing costs during the course of performance after the costs have been incurred.

The contract auditor may be authorized to receive reimbursement vouchers directly from contractors, approve for payment those vouchers found acceptable, and suspend payment of questionable costs. The auditor forwards approved vouchers for payment to the cognizant contracting, finance, or disbursing officer, as appropriate under the agency's procedures.

If the examination of a voucher raises a question regarding the allowability of a cost, the auditor may issue a notice of contract costs suspended and/or disapproved simultaneously to the contractor and the disbursing officer for deduction from current payments with respect to costs claimed but not considered reimbursable. If the contractor disagrees with the deduction, the contractor may: (1) submit a written request to the contracting officer to consider whether the unreimbursed costs should be paid; and/or (2) file a claim under the disputes clause.

PERFORMANCE ASPECTS

Events that occur during contract performance can create significant contract administration problems. One such event is a government suspension or delay of work. Because past performance is more important

than ever in obtaining new contract awards, it is essential that that contractor handle such an occurrence properly. The government may also modify a contract—sometimes unilaterally. Subcontracting and government property are two additional contract administrative matters that should be considered. Finally, the government may terminate a contract for its convenience at any time.

Suspension of Work, Stop-Work Orders, and Government Delay of Work

A contracting officer may issue a suspension of work under a construction or architect-engineer contract. If the suspension is unreasonable, the contractor may submit a written claim for increases in the cost of performance, excluding profit. Stop-work orders may be used, when appropriate, in any negotiated fixed-price or cost-reimbursement supply, research and development, or service contract if work stoppage is required for reasons such as advancement in the state-of-the-art, production or engineering breakthroughs, or realignment of programs.

Generally, the contracting officer will issue a stop-work order if he or she determines that work should be suspended pending a decision by the government. Issuance of a stop-work order must be approved at a level higher than the contracting officer. Stop-work orders are not to be used in place of a termination notice after a decision to terminate has been made.

Stop-work orders include a description of the work to be suspended, instructions concerning the contractor's issuance of further orders for materials or services, guidance to the contractor on action to be taken on any subcontracts, and other suggestions to the contractor for minimizing costs. Generally, after issuing a stop-work order, the contracting officer should discuss the order with the contractor and modify it if necessary. As soon as feasible after a stop-work order is issued, but before its expiration, the contracting officer should take appropriate action to terminate the contract, cancel the stop-work order, or extend the period of the stop-work order if it is necessary and if the contractor is in agreement with an extension.

The clause at FAR 52.242-17, Government Delay of Work, provides for the administrative settlement of contractor claims that arise from delays and interruptions in the contract work caused by the acts, or failures to act, of the contracting officer. This clause is not applicable if the contract otherwise specifically provides for an equitable adjustment because of the delay or interruption (i.e., when the changes clause is applicable).

The clause does not authorize the contracting officer to order a suspension, delay, or interruption of the contract work. If the contracting officer has notice of an unordered delay or interruption covered by the clause, the contracting officer must act to end the delay or take other appropriate action as soon as practicable.

Past Performance Evaluations

Agency procedures for the past performance evaluation generally provide for input from the technical office, contracting office, and, where appropriate, end users of the product or service. Agency evaluations of contractor performance are to be provided to the contractor as soon as practicable after completion of the evaluation. Contractors are given a minimum of 30 days to submit comments, rebut statements, or provide additional information. Agencies will provide for review at a level above the contracting officer to consider disagreements between the parties regarding the evaluation.

The ultimate conclusion on the performance evaluation is a decision of the contracting agency. These evaluations may be used to support future award decisions and are designated "source selection information." For the period during which the information may be used to provide source selection information,

the completed evaluation may not be released to other than government personnel and the contractor whose performance is being evaluated. Disclosure of such information could cause harm both to the commercial interest of the government and to the competitive position of the contractor being evaluated, as well as impede the efficiency of government operations. Evaluations used in determining award or incentive fee payments may also be used. A copy of the annual or final past performance evaluation should be provided to the contractor as soon as it is finalized.

Departments and agencies share past performance information with other departments and agencies when requested to -support future award decisions. The information may be provided through interview and/or by sending the evaluation and comment documents to the requesting source selection official. Past performance information systems are intended to include appropriate management and technical controls to ensure that only authorized personnel have access to the data. The past performance information is not retained to provide source selection information for longer than three years following completion of contract performance.

Contract Modifications

Contract modifications can be either bilateral or unilateral. A bilateral modification (supplemental agreement) is a contract modification that is signed by the contractor and the contracting officer. Bilateral modifications are used to make negotiated equitable adjustments resulting from the issuance of a change order; they definitize letter contracts and reflect other agreements of the parties modifying the terms of contracts.

A unilateral modification is a contract modification that is signed only by the contracting officer. Unilateral modifications are used to make administrative changes, issue change orders, make changes authorized by clauses other than a changes clause (e.g., property clause, options clause, suspension of work clause), and issue termination notices.

When a contractor considers that the government has effected or may effect a change in the contract that has not been identified as such in writing and signed by the contracting officer, the contractor should notify the government in writing as soon as possible. This will permit the government to evaluate the alleged change and confirm that it is in fact a change, direct the mode of further performance and plan for its funding, countermand the alleged change, or notify the contractor that no change is considered to have occurred.

Constructive changes (i.e., situations where government actions cause a change in contract performance) are a key element for profitable contract performance. If such changes increase the cost of contract performance, the contractor should request an increase in the contract price. Contractors often neglect to seek price increases for various reasons (e.g., the cost increase is minor, the customer might not appreciate a price adjustment request). However, contractors are well-advised to accumulate the additional cost of performance and request a price adjustment where appropriate.

Subcontracting

If the contractor has an approved purchasing system, consent is required for subcontracts specifically identified by the contracting officer in the subcontracts clause of the contract. The contracting officer may require consent to subcontract if the contracting officer has determined that an individual consent action is required to protect the government adequately because of the subcontract type, complexity, or value, or because the subcontract needs special surveillance. These can be subcontracts for critical systems, subsystems, components, or services. Subcontracts may be identified by subcontract number or by class of items (e.g., subcontracts for engines on a prime contract for airframes).

If the contractor does not have an approved purchasing system, consent to subcontract is required for cost-reimbursement, time-and-materials, labor-hour, or letter contracts, as well as for unpriced actions (including unpriced modifications and unpriced delivery orders) under fixed-price contracts that exceed the simplified acquisition threshold:

- For DOD, the Coast Guard, and NASA, the greater of the simplified acquisition threshold or 5 percent of the total estimated cost of the contract
- For civilian agencies other than the Coast Guard and NASA, either the simplified acquisition threshold or 5 percent of the total estimated cost of the contract.

Consent also may be required for subcontracts under prime contracts for architect-engineer services.

Government Property

Contractors are responsible and liable for government property in their possession, unless otherwise provided by the contract. Generally, contracts do not hold contractors liable for loss of or damage to government property when the property is provided under negotiated fixed-price contracts, cost-reimbursement contracts, facilities contracts, or service contracts performed on a government installation.

A contract may require the contractor to assume greater liability for loss of or damage to government property. For example, this may be the case when the contractor is using government property primarily for commercial work rather than for government work. Contractor records of government property established and maintained under the terms of the contract are the government's official property records.

Issues relating to government property arise when a contractor purchases materials, equipment, supplies, etc., for a government cost-reimbursement contract. The property must be used only for that contract unless permission is obtained from the contracting officer. Property tagging, storage, and records must be properly maintained for these items.

Earned Value Management Systems

Earned value management systems (EVMS) are basically budgeting systems that focus on tracking performance to budgets. They feature estimates to complete for purposes of ensuring early notification of potential program overruns. These requirements are incorporated in contracts on a case-by-case basis.

Termination for Convenience

Unique to government contracts is the ability of the government to terminate a contract for its own "convenience." In a commercial environment, a buyer generally cannot unilaterally cancel a contract without committing a breach of contract. If the government terminates a contract for convenience, the government will reimburse a contractor for costs incurred plus a reasonable profit for work performed.

A contractor must submit a settlement proposal to receive this reimbursement. Whenever a contract is terminated, the contractor should cease all work on the contract. Normally, a settlement proposal is required within one year of the termination notice. When a termination notice is received, a contractor should begin to accumulate the costs of the termination administration. These settlement costs are reimbursable as part of the settlement proposal.

Two basic types of termination settlements are used: (1) the inventory method; and (2) the total cost method. Cost-reimbursement and certain fixed-price contracts are settled using the total cost method. Under the inventory method, the contractor is paid the contractual price for completed/accepted items and is reimbursed on a total cost basis for the remaining contract items. The inventory method can be used only when unit prices and costs are available and some items have been completed and accepted by the government. If a contract would have resulted in a loss, the government may not permit recovery of any profit on the termination settlement. In fact, a loss factor will be applied in lieu of profit for the work performed.

Ethics

In late 2008, the FAR was revised to expand the requirements for (1) a contractor code of business ethics and conduct, (2) an internal control system, and (3) disclosure of significant overpayments, certain criminal violations, or False Claims Act (FCA) violations. Contractors must establish and maintain internal controls to detect and prevent improper conduct in connection with a government contract or subcontract. Whenever a contractor or subcontractor has "credible evidence" of an FCA violation or a federal criminal violation involving fraud, conflict of interest, bribery, or a gratuity, that evidence must be disclosed to the agency's inspector general and the contracting officer. Knowing failure by a contractor principal to comply with these disclosure requirements is cause for suspension or debarment.

The FAR rule limits mandatory disclosures to a period of three years after contract completion because it would be difficult to locate evidence and responsible parties for older contracts. The final rule was revised to require reporting only of significant overpayments, which depends on both dollar value and circumstances. A suspension and debarment official may determine whether an overpayment is significant and whether suspension or debarment is the appropriate outcome for failure to report such overpayment.

	Figure 31 TABLE OF CONTENTS FY 20XX YEAR ENDED JUNE 30, 20XX	
Schedule	**Title**	
A	Rate Summary	
B	General and Administrative Costs Expenses (Final Cost Pool)	
C	Overhead Expenses (Final Cost Pool)	
D	Fringe Benefit Expenses (Intermediate Cost Pool)	
E	Claimed Direct Costs	
F	FACILITIES CAPITAL COST OF MONEY FACTORS COMPUTATION	
G	RESERVED	
H	Total Costs by Contract and Contract Type	
H-1	Government Participation in Costs	
I	Schedule of Cumulative Direct and Indirect Costs Claimed and Billed	
J	Subcontract Information	
K	Summary of Hours and Amounts on T&M/Labor Hour Contracts	
L	Reconciliation of Total Payroll to Total Labor Distribution	
M	List of Decisions/Agreements or Approvals Affecting Direct/Indirect Costs and Description of Accounting and Organizational	
N	Certificate of Final Indirect Costs	
O	Contract Closing Information	
P	RESERVED	
Q	RESERVED	
R	RESERVED	
S	Contract Briefs	
T	Executive Compensation Data	

COST POOL	RECORDED	ADJUSTMENTS	CLAIMED	REFERENCE
				SCHEDULE A
		Summary of Claimed Indirect Cost Rates		
		FY 20xx		
		YEAR ENDED JUNE 30, 20xx		
FRINGE BENEFITS				
EXPENSE	$2,177,040	$0	$2,177,040	SCHEDULE D
BASE	$5,992,699	$0	$5,992,699	SCHEDULE D
RATE	36.33%	0.00%	36.33%	
OVERHEAD				
EXPENSE	$930,728	$23,224	$907,504	SCHEDULE C
BASE	$5,992,699	$0	$5,992,699	SCHEDULE C
RATE	15.53%	−0.39%	15.14%	
GENERAL AND ADMINISTRATIVE				
EXPENSE	$1,853,113	$81,225	$1,771,888	SCHEDULE B
BASE	$11,101,258	$0	$11,101,258	SCHEDULE B
RATE	16.69%	−0.73%	15.96%	

				SCHEDULE B
General and Administrative Costs Expenses (Final Cost Pool)				
FY 20xx				
DESCRIPTION	RECORDED	ADJUSTMENT	CLAIMED	NOTES
Indirect Labor	$770,931	$0	$770,931	
Professional fees	143,048	0	143,048	
Travel, Lodging and Per Diem	26,750	5,350	21,400	Note 1
Bid and Proposal	406,121	0	406,121	
Consulting Fees	35,314	0	35,314	
Rent	82,450	0	82,450	
Marketing	80,168	20,137	60,031	Note 2
Management Committee	32,601	0	32,601	
Office supplies	42,461	0	42,461	
Insurance	40,464	0	40,464	
Depreciation	23,537	0	23,537	
Recruiting	6,745	0	6,745	
Interest Expense	16,754	16,754	0	Note 3
Telephone and Utilities	17,890	0	17,890	
Legal Fees	20,236	0	20,236	
Plan Fees	27,074	0	27,074	
Maintenance and Repairs	6,060	0	6,060	
Dues and Subscriptions	13,447	0	13,447	
Continuing Education	4,080	0	4,080	
Taxes and Licenses	7,698	0	7,698	
Miscellaneous	33,346	23,045	10,301	Note 4
Entertainment	204	204	0	Note 5
Donations	2,980	2,980	0	Note 6
Fines and Penalties	12,755	12,755	0	Note 7
Total General and Administrative	$1,853,113	$81,225	$1,771,888	
Allocation Base				
Direct Labor	$5,932,699	$0	$5,932,699	Schedule E
Fringe Benefits	2,155,243	0	2,155,243	DL$ x FB Rate
Subcontracts	1,063,265	0	1,063,265	Schedule E
Materials	1,325	0	1,325	Schedule E
Equipment	77,878	0	77,878	Schedule E
Other Direct Costs	949,206	0	949,206	Schedule E
Overhead	898,418	0	898,418	DL$ x OH Rate
Unallowable Overhead	23,224	0	23,224	Schedule C
Total Cost Input	$11,101,258	$0	$11,101,258	

Note 1–Unallowable per FAR 31.205-36, Travel.
Note 2–Unallowable per FAR 31.205-1, Advertising and Public Relations
Note 3–Unallowable per FAR 31.205-20, Interest and Other Financial Costs
Note 4–Unallowable per FAR 31.2, Cost Principles.
Note 5–Unallowable per FAR 31.205-14, Entertainment
Note 6–Unallowable per FAR 31.205-8, Contributions or Donations
Note 7–Unallowable per FAR 31.205-15, Fines and Penalties

				SCHEDULE C
Overhead Expenses (Final Cost Pool) **FY 20xx**				
DESCRIPTION	RECORDED	ADJUSTMENT	CLAIMED	NOTES
Indirect Labor	$621,208	$0	$621,208	
Travel, Lodging and Per Diem	116,119	23,224	92,895	Note 1
Consulting Fees	8,187	0	8,187	
Rent	16,139	0	16,139	
Office supplies	24,523	0	24,523	
Insurance	89,359	0	89,359	
Depreciation	23,139	0	23,139	
Telephone and Utilities	10,330	0	10,330	
Recruiting	3,448	0	3,448	
Maintenance and Repairs	188	0	188	
Dues and Subscriptions	10,631	0	10,631	
Continuing Education	3,731	0	3,731	
Miscellaneous	3,726	0	3,726	
Shared Services Allocation	0	0	0	
TOTAL OVERHEAD	$930,728	$23,224	$907,504	
Allocation Base				
Direct Labor	$5,932,699	$0	$5,932,699	Schedule E
Independent Research and Development	50,000	0	50,000	Schedule D
Bid and Proposal	10,000	0	10,000	Schedule D
Total Labor Dollars	$5,992,699	$0	$5,992,699	
Note 1–Unallowable per FAR 31.205-36, Travel. Use additional Schedule Cs for additional final cost pools such as Engineering, Material Handling, Subcontract Administration				

				SCHEDULE D
Fringe Benefit Expenses (Intermediate Cost Pool)				
FY 20xx				
DESCRIPTION	RECORDED	ADJUSTMENT	CLAIMED	NOTES
Paid Time Off	672,399	0	672,399	
Benefits	1,504,641	0	1,504,641	
TOTAL OVERHEAD	$2,177,040	$0	$2,177,040	
Allocation Base				
Direct Labor	$5,932,699	$0	$5,932,699	Schedule E
Independent Research and Development	50,000	0	50,000	
Bid and Proposal	10,000	0	10,000	
Total Labor Dollars	$5,992,699	$0	$5,992,699	
Use additional Schedule Ds for additional intermediate cost pools such as Occupancy, Human Resources, Information Technology, Communications				

				SCHEDULE E
Claimed Direct Costs				
FY 20xx				
DESCRIPTION	RECORDED	ADJUSTMENTS	CLAIMED	Notes
Direct Labor	$5,932,699	$0	$5,932,699	
Fringe Benefits	2,155,243	0	2,155,243	
Subcontracts	1,063,265	0	1,063,265	
Material	1,325	0	1,325	
Equipment	77,878	0	77,878	
Other Direct Cost	949,206	0	949,206	
TOTAL DIRECT COSTS	$10,179,616	$0	$10,179,616	

Schedule F

FACILITIES CAPITAL
COST OF MONEY FACTORS COMPUTATION

Contractor: **Address:**
Business Unit:

COST ACCOUNTING PERIOD						
1. Applicable Cost of Money Rate	5.000%					
Business Unit Facilities Capital	2. Accumulation and Direct Distribution of N.B.V.	3. Basis of Allocation	4. Total Net Book Value	5. Cost of Money for the Accounting Period	6. Allocation Base for the Period	7. Facilities Cost of Money Factor
Recorded	$700,000					
Leased Property	100,000					
Corporate and/or Group	10,000					
Total	$810,000					
Undistributed	100,000					
Distributed	$710,000					
Indirect Cost Pools						
Overhead	$600,000	$80,000	$680,000	$34,000	$5,992,699	$0.006
G&A	110,000	20,000	130,000	6,500	11,101,258	0.001
Total	$710,000	$100,000	$810,000	$40,500		

SCHEDULE H

Direct Cost by Contract/Subcontract, IR&D/B&P Direct Incurred, and Indirect Expense Applied at Claimed Rates
FY 20xx

CONTRACT NUMBER/DELIVERY ORDER	CONTRACT NO.	JOB NO.	LABOR	FRINGE BENEFITS 36.33%	SUB-CONTRACTS	MATERIAL	EQUIPMENT	OTHER DIRECT COSTS	OVERHEAD 15.14%	TOTAL COST INPUT	G&A 15.96%	TOTAL COSTS
A. COST TYPE (None)			$0	$0	$0	$0	$0	$0	$0	$0	$0	$0
B. TOTAL OTHER FLEXIBLY PRICED (None)			$0	$0	$0	$0	$0	$0	$0	$0	$0	$0
C. TIME AND MATERIAL												
		5001-39	$1,627,430	$591,216	$0	$0	$11,989	$586,523	$246,450	$3,063,608	$488,987	$3,552,595
		5000-39	1,857,991	674,975	0	0	0	23,753	281,365	2,838,084	452,991	3,291,075
C. TOTAL TIME AND MATERIAL			$3,485,422	$1,266,191			$11,989	$610,275	$527,815	$5,901,692	$941,978	$6,843,670
D. TOTAL FIXED PRICE			$2,447,277	$889,052	$1,063,265	$1,325	$65,889	$338,931	$370,603	$5,176,342	$826,204	$6,002,546
E. COMMERCIAL WORK (None)			$0	$0	$0	$0	$0	$0	$0	$0	$0	$0
SUBTOTAL			$5,932,699	$2,155,243	$1,063,265	$1,325	$77,878	$949,206	$898,418	$11,078,034	$1,768,182	$12,846,216
Independent Research and Development			$50,000	$18,164	$0	$0	$0	$0	$7,572			$75,736
Bid and Proposal			10,000	3,633	0	0	0	0	1,514			15,147
SUBTOTAL			$60,000	$21,797					$9,086			$90,883
TOTAL COSTS			$5,992,699	$2,177,040	$1,063,265	$1,325	$77,878	$949,206	$907,504	$11,078,034	$1,768,182	$12,937,099
UNALLOWABLE/UNCLAIMED COSTS												
Unallowable/Unclaimed Direct Costs			0	0	0	0	0	0	$0	$0	$0	$0
Unallowable/Unclaimed Fringe Benefits				0					0	0	0	0
Unallowable/Unclaimed Overhead									23,224	23,224	3,707	26,931
Unallowable/Unclaimed G&A											81,225	81,225
TOTAL INCLUDING UNALLOWABLE/UNCLAIMED COSTS			$5,992,699	$2,177,040	$1,063,265	$1,325	$77,878	$949,206	$930,728	$11,101,258	$1,853,113	$13,045,254

SCHEDULE H-1

Government Participation in Costs
FY 20xx

COST ELEMENTS	TIME & MATERIALS	COST TYPE	FLEXIBLY PRICED	FIRM FIXED PRICE	TOTAL COMMERCIAL	TOTAL COMPANY BASE	GOVERNMENT PERCENTAGE					
							T&M	CPFF	FLEX	FFP	COMM'L	TOTAL
DIRECT LABOR	$3,485,422	$0	$0	$2,447,277	$0	$5,932,699	59%	0%	0%	41%	0%	100%
FRINGE BENEFITS	1,266,191	0	0	889,052	0	2,155,243	59%	0%	0%	41%	0%	100%
OVERHEAD	527,815	0	0	370,603	0	898,418	59%	0%	0%	41%	0%	100%
SUBCONTRACTS	0	0	0	1,063,265	0	1,063,265	0%	0%	0%	100%	0%	100%
MATERIAL	0	0	0	1,325	0	1,325	0%	0%	0%	100%	0%	100%
EQUIPMENT	11,989	0	0	65,889	0	77,878	15%	0%	0%	85%	0%	100%
OTHER DIRECT COSTS	610,275	0	0	338,931	0	949,206	64%	0%	0%	36%	0%	100%
GENERAL AND ADM.	941,978	0	0	826,204	0	1,768,182	53%	0%	0%	47%	0%	100%
TOTAL	$6,843,670	$0	$0	$6,002,546	$0	$12,846,216	53%	0%	0%	47%	0%	100%
TOTAL ADV DOLLARS	$1,564,242	$0	$0	$0	$0	$1,564,242	100%	0%	0%	0%	0%	100%

SCHEDULE I

SCHEDULE OF CUMULATIVE DIRECT AND INDIRECT COSTS CLAIMED AND BILLED ON COST/FLEXIBLY PRICED AND T&M CONTRACTS AND SUBCONTRACTS THROUGH 06/30/xx

Contract No./Delivery Order	Subject To Penalty Clause	Prior Years Settled Total Costs	Unsettled/Claimed Direct And Indirect Costs Using Claimed Rates			Less Contract Limitations	Voluntary Deletions	Rebates/ Credits	Net Cumulative Settled or Claimed	PV No./ Inv. No.	Cumulative Billed			Over (Under) Billing
			FYE 6/30/20xx	FYE 6/30/20xx							Date Cost Billed Through	Amount		
Cost Type (None)														
Time & Material (Material portion only)														
	N	$466,142	$576,480	$598,511		$107,790	$0	$0	$934,832			$934,832		$0
	Y	2,461	16,770	23,753		17,865	0	0	1,365			1,365		0
Total- Cost Type and Time & Material Contracts		$468,603	$593,250	$622,264		$125,655	$0	$0	$936,198			$936,198		$0

SCHEDULE J

SUBCONTRACT INFORMATION
FY 20xx

SUBCONTRACT NO.	PRIME CONTRACT NO.	SUBCONTRACTOR'S NAME & ADDRESS	POINT OF CONTACT AND PHONE NO.	SUBCONTRACT VALUE	COSTS INCURRED IN FY	AWARD TYPE

SCHEDULE K

Summary of Hours and Amounts on T&M/Labor Hour Contracts
FY 20xx

Contract Labor Category LABOR	Contract No. July 20xx – December 20xx			Contract No. January 20xx – June 20xx			Contract No. July 20xx – June 20xx			Amount
	Rate	Hrs	Amount	Rate	Hrs	Amount	Rate	Hrs	Amount	
Project Manager	$78.44	869.00	$68,164	$81.58	970.00	$79,133				$147,297
Technical Writer	59.32	2,674.50	158,651	61.69	2,820.00	173,966				332,617
Technical Writer OT	88.98	30.00	2,669	92.54	0.00	0				2,669
Library Technician	27.61	922.50	25,470	28.72	930.50	26,724				52,194
Word Processor I	25.00	931.00	23,275	26.00	0.00	0				23,275
Word Processor II	28.42	4,817.35	136,909	29.55	6,591.35	194,774				331,683
Word Processor II OT	42.62	54.10	2,306	44.33	12.60	559				2,864
Word Processor III	32.47	12,336.50	400,566	33.77	12,248.75	413,640				814,206
Word Processor III OT	48.71	121.00	5,894	50.66	50.50	2,558				8,452
General Clerk III	27.59	4,106.80	113,307	28.70	5,027.30	144,284				257,590
General Clerk III OT	41.39	0.00	0	43.04	0.00	0				0
General Clerk IV	30.44	2,745.50	83,573	31.65	2,827.20	89,481				173,054
General Clerk IV OT	45.65	10.00	457	47.48	0.00	0				457
Security Clerk III	29.55	4,115.70	121,619	30.73	4,048.50	124,410				246,029
Security Clerk III OT	44.33	76.00	3,369	46.10	105.00	4,841				8,210
Illustrator I	34.51	0.00	0	35.89	0.00	0				0
Drafter I	24.12	903.50	21,792	25.09	905.50	22,719				44,511
Drafter I OT	36.18	18.50	669	37.63	0.00	0				669
Accounting Clerk II	25.00	1,183.00	29,575	26.00	1,348.50	35,061				64,636
Accounting Clerk II OT	37.50	21.50	806	39.01	0.00	0				806
Accounting Clerk III	28.42	2,753.50	78,254	29.55	2,771.00	81,883				160,138
Accounting Clerk III OT	42.62	54.00	2,301	44.33	13.00	576				2,878
Accounting Clerk IV	32.36	3,851.00	124,618	33.65	3,265.00	109,867				234,486
Accounting Clerk IV OT	48.54	82.00	3,980	50.48	0.00	0				3,980
Messenger	29.18	1,775.00	51,795	30.35	1,886.00	57,240				109,035
Warehouse Specialist	29.63	2,426.00	71,882	30.82	2,834.00	87,344				159,226
Warehouse Specialist OT	44.45	0.00	0	46.22	4.00	185				185
Supply Technician	40.24	2,685.05	108,046	41.85	2,795.00	116,971				225,017
Supply Technician OT	60.36	0.00	0	62.78	23.50	1,475				1,475
Laborer	28.60	2,323.00	66,438	29.75	2,311.00	68,752				135,190
Laborer OT	39.64	0.00	0	41.22	3.00	124				124
Technical Writer Asst II	32.36	930.50	30,111	33.65	901.00	30,319				60,430
Technical Writer Asst II OT	48.54	11.50	558	50.48	0.00	0				558
Project Liaison	34.32	7,238.00	248,408	35.69	8,221.00	293,407				541,816

Contract Labor Category LABOR	Contract No. July 20xx – December 20xx			Contract No. January 20xx – June 20xx			Contract No. July 20xx – June 20xx			Amount
	Rate	Hrs	Amount	Rate	Hrs	Amount	Rate	Hrs	Amount	
Project Liaison OT	51.48	90.50	4,659	53.54	35.00	1,874				6,533
Driver	0.00	0.00	0	47.42	20.00	948				948
Driver OT	0.00	0.00	0	71.13	0.00	0				0
Logistic Coordinator							$29.29	0.00	$0	0
Quality Manager Program Adm							37.22	0.00	0	0
Risk Program Administ							37.22	0.00	0	0
Secretary							30.42	0.00	0	0
Security Assistant							29.29	0.00	0	0
Security Assistant (overtime)							0.00	0.00	0	0
Chauffer - Escort - Messenger							16.22	1,408.00	22,838	22,838
Chauffer - Escort - Messenger							16.34	344.00	5,621	5,621
Chauffer - Escort - Messenger							22.33	8.00	179	179
Chauffer - Escort - Messenger							22.50	8.00	180	180
Program Assistant							0.00	0.00	0	0
Program Director							0.00	0.00	0	0
Research Specialist Junior							0.00	0.00	0	0
Research Specialist Senior							0.00	0.00	0	0
Research Specialist Senior							0.00	0.00	0	0
Logistic Assistant							35.68	0.00	0	0
Night Vision Instructor							48.90	1,112.00	54,377	54,377
Night Vision Instructor (Overtime)							0.00	0.00	0	0
Night Vision Instructor							49.27	472.00	23,255	23,255
Night Vision Instructor							29.67	296.00	8,782	8,782
Night Vision Instructor (Overtime)							40.84	56.00	2,287	2,287
Accounting Clerk							46.72	464.50	21,701	21,701
Accounting Clerk							46.37	1,370.00	63,527	63,527
Aviation Fuel Technician							32.43	1,296.00	42,029	42,029
Aviation Fuel Technician							32.19	4,296.00	138,288	138,288
Colar aviation advisor							60.07	0.00	0	0
Driver Messenger							12.83	0.00	0	0

Contract Labor Category LABOR	Contract No. July 20xx – December 20xx			Contract No. January 20xx – June 20xx			Contract No. July 20xx – June 20xx			Amount
	Rate	Hrs	Amount	Rate	Hrs	Amount	Rate	Hrs	Amount	
Driver Messenger (overtime)							17.66	0.00	0	0
NAS Aviation Unit Driver							12.83	0.00	0	0
NAS Aviation Unit Driver (overtime)							17.66	0.00	0	0
NAS Aviation Unit Receptionist							14.42	0.00	0	0
NAS Colar Logistic Exp							0.00	0.00	0	0
NAS Colar Logistic Exp							32.19	0.00	0	0
NAU Bus Driver for Larandia							15.21	1,248.00	18,982	18,982
NAU Bus Driver for Larandia (overtime)							20.93	418.00	8,749	8,749
NAU Bus Driver for Larandia							15.09	3,848.00	58,066	58,066
NAU Bus Driver for Larandia (overtime)							20.78	1,289.00	26,785	26,785
Office Administrator							33.52	472.00	15,821	15,821
Office Administrator							33.26	1,400.00	46,564	46,564
Plan Colombia Helicopter Aviation Program Advisor							53.68	952.00	51,103	51,103
Plan Colombia Helicopter Aviation Program Advisor							54.09	472.00	25,530	25,530
Aviation Advisor							37.92	1,056.00	40,044	40,044
Aviation Advisor							38.21	464.00	17,729	17,729
POL Fuel Specialist							33.69	1,376.00	46,357	46,357
POL Fuel Specialist							32.43	1,416.00	45,921	45,921
POL Fuel Specialist							33.44	4,211.00	140,816	140,816
POL Fuel Specialist							32.19	4,198.00	135,134	135,134
Rotating Fuel Assistant							14.22	2,584.00	36,744	36,744
Rotating Fuel Assistant (Overtime)							19.57	1,418.00	27,750	27,750
Rotating Fuel Assistant							14.11	7,422.00	104,724	104,724
Rotating Fuel Assistant (Overtime)							19.43	3,329.00	64,682	64,682
Secretary							11.55	535.00	6,179	6,179
Secretary							35.68	0.00	0	0
Legal Assistant							31.15	472.00	14,703	14,703
Legal Assistant							30.92	680.00	21,026	21,026
Scientific Assistant							28.39	640.00	18,170	18,170
Scientific Assistant							29.60	0.00	0	0
Project Evaluation Analyst							0.00	0.00	0	0

Contract Labor Category LABOR	Contract No.			Contract No.			Contract No.			Amount
	July 20xx – December 20xx			January 20xx – June 20xx			July 20xx – June 20xx			
	Rate	Hrs	Amount	Rate	Hrs	Amount	Rate	Hrs	Amount	Amount
Environmental Auditor							38.70	558.00	21,595	21,595
Toxicology Physician							38.99	472.00	18,403	18,403
Toxicology Physician							38.70	1,385.50	53,619	53,619
Eradication Driver							12.83	0.00	0	0
Eradication Driver (overtime)							17.66	0.00	0	0
Eradication Receptionist							14.75	0.00	0	0
Eradication Receptionist OT							20.31	0.00	0	0
Program Operat. and Stand. Advisor Training							73.35	456.00	33,448	33,448
Program Operas. and Stand. Advisor Training							72.80	1,344.00	97,843	97,843
Eradication Secretary (Eliana´s Replacement)							26.13	0.00	0	0
Secretary (Bilingual)							31.58	0.00	0	0
Air Condition Technician							15.21	408.00	6,206	6,206
Air Condition Technician (overtime)							20.93	194.00	4,060	4,060
Air Condition Technician							11.28	896.00	10,107	10,107
Air Condition Technician (overtime)							15.53	369.00	5,731	5,731
Air Conditioner Technician							15.09	1,280.00	19,315	19,315
Air Conditioner Technician (overtime)							20.78	488.50	10,151	10,151
Air Conditioner Technician							12.53	0.00	0	0
Air Conditioner Technician (overtime)							17.25	0.00	0	0
Air Conditioner Technician							11.20	2,512.00	28,134	28,134
Air Conditioner Technician (overtime)							15.41	906.50	13,969	13,969
Air Operations Assistant							37.22	0.00	0	0
Architect							50.13	472.00	23,661	23,661
Architect							49.75	1,359.00	67,610	67,610
Civil Engineer							0.00	0.00	0	0
Civil Engineer							49.75	0.00	0	0

Contract Labor Category LABOR	Contract No. July 20xx – December 20xx			Contract No. January 20xx – June 20xx			Contract No. July 20xx – June 20xx			Amount
	Rate	Hrs	Amount	Rate	Hrs	Amount	Rate	Hrs	Amount	
Driver Messenger							0.00	0.00	0	0
Driver Messenger (overtime)							0.00	0.00	0	0
Driver Messenger							12.83	0.00	0	0
Driver Messenger (overtime)							17.66	0.00	0	0
Driver Messenger							13.35	0.00	0	0
Driver Messenger (overtime)							18.38	0.00	0	0
Electrical Technician							11.28	856.00	9,656	9,656
Electrical Technician (overtime)							15.53	435.00	6,756	6,756
Electrical Technician							12.53	0.00	0	0
Electrical Technician (overtime)							17.25	0.00	0	0
Electrical Technician							19.41	0.00	0	0
Electrical Technician (overtime)							26.72	0.00	0	0
Electrical Technician							11.20	2,448.00	27,418	27,418
Electrical Technician (overtime)							15.41	944.50	14,555	14,555
Master Electrician							17.48	296.00	5,174	5,174
Facilities Maint. Tech. (handyman)							16.89	0.00	0	0
Facilities Maint. Tech. (handyman) (overtime)							23.25	0.00	0	0
Facilities Maint. Manager							32.13	265.50	8,531	8,531
Handyman							19.41	0.00	0	0
Handyman (overtime)							26.72	0.00	0	0
Installations & Vehicle Manager							41.72	424.00	17,689	17,689
Installations & Vehicle Manager							41.41	1,356.00	56,152	56,152
Logistic Expediter							0.00	0.00	0	0
Logistic Expediter							0.00	0.00	0	0
Logistic Expediter							32.19	0.00	0	0
Logistic Expediter							28.22	24.00	677	677
Maintenance Technician							11.28	872.00	9,836	9,836
Maintenance Technician (overtime)							15.53	306.00	4,752	4,752
Maintenance Technician							12.53	0.00	0	0
Maintenance Technician (overtime)							17.25	0.00	0	0

Contract Labor Category LABOR	Contract No. July 20xx – December 20xx			Contract No. January 20xx – June 20xx			Contract No. July 20xx – June 20xx			Amount
	Rate	Hrs	Amount	Rate	Hrs	Amount	Rate	Hrs	Amount	
Maintenance Technician							11.20	2,408.00	26,970	26,970
Maintenance Technician (overtime)							15.41	740.00	11,403	11,403
Operations Specialist							38.99	472.00	18,403	18,403
Operations Specialist							38.70	1,416.00	54,799	54,799
Deployment/Quality Assurance Manager							50.13	57.00	2,857	2,857
Procurement Specialist							35.68	0.00	0	0
Senior Maintenance Technician							31.58	0.00	0	0
Senior Office Administrator							0.00	0.00	0	0
Senior Office Administrator							46.51	801.50	37,278	37,278
Small Engine Mechanic							15.02	0.00	0	0
Small Engine Mechanic (overtime)							20.68	0.00	0	0
Vehicle Dispatcher							19.41	0.00	0	0
Vehicle Dispatcher (overtime)							26.72	0.00	0	0
Vehicle Mechanic							16.89	0.00	0	0
Vehicle Mechanic (overtime)							23.25	0.00	0	0
Geographic Information Systems Instructor							32.78	464.00	15,210	15,210
Geographic Information Systems Instructor							32.53	992.00	32,270	32,270
IPL Network Systems Asst. Administrator							32.78	447.50	14,669	14,669
IPL Network Systems Asst. Administrator							32.53	1,424.50	46,339	46,339
IPL Network Systems Asst. Administrator (librarian)							27.14	0.00	0	0
File Clerk							11.93	960.00	11,453	11,453
File Clerk							16.42	13.00	213	213
Legal Assistant							18.38	0.00	0	0
NAS Vehicle Maintenance Advisor							0.00	0.00	0	0

Contract Labor Category LABOR	Contract No. July 20xx – December 20xx			Contract No. January 20xx – June 20xx			Contract No. July 20xx – June 20xx			Amount
	Rate	Hrs	Amount	Rate	Hrs	Amount	Rate	Hrs	Amount	
NAS Vehicle Maintenance Advisor (overtime)							0.00	0.00	0	0
NAS Vehicle Maintenance Advisor							17.17	96.00	1,648	1,648
NAS Vehicle Maintenance Advisor (overtime)							23.64	0.00	0	0
Secretary							31.14	0.00	0	0
Advisory Canine Program							0.00	0.00	0	0
Legal Advisor							0.00	0.00	0	0
Contracting Legal Assistant							43.33	472.00	20,452	20,452
Contracting Legal Assistant							43.00	1,388.00	59,684	59,684
Criminal Law/Legal Assistant							43.33	171.00	7,409	7,409
Criminal Law/Legal Assistant							43.00	1,432.00	61,576	61,576
Communication Director							49.27	447.00	22,024	22,024
Communication Director							48.90	1,408.00	68,851	68,851
Communication Assistant							29.48	411.00	12,116	12,116
Communication Assistant							29.26	472.00	13,811	13,811
Communication Assistant							22.34	0.00	0	0
Program Advisor							72.80	463.00	33,706	33,706
Group Coordinator							32.13	944.00	30,331	30,331
Group Coordinator							31.89	2,283.00	72,805	72,805
Strategic Planning Analyst							32.43	472.00	15,307	15,307
Strategic Planning Analyst							32.19	947.00	30,484	30,484
International Affairs Analyst							12.02	472.00	5,673	5,673
International Affairs Analyst							11.93	222.00	2,648	2,648
Defense Budget Analyst							18.07	944.00	17,058	17,058
Defense Budget Analyst							17.93	2,110.00	37,832	37,832
Administrative Assistant							0.00	0.00	0	0
Administrative Assistant OT							0.00	0.00	0	0
Administrative Assistant							14.11	1,368.00	19,302	19,302

Contract Labor Category LABOR	Contract No. July 20xx – December 20xx			Contract No. January 20xx – June 20xx			Contract No. July 20xx – June 20xx			Amount
	Rate	Hrs	Amount	Rate	Hrs	Amount	Rate	Hrs	Amount	
Administrative Assistant OT							0.00	0.00	0	0
VIP Protection Technical Interpreter							19.60	456.00	8,938	8,938
VIP Protection Technical Interpreter (overtime)							26.96	27.00	728	728
VIP Protection Technical Interpreter							23.45	448.00	10,506	10,506
VIP Protection Technical Interpreter (overtime)							32.28	49.00	1,582	1,582
VIP Protection Technical Interpreter							19.45	1,272.00	24,740	24,740
VIP Protection Technical Interpreter (overtime)							26.78	117.50	3,147	3,147
VIP Protection Logistics Interpreter							0.00	0.00	0	0
VIP Protection Logistics Interpreter (Overtime)							0.00	0.00	0	0
VIP Protection Logistics Interpreter							0.00	0.00	0	0
VIP Protection Logistics Interpreter (Overtime)							0.00	0.00	0	0
VIP Protection Logistics Interpreter							23.27	1,336.00	31,089	31,089
VIP Protection Logistics Interpreter (Overtime)							32.04	106.50	3,412	3,412
Training Coordinator							29.48	472.00	13,915	13,915
Training Coordinator							0.00	0.00	0	0
Training Coordinator							29.26	1,377.00	40,291	40,291
Fuel Specialist							22.34	1,424.00	31,812	31,812
Fuel Specialist							30.76	54.00	1,661	1,661
Fuel Specialist							23.52	408.00	9,596	9,596
Fuel Specialist							32.39	8.00	259	259
Fuel Specialist							22.51	472.00	10,625	10,625
Fuel Specialist							30.99	16.00	496	496
Fuel Specialist							23.35	1,408.00	32,877	32,877
Fuel Specialist							32.14	0.00	0	0
Safety Specialist							44.45	373.00	16,580	16,580
Safety Specialist							44.12	1,432.00	63,180	63,180
Administrative Assistant							14.22	464.00	6,598	6,598
Administrative Assistant (Overtime)							19.57	0.00	0	0

Contract Labor Category LABOR	Contract No. July 20xx – December 20xx			Contract No. January 20xx – June 20xx			Contract No. July 20xx – June 20xx			Amount
	Rate	Hrs	Amount	Rate	Hrs	Amount	Rate	Hrs	Amount	
Administrative Assistant							11.20	912.00	10,214	10,214
Receptionist							10.10	232.00	2,343	2,343
Chief Nurse Instructor							28.44	472.00	13,424	13,424
Chief Nurse Instructor							0.00	0.00	0	0
Chief Nurse Instructor							28.22	1,432.00	40,411	40,411
TOTAL		60,156.50	$1,990,124		62,968.20	$2,163,115		113,843.50	$3,112,700	$7,265,939
OTHER COSTS										
CONTRACT LIMITATIONS										
Material Costs			$0						$0	
Subcontracts			0						0	
Equipment			11,989						0	
Other Direct Costs			586,523						23,753	
Subtotal			$598,511						$23,753	
Unallowable per Contract terms			0						0	
TOTAL			$598,511						$23,753	$622,264
G&A per contract	0.00%	598,511	$0				4.40%	$23,753	$1,045	$1,045
G&A @actual	15.96%	598,511	95,529				15.96%	$23,753	3,791	$99,321
TOTAL ALLOCABLE			$694,041						$27,544	$721,585
TOTAL BILLABLE			$598,511						$24,798	$623,309

				SCHEDULE L
Schedule L - Reconciliation of Total Payroll to Total Labor Distribution FY 20xx				
DESCRIPTION	CLAIMED	IRS 941's	DIFFERENCE	NOTES
Direct Labor				
Indirect Labor				
Paid Time Off				
Reverse Payroll Accrual January 1				
Payroll Accrual December 31				
941 Q 1				
941 Q 2				
941 Q 3				
941 Q 4				
TOTALS	$0	$0	$0	

SCHEDULE M

LISTING OF DECISIONS/AGREEMENTS, OR APPROVALS AFFECTING DIRECT/ INDIRECT COST AND DESCRIPTION OF ACCOUNTING and ORGANIZATIONAL CHANGES FY 20xx

A. Decisions/Agreements
   None

B. Accounting Changes
   None

C. Organizational Changes
   None

SCHEDULE N

CERTIFICATE OF FINAL INDIRECT COSTS

This is to certify that I have reviewed this proposal to establish final indirect cost rates and to the best of my knowledge and belief:

1. All costs included in this proposal dated June 30, 20xx, to establish final indirect cost rates for the fiscal year 20xx (year ended June 30, 20xx) are allowable in accordance with the costprinciples of the Federal Acquisition Regulation (FAR) and its supplements applicable to the contractsto final indirect cost rates will apply; and

2. This proposal does not include any costs which are expressly unallowable under applicable cost principles of the FAR or its supplements.

Firm: _____

Signature:_____

Name of Certifying Official: _____

Title: _____

Date of Execution:_____

CONTRACT BRIEFING CARD **A. General Information**					Page 1 of 4

CONTRACT BRIEFING CARD

A. General Information — Page 1 of 4

1. Contractor Name:

2. Contract Number:	Date of Award:
Contractor Job No.	FY Funds:
3. Briefed through Mod. No.	Dated:

4. Contract Type

CPFF CPIF CPAF CS CR
T&M FPI FFP IDIQ Other (Specify) _____

5. Estimated Cost $ _____   Estimated Fee $ _____   Total Price $ _____

6. Period of Performance _____ To _____

7. Is this a Subcontract?	Yes (Go to Item 8)	No (Go to Item 9)

8. Prime Contractor

Prime Contract No.	Contract Type
Address	
Point of Contact	Phone

Cognizant DCAA Office

CONTRACT BRIEF	Page 2 of 4

9. Acquisition Agency

Address:

Point of Contact:	Phone

10. Administrative Contract Office

Address:

Point of Contact:	Phone

11. Procurement Regulations: Check All that Apply.

☐ FAR   ☐ DFARS   ☐ NASA   ☐ Other (Specify) _____

12. Cost Accounting Standards (CAS)	Identify the CAS clauses contained in the contract. ☐ FAR 52.230-1 ☐ FAR 52.230-2 ☐ FAR 52.230-3 ☐ FAR 52.230-4 ☐ FAR 52.230-5 ☐ FAR 52.230-6

13. Truth In Negotiation Act (TINA)	Identify the TINA clauses contained in the contract. ☐ FAR 52.215-22 (FAR 52.215-10, effective 10/10/97) ☐ FAR 52.215-23 (FAR 52.215-11, effective 10/10/97) ☐ FAR 52.215-24 (FAR 52.215-12, effective 10/10/97) ☐ FAR 52.215-25 (FAR 52.215-13, effective 10/10/97)

14. Brief Statement of Scope of Work:

CONTRACT BRIEF		Page 3 of 4
B. Contract Clauses and Special Provisions		
15. Identify the contract clauses incorporated by reference.		
16. If this is a Time and Material (T&M) or fixed unit price contract, attach the schedule of negotiated rates.		
17. If this is a cost sharing contract, identify the terms of the cost sharing arrangement.	YES	NO
18. Does the contract contain a level of effort clause? If yes, identify the limitations specified in the contract.		
19. Does the contract contain ceilings on the indirect rates? If yes, identify the ceiling rates (attach relevant portions of the contract).		
20. Is Facilities Capital Cost of Money (FCCM) allowable on this contract? (FAR 52.215-30) (FAR 52.215-16 effective 10/10/97)		
21. Does the contract contain the FAR Penalty Clause (52.242-3)?		
22. Does the contract contain precontract or cost allowability restrictions? If yes, identify the relevant portions of the contract.		
23. Does the contract contain restrictions on overtime (FAR 52.222-2)?		
24. Does the contract contain restrictions or special requirements for subcontracts? If yes, identify the relevant portions of the contract.		
25. Identify any costs made specifically unallowable by the terms of the contract.		
26. Identify any profit or fee provisions in the contract.		
27. Identify other special provisions/limitations specified in the contract.		

CONTRACT BRIEF					Page 4 of 4	
Contractor Name:						
Contract Number:						
Summary of Contract Modifications						
Modification Number	**Date**	**Change in Funding**	**Total Funding**	**Cost**	**Profit/Fee**	**Total**
Original Contract						

SCHEDULE OF CONTRACT CLOSING INFORMATION FOR THOSE CONTRACTS ON WHICH WORK EFFORT WAS COMPLETED DURING FY 20xx

SCHEDULE O

| Contract No. | Order No. | Performance Period | | Ready To Close | Contract Ceiling Amount | Fee | Level of Effort Cumulative Hours | | Notes |
		From	To				Required	Actual	
Cost Type:									
Time & Material									

SCHEDULE T

Executive Compensation Data
FY 20xx

Year	Total Sales	% Gvt.	% ADV	Net Income	No. of Employees	
						Primary NAIC xxxxxx
2005	11,198,923	100.00%	4.17%	342,033	128	Corporation–Private
2006	13,142,934	100.00%	6.14%	451,629	121	
2007	12,514,317	100.00%	4.79%	(305,553)	117	

Name	Position	Direct Charges (Y/N)	Ownership %	Base Salary	Bonus	Pension	Life/Health Ins.	Auto	Stock Options	Other (Identify)	Total Compensation
20xx											
Al Aberts	CEO	N	0%	$102,000	$0	$4,080	$1,342	$0	$0	$0	$107,422
Bob Brown	CFO	N	0%	129,900	0	5,196	1,342	0	0	0	136,438
Carl Carlson	Vice President–Operations	N	0%	94,360	0	3,000	1,342	0	0	0	98,702
Don Dailey	Vice President–Sales	N	0%	90,000	0	3,000	1,342	0	0	0	94,342
Earl Edwards	Vice President–Administration	N	0%	85,000	0	3,000	1,342	0	0	0	89,342
20xx											
Al Aberts	CEO	N	0%	$150,000	$0	$4,000	$1,500	$0	$0	$0	$155,500
Bob Brown	CFO	N	0%	135,092	0	5,000	1,500	0	0	0	141,592
Carl Carlson	Vice President–Operations	N	0%	99,999	0	3,000	1,500	0	0	0	104,499
Don Dailey	Vice President–Sales	N	0%	95,000	0	3,000	1,500	0	0	0	99,500
Earl Edwards	Vice President–Administration	N	0%	90,000	0	3,000	1,500	0	0	0	94,500
20xx											
Al Aberts	CEO	N	0%	$166,867	$0	$5,000	$1,500	$0	$0	$0	$173,367
Bob Brown	CFO	N	0%	133,118	0	55,000	1,500	0	0	0	189,618
Carl Carlson	Vice President–Operations	N	0%	112,000	0	4,000	1,500	0	0	0	117,500
Don Dailey	Vice President–Sales	N	0%	100,000	0	4,000	1,500	0	0	0	105,500
Earl Edwards	Vice President–Administration	N	0%	95,000	0	4,000	1,500	0	0	0	100,500

CHAPTER 11

Government Contract Audits

Any audit can be cause for anxiety. Being familiar with the various types of audits that may be conducted, however, will help a contractor be prepared. When an audit is to occur, a contractor should: (1) be aware of why the audit is a requirement, (2) understand what the auditor will be looking for, and (3) request an entrance and exit conference with the auditor to avoid any misunderstandings.

For contractors audited by DCAA, the auditing concept and process changed significantly in 2010. Formerly, DCAA's mission was to provide financial advice in the administration of contracts. In response to criticism by the Government Accountability Office (GAO), the DCAA mission has shifted emphasis and added that DCAA is to "protect the interest of the taxpayer." This seemingly minor addition to the mission has created a much more independent audit organization. Recently, DCAA has rejected systems as inadequate that the agency had accepted for many years. In addition, audit recommendations may now be based on an individual auditor's opinion of how much the taxpayer should pay rather than on rules, regulations, and contract terms. For example, one auditor reported "excessive profits" when related rules, regulations, and laws had been removed from the books three decades earlier. It is now DCAA policy not to cancel an audit request if the agency believes the contracting officer is attempting to avoid a negative report. DCAA also now encourages its auditors to report contracting officers who do not accept DCAA's recommendations for suspected irregular conduct.

A rule proposed in late 2010 would require adequate internal controls for six key contractor business systems. Three of these systems would be within the purview of DCAA: accounting, estimating, and material management and accounting. These three systems are discussed in this chapter. The other three systems would be within the purview of DCMA: purchasing, earned value management, and property. Purchasing is addressed in this chapter as well as in Chapter 10; earned value management and property are addressed in Chapter 10. This rule would permit the government to withhold up to 5 percent (2 percent for small businesses) when a system is declared inadequate. After a contractor submits an acceptable corrective action plan, the withholdings may be reduced to 2 percent (1 percent for small businesses).

ACCOUNTING SYSTEM REVIEW

An accounting system review typically occurs when the government contract auditor makes his or her first review of an accounting system to determine whether that system is adequate for accumulating costs under cost-type contracts, for determining progress payments under fixed-price contracts, and for estimating future costs on new contracts. This review tends to be quite difficult for smaller companies that are facing it for the first time.

It is essential to the success of the accounting system review that the contractor have an accounting policy and procedures manual. The disadvantages of not having written policies are twofold. First, when the auditor begins an accounting system review, he or she wants to see what the contractor's ground rules are for cost accounting. The auditor will test the accounting system to determine whether the company's practices are what the written procedures require. If the company does not have these procedures clearly documented, the auditor will have to review a myriad of detailed accounting records to determine what the procedures actually are. The second disadvantage of not having clearly written procedures is that a company runs the risk of not having consistent practices for booking costs. If an accounting practice is in writing, it will provide more consistency to the company's internal operations for charging costs.

The accounting for unallowable costs should also be explained clearly in the accounting procedures because when auditors make their review, they want to see such segregations. If the written procedures do not have separate classifications for what are clearly unallowable costs, government auditors might perform an account-by-account analysis and remove any unallowable costs that might have inadvertently been included in another type of account.

The internal controls of an accounting system are also quite important. The government auditor looks for different internal controls than do most external auditors. For example, the government auditor will look for an assurance that the accounting system has detailed written procedures and works effectively in practice; that is, that the costs (both direct and indirect) charged against the individual contracts are valid as charges against those contracts. The government is concerned that the direct costs by contract are proper because different government agencies buy under different contracts, using many different contract types. Similarly, contracts can share differently in indirect costs from the various pools. As a result, if the indirect costs are not charged to the proper pool, the charges against the contracts may be distorted.

An adequate accounting system for tracking costs and providing vital financial information to management is not only important, but is required for the performance of government contracts. An accounting system represents a combination of records, internal controls, and written policies and procedures that function together in the process of accumulating and reporting financial data. During the performance of government contracts, the contractor is required to develop its accounting systems in a manner consistent with generally accepted accounting principles (GAAP). However, government regulations, particularly FAR Part 31 and the CAS, play a significant role in the tailoring of a contractor's accounting system.

Typically, an adequate accounting system for the accumulation of costs under government contracts has to include: (1) segregation of costs by contract and by contract line item; (2) data at interim periods to allow for contract repricing or negotiating revised contract targets; (3) accounting for specific unallowable costs as established in FAR Subpart 31.2; (4) separation of preproduction costs from production costs; and (5) reliable data for purposes of pricing follow-on procurements.

Basic Record Keeping

The types of books and records used in an accounting system are based on what is most suitable for a contractor's business. The objective is to provide accounting and financial data that are adequate for government contract costing purposes. At the very least, the basic record keeping system must provide visibility of contract costs at a sufficiently detailed level so that costs can be determined at interim levels for purposes of repricing, negotiating revised targets, and determining billings. The use and design of certain specific accounting records will vary from contractor to contractor; however, a standard requirement for essentially all companies involved in government contracts is that their books and records include a general ledger, job cost ledger, labor distribution, time records, subsidiary journals, chart of accounts, and financial statements.

Several key factors are essential to the adequacy of any basic record keeping system: (1) segregation of direct costs by contract or job, and indirect costs by account and title; (2) accumulation of costs on a current and cumulative basis; (3) periodic reconciliation of time sheets to labor costs included in job cost ledgers and basic cost records to the general books of account; (4) posting of costs to the books on a current basis; and (5) separation of unallowable costs in the regular books of account or by means of any less formal cost accounting technique that establishes and maintains adequate cost identification.

Internal Controls and Written Policies and Procedures

Good internal controls—established in written policies and procedures and followed by management—are the backbone of any accounting system. The government regulations do not prescribe specific internal control procedures; however, the CAS require the establishment and use of written procedures for several areas of cost accumulation and allocation, including depreciation, capitalization of tangible assets, accounting for acquisition of material costs, and allocation of direct and indirect costs. In addition, government auditors will be evaluating the strengths and weaknesses of contractor internal control systems in determining the overall adequacy of the contractor's accounting system. If they find significant deficiencies, the auditors will qualify their audit reports submitted to gov-

ernment procurement officials by citing the inadequacy of the contractor's record keeping system for government contract costing purposes.

Every good accounting system requires adequate internal controls if it is to operate in an efficient and effective manner. The following are some of the more significant positive internal control features, identified in generic form, of an acceptable accounting system for government contract costing purposes:

1. Separation of authority between key accounting functions (e.g., payroll vs. timekeeping, requisitioning of materials and services vs. purchasing vs. accounts payable)

2. Policies and procedures establishing the purposes and requirements of the accounting system (e.g., timekeeping, payroll, purchased services and materials, direct and indirect cost control, asset capitalization and utilization)

3. Internal reviews by management to ascertain employee compliance with policies and procedures

4. Periodic reconciliation of cost control records from the point of original entry through the cost accumulation summaries to the billing records

5. Management authorizations of critical accounting functions and events (e.g., issuance of payroll checks, signing of timesheets, purchasing of materials and services)

6. Budget control procedures established for comparison of actual costs to budgets and contract financial status

7. Productivity measurement techniques used to allow management to focus on problem areas and improve overall

economy and efficiency (e.g., application of work measurement techniques)

8. Organizational charts created to define lines of authority and responsibility and to provide for division of responsibility in operating, recording, and custodial functions

9. In-house "hotlines" established to encourage employees to inform management of possible areas of fraud, waste, or abuse.

Payment Requests

A contractor usually obtains payment from the government during contract performance by submitting either standard public vouchers or progress payments. Public vouchers are used to obtain payment for cost-reimbursable and time-and-materials contracts. Progress payments apply to fixed-price contracts. In either case, the contractor's accounting system must be adequate to support the payment of costs incurred on a current basis.

When submitting a standard public voucher, the contractor must ensure that the costs included reflect costs incurred in the current period and cumulative to date. Direct costs should be included as actually incurred, and the applied indirect costs should reflect a billing rate based on an estimate of year-end allowable actual costs, or contractually established provisional costs. Any cost reductions resulting from contractually established cost ceilings or limitations must also be reflected in the voucher. As a general rule, cost-reimbursable contracts are subject to a withholding of 15 percent of fee until the contract is completed and the contractor submits its final voucher.

A fixed-price contractor's submittal of progress payments is governed by FAR 52.232-16. The government requires that the claimed costs must have been incurred or actually paid, depending on the contract terms. For example, the standard progress payment clause requires that the costs of "supplies and services" purchased by the contractor directly for the contract may be included in the progress payment claim only after actual payment. Costs for such items as direct labor, materials issued from inventory, and properly allocable and allowable costs must only be incurred, not necessarily paid, at the time the progress payment is submitted. However, the contractor must not be delinquent in making payment on these items. Government auditors will review a contractor's historical payment record to ascertain whether delinquency is a problem. As of October 1, 1999, the requirement that subcontractors be paid before a prime contractor could seek reimbursement from the government was being considered for deletion.

The government also requires that the contractor provide a reasonable indication of the percentage of contract completion. This requirement underscores the need for the contractor's accounting system to accumulate costs by contract and allows for the visibility of actual costs incurred compared to budgeted costs. The accounting data will have to be merged with the engineering estimates to enable management to assess project status fully.

Limitation of Cost Clause

An adequate accounting system must provide sufficient financial information to allow management to comply with the reporting requirements of the limitation of cost (LOC) clause (FAR 52.232-20). The LOC clause requires the contractor to give the government notice whenever the costs incurred on a cost-reimbursable contract reach a certain percent of completion (generally, 75 percent or 85 percent), or whenever estimated costs on the contract are expected to be either greater or substantially less than the contractual estimated cost. The burden is on the contractor not only to track its actual costs incurred on a periodic and regular basis, but to project, within reason, year-end "allowable" costs. Once the required percent of contract cost completion is reached, and at any time the contractor expects an overrun on the contract, the contractor must provide notice to the government that it is stopping work on the contract until additional funds are provided.

It is essential that contractors comply with the LOC clause and develop a system of accounting that will keep management abreast of project status as well as actual and projected indirect rate fluctuations at all times throughout the cost accounting -period. The company must establish a procedure whereby a letter of notification is submitted to the contracting officer im-mediately upon the incurrence of the applicable percent of completion and potential overrun events. The letter must state—and the contractor must be prepared to initiate action—that formal notice is given accordingly and contract work will be stopped unless further authorization is received from the contracting officer to exceed total estimated costs.

ESTIMATING SYSTEM REVIEW

An estimating system review has a direct effect on the acceptability of any cost proposal submitted. The ability to develop a system for the purpose of preparing a cost proposal should be a high priority in any company, especially in light of the significant cost of proposal preparation. This audit may involve many government reviewers, not just the auditors, and is usually quite comprehensive.

When a contractor is required to submit cost or pricing data with a proposal for a negotiated contract, the contractor will have to certify that the data are current, accurate, and complete. The contractor's cost accounting system serves as the basis for deriving cost estimates for input to the proposal. The overall adequacy of the cost accounting system and the statistical data it contains are primary factors contributing to the sufficiency of the contractor's estimating system.

Proposals require the input of cost estimates based on historical data as recorded in the accounting system, plus an application of escalation and projected future amounts based on the contractor's policy on pay raises and expected economic factors. For example, proposed direct material units may be based on directly applicable experience by product or task, plus an application of scrap/attrition as realized on similar work, all of which are supported in the accounting records.

An optimal estimating system is one where the estimating procedures are firmly established and consistently applied, but allow sufficient flexibility for changes. Factors such as the dollar size of the proposal, anticipated contract type, clarity of government specifications, and availability of information from a similar proposal or contract may influence a contractor's methods of estimating. The particular estimating methods used are of key importance when developing a proposal because they will impact the accumulation of costs subsequent to contract award.

If a contractor has a contract covered under the CAS, CAS 401 requires that the methods used for estimating costs be consistent with the methods used for accumulating and reporting costs. Therefore, a contractor who estimates costs, for example, using "no actual" costs will not be able to accumulate costs after contract award on the basis of "standard" or "average" costs.

Effective implementation of a cost estimating system is based on a team concept. Participants from various functional areas of the company—such as engineering, marketing, quality control, purchasing, pricing, and accounting—should be involved in developing the proposed cost and quantitative estimates. The proposal manager should coordinate interactions between and among the various participants, providing input that is guided by established written procedures.

A comprehensive budgeting system is another critical factor in the development of an adequate estimating capability. The purpose of a budgeting system is twofold: (1) to control costs during contract performance; and (2) to provide necessary information to develop forecasts of sales and rate data. An accounting system that tracks contract costs on the basis of actual costs incurred to date and compares the information to established budgetary amounts will provide valuable information not only on contract financial status, but also on areas of inefficiency that need improvement. The end objective in the budgetary process is to obtain optimal use of resources. Historical budgetary data, combined with various marketing and economic considerations, provide the basis for developing sales and rate forecasts.

An effective estimating system—from the government's viewpoint, an acceptable system—requires the establishment of written policies and procedures. Written procedures are necessary to provide guidance to the various participants of the proposal estimating team in developing the cost and quantity estimates, as well as to create a communication network that includes various checks and balances to ensure that current, accurate, and complete data are being developed. Of course, written policies and procedures are of no value unless management implements them. Contractors can be sure that government auditors will be reviewing their estimating systems for both the adequacy of the written policies and procedures and for related compliance.

Organizational Relationships

A full and complete description of organizational relationships among the various contributors to the estimating team (e.g., engineering, marketing, manufacturing, quality control, purchasing, accounting) is absolutely essential if the estimating system is to operate effectively and efficiently. Contributors need to appreciate the purpose of their role in proposal formulation, how it relates to the total proposal effort, and what is expected of them. Effective lines of communication between and among the primary proposal participants need to be established so that the proposal team operates in harmony to the maximum extent practicable.

Review Requirements

Any proposal development system requires a quality control or review system. Ideally, independent reviews of work accomplished should be conducted at each functional area prior to submittal to the proposal manager for incorporation into the final product. The objective of this review is to determine that all the necessary steps have been taken consistent with policies and procedures, and that the quality of the output is at an acceptable level. The proposal manager should perform another quality control check prior to submitting the proposal. Some contractors like to establish a quality control team consisting of members from management of the various functional areas and administration to provide final approval to large dollar proposals.

Make-or-Buy Decisions

The make-or-buy decision is a very important concept for proposal estimating. A "buy" means that an item or work effort will be produced or performed by a subcontractor. A "make" item means that an item or work effort will be produced by the prime contractor or its affiliates, subsidiaries, or divisions. The FAR requires contractors to submit make-or-buy programs for all negotiated acquisitions whose estimated value is $10 million or more, except when the proposed contract is: (1) for research or development and, if prototypes or hardware are involved, no significant follow-on production is anticipated; or (2) the price is based on adequate competition or is established by catalog or market. The government reserves the right to review and agree on the contractor's make-or-buy program whenever deemed appropriate to ensure a fair and reasonable contract price.

The reporting requirements place a significant burden on the contractor to establish an adequate make-or-buy program, and to define its requirements in written policies and procedures. The FAR requires that specific information be provided in a contractor's make-or-buy program. This information should be clearly defined in a contractor's written policies and procedures, and should include: (1) description of the factors to be used in evaluating the proposed program; (2) description of each major acquisition item or work effort involved; (3) categorization of each major item or work effort as "must make," "must buy," or "can either make or buy"; and (4) reasons for categorizing items as "make" or "buy" balanced against the evaluation factors.

Updating Cost or Pricing Data

It is important for a contractor to establish procedures that require management to update cost or pricing data up to a negotiated agreement on price. The Truth in Negotiations Act requires that contractors certify certain cost or pricing data. The certification states that the cost or pricing data as submitted are current, accurate, and complete. The certification requirement applies to most negotiated contracts and subcontracts as well as to modifications, except when price is based on adequate competition or established by law, or where the acquisition is for a commercial item.

FAR Subpart 15.4, Contract Pricing, addresses what data no longer require certification. (See Chapter 9 for a complete discus-

sion.) *If certification is not required, contractors should not provide any type of certification.* The consequences of defective certification are onerous, and contractors who are unsure of their position should seek professional advice and assistance.

The government's remedy against the contractor's submittal of noncurrent, incomplete, or inaccurate cost or pricing data is significant. The government has the authority to make price adjustments, including profit or fee, of any significant amount by which the price was increased because of the defective data.

Given the significance of a defective pricing allegation, it is very important for the contractor to establish effective written policies and procedures—and associated internal controls—to protect against the submittal of inaccurate, incomplete, or noncurrent cost or pricing data. The contractor's procedures should cover such subjects as changes in the make-or-buy decisions, submittal of updated forward-pricing rates, changes in escalation factors, updated vendor quotes or purchase orders, anticipated alterations in production methods, and availability of residual materials from previous contracts.

DOD Estimating System Requirements

All contractors submitting cost or pricing data to DOD must have an estimating system that produces well-supported proposals that establish an acceptable basis for negotiating fair and reasonable prices. A clause requiring such a system will be included in all solicitations and contracts to be awarded on the basis of certified cost or pricing data. In addition, large contractors (i.e., those with more than $50 million per year in negotiated contracts) must disclose in writing their estimating systems to the contracting officer responsible for contract administration.

"Estimating system" is a term used to describe a contractor's policies, procedures, and practices for generating cost estimates that forecast costs based on the information available at the time. It includes the: (1) organizational structure; (2) established lines of authority; (3) duties and responsibilities; (4) internal controls and managerial reviews; (5) flow of work, coordination and communication, and estimating methods and techniques for the accumulation of historical costs; and (6) analyses used to generate estimates of costs and other data included in proposals submitted in the expectation of receiving contract awards.

An estimating system should be consistent with and integrated into the contractor's related management system and should be subject to applicable financial control systems. To be considered adequate, a contractor's estimating system must be established, maintained, reliable, and consistently applied, and must produce verifiable, supportable, and documented cost estimates.

As noted, it is DOD policy that all contractors have adequate estimating systems. In addition, certain large contractors must disclose their estimating systems to the ACO and must respond to any reports that identify deficiencies in the systems. A contractor is subject to the disclosure and response provisions if: (1) it is a large business, and in its prior fiscal year received DOD contracts or subcontracts totaling $50 million or more for which certified cost or pricing data were required; or (2) in its prior fiscal year, received such DOD contracts totaling $10 million or more when the contracting officer determines it is in the best interest of the government.

If a contractor is required to disclose its estimating system to the ACO, the disclosure must be adequate. A disclosure is adequate when the documentation: (1) accurately describes the policies, procedures, and practices used in preparing cost proposals; and (2) provides sufficient detail for the government to reasonably make an informed judgment regarding the accuracy of the contractor's estimating practices. To meet the maintenance

requirement, the contractor must disclose any significant changes to the cost estimating system on a timely basis to the ACO.

The DOD rule does not spell out specific requirements for adequate estimating systems, but instead provides general guidance. The rule states that adequacy is dependent on the successful interrelationship of many variables. The relative importance of each is determined by the particular circumstances facing each contractor. In general, adequate systems should: (1) provide for the use of appropriate source data; (2) use sound estimating techniques and appropriate judgment; (3) maintain a consistent approach; and (4) adhere to established policies and procedures.

The rule also lists examples of the types of characteristics that the ACO should consider when evaluating a system. Though not intended as a checklist, these examples are useful for both government and contractor personnel. Specifically, the ACO should consider whether the contractor's estimating system:

1. Establishes clear responsibility for the preparation, review, and approval of cost estimates

2. Provides a written description of the organization and the duties of personnel responsible for preparing, reviewing, and approving estimates, and the various functions that contribute to the process (e.g., accounting, planning)

3. Ensures that personnel have sufficient training, experience, and guidance to perform estimating tasks in accordance with established procedures

4. Identifies the sources of data and the estimating methods and rationale used in developing cost estimates

5. Provides for appropriate supervision throughout the estimating process

6. Provides for consistent application of estimating techniques

7. Provides for detection and timely correction of errors

8. Protects against cost duplication and omissions

9. Provides for the use of historical experience where appropriate

10. Requires the use of appropriate analytical methods

11. Integrates information available from other management systems as appropriate

12. Requires management review, including verification that the company's estimating policies, procedures, and practices comply with the regulation

13. Provides for internal review of, and accountability for, the adequacy of the estimating system, including the comparison of projected results to actual results and an analysis of any differences

14. Provides procedures to update cost estimates in a timely manner throughout the negotiation process

15. Addresses responsibility for review and analysis of the reasonableness of subcontract prices.

The DOD rules provide further guidance on estimating systems by listing some indicators of conditions that may produce or lead to significant estimating deficiencies:

1. Failure to ensure that relevant historical experience is available and used

2. Continuing failure to analyze material costs or to perform subcontractor cost reviews as required

3. Consistent absence of analytical support for significant proposed cost amounts

4. Excessive reliance on personal judgment where historical experience or commonly used standards are available

5. Recurring significant defective pricing findings within the same cost elements

6. Failure to integrate relevant parts of other management systems

7. Failure to provide established policies, procedures, and practices to persons responsible for preparing and supporting estimates.

The DOD regulation specifies detailed government review procedures. Audit and contract administration activities are required to establish and maintain regular programs for reviewing selected contractors' estimating systems. Reviews are to be on a team basis, with the contract auditor designated team leader. Teams will include audit, contract administration, and technical specialists.

Reviews will be conducted at least every three years of contractors who meet the criteria for disclosure and maintenance requirements. This period may be extended if the auditor and the ACO determine that past experience and a current vulnerability assessment indicate low risk. On the other hand, reviews will be performed more frequently if the auditor and the ACO determine that the government is at high risk.

The auditor will issue to the ACO a report outlining the findings and recommendations of the review team. If the team identifies significant estimating deficiencies, the report will recommend disapproval of all or part of the estimating system. Field pricing reports will also note any significant deficiencies that remain unresolved.

The ACO will provide a copy of the audit report to the contractor and allow 30 days for submission of its written response. If the contractor agrees with the report findings and recommendations, it should make corrections to identified deficiencies or submit a plan of action for doing so. If the contractor disagrees with the report findings, its response should provide its rationale for the disagreement.

The ACO, in consultation with the auditor, will evaluate the contractor's response and determine whether: (1) the estimating system contains deficiencies that need correction; (2) any of the deficiencies are so significant as to result in disapproval of all or a portion of the system; and (3) any proposed corrective actions are adequate to correct the deficiencies.

If such deficiencies are found, the ACO will notify the contractor that corrections or a corrective action plan is due within 45 days. The auditor and the ACO will monitor the contractor's progress toward correction. If adequate progress is not made, the ACO can consider the following actions: (1) bringing the issues to the attention of higher level management; (2) reducing or suspending progress payments; and (3) recommending nonaward of potential contracts.

If, within 45 days, the contractor has neither submitted an acceptable corrective action plan nor corrected significant deficiencies, the ACO will disapprove all or a portion of the estimating system in writing. A copy of the notice of disapproval will be sent to each contracting office and contract administration office that has substantial business with the contractor.

Under the regulation, when a contracting officer determines that an estimating system deficiency has a significant impact on a contract under negotiation, he or she should consider pursuing such alternatives as: (1) allowing the contractor additional time to correct the deficiency and submit a corrected proposal; (2) considering another type of contract; (3) segregating the questionable areas as a cost-reimbursable line; (4) reducing the profit or fee objective; or (5) including a

contract clause that provides for adjustment of the contract amount after award.

LABOR RECORDING SYSTEM AUDIT

The cost of labor at many contractor locations is often the most sensitive cost element that the government is required to audit. Labor costs have various impacts on a contractor's cost structure, and thus the price paid by the government. Direct and indirect labor costs are generally the single most significant cost element charged to government contracts. In addition, certain areas of labor (e.g., direct labor dollars or hours) are commonly used as the base element for indirect (i.e., overhead) cost applications. Labor costs and/or hours are also an essential element in a contractor's estimating system used in providing quantitative and qualitative historical data necessary for determining estimated costs for follow-on government contracts.

Accordingly, the accurate recording of labor costs by contractor employees is of utmost importance. Unlike other cost elements, labor is not supported by third-party documentation such as an invoice, purchase order, or other receipt. The key document in a manual timekeeping system is the time reporting by individual employees. Time reporting can be either by a timecard or by an automated time reporting system. Since time reporting can be altered or controlled by other persons, it is essential that individual employees be made aware of their responsibility and realize the importance of accurate time reporting. The government relies heavily on basic internal controls to ensure the propriety of labor costs presented for payment, contract costing, and estimating. It is essential that the internal controls related to labor recording and distribution be firmly established and reviewed periodically by management.

In recognition of the overall sensitivity of labor charging in the pricing of government contracts, and as a part of the government's overall program on fraud, waste, and abuse in government contracting, DCAA has developed a specialized audit to respond to these concerns. This audit, called a "comprehensive labor audit," is intended to analyze labor-charging patterns. The basic objectives of a comprehensive labor audit are to determine: (1) the propriety of labor costs (i.e., are employees accurately charging what they work on?); (2) the adequacy and reliability of the contractor's labor cost accounting and time-keeping system; and (3) the contractor's compliance with established internal controls. DCAA claims that the discovery of unlawful or fraudulent activities is not its primary audit objective; nonetheless, fraudulent activity is often uncovered during such an audit. Regardless of the written objective, contractors should be aware that many auditors conducting this review are actively searching for labor mischarging.

Two fundamental themes of a labor audit are that the audit is both current and comprehensive. DCAA's objective is to review labor costs as close to the date of their incurrence as possible. The intent is to identify problems close to their onset and to have ready access to current documentation. A labor audit involves not only the basic verification of costs incurred, but also includes a detailed analysis of existing policies, procedures, and internal controls, as well as employee compliance in these areas. The auditors also review the propriety of labor charging. Audit emphasis is on comparing recorded labor charging to actual work accomplished.

Comprehensive labor audits are usually conducted at larger contractor locations. However, any contractor can potentially be selected for one of these reviews. In addition, DCAA has increased its review of contractor off-site locations where activity is distant from normal audit scrutiny. Specific guidance has been provided to auditors from DCAA headquarters on exactly how to conduct one of these "off-site" reviews. The audit may be performed by representatives from a local audit office on an independent basis, or under the general supervision of regional management. The agency has also established labor audit teams in which the auditors are specifically trained in such special audit techniques as risk assessment, intensified audit analysis of accounting data, and employee interviews.

The comprehensive labor audit consists of a series of analytical steps:

1. Risk assessment

2. Employee interviews

3. Audit report (and possible referral to an investigative agency).

Methods are available for a contractor to strengthen its accounting system against potential problems that may be encountered during these steps.

Risk Assessment

The initial phase in determining audit risk is for the auditor to become familiar with a contractor's organization, its budgetary controls, and its direct/indirect labor charging policies and procedures. An auditor's basic understanding of a contractor's operations serves as the initial starting point toward further evaluation. The auditor will begin to develop basic notions regarding the adequacy of a contractor's accounting system for labor recording purposes. If the auditor's initial impressions are favorable, it is likely that the risk assessment will progress at a faster pace, perhaps with less detailed evaluation.

It is thus essential for a contractor to have a well-defined, documented labor accounting system with adequate internal controls. The chances are that contractors with such systems may receive less audit scrutiny because the auditors may tend to place greater reliance on the accounting system's established procedures. A carefully developed labor accounting system should help protect the contractor from potential problem areas.

The types of documents that the auditors will be reviewing during their preliminary audit work may include the following: (1) company organizational charts; (2) listing of contracts; (3) policies and procedures relating to labor charging and basic timekeeping requirements; (4) flowcharts establishing how labor costs are processed through the accounting system; (5) listings of all labor-related management reports, both manual and automated; (6) timecards, or review of the automated time reporting system; (7) internal audit reports; and (8) details on the existing workforce (i.e., number, location and type of employees).

At this stage of the audit, the auditor should conduct a formal entrance conference. At the conference, the auditor has the responsibility to advise the contractor on a number of areas, including: (1) areas of audit coverage and potential duration of the audit; (2) potential for employee interviews to be conducted; and (3) required contractor involvement during the audit. The entrance conference is a critical point for the contractor. At this stage of the review, it is absolutely essential that the basic ground rules be established for conducting the audit. The contractor should establish a liaison or contact point through whom all audit requests must be coordinated. The contractor should also request that the auditor identify the types of all accounting and related records that are anticipated to be reviewed. A control mechanism for reviewing these records may be established, and particular rules regarding access can be formalized.

In addition, it is advisable that the contractor obtain an agreement with the auditor regarding the performance of employee interviews. Areas of contractor concern may include: (1) prior notification of interview dates; (2) advance notification of employees to be interviewed; (3) identification of employees to be interviewed; (4) limitation of interview . questions; (5) requirement for contractor rep-

resentation at employee interviews; (6) reasonable time length of interviews; and (7) acceptable documentation to be reproduced during an interview. Auditors generally are not amenable to any form of restriction in their audits. However, these areas are of critical importance to the contractor in properly monitoring the audit. As long as the contractor neither refuses access to relevant audit documents, nor impedes audit performance, the company has a right to place certain reasonable controls on auditors in terms of their relations with employees and proprietary records.

Once the auditor understands the contractor's labor accounting system, he or she will identify any risks to the government. The basic audit risk assessment as it applies to a contractor's labor accounting system involves: (1) a risk analysis of problem areas that may result in a significant adverse cost impact to the government; and (2) an assessment of this analysis to determine the extent of exposure to "suspected irregular conduct"—or fraud. The results of this analysis are critical, as they determine not only the direction of the audit, but also the scope of audit effort. A contractor with "high" risk indicators that are not otherwise moderated (e.g., by solid internal controls and historical "high" audit marks relating to proper employee compliance) will be subject to closer and more intense audit scrutiny than will a contractor with relative low risk.

The auditor generally considers a number of factors during the risk assessment. Some of the more significant areas are discussed below.

Adequate internal controls are essential for the auditor to place any reliance on the contractor's labor system regarding contract pricing and forward-pricing estimating purposes.

If a contractor has had a history of timekeeping problems (i.e., employees not completing timecards or not using the time reporting system properly), the risk indicators in this area will be graded as high. Proper timekeeping practices and basic employee awareness of their responsibilities in this area are absolutely essential to an adequate labor charging system.

Overrun (or potentially overrun) contracts are of concern to government auditors. When contract costs exceed the established contract values, contractors might tend to divert these excess costs to other contracts or to indirect accounts. As a general rule, contractors with established procedures and safeguards relating to the accounting for costs in overrun situations will be viewed more favorably in terms of audit reliance and risk than those with poor, or no, controls.

Auditors might prepare trend analyses to monitor changes in independent research and development and bid and proposal (IR&D/B&P) versus marketing/selling costs to identify significant changes, which may indicate possible switching of costs. The recent elimination of the formula limitation has greatly relieved this problem.

Auditors and contractors often disagree on the interpretation of what constitutes an IR&D/B&P cost as opposed to a marketing/selling expense. Questions also arise regarding when an IR&D or B&P project is actually started, what costs should be included, and over what basis they should be allocated. Numerous considerations come into play in evaluating this area, and the requirements provided in FAR 31.205-18 and CAS 420 should be evaluated closely in determining a corporate policy for classifying and controlling these costs.

The contractor's mix of contracts refers to the relative composition of government cost-type, government fixed-price, and commercial work as a percentage of total contracts. A particular mix of work will have a direct bearing on the level of audit risk a contractor is assigned. For example, if a contractor has all cost-type or all fixed-price work, the perceived risk is considered low. The highest theoretical risk is a contractor with a 50/50 mix of government cost-type work and gov-ernment fixed-price work, or government work and commercial work. The reason for a high risk assessment in a 50/50 contract mix situation is that auditors believe that contractors have a high motivation to allocate fixed-price costs to cost-type work, or commercial costs to government work.

Time-and-materials (T&M) contracts are assessed a high risk because of their inherent nature. T&M contracts provide for the procurement of supplies and services on the basis of direct labor hours at specified fixed hourly rates and material at actual cost. As referenced in FAR 16.601, particular care should be exercised in the use of this type of contract since its nature does not encourage management controls.

Various areas of audit concern are expressed relating to T&M contracts, including: (1) employees promoted to higher labor categories without the required government authorization; (2) transfers between task orders in which no credit was given to the "transferor" task order; (3) contractors billing costs by applying the estimated percentage of physical completion to the ceiling amount of the delivery order without regard to the actual costs incurred on the order; (4) employees not meeting the skill qualifications required by the contract; (5) employees charging specific task orders without performing any labor effort in order to use up available funds; (6) transfers between task orders made to avoid overruns; (7) precontract costs incurred without required contracting officer approval; and (8) employees billed outside of their respective labor categories, resulting in excess costs paid by the government.

Auditors also monitor the charging of labor to indirect accounts (e.g., marketing), which may represent employee idle time. The objective is to identify significant changes in cost levels. Such changes require further evaluation to determine the reasons behind the changes.

Changes in a contractor's organization or classification of employees may present a high-risk situation. Auditors are particularly sensitive to this type of activity if it alters the allocation of costs between contract types. The bottom-line impact to the government will be closely evaluated. What this says to contractors is that any proposed change in organization, cost structure, or employee classification needs to be justified properly if it is to receive acceptance and reliance by government auditors.

A very important area in terms of audit review is the evaluation of labor transfers through journal entries. The quantity and type of labor transfers will directly impact the risk assessed for that activity. For example, frequent transfers, or transfers between different contracts, particularly if one is cost-type and the other is fixed-price, will be reviewed very closely. In an effort to reduce risk in this area, contractors should have a strict policy on how and for what purpose journal entries are to be used. Furthermore, proper justification for any journal entry—labor transfer or otherwise—is essential.

Contractors often have numerous different physical locations where substantial labor charges are incurred. However, the accounting books and records relating to the costs incurred at these locations are usually maintained at the contractor's main facility. Because of this, the actual labor activity at the off-site location receives less direct audit scrutiny. Consequently, with regard to the comprehensive labor audit, increased emphasis is now being placed on off-site locations. Contractors should take steps to strengthen their labor-charging practices at these locations.

Employee Interviews

Once an auditor has selected an area of perceived high risk to review in detail, the pre-interview analysis begins. The purpose of this part of the audit is to gather the necessary accounting and related data to evaluate more

fully the propriety of labor charges relating to the area under review. Various types of contractor documents will be analyzed during this portion of the audit, depending on the nature of the area under review. Some of the more commonly reviewed records include: (1) timecards and/or time reporting systems reports; (2) travel reports; (3) labor reports; (4) contractual documents; (5) project status reports; (6) budgetary data; and (8) corporate memoranda.

As mentioned, the contractor should be careful to establish control procedures at the beginning of the audit with regard to the monitoring and release of records to auditors. The closer a contractor monitors the records being used by the auditors, the more aware management will be with respect to the audit areas being evaluated. It is to the contractor's advantage to understand problems uncovered early so that resolution can be sought before a possible misinterpretation of the facts by the auditor, which could result in the unnecessary referral of an audit finding to a criminal investigator.

Auditors are often very sensitive about providing specific details regarding their audit findings, particularly in the area of labor mischarging. They will identify any apparent discrepancies found between labor charges, but not a great deal more. The purpose of their secretive nature is to avoid interfering with the results of any potential future criminal investigation. Therefore, it is incumbent upon the contractor to gather as much information as possible both from the auditor and independently to be able to respond to audit inquiries most effectively, and thereby potentially settle an issue before it gets passed along to investigators.

Auditors use various techniques in conducting their pre-interview analysis in an effort to complete their review in an effective and efficient manner. One technique of particular significance is the use of automated data retrieval software programs. The auditor will want to install these program(s) on a contractor's computer system and use them to gather labor-charging data in a certain manner. Basically, these programs allow the auditor to retrieve labor charges over a particular period of time and accumulate them in a workable format—generally, by contract, account, or employee. Many contractors allow the auditors to use these programs on their computer systems while others simply refuse. The major risk involved in refusing to accept the use of these "retrieval" programs is that the government may allege a breach of its access-to-records audit rights.

Contractors should be aware that auditors will be using the results of their pre-interview analysis as a basis for questions while conducting employee interviews. The interview questions generated under this type of audit are specifically directed and much more effective than questions asked during DCAA's standard periodic "floorchecks" used in conjunction with the annual incurred cost audit.

Upon completion of the pre-interview analysis, the auditor will want to start the interview process. The audit interview of employees represents the culmination of the labor analysis on select area(s) of high risk.

DCAA states that its primary authority to conduct employee interviews is based on generally accepted auditing standards (GAAS) as established by the American Institute of Certified Public Accountants (AICPA). Under GAAS, the third standard of fieldwork requires that significant competent evidential matter be obtained through inspection, observation, inquiry, and confirmation to afford a reasonable basis for an opinion on costs recorded.

Contractors should view the audit interview as a very significant part of the labor audit and treat it accordingly. That is, management should carefully evaluate the purpose and objective of the interview, and place adequate controls on its auditors' conduct. Numerous areas of concern are often raised between contractors and auditors regarding interview procedure.

For example, DCAA's standard audit procedure is to provide two auditors and to request a contractor representative. From the contractor's perspective, and for its own protection, the company representative should be very knowledgeable about government contract costing issues.

Auditors do not like to provide advance notification of interview dates or individuals selected to be interviewed. They believe that the element of surprise is essential to the credibility of their review. Some contractors require that some reasonable degree of notice be provided so that they can plan for the proper representative to attend. This can sometimes be an area of compromise between the auditor and the contractor.

Auditors are not investigators; it is outside their charter of responsibility to "investigate." However, sometimes contractors feel that certain questions asked and methods used by auditors are investigatory in nature. In fact, auditors are not to ask such questions as "Do you ever mischarge?" Perhaps the best policy for a contractor who has doubts regarding the nature of an audit question is to refuse to allow an employee to answer the question until legal advice can be sought. Various legal and constitutional rights may come into play, particularly if a contractor is actually under investigation, with respect to the inquiry of employees.

In fact, the auditor may actually be doing work for an investigator and the contractor may not know about it. For this reason, some lawyers have advised contractors that, prior to allowing any audit interviews, a contractor should ask the auditor if his or her work is in conjunction with an investigation. If the answer is yes, the contractor should seek legal assistance before allowing the auditor to proceed.

Auditors are hesitant to release any questions to the contractor before the interview. They may respond that they don't know what the next question will be until an employee provides an answer. Some contractors have requested that DCAA provide them with at least the general type of questions to be asked. Other contractors have acted more aggressively and actually tried to limit the specific questions that may be asked during an interview. This is a sensitive area and may be tied into an access-to-records issue; however, a compromise can usually be reached with DCAA.

The interview process can be an intimidating experience for an employee. Auditors are often trained in specific interview techniques. Questions may be very effective, and are based on their pre-interview analysis. Auditors want to obtain a significant amount of documentation during the course of the interview (e.g., current time records, engineering logs, samples of work performed). The audit purpose is to verify that direct projects or indirect accounts charged are actually what is being worked on. Of primary concern to the contractor should be the auditor's proper interpretation of the documents being received as they relate to particular projects. In addition, there is no obligation that employees provide personal documentation to auditors as long as these documents are not used as an official accounting record or as the primary basis for an official record (e.g., daily logs).

After completing the initial interview process, auditors will assess the impact of any problem areas uncovered and determine whether further analysis is warranted. If not, and if the auditor is satisfied with the scope of his or her work, an audit report will be written and the review completed. However, if the auditor believes that a particular area needs further development in terms of understanding the issue or assessing the full magnitude of the problem, additional analysis and another series of interviews may be conducted. From the contractor's standpoint, as much information as possible should be obtained from the auditor to evaluate the problem area(s) and determine the auditor's status of audit completion. Since a contractor representative should have attended the interviews along with the auditor, he or she should be generally aware of any problem areas.

The contractor would be well-advised to conduct its own internal review of the circumstances or to hire an independent accounting firm familiar with the issues to assist in this analysis if audit findings appear serious. It is critical that a contractor appreciate the full magnitude of any labor-related internal control weaknesses or possible areas of mischarging to be able to respond effectively to government auditors and protect itself against any possible allegations of fraudulent activity.

Audit Report

The results of a labor audit are formalized in a report addressed to the applicable ACO. The contractor should receive the results of this report through an exit conference; in some cases, the company may receive a draft copy of the report. The report will include discussions regarding the adequacy of the contractor's overall timekeeping system and the propriety of its labor-charging practices. If the auditor identifies possible labor mischarging, then the contractor will be provided a general description of the mischarge and its associated dollar impact. Further particulars of the audit findings (e.g., documentation received during the course of the review that could implicate the contractor) will generally not be disclosed to management. The contractor will be asked to respond in writing to the audit report. The response should be carefully prepared so as not to damage the company's position. At this point, it may be advisable to seek independent accounting and/or legal counsel.

PROCUREMENT SYSTEM REVIEW

The procurement system review is conducted by several different groups in the government, including procurement experts, auditors, and technical experts. The main purpose of the review is to determine the effectiveness of the company procurement system as it relates to a broad range of issues such as: (1) competition in buying; (2) sources of supply; (3) lead-time considerations; (4) inventory control; (5) production control; (6) price negotiation documentation; (7) compliance with regulations; (8) make-or-buy decisions; (9) quality control; (10) payment to suppliers; and (11) intercompany purchases.

For some contractors, the material content of cost proposals is higher than labor costs. Therefore, the cost of acquiring material in the most economical and efficient manner is of concern to the government auditors. The results of the review will influence the credibility of material cost amounts in future cost proposals. Poor marks in this review will cause the government to review proposed material costs in future proposals in more detail.

COMPENSATION SYSTEM AUDIT

The compensation system audit deals with two key areas: (1) reasonableness of compensation; and (2) uncompensated overtime.

Reasonableness of Compensation

The government's efforts in assessing the reasonableness of compensation costs are for the most part conducted by DCAA auditors in a compensation review. A typical -result in the audits performed by DCAA is allegations of unreasonableness. These allegations are based on the results of the use of a data bank of information that DCAA has developed for different geographic areas. In applying this information, DCAA is comparing similar companies and services with similar sales volumes, in the same geographic area, to identify unreasonable amounts.

The cost principle that addresses the allowability of compensation costs is FAR 31.205-6. Compensation for personal services will be considered reasonable if total compensation is similar to that paid by other firms of the same size and in the same industry. Special circumstances may apply in evaluating the reasonableness of individual compensation if one or more of the following criteria apply:

1. Compensation of owners of closely held corporations (i.e., partners, sole proprietors, members of the immediate family, or persons having a substantial financial interest in the enterprise) must be reasonable for the services rendered and not reflective of a distribution of profits. Closely held corporation compensation amounts may not exceed those recognized under the Internal Revenue Code.

2. The nature of the contractor's business is such that compensation levels are not subject to the normal restraints of a competitive business.

3. Changes in compensation plans are concurrent with changes in the mix of government contracts.

4. Compensation costs are in excess of amounts deductible for income tax purposes.

5. Compensation costs are not significant deviations from the contractor's established practices.

If DCAA alleges that compensation, or a particular element thereof, is unreasonable, the "burden of proof" passes to the contractor to support reasonableness. However, as a practical matter, since DCAA has rarely made available the details of its database, the proof that its auditors are using all the criteria set forth in the regulation is lacking. Additionally, DCAA at times appears to use the median of its statistics as the ceiling and questions all compensation that exceeds the median. Clearly, this application of the FAR criteria might be susceptible to challenge.

In considering reasonableness of compensation, numerous factors should be evaluated. These factors apply equally to a challenge of the government's allegation of unreasonableness as to the development of a contractor's position. The highlights of some of the more significant areas are:

- **Validity of data used**—Are the companies comparable? Are they producing similar services or products? Are they in the same industry? Are they in the same geographic area? Are they similar in size? How measured? By sales only? By numbers of employees? Are they performing a similar mix of government work relative to commercial? Fixed-price vs. CPFF?
- **Uniqueness of contractor**—Has the company experienced unusual sales growth? Noteworthy growth or profitability? Noteworthy growth measured by return on investment or return on assets? Does the company perform work for a large variety of government agencies and contracting officers (requiring officials to be more efficient than other types of clientele or customers)?
- **Uniqueness of personnel**—Does the company's staff show evidence of great leadership, scientific renown, or other specialized skills?

Uncompensated Overtime

The issue of uncompensated overtime has historically caused numerous problems between contractors and auditors. The greatest problem arises when exempt employees are working uncompensated overtime, but are only recording and allocating their time to cost objectives based on the standard 40-hour work week. In other words, no recognition of costs incurred is associated with the excess hours. The concern of government auditors is that this practice might lead to an inequity in allocating costs to final cost objectives. In particular, there is the perceived risk of "gaming," which could negatively impact government contracts.

The concept of "gaming" generally refers to the: (1) maximization of time charged to government cost-reimbursable contracts to fulfill the standard 40-hour cost allocation requirement; and (2) minimization of time allocated to government fixed-price and commercial contracts. In other words, assume an employee works 50 hours during a week and charges 40 hours to cost-reimbursable contracts and 10 hours to fixed-price contracts. Under this scenario, at least two potential problems arise: (1) improper cost allocation; and (2) fraudulent time charging. In the cost allocation area, the government auditors will state that if only 40 hours of work receive the full allocation of costs, then other cost objectives associated with the extra 10 hours are not receiving a fair cost allocation. Furthermore, if the charging of 40 hours is related to cost-reimbursable contracts, system complications arise that present unacceptable conditions to contractors.

The issue of uncompensated overtime requires an evaluation on a case-by-case basis before the most appropriate allocation procedure can be identified. Before deciding on any system for controlling and recording uncompensated overtime, a contractor should direct special consideration to the materiality of results. Government auditors should be concerned with the same issues. For example, would there be a significant difference between present and revised allocations of costs to final cost objectives? Is the government (as a whole or on particular programs) suffering inequities because of the present allocations? Would the cost of controlling and recording uncompensated overtime exceed the benefits of improved accounting?

In light of these considerations, the following is a sample list of methods that contractors use to account for uncompensated overtime. The first method listed is generally the least acceptable to government auditors; the second method usually represents the auditors' preference. Auditors and contractors generally have the exact opposite preferences in this area.

1. Labor costs are distributed only to cost objectives worked on during the first 8 hours of the day; no accounting is made for hours worked in excess of 8 hours per day or 40 hours per week.

2. Costs are distributed to all cost objectives worked on during the week based on an average weekly labor rate (i.e., weekly salary divided by total actual hours worked during the week).

3. Costs are distributed to all cost objectives worked on during the week based on a labor rate predicated on a 40-hour workweek. Amounts distributed that are in excess of salaries paid are credited to overhead.

4. All cost objectives worked on during the day are charged an amount representing a pro rata allocation of the total hours worked. For example, if an employee worked 3 hours each on three different cost objectives during the day, each cost objective would be charged with one-third of the employee's daily salary.

5. Costs are distributed to all cost objectives worked on at an estimated hourly rate. The estimated hourly rate is calculated by dividing the employee's annual salary by the total hours the employee is expected to work during the year. Any variance between actual salary cost and the amount distributed is charged/credited to overhead.

PRICE PROPOSAL REVIEW

Cost or pricing data submitted by a contractor enables the government to perform cost or price analysis that will ultimately enable the two parties to negotiate fair and reasonable contract prices. In connection with this analysis, a contracting officer should request an audit review of a contractor's price proposal by the contract auditor when the information available is inadequate to determine the reasonableness of the proposed cost or price. Legislation also has exempted certain categories (e.g., commercial products and services) from submittal of cost or pricing data for audit. Contractors need to be aware of exactly what data are required to be submitted and what data are exempt.

Developing Cost Estimates

Developing cost estimates can be a complicated and involved process. The contractor is concerned with maintaining a competitive posture, as well as responding to the government in a timely fashion with minimal costs questioned by the auditors. Often, problems arise in the estimating process with respect to: (1) developing labor hours; (2) obtaining necessary and timely quotes from vendors and subcontractors; (3) applying scrap and attrition factors; and (4) computing escalation rates and indirect cost rates. A high degree of coordination is required between the proposal pricing staff and the various contributing functional groups. The propriety of the estimates may be subject to review by government auditors. If this happens, all estimates will have to be supported by documentation, such as: (1) multiple price quotes; (2) rate information supported by the accounting records; (3) budgetary data; and (4) production records relating to similar units produced.

Key areas relating to the development of cost estimates include the following:

Direct Labor Costs

- Period of time during which the contract is going to be performed
- Method of determining labor rates (i.e., average vs. actual) and applying associated escalation
- Categories of labor that will be used on the job
- Mix of labor categories required to accomplish the work
- Experience on prior similar work and the potential application of a learning curve
- Application of manufacturing labor standards (i.e., engineered or estimated work measurement standards)

Indirect Cost Rates

- Budgeted overhead expenses with offsets for anticipated unallowable costs
- Planned changes in the indirect cost base (i.e., growth or decline of direct labor dollars associated with a particular overhead pool or changes in total costs for a G&A pool)
- Mix of variable and fixed indirect expenses and their associated impact as a result of changes in the indirect base
- Forecast increases or decreases in business volume and anticipated creation of new product lines or organizations, which may require new indirect rates

Materials, Subcontracts, and Other Direct Costs

- Experienced usage factors (i.e., number of units required in the end product) and loss factors (e.g., attrition, scrap)
- Availability and accuracy of price quotations (government auditors often like to see two or three current quotations for each significant item of material/ subcontract)
- Determination of prices from catalogs or established markets (e.g., travel costs from airline guides)
- Development and support relating to decrement factors (i.e., experienced reduction in price)

Auditor Approaches

The best way to prepare for an audit of a cost proposal is to prepare the backup to the proposal before the auditor arrives. In other words, if the company assumes that all its proposals will be audited, supporting documentation will be prepared on a recurring basis by all the individual company elements. This discipline is required to minimize, to the extent possible, any audit problems concerning lack of audit support. The government auditor will typically review the following areas of a cost proposal: (1) direct labor rates; (2) direct labor hours; (3) material prices; (4) indirect cost rate projections (i.e., overhead, fringe benefits, and G&A); and (5) other direct costs, including cost of money.

The audit entrance and exit conferences are the most important parts of the audit from a contractor's point of view. The DCAA guidance in DCAM 4-302 requires the auditor to hold a formal entrance and exit conference on each audit performed. The contractor has a right to know the purpose of the audit, the expected duration of the audit, and what the auditor will need to accomplish the audit. At the conclusion of the audit (and preferably throughout the course of the audit), the auditor is required to discuss any factual matters concerning the results of audit—such as items that do not add up, whether or not a quote is adequate, etc. The auditor is not required to discuss judgmental findings—such as the escalation is too high, the proposed overhead is 6 points too high, etc. However, most auditors are willing to discuss the audit in general terms, like the labor rates are a bit high, a lot of prior prices need to be updated, etc.

Direct Labor Rates

- Basis of the proposed labor rates (e.g., average category, weighted average)
- Reasonableness of current compensation
- Verification of the midpoint of effort
- Actual labor rates for the prior year and current fiscal year to date

- Impact of any additional hires on projected labor rates

Direct Labor Hours
- Basis of the proposed labor hours
- Whether the proposed hours are based on historical data and how reliable the historical records are
- Whether all nonrecurring effort is eliminated for projection purposes
- If hours are based upon estimates, the basis of the estimates (i.e., do the hours reflect current practices?)
- Whether any direct labor is proposed that could be recorded as indirect
- Whether any contingencies are included in the proposed hours

Material Costs
- Whether a combined bill of material has been prepared
- Basis of the proposed unit prices and their validity (generally using statistical sampling)
  - If pricing is based on current or prior purchases, comparison of proposed quantities to previously acquired quantities
  - Age of purchase orders used and applicability of escalation
- If pricing is based on vendor quotes, reasonableness and competitiveness
- Whether material requirements have been combined with other contracts to obtain lower prices
- Whether contractor performed a cost or price analysis on major subcontractors
- Whether proposed quantities include scrap and attrition

Indirect Cost Rates
- Whether allocation bases for various cost pools are consistent with prior history, and adequately reflect anticipated business volume

- Whether proposed indirect costs are compatible with prior periods and years (i.e., ratio analysis)
- Whether direct and indirect costs are classified correctly
- Whether all expressly unallowable costs have been specifically excluded (e.g., interest, bad debts)
- Whether bid and proposal and independent research and development costs have been segregated properly

Other Direct Costs
- Travel costs (e.g., number of trips, costs per trip)
- Reproduction or computer services (e.g., are those tasks proposed in-house or by outside vendors?)
- Cost-of-money calculations (e.g., are the allocation bases and net book values used the same as those used for indirect expense rates?)

INCURRED COST AUDIT

The purpose of an incurred cost audit is to establish final, government-approved direct and indirect costs for the cost accounting period under review to facilitate the final closeout of cost-reimbursable contracts. An auditor's primary objective in conducting an incurred cost audit is to examine the contractor's cost representations, and to express an opinion on whether the incurred costs are reasonable, allocable, and not prohibited by the contract, by government statute or regulation, or by previous agreement with or decision of the government contracting officer. In addition, the auditor is interested in determining whether the contractor's accounting system is adequate for subsequent cost determinations that may be required for the current contract or for subsequent contracts.

According to FAR 42.703, if a contractor has a cost-reimbursable contract with the government, the contractor is required to submit a summary of actual indirect and direct contract charges on a fiscal year basis. This "cost submission" is supposed to be submitted to the contracting officer, or auditor, within six months after the close of the fiscal year. The cost submission is to show a summary of costs incurred under flexibly priced contracts, detailing incurred costs for direct labor, material, overhead, and other direct costs for each auditable contract. The submission should also include the details of the overhead rates for the fiscal year showing the rate(s) developed, supported by indirect expense schedules for each cost pool. DCAA also requires that a copy of financial statements and the general ledger trial balance be submitted.

The Department of Defense has given the contracting officer the authority to determine final rates. Alternatively, DOD has given DCAA auditors the authority to set final indirect rates through "audit determination." The parameters for audit-determined rates are set forth in FAR 42.705. If a contractor does not agree with the auditor's conclusion (in an audit-determined situation), the contractor has the right to appeal to the contracting officer or an appropriate court of appeals to settle the disputed costs. This practice differs from the practice of "audit-negotiated" rates, where the DCAA auditor was advisory to the contracting officer and the contracting officer would set the rate (after negotiation with the contractor). In addition, DOD contractors must certify that their overhead submissions do not contain expressly unallowable costs. Most larger contractors have indirect cost settlements by negotiation.

Labor Costs

In determining the propriety of labor costs for any given cost accounting period, auditors are interested primarily in reviewing the contractor's labor and accounting policies, internal control procedures, and organizational responsibilities. The purpose of this part of the audit is to ascertain whether the policies, procedures, and internal controls are well-defined and reasonable in concept, and whether they are being implemented effectively by contractor personnel.

The auditor is generally interested in determining whether or not: (1) time charges are being recorded on a current basis; (2) the work performed reflects the confirmation of the supervisor in charge or of an independent timekeeper; (3) the rates paid to employees are commensurate with the type of work being performed; (4) the labor distribution or other records prepared by the contractor are prepared on a current basis, and labor costs chargeable to contracts are recorded accurately and in accordance with the price proposal submission; (5) indirect labor costs consist of types of items acceptable under the contract and meet the criteria of cost interpretations established by current directives and generally accepted accounting principles; and (6) management policies governing the hiring, assignment, reassignment, and control of the labor force are consistent with prudent business management practices.

Typically, in the auditor's review of labor in the annual incurred cost audit, both direct labor as well as indirect labor categories are reviewed. Some of the techniques that the auditor will use in testing labor are:

1. Review policies and procedures for any changes in direct/indirect time charging procedures (e.g., engineering, program management, idle time).

2. Perform a comparative analysis of "sensitive" labor accounts to identify any areas for an in-depth review (e.g., bid and proposal costs dropping off near the end of the year, a large increase in idle time).

3. Verify that the labor cost distributions reconcile to payroll accruals and disbursements.

4. Review adjusting journal entries and exception reports for labor costs to identify any adjustments and/or exceptions that require further review (e.g., transfers of charges between contracts).

5. Perform a "floorcheck" to determine whether timekeeping policies and procedures (e.g., timecards are completed in ink with no "whiteouts," proper corrections are made on time reporting systems, supervisors approve time reported either on cards or on a system) are being observed.

6. Sample selected employee-prepared records and trace their time for an entire transaction (e.g., the time reported by either a card or time reporting system), and payroll records to determine the actual pay rate, pay checks, job distributions, etc. (Usually this type of procedure is done on a statistical basis. If any problems are encountered in this audit step, the auditor will not be able to place a great deal of reliance on the labor accounting system, and will be required to extend this phase of testing.)

Material and Subcontract Costs

An auditor's primary objective in reviewing material and subcontract costs is to determine whether the contractor's accounting policies, procedures, and internal controls are well-defined, reasonable in concept, and effectively implemented. The auditor is also concerned with determining that costs were accurately charged to benefiting contracts. In performing the tests, the auditor will generally attempt to ascertain that the material was: (1) needed for the contract; (2) properly considered for "make" or "buy"; (3) purchased in reasonable quantity; (4) purchased at a prudent price; (5) used on the contract; and (6) properly accounted for in terms of both initial charge and residual value.

Generally, the auditor will perform some sort of transaction testing of selected items through the accounting system—from invoice, to voucher, to check, to job cost records—to determine the accuracy of the transactions tested. Unless problems are encountered, little audit effort is spent on this area.

Indirect Costs

In reviewing indirect costs in an incurred cost audit, the auditors are primarily interested in the following areas: (1) allowability of the costs allocated to government contracts based on FAR Subpart 31.2; (2) accuracy of the methods used to accumulate indirect costs; (3) propriety of the bases used to allocate indirect costs; (4) consistency in applying policies and procedures to governmental and to other operations; (5) mathematical accuracy of the computed amount of indirect costs allocated; and (6) reasonableness of indirect costs allocated to government contracts.

When evaluating issues of indirect cost allowability, auditors use FAR Subpart 31.2. as their primary regulatory source. During the course of applying these regulations, controversy often arises between the auditor and the contractor regarding the proper interpretation of an "allowable cost." Conflicting positions are not unusual, particularly in those areas generally classified as "grey." Grey areas often include selling costs, public relations, employee morale, and technical/professional activities. The following is a sample checklist of some of the more common questions raised by auditors relating to indirect costs. A "yes" answer to any of these questions would prompt an audit concern.

1. FAR 31.203, Indirect Costs—Did the company fail to include unallowable costs as part of its allocation base(s)?

2. FAR 31.205-1, Public Relations and Advertising Costs—Did the company

advertise in newspapers, magazines, on radio, etc., for other than help wanted? Is the company involved in trade, exhibit booths, etc., relative to the products and/or services the company offers?

3. FAR 31.205-3, Bad Debts—Does any person spend the majority of his or her time involved in the collection of bad debts?

4. FAR 31.205-6, Compensation for Personal Services—Did the contractor defer any employee compensation? Are bonuses paid without the basis of a formal agreement between the company and the employees? Did the company terminate any pension, profit-sharing, bonus plans, etc.? Did the company fail to fund profit-sharing, bonus, or retirement plans? Were the plans funded on other than a quarterly basis? Does the leave policy allow employees to carry over hours to a future year?

5. FAR 31.205-11, Depreciation—Does the company use the accelerated cost recovery system (ACRS) for income tax and/or financial accounting purposes?

6. FAR 31.205-13, Employee Morale, Health, Welfare—Is a cafeteria maintained for employees? Is it operated on other than a break-even basis?

7. FAR 31.205-14, Entertainment Costs—Are there any noted weaknesses in the contractor's support for luncheons, meetings, etc.?

8. FAR 31.205-15, Fines and Penalties—Were any tax returns filed late?

9. FAR 31.205-17, Idle Facilities and Idle Capacity Costs—Have any reductions in force resulted in unoccupied space?

10. FAR 31.205-19, Insurance and Indemnification—Does "key man" life insurance exist?

11. FAR 31.205-27, Organization Costs—Has the company reorganized, established a new division, merged with another company, etc.?

12. FAR 31.205-30, Patent Costs—Are patent costs incurred for other than a direct requirement of the contract?

13. FAR 31.205032, Precontract Costs—Does the company ever start working on a contract prior to its effective date? If so, was approval obtained from the contracting officer?

14. FAR 31.205-33, Professional & Consulting Service Costs—Did the company require legal services for organizing, reorganizing, antitrust suits, claims against the government, or bad debts? Does the company maintain supporting evidence for services rendered?

15. FAR 31.205-34, Recruitment Costs—Were any new people hired who left the company within 12 months of their hire date?

16. FAR 31.205-35, Relocation Costs—Does the relocation policy allow for payment of income taxes? Loss on sale of a home? Continuing mortgage principal on residence being sold?

17. FAR 31.205-36, Rental Costs—Did the company enter into any new leases or renegotiate any existing leases during the year? If so, was FASB #13 considered? Are there any rental payments for property leased from an owner, stockholder, or affiliate of the contractor?

18. FAR 31.205-41, Taxes—Have more taxes (state income taxes mainly) been accrued than paid?

19. FAR 31.205-42, Termination Costs—Were any contracts terminated during the year? If so, were any indirect costs charged direct as part of the termination?

20. FAR 31.205-43, Trade, Business, Technical and Professional Activities Costs—Does the company belong to any professional association? Is technical information discussed at meetings? Are any management meetings held at sites other than the main office? Did the company pay any costs for guests?

21. FAR 31.205-44, Training and Educational Costs—Were any grants, scholarships, fellowships, etc., provided to anyone? Did the company provide training and education to people other than employees?

22. FAR 31.205-46, Travel Costs—Have per diem ceilings been exceeded? Did any employee travel on first class airfare? Were any rebates, credits, or discounts given to the company by airlines, car rental firms, motels, etc.?

23. FAR 31.205-51, Cost of Alcoholic Beverages—Were alcoholic beverages served at any company functions?

The auditor will most likely spend the majority of his or her time in an incurred cost audit reviewing indirect costs. To accomplish the review, the auditor will perform the following analyses:

1. **Indirect account analyses**—The auditor will analyze selected indirect cost accounts or transactions, such as sensitive accounts, new accounts, and accounts with large variances to determine allowability, allocability, and reasonableness.

2. **B&P/IR&D compliance**—The auditor will review the bid and proposal and independent research and development costs for proper classification and completeness.

3. **Indirect allocation bases**—The auditor will review the various indirect cost pool allocation bases for consistency with prior years and applicable CAS.

4. **Indirect rate computations**—The auditor will test the accuracy of the various rate calculations.

5. **Indirect adjusting entries**—The auditor will review the adjusting journal entries related to indirect costs to identify any adjustments that require additional explanations.

6. **Testing of indirect accounts**—The auditor will select certain accounts to be reviewed in detail to test for any unallowable costs. The auditor will usually concentrate on sensitive (or controversial) areas such as business meals, travel, and corporate aircraft.

Other Direct Costs

In addition to direct labor and material (prime costs), which can be readily identified with a specific contract, there are other types of expenses that, under certain circumstances, may be charged directly to a specific job. These are generally referred to as "other direct costs." Examples are: (1) special tooling, dies, jigs, and fixtures; (2) plant rearrangement; (3) packaging and packing; (4) consultants' fees; (5) outbound freight; (6) expediting; (7) travel; (8) long distance telephone; and (10) cost of money. Costs of this nature may be charged direct to jobs, allocated on some representative basis, or charged partially direct and partially by allocation.

The auditor's objectives in reviewing these costs are generally to determine whether: (1)

the contractor's cost representations are reliable and accurate; (2) the amounts charged to government contracts are reasonable in amount and are allocable to government contracts; (3) costs have been accumulated in accordance with generally accepted accounting principles appropriate in the circumstances; and (4) the contractor has been consistent in allocating such costs to commercial and government work.

POSTAWARD REVIEW (DEFECTIVE PRICING)

The Truth in Negotiations Act requires that contractors involved in negotiated procurements submit to the government details concerning costs anticipated to be incurred during performance of the contract. This disclosure, coupled with sanctions that can be brought against the contractor if the contractor fails to satisfy this obligation, permits the government to negotiate a price that is based on a realistic assessment of the contractor's cost expectations. The Truth in Negotiations Act offers protection against what is commonly referred to as "defective pricing."

The act's provisions pertaining to defective pricing have been strengthened over the years as the government has recognized their effectiveness. Fundamentally, TINA requires contractors to disclose certain cost or pricing data and to certify that these data are current, accurate, and complete as of the date of the certification. To the extent that the certification is erroneous—that is, the data are not current, accurate, or complete—the government, in accordance with a price reduction clause inserted into government contracts, obtains a reduction in the contract price to the extent that the price was overstated as a result of inaccurate, incomplete, or noncurrent disclosure.

Certain cost or pricing data submitted for a contemplated negotiated contract $500,000 or greater must be certified as current, accurate, and complete. FAR 15.406-2 details the content of the required certificate, as follows: "This is to certify that, to the best of my knowledge and belief, the cost or pricing data (as defined in section 15.401 of the Federal Acquisition Regulation (FAR) and required under FAR subsection 15.403-4) submitted, either actually or by specific identification in writing, to the contracting officer or to the contracting officer's representative in support of [the proposal] are accurate, complete and current as of [date]. This certification includes the cost or pricing data supporting any advance agreements and forward pricing rate agreements between the offeror and the Government that are part of the proposal."

The contracting officer will specify whether cost or pricing data are required and whether or not certification is required. Generally, Table 15-2 in FAR Subpart 15.408 outlines how cost and pricing data will be submitted to the contracting officer.

Audit Emphasis

During the 1960s, both DCAA and GAO performed defective pricing audits. DCAA gradually assumed the predominant responsibility in this area, with GAO performing fewer and fewer reviews. GAO has historically been critical of DCAA's efforts in performing defective pricing reviews because GAO believes that DCAA should perform more of these audits.

Since DCAA cannot review every pricing action for possible defective pricing, the agency has used various contract selection techniques for the past several years. Initially, DCAA developed a sampling plan, which required a review of contracts over a specific dollar level and a random sample of contracts below that level.

In an attempt to refine the selection process, DCAA abandoned the random sampling approach and added two judgmental approaches. One method considers the effectiveness of the contractor's estimating system as an indicator of the need for more or fewer audits. The second method is a list of eight criteria that may indicate the need for a review. These criteria are:

1. Has significant time elapsed between the time the proposal was submitted and negotiations?

2. Were accounting changes made after the proposal was submitted?

3. Were supporting data introduced at the negotiation, but not audited?

4. Were there significant price differences between the proposed and negotiated amounts?

5. Was there adequate time for the contractor to prepare the cost proposal?

6. Was there adequate lead-time for an audit to be performed on the proposal?

7. Were there any unsupported costs in the audit review?

8. Does the contractor have any outstanding estimating system problems?

Applicability of the Truth in Negotiations Act

The Truth in Negotiations Act originally covered contracts entered into by DOD and NASA. Recognizing the benefits of the requirements of TINA for their own negotiated contracts, civilian agencies sought to implement the statutory provisions by regulation. Currently, both civilian agencies and the military have similar provisions with regard to defective pricing.

The defective pricing provisions in FAR 15.403-4 are applicable to the following types of contracts: (1) negotiated prime contracts $500,000 or greater; (2) contract modifications or changes over $500,000; (3) subcontracts $500,000 or over at any tier, but only in the event that the prime and higher-tier subcontractors have also provided cost or pricing data; and (4) any modification or change to a subcontract covered in (3) above. The provisions apply to modifications or changes to a contract over the threshold amount not only for negotiated contracts, but also for contracts that were initially the product of sealed bidding procedures. This application makes sense in light of the overall concern that the cost or pricing disclosure requirements be imposed in situations in which the government does not have adequate assurance that competitive forces will obtain a reasonable price. Usually when a contractor is undertaking a modification, no real competitive forces can be brought to bear, and so the government seeks the benefits provided through the disclosure of data.

TINA sets forth four exemptions from coverage, even in those cases in which the requisite dollar amount has been satisfied and the modification or contract award is the result of negotiated procedures. These exemptions (found in FAR 15.403-1) for contracts and subcontracts are applied when the price is based on: (1) adequate price competition; (2) commercial items; (3) prices set by law or regulations; or (4) in exceptional cases, where the head of the agency determines that the requirements may be waived and states in writing the reasons for such determination.

Price Reduction

The result of not providing current, accurate, or complete data will be a price reduction in the contracted value for the defective amount: "If any price, including profit or fee, negotiated in connection with this contract, or any cost reimbursable under this contract, was increased by any significant amount because the contractor or a subcontractor furnished cost or pricing data that were not complete, accurate and current as certified. . .the price or cost shall be reduced accordingly and the contract shall be modified to reflect the reduction." (FAR 52.215-10)

The elements of this statutory provision and its regulatory implementation have been the subject of a multitude of decisions in the Claims Court and the various Boards of Contract Appeals. The significant decisions offer insight into the magnitude of a contractor's responsibility for disclosure pursuant to the Truth in Negotiations Act.

Fraud in Defective Pricing

For a contractor to be guilty of fraud in the submission of defective data, it must have had "knowledge" of the defects. Under the False Claims Act, any one of three criteria may be applied to support a determination of culpable knowledge in an appropriate case: (1) intent to deceive; (2) misrepresentation; and (3) actual knowledge.

Situations of "intent to deceive" and "actual knowledge" are often difficult to prove since they require an inquiry into a person's state of mind to determine liability. However, such factual areas as verbal admissions and documented items (e.g., correspondence, memoranda) may prove sufficient to support this test.

Under the "misrepresentation" standard, the courts have set forth two criteria: (1) intentional misrepresentation; and (2) negligent misrepresentation. Intentional misrepresentation, the more stringent criterion, may occur as a result of a contractor's reckless disregard for the truth or falsity of a belief. Negligent misrepresentation, a less stringent criterion, has been defined as a lack of reasonable care in ascertaining the facts. However, carelessness that resembles a mistake will not meet the negligent misrepresentation definition. The negligence must be extreme enough

to be considered functionally equivalent to actual knowledge.

Government auditors, in particular DCAA auditors, review defective pricing cases for any indications of possible fraud. Some of the key areas of auditor concern, which may trigger additional audit analysis and prompt an investigative referral, are:

1. High incidence of persistent defective pricing

2. Repeated defective pricing involving similar patterns or conditions

3. Continued failure to correct known system deficiencies

4. Consistent failure to update cost or pricing data with the knowledge that prices have changed

5. Specific knowledge that is not disclosed regarding significant cost issues that will reduce proposal costs (e.g., revising the price of a major subcontract, combining material requirements)

6. Denials by responsible contractor employees of the existence of historical records, which are subsequently found to exist

7. Use of unqualified personnel to develop cost or pricing data used in the estimating process

8. Indications of falsification or alteration of supporting data

9. Distortion of the overhead accounts or base information by the transfer of charges that have a material impact on government contracts

10. Failure to make complete disclosure of data known to responsible contractor personnel

11. Employment of people known to have previously perpetrated fraudulent acts against the government.

If the DCAA auditor reasonably concludes that a fraudulent act may have occurred, the agency guidelines state that the field auditor should notify the local investigative organization regarding what course of action he or she should pursue. Once the auditor suspects fraud, and the contractor becomes aware of a problem, the contractor may wish to seek legal advice. In most cases, the contractor is not even aware that an investigator has been called until records are subpoenaed or officials are questioned by an investigator.

Audit Techniques

The auditor's main concern in performing a defective pricing review is to determine whether the costs proposed to the government were the most accurate, complete, and current when the contract was negotiated. Under "ideal" conditions, an auditor would prefer to perform this audit shortly after a contract has been negotiated. In this situation, both parties should easily remember what actually transpired at negotiations. However, in the current environment, a defective pricing audit generally takes place many months after contract award.

The auditor will review contractor cost performance records to identify any differences between costs as proposed/negotiated and costs as incurred. The auditor therefore considers performance records to be a valuable tool in determining what elements of costs are most susceptible in the defective pricing audit. The auditor will attempt to identify any overruns or underruns on a cost-element-by-cost-element basis to find out whether there were any "make-or-buy" changes, changes in production methods, changes in subcontractors proposed, different material prices, different labor mix, etc.

Generally, if the overrun or underrun exceeds 5 percent of the negotiated cost of the cost element, the auditor will conduct further reviews. If the incurred costs are similar to the costs proposed, the auditor will perceive a low risk of defective pricing—and might even curtail the review. The auditor rarely performs a defective pricing review on each and every cost element within a selected contract. Usually, cost elements that are perceived to be "high" risk are reviewed.

If judgment factors are prevalent in the estimation of direct labor hours, and if no other basis was available regarding how the hours were established, further review will not be likely. If prior actual hours were used, the auditor will perform a review to determine that the history was current at the time of price agreement. If an improvement curve was used, the auditor will verify the historical basis for accuracy as of the agreement date.

The auditor will review the basis of the proposed direct labor rates (e.g, weighted average, departmental, factorywide) and compare the proposed rates to the actual rates at the certification date. The auditor will also check to determine any impact of pending labor union agreements.

Statistics on completed defective pricing reviews have shown that materials and subcontracts are the most susceptible areas for defective pricing. The auditor will perform a statistical sample of large dollar items to determine whether the quoted price was the most current price. This is done by reviewing purchase order history files, "buy cards," or other similar records that detail purchase history. The auditor will also review the actual quantities being purchased to determine if the company is combining material requirements to obtain lower-than-bid prices. Any changes in "make-or-buy" decisions will most likely be reviewed.

The auditor will compare the proposed indirect cost rates to the actual incurred rates. If there has been a substantial change—such as in the burden pool structure, or projected sales were greater than expected—a further review will be conducted.

The results of the auditor's review are provided to the contracting officer for disposition. Usually, the company will be provided the opportunity to respond formally to any defective pricing allegations before the government's decision is made.

COST ACCOUNTING STANDARDS

Although the ACO is responsible for administration of the CAS, the government auditor plays an important part in this administrative effort. Two major areas of government auditor involvement in CAS matters are: (1) conducting reviews of CAS disclosure statements for adequacy and compliance; and (2) assisting the ACO in analyzing cost impact proposals submitted in connection with changes to disclosed or established cost accounting practices.

Disclosure Statement

The disclosure statement (CASB-DS-1) was designed to provide the government with a detailed, authoritative description of a contractor's cost accounting practices. The government's objective is to use this disclosure statement to establish a clear understanding of the accounting practices used, or to be used, particularly practices related to direct vs. indirect costs and the allocation of costs to cost objectives.

The auditor will review a completed disclosure statement for adequacy of the descriptions and then for compliance with the CAS and the FAR. To be adequate, the disclosure statement must be current, accurate, and complete. "Current" is not restricted to present practices, but may be the practices that the contractor intends to follow if a contract is awarded. The "accurate" criterion is self-explanatory and seldom causes problems. The

"complete" criterion is subject to considerable auditor judgment and controversy.

Several general cautions about completing the disclosure statement should be noted. These include the use of "not applicable," the use of "other," any response that requires a narrative explanation, and responses that are in obvious noncompliance with the CAS or the FAR. The use of "not applicable" is acceptable if the question pertains to a cost that currently does not exist. However, subsequent use of this cost category might lead the government to allege that an accounting change has occurred. Under these circumstances, the contractor should point out that this is a new cost practice and not a changed practice. Before any question is checked "not applicable," the contractor should consider the need for a new or revised policy related to that question.

The response "other" and certain combinations of responses will require a narrative supplement. Generally, narratives should be avoided because of the judgmental factors in establishing what is considered to be a complete response. Narratives must be carefully written to describe the practice completely enough to meet the government's requirements, but not limit the flexibility available to the contractor under the regulations.

Changes in Cost Accounting Practices

48 CFR 9903.302-1 states that "cost accounting practice" means any disclosed or established accounting method or technique that is used to measure cost, assign cost to cost accounting periods, or allocate cost to cost objectives. A contractor's cost accounting practices can be revised for a number of reasons, including: (1) to implement the requirements of newly applicable standards; (2) to implement negotiated changes, involuntary or sanctioned, to accounting practices; and (3) to correct noncompliant practices.

48 CFR 9903.302-2 defines a "change" to a cost accounting practice as any alteration in

a cost accounting practice, as defined above, whether or not such practice is covered by a disclosure statement, except for situations where:

1. The initial adoption of a cost accounting practice for the first time a cost is incurred, or a function is created, is not a change in cost accounting practice.

2. The partial or total elimination of a cost or the cost of a function is not a change in cost accounting practice. (As used here, "function" is an activity or group of activities that is identifiable in scope and has a purpose or end to be accomplished.)

3. The revision of a cost accounting practice for a cost that previously had been immaterial is not a change in cost accounting practice.

Once a change in a cost accounting practice has been initiated, the standard contract clause entitled "Administration of Cost Accounting Standards" requires the contractor to submit to the cognizant contracting officer: (1) a description of the change; (2) the potential impact of the change on contracts containing the clause; and (3) if not obviously immaterial, a general dollar magnitude cost impact analysis of the change that displays the potential shift of costs between CAS-covered contracts by contract type and other contractor business activity. If deemed necessary by the contracting officer, the contractor may be required to submit a cost impact proposal within 60 days after the date of determination of the adequacy and compliance of the change.

Adjustments to contract prices resulting from a change in cost accounting practice are governed by the CAS clause in 48 CFR 9903.201-4. Classification of the accounting change and the required treatment of costs are summarized as follows:

Contract Price Adjustment

Type of Accounting Change	Increased Costs	Offsets
1. Equitable Adjustment Change to comply with new CAS	yes	yes
2. Voluntary Change— negotiated revision that the government does not consider necessary and/or beneficial to its interest	no	yes
3. Sanctioned Change— negotiated revision that the government considers desirable and beneficial	yes	yes
4. Noncompliance change to comply with CAS	no	yes

"Increased costs" as interpreted in 48 CFR 9903.306(a) are deemed to have resulted whenever: (1) the cost paid by the government results from a change in a contractor's cost accounting practices or from a failure to comply with applicable CAS; and (2) such cost is higher than it would have been had the practices not been changed or compliance with the applicable CAS had been maintained. Special attention is given to the interpretation of an "increased cost to the government" when referring to fixed-price contracts. FAR 9903.306(b) and the DOD CAS Working Group Guidance Paper No. 76-4 address this issue and define this situation to exist when costs allocated to the contract are less than would have been allocated if the method of allocation had not been changed. Just the opposite situation exists for a cost-reimbursable contract:

Increased/Decreased Cost to the Government

Contract Type	Old Method	New Method	Increase (Decrease)
FP	$100,000	$110,000	$(10,000)
FP	100,000	90,000	10,000
Total	$200,000	$200,000	$ 0
CP	$100,000	$ 110,000	$ 10,000
CP	100,000	$ 90,000	(10,000)
Total	$200,000	$ 200,000	$ 0

Regarding "offsets," 48 CFR 9903.306(e) generally encourages the use of them in the course of determining a bottom-line price adjustment/impact. Offsets are described as: "The change or failure may increase the cost paid under one or more of the contracts, while decreasing the costs paid under one or more of the contracts. In such case, the government will not require price adjustment for any increased cost paid by United States so long as the cost decreased under one or more contracts are at least equal to the increased cost under the other affected contracts, provided that the contractor and all affected contracting officers agree on the method by which the price adjustments are to be made. . . ." The DOD CAS Working Group Guidance Nos. 76-8 and 79-23 interpret the application of offsets to be generally allowed for all types of accounting changes.

CONTRACT TERMINATION AUDIT

The government may terminate a contract for default or for the convenience of the government. In the former situation, the government may attempt to recover money paid to the contractor and reprocurement costs. In the latter situation, the contractor must submit a termination claim settlement proposal, usually within one year of termination. When a termination for convenience occurs, the cost principles are not applied in the normal fashion. This requires special audit attention.

Frequently, government auditors are not familiar with termination claims. When this situation occurs, it may be necessary to spend time educating the auditor on the cost principles involved in a termination for convenience.

EQUITABLE CONTRACT PRICE ADJUSTMENT AUDIT

When the government directs a change to a contract, the contractor may submit a price proposal reflecting the impact of the change. This proposal is reviewed much like any price proposal. The exception is that sometimes the pricing occurs after the work has been performed. In such instances, it is necessary for the auditor to review incurred costs related to the change as well.

In addition to the formally directed contract changes, the government may—by action or inaction—cause a contract to be changed. The contractor may then submit a claim that ultimately is settled by the courts.

Two of the most common changes relate to delay and disruption by the government. These can be either acknowledged or denied by the government. If the government issues a stop-work order, the delay is seldom disputed and must be quantified for negotiations. If the government is late in delivering equipment or materials, it may argue that the cause of the delay is other than its own actions. In these instances, the delay claim is disputed and settled through litigation.

A disruption may occur if the government directs the work to be performed in a different manner. A disruption may also occur and not be acknowledged by the government. Like a disputed delay, this may result in litigation.

Auditors are very suspicious of any disputed claim. Often the auditor will refuse to audit the claim because the extra costs caused by the delay or disruption were not segregated at the time the cost was incurred. The auditor will cite a contract clause that requires separate accounting for changes in excess of $100,000. The auditor will challenge estimates as unauditable and refuse to audit, or will qualify the audit report as unacceptable for negotiations.

FINANCIAL CAPABILITY AUDIT

The government wants some assurance that its contractors are financially solvent and are thus able to perform the contract. If the contractor goes out of business while the contract is in process, the government has to locate another contractor to complete the contract. Small companies and those doing business with the government for the first time are prime targets for this type of review.

In a financial capability audit, the auditor will review the external financial statements, as either certified or reviewed by a CPA firm. Particular attention will be paid to the types of financial circumstances that could lead to insolvency, such as poor cash flow, lack of orders, excessive debt and/or lines of credit, and insufficient working capital and equity. If the auditor's review is unfavorable, the government might not award the contract until the company takes some kind of corrective action.

OPERATIONS AUDIT

DCAA performs reviews of contractor operations to identify significant opportunities for reducing costs through improved economy and efficiency. These operations audits involve the systematic examination of particular organizational units or functions within a contractor's business to determine whether efficient and economical methods are employed in the performance of government contracts.

An operations audit generally relates to specific areas of a contractor's operations and usually results in recommendations to contractors for eliminating unnecessary costs or waste through contractor-initiated corrective actions. The two basic types of operations audits are "high technology" and "traditional." "High technology" operations audit recommendations typically provide for the implementation of new, emerging technologies and usually require the acquisition of capital equipment associated with the new technology. Examples of high technology types of operations audits are computer-aided design/computer-aided manufacturing (CAD/CAM),

or the use of robotics or lasers in manufacturing. "Traditional" operations audits generally recommend changes to existing contractor functions, policies, procedures, or practices to improve the effectiveness or efficiency of contractor operations. Some examples of traditional types of operations audits are repair/rework/scrap, equipment utilization and maintenance, and subcontract management.

DCAA performs follow-up reviews to confirm whether the contractor has initiated corrective action. During the follow-up reviews, the approximate cost impact of the corrective measures is assessed. Actions taken by contractors in response to operations audit recommendations may represent a change in procedure or process, or an investment in capital equipment to automate a function or operation previously performed manually. DCAA's policy is not to report any contractor savings until the contractor has implemented the procedural or process change, or has issued a purchase order for the capital equipment. If the contractor does not implement the audit recommendation, the auditor's only remedy is to question "wasteful" practices in accordance with the FAR contract cost principle on reasonableness.

In one operations audit, for example, DCAA recommended that a contractor affiliate with an independent travel agency to provide its travel needs. Use of an in-plant travel agency reduced the contractor's operating expenses and provided commissions to its travel service department. The contractor's implementation of DCAA's recommendations resulted in an estimated annual cost avoidance of $700,000.

In another operations audit, DCAA recommended that the contractor upgrade its current interactive computer graphics system and acquire, on a time-phased implementation plan, sufficient equipment to accomplish those manual engineering and drafting operations susceptible to this technology. Contractor representatives at the business unit level agreed with DCAA's recommendation and used the audit to convince their senior management of the need to expand and upgrade the graphics system. The contractor's implementation of this recommendation resulted in cost savings of $650,000.

In another instance, DCAA recommended that the contractor solicit various vendors to obtain energy management surveys and, based upon the results, evaluate the feasibility and potential effectiveness of installing computerized energy management systems at its facilities. The contractor responded by including a computerized energy management system in its capital budget and issuing the initial purchase order for the complete design of such a system. Annual cost avoidance associated with this recommendation amounted to $1,600,000 for one of the contractor's business units and $875,000 for another business unit.

For another contractor, DCAA recommended that management: (1) improve the system for measuring the cost of replacement material; (2) provide more detailed explanations in the supporting documentation for replacement material orders to identify specific reasons and individuals responsible for the orders; and (3) monitor the cost and reasons for replacement material to identify instances where corrective action can be taken to reduce replacement material cost. The contractor concurred with DCAA's recommendations and improved its practices in controlling the level of replacements of direct material. Replacement material orders were reduced significantly during a representative period subsequent to the contractor's implementation of DCAA's recommendations, resulting in annual cost avoidance of approximately $1,000,000.

While many operational audits conclude with recommendations for cost avoidance, many contractors contend that there is no contractual requirement for DCAA to perform these types of audits. Recently, contractors have been expressing resistance to DCAA performing these types of audits.

MATERIAL MANAGEMENT AND ACCOUNTING SYSTEM

This contractor system relates to planning, controlling, and accounting for the acquisition, use, issuance, and disposition of materials. The DOD FAR Supplement at 252.242-7004 details the requirements for an acceptable material management and accounting system (MMAS). Generally these requirements include: (1) written policies and procedures; (2) a 98 percent bill of material accuracy and a 95 percent master production schedule accuracy; (3) a system for identifying, reporting, and resolving system weaknesses and manual overrides; (4) adequate audit trails; (5) 95 percent accuracy in inventory counts; (6) details on the process of transferring parts between cost objectives; (7) consistent criteria for pricing part transfers; (8) written procedures on the transfer of parts process; (9) adequate controls to identify specific materials as required by contract terms; and (10) periodic internal control reviews.

DCAA CONTRACT AUDIT MANUAL

DCAA updates its Contract Audit Manual (DCAM) every six months. Published by the U.S. Government Printing Office, this document is an important item for contractors to have in dealing with auditors from any organization. The DCAM is also available at the DCAA website: www.dcaa.mil/.

Chapter 1 of the manual addresses DCAA responsibilities and interactions with other government organizations, contractors, and the public. Chapter 2 describes audit standards and ties DCAA standards to the AICPA and the GAO standards. The chapter also provides DCAA's justification for operations audits. Chapter 3 provides guidance to DCAA auditors on audit planning and on selecting areas for audit. Chapter 4 expands on the audit standards. Chapter 5 provides guidance to DCAA auditors on reviewing internal controls for all types of audits. Chapter 6 covers incurred cost audit procedures, including direct and indirect cost audits and suspension and disallowance of costs.

DCAA expands on the FAR cost principles in Chapter 7. This chapter addresses such costs as: computer cost allocations; leasing costs; allocation of special facilities operating costs; depreciation costs; insurance costs; pension costs; patent and royalty costs; labor settlement and strike period costs; employee training and educational costs; employee travel and relocation costs; dues, memberships, and professional activity costs; public relations and advertising costs; selling costs; taxes; independent research and development and bid and proposal costs; warranty and/or correction of defect costs; business combinations costs; and joint venture, teaming arrangements, and special business units.

Chapter 8 addresses the CAS. Chapter 9 covers the DCAA review of cost estimates and price proposals, detailing what the auditor is expected to do during these audits. Chapter 10 describes how DCAA audit reports are to be presented. Chapter 11 addresses such matters as limitation of cost clauses, C/SCSC (cost/

schedule control system criteria) reviews, and DOD program management systems reporting requirements.

Chapter 12 addresses contract terminations, delay/disruption claims, and other claims. Chapter 13 provides special guidance regarding educational and nonprofit organizations. Chapter 14 covers several areas, including postaward reviews, progress payment audits, financial capability audits, government property audits, operations audits, contractor capital investment projects, and other operations areas. Chapter 15 addresses miscellaneous DCAA functions.

Appendix A contains the cost principles from the FAR, DAR, and DFARS. Appendix B provides guidance on statistical sampling. Appendix C provides guidance on auditing computer systems. Appendix D addresses obtaining technical assistance. Appendix E provides guidance on graphic and computational analysis. Appendix F provides guidance on improvement curve analysis. Appendix G is internal guidance on mobile audits, Appendix H is internal guidance on resident audits, and Appendix I addresses work sampling.

Acronyms

ABC	activity-based costing	C/SCSC	cost/schedule control system criteria
ACO	administrative contracting officer	DAR	Defense Acquisition Regulation
ACRS	accelerated cost recovery system	DCAA	Defense Contract Audit Agency
AICPA	American Institute of Certified Public Accountants	DCMA	Defense Contract Management Agency
ASBCA	Armed Services Board of Contract Appeals	DD	Department of Defense
		DFARS	Department of Defense Federal Acquisition Regulation Supplement
ASPR	Armed Services Procurement Regulation		
BCA	Board of Contract Appeals	DLA	Defense Logistics Agency
BOA	basic ordering agreement	DOD	Department of Defense
B&P	bid and proposal	DOE	Department of Energy
CAD/CAM	computer-aided design/ computer-aided manufacturing	EPA	Environmental Protection Agency
CAS	cost accounting standards	ERISA	Employee Retirement Insurance Security Act
CASB	Cost Accounting Standards Board		
		ESOP	Employee Stock Ownership Plan
CICA	Competition in Contracting Act	EVMS	Earned Value Management System
CLIN	contract line item number		
Cls Ct	Court of Claims	FAR	Federal Acquisition Regulation
CO	contracting officer	FARA	Federal Acquisition Reform Act
CPA	certified public accountant	FASA	Federal Acquisition Streamlining Act
CPAF	cost plus award fee		
CPFF	cost plus fixed fee	FFP	firm fixed price
CPIF	cost plus incentive fee	FIFO	first-in, first-out
		FMS	foreign military sales

FPI	fixed-price incentive	LOC	limitation of cost
FPIF	fixed-price incentive fee	LOCC	limitation of cost clause
FPIS	fixed-price incentive successive targets	LOE	level of effort
FP-LOE	firm fixed-price, level of effort	MMAS	Material Management and Accounting System
FPR	fixed-price redeterminable	NASA	National Aeronautics and Space Administration
FPR	Federal Procurement Regulation	NASA BCA	National Aeronautics and Space Administration Board of Contract Appeals
FPRA	forward-pricing rate agreement		
FPRR	forward-pricing rate recommendation	NPR	National Performance Review
FTR	Federal Travel Regulation	NTE	not to exceed
FY	fiscal year	OFPP	Office of Federal Procurement Policy
G&A	general and administrative	OMB	Office of Management and Budget
GAAP	generally accepted accounting practices		
GAAS	generally accepted accounting standards	OT	other transaction
		PPA	Pension Protection Act
GAO	Government Accountability Office	RFP	request for proposals
		RFI	request for information
GSA	General Services Administration	PHM	Plastic Hull Minesweeper
ICE	Incurred Cost Electronically	PL	public law
ID	indefinite delivery	PNM	price negotiation memorandum
IDIQ	indefinite delivery, indefinite quantity	PRB	postretirement benefit
IFB	invitation for bids	SDB	small disadvantaged business
IG	Inspector General	SF	standard form
IQ	indefinite quantity	TCI	total cost input
IRAN	inspect and repair as needed	TD	Treasury Decision
IRS	Internal Revenue Service	TINA	Truth-in Negotiations Act
IR&D	independent research and development	T&M	time and materials
		US	United States
JTR	Joint Travel Regulations	USC	United States Code
LIFO	last-in, first-out	VA	value added

Index

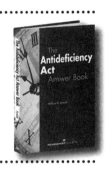

Federal Acquisition ActionPacks

Federal Acquisition ActionPacks are designed for busy professionals who need to get a working knowledge of government contracting quickly—without a lot of extraneous detail. This ten-book set covers all phases of the acquisition process, grounds you firmly in each topic area, and outlines practical methods for success, from contracting basics to the latest techniques for improving performance.

Each spiral-bound book contains approximately 160 pages of quick-reading information—simple statements, bulleted lists, questions and answers, charts and graphs, and more. Each topic's most important information is distilled to its essence, arranged graphically for easy comprehension and retention, and presented in a user-friendly format designed for quick look-up.

Order the full set of *Federal Acquisition ActionPacks* to get a comprehensive knowledge of government contracting today.
Full set: ISBN 978-1-56726-198-1 ■ Product Code B981

Or order the single titles that are most important to your role in the contracting process. Either way, this is the most effective, affordable way for both buyers and sellers to get a broad-based understanding of government contracting—and proven tools for success.

Earned Value Management *Gregory A. Garrett* ISBN 978-1-56726-188-2 ■ Product Code B882 173 Pages	**Best-Value Source Selection** *Philip E. Salmeri* ISBN 978-1-56726-193-6 ■ Product Code B936 178 Pages
Performance-Based Contracting *Gregory A. Garrett* ISBN 978-1-56726-189-9 ■ Product Code B899 153 Pages	**Government Contract Law Basics** *Thomas G. Reid* ISBN 978-1-56726-194-3 ■ Product Code B943 175 Pages
Cost Estimating and Pricing *Gregory A. Garrett* ISBN 978-1-56726-190-5 ■ Product Code B905 161 Pages	**Government Contracting Basics** *Rene G. Rendon* ISBN 978-1-56726-195-0 ■ Product Code B950 176 Pages
Contract Administration and Closeout *Gregory A. Garrett* ISBN 978-1-56726-191-2 ■ Product Code B912 153 Pages	**Performance Work Statements** *Philip E. Salmeri* ISBN 978-1-56726-196-7 ■ Product Code B967 151 Pages
Contract Formation *Gregory A. Garrett and William C. Pursch* ISBN 978-1-56726-192-9 ■ Product Code B929 163 Pages	**Contract Terminations** *Thomas G. Reid* ISBN 978-1-56726-197-4 ■ Product Code B974 166 Pages